College Guide for Students with Learning Disabilities

Sixteenth Edition

Annette Joy Sclafani
and
Michael J. Lynch

Laurel Publications
Miller Place, Long Island, New York 11764

For further information, contact
Laurel Publications
595 Route 25A – Suite 18
Miller Place, NY 11764

Library of Congress Catalog Number: 86-62574
ISBN: 0933243-13-8

Published and distributed by
Laurel Publications
595 Route 25A – Suite 18
Miller Place, NY 11764
(631) 209-1894
www.laurelpublications.net

College Guide for Students with Learning Disabilities

This guide was prepared to assist high school students with learning disabilities, their parents and their guidance counselors in the identification of options for post-secondary education and the steps to get there.

CONTENTS

INTRODUCTION

Many colleges today offer services for students with learning disabilities. Students enroll in the college and take courses that lead to chosen degrees. However, during their college careers, students with learning disabilities can receive academic and tutorial support services. No indication is made on a student's degree or transcript that he or she participated in a program for students with learning disabilities. For students who enter college and later decide that they would benefit from the services of a Learning Disabilities Program, there is the option of applying to such a program at that time. All decisions regarding acceptance into the Special Program are made on an individual basis.

This updated 16th edition of the *College Guide for Students with Learning Disabilities* includes descriptive information about four-year and two-year colleges with programs for students with learning disabilities, including academic majors and vocational programs. There is also a section with information about colleges that offer expanded and detailed services, as well as a comprehensive list of colleges that offer these services to students with learning disabilities. A separate section describes summer transition programs for students with learning disabilities. Profiles of scholarships offered exclusively to students with learning disabilities at various colleges are also listed in this guide. Please contact the college for more specific information about the scholarships mentioned.

The factor that differentiates a program from services in the *College Guide for Students with Learning Disabilities* is the requirement that a sufficient number of certified learning disabilities specialists be on staff to work with the students. For a college to be described in the Program category, these learning disabilities specialists should be available full-time for a one-on-one counseling approach for the students enrolled in the Program.

Before making a final decision about college, it is important to visit the school to be sure the services offered are compatible with the individual student's needs. Ask for a list of the services that are available; the fee for the special program (if any); and try to meet the staff that will be working directly with the student. The College Guide also covers many additional details to consider when choosing a college that has a special program for the student with learning disabilities.

The College Guide is current, well-organized and easy to use — an ideal reference book for students, parents, counselors and resource teachers. It is important to review these programs annually, since many are supported by federal funds which change from year to year.

CHOOSING A COLLEGE

There are nearly 3,000 colleges and universities (plus hundreds of vocational and technical schools) in the United States and no two are quite the same. Colleges can be . . .

- large or small
- coed or single sex
- specialized or diversified in their curriculums
- affiliated with a particular religion or nonsectarian
- expensive or low cost
- near your home or far away
- in a suburban, urban or rural setting

How do you sort out all the possibilities and finally make a choice? Work with your counselor in making this decision. The considerations listed above should be reviewed now before thinking about specific colleges. When you have done so, your counselor can assist you in identifying colleges that will offer the kind of experience you would like.

Questions to Ask Yourself

THINK ABOUT YOUR GOALS

What do you want from your college experience?

- Preparation for a particular career?
- An opportunity to meet new people from different backgrounds?
- A diversified education in the liberal arts?
- Vocational training?
- A chance to live in another part of the country?
- An opportunity to participate in intercollegiate athletics or amateur theater productions?

THINK ABOUT THE KINDS OF SITUATIONS IN WHICH YOU LEARN BEST AND FEEL MOST COMFORTABLE

- Do you think you can handle large classes or do you need more individual attention from your teachers?
- Do you like doing special projects and independent study on your own, or do you work better in a very structured classroom situation when everyone is working on the same subject matter?
- Do you like a very competitive environment or are you happier in a more relaxed learning situation?
- Do you like being with lots of different kinds of people or are you more comfortable with people whose interest and abilities are pretty similar to your own?

How you want to learn is just as important a factor as *what* you want to learn in choosing a college. There are certainly many questions to ask yourself. But you should RELAX.

With good planning, BEGINNING NOW, and consultations with your counselor and parents, you stand a pretty solid chance of making a good decision.

Timetable for Post-Secondary Planning

GRADE 9

- This year begins your official high school record. Your grades will be recorded on the permanent record card (PRC) transcript.
- Get to know your counselor and let your counselor get to know you. Visit with your counselor frequently so your adjustment to high school will be the best possible. Take advantage of all the services offered through the school's counseling program.
- Do as well as you can academically, seek assistance whenever you feel you need it.
- Participate in the career exploration program that your guidance counselor conducts.
- Participate in extracurricular activities.

GRADE 10

- Continue working with your counselor, communicate frequently.
- Work hard at your academics, seeking assistance whenever needed, and continue your involvement in extracurricular activities.
- Research career areas related to your interests.
- Consider the Vocational Education Program available to your district as a route to your goal.

GRADE 11

- Continue to communicate with your counselor because this communication becomes more important in the second half of your high school experience.
- Continue your involvement in extracurricular activities.
- Work hard at giving a solid academic performance. Eleventh grade is particularly important so make your best efforts.
- Continue your career research and begin matching your interests with career possibilities.
- Begin your college research.
- Register to take the Preliminary Scholastic Aptitude Test (PSAT) in October at your school. Let your counselor know if you plan to take the test untimed.

- Consider taking the Armed Services Vocational Aptitude Battery (ASVAB); see your counselor about this test.

SUMMER BETWEEN GRADE 11 AND GRADE 12

- Plan your summer.
- Visit colleges you have identified for yourself.
- Have an interview with an admissions representative.
- Take advantage of the various summer experiences available for eleventh graders conducted at colleges and other educational institutions. (See your counselor for information.)

GRADE 12

- Continue communication with your counselor.
- Maintain a solid, quality, academic program.
- Continue your involvement in extracurricular activities.
- Colleges are interested in your progress in your final year of high school. They consider seventh semester grades (first half of your senior year) when processing your application for admission.
- Acceptance for admission at most colleges is provisional, pending receipt of your final grades.
- Complete college visits early in your senior year.
- Pay close attention to the announcements from your guidance office.
- Complete applications on line and give a copy of them to your counselor by mid-November.
- Be aware of early application deadlines, especially applications to special programs.
- Be aware that two-year agricultural and technical schools accept students on a first come - first serve basis as long as they meet minimum entrance requirements.
- Meet college representatives who visit your school
- Take the necessary tests required by the colleges in which you are interested (SAT, ACT). Be sure to make arrangements with your counselor if you plan to take the untimed SAT or ACT.
- Inform your counselor when you have made a decision as to what you will do after graduation.

Graduate and feel comfortable about your plans because you know you have put effort into the decision-making process.

Criteria for Comparing and Selecting Colleges

You and your parents can use the following list of criteria to compare colleges and then make a selection of colleges to consider further. Under each heading in the list below are found questions to answer and items to consider when you look at college information brochures and catalogs. You may fill out the College Comparison Worksheet (on page 31) with the information required or you may prepare a comparison worksheet of your own.

When you are finished with this information-gathering process, you will be ready to narrow down the choice of colleges to which you wish to send applications.

PROGRAM FOR STUDENTS WITH LEARNING DISABILITIES

You should learn. . . .

How long has the program been in existence?
How many students are admitted to the program each year?
How many students are presently in the program?
What types of support services are offered?
What curriculum modifications are available?
What is the success rate of the program (that is, the percentage of students with learning disabilities who successfully complete the course of study)?

SERVICES AVAILABLE THROUGH THE LEARNING DISABILITIES PROGRAM

Basic Study Courses: Basic Study courses in Math Skills, Reading Skills, Spelling Skills, Study Skills, Organization of Study Skills, Writing Skills, Listening Skills, Speech Skills, and Development of Long and Short Term Memory.

Resource Center: Special Resource Centers where students can be given remediation, alternative methodology, and tutorial services.

Types of Lesson Presentation: Multisensory Lesson Presentations — auditory, visual, tactile, kinesthetic.

Curriculum Modifications: Taping of lectures and textbooks for students with reading or visual memory problems.

Individualized and Self-paced Instructional Programs. (Alternative freshman year —self-paced program.)

Individualized Instruction
Individualized assessments of strengths and weaknesses
Individualized learning plans
One-to-one tutoring

Individualized testing
Oral and untimed exams (if needed)
Career planning
Social adjustment
Course scheduling
Realistic goals
Structure in realizing short-term and long-range goals
Social and family evaluation

Faculty: Number of staff working in the Program; degrees; past experience. Special education and selected training for instructors (certified learning disability specialists).

Faculty/Student Relationships: Faculty/student ratio. Will student work with same counselor and learning disabilities specialist throughout college career?

STUDENT ENROLLMENT

Enrollment: Total % Undergraduate students. Freshman class size.

Retention: % Freshmen who graduate.

Background: Male/Female ratio. % Commuter/Resident. Geographic origin. % with Financial Aid.

Transfer: % of students who transfer into 4-year colleges from 2-year colleges. % of transfer students accepted into 4-year colleges.

LOCATION AND SURROUNDINGS

Location: Geographic region. Distance from home. Travel costs and convenience.

Setting: Urban or rural. Weather. Nearest city or countryside. Recreational opportunities.

Facilities: Library. Laboratories. Studies and practice rooms. sports. Student Center.

COLLEGE TYPE AND PHILOSOPHY

Type: Two- or four-year school. Church, state or private control. College or university. Liberal arts. Preprofessional for business, education, engineering, fine arts, etc. Technical or vocational institute. Degrees offered.

Philosophy: Traditional or progressive. Academically career-oriented. Comprehensive.

Calendar: Semester/trimester/quarter/module.

CURRICULUM

Academic Requirements: Proportion of study to general education/concentration/student choice. Required freshman courses or curriculum/distribution requirements in curricular areas/electives.

Academic Offerings: Majors offered in student's areas of interest. Interdisciplinary courses and majors. Strong departments.

Independent Study: Individual tutorials. Seminars. Research opportunities.

Special Study Programs: Field work. Internships. Exchange programs. Foreign study. Joint degree programs. Cooperative work/study plan. Preprofessional programs.

Standards: Accreditation. Degree requirements. Grading systems. Grading/distribution. Honor system.

Course Descriptions: Sequential/open order. Introductory/advanced/specialized courses. Courses for majors/non-majors. Number of courses required for major.

TECHNOLOGY

Many colleges have developed Adaptive Technology Laboratories (ATL) for the expressed purpose of providing professional services in adaptive technology for persons with disabilities. Technology is available to accommodate learning disabilities assistance in word processing with spell check, word finding, and cut-and-paste features – to facilitate writing and revising; outlining and brainstorming programs – to aid with organization of ideas; speech output – to provide auditory feedback of written text; word prediction – to help people with some types of spelling or word retrieval difficulties; and electronic dictionaries and encyclopedias. When checking on services available at various colleges, be sure to investigate what the college provides regarding ATL.

ADMISSIONS

Deadlines: Notification of Decision. Reply to offer of Admission.

Entrance Requirements: Fee. Information forms. Specific high school courses. Transcript. Secondary school reports which show evidence of specialized learning need. Recommendations. Interview. Other.

Most Learning Disabilities Programs require a letter from the student's Special Education Guidance Counselor stating nature of disability; recent WAIS and Achievement tests.

SAT or ACT Tests Required: SAT/ACT. Are untimed SAT's preferred?

Admissions Selectivity: % applicants offered admission. Average SAT/ACT scores of freshmen.

PRE-ADMISSION SUMMER PROGRAM

Those students who enroll in the pre-admission summer program have an easier adjustment period if they are gradually introduced to the program. There are fewer students during the summer and they take only one or two academic courses to give them an idea of what to expect in September. Taking academic courses during the summer enables the student to take a more limited course load during the school year, thereby increasing the opportunity to perform well. Students are with students who have similar disabilities so they do not feel alone. Another plus is that students can choose their own roommates after the summer session.

The pre-admission summer program is highly recommended to familiarize students with the college staff and with other students in the program. The transition to college life and studies will be that much smoother.

ACADEMIC ENVIRONMENT

Faculty: Number of full-time/part-time faculty; degrees; past experience.

Faculty/Student Relationships: Faculty/student ratio. Advising. Accessibility for conferences, assistance. Average class size. Number of classes under 20 students/over 50 students. Opportunities for discussion/student presentation/exchange of ideas.

Academic Demands: Workload. Course expectations. Type of assignments. Academic pressures/competition.

Career Preparation: Preprofessional programs. Career advising and information programs. % who go to graduate school. Graduate school and job placement success rates.

CAMPUS

Living Arrangements: Predominantly large dorms/housing clusters/small houses. Availability of single rooms/doubles/suites/multiple rooms. System of housing allocation/roommate selection. Centralized/decentralized dining. Alternative dining programs.

Campus Activities: Activities related to student's interests. Emphasis on social life, fraternities, sports or other dominant interests.

Clubs and Organizations: Traditional/creative/competitive/issue-oriented. Presence of religious, ethnic or cultural groups. Cultural opportunities on campus or in community. Focus of social life on campus/fraternities/community/other college/camps/home.

COSTS AND FINANCIAL AID

Costs: Minimum-maximum total costs per year. Student budget for tuition and fees/room and board/books and personal expenses/travel costs. Admission and enrollment fees. ***Is there an extra fee for Special Services for Students with Learning Disabilities?***

Family Resources: What does the student's family pay toward college expenses? Student's earnings and savings.

Awards: % students receiving aid. Range of awards. Average award.

Financial Aid: Based on need/merit/or funds available. Loan and job expectation.

Application: Forms required. Deadlines.

HOW COLLEGES SELECT STUDENTS

Before they decide they will admit a student, college admissions directors and their committees consider the following:

1. The student's high school academic record.
2. The type of course pursued by the student during high school.
3. Marked improvement by the student in scholastic achievement from year to year.
4. SAT, ACT, or other entrance examination scores (if required).
5. The high school's rating on the student's personality and character.
6. Indication of the student's special ability: art, music, or leadership.
7. Service to the school by the student.
8. Service to the community by the student.
9. Extracurricular activities pursued by the student: dramatics, sports, band, publications.
10. Attendance record and personal profile of the student.
11. Neatness and accuracy of the college application.
12. Letters of recommendation from the high school principal, counselors, teachers, and others.
13. The personal interview (if required). The personal interview can be particularly helpful in applying to a program for students with learning disabilities. Carefully review the section on the personal interview (page 27).

CALENDAR FOR COLLEGE PLANNING

Active College Planning During the High School JUNIOR Year

DATE	ACTIVITY	TESTING & COURSES	APPLICATIONS
SPRING/JUNIOR YEAR			
March -May	Self-Assessment. Determine college criteria. Discuss plans with parents.	Take the May SAT. Make arrangement with your counselor by January if you plan to take the untimed SAT.	
	Review college web sites. Make a preliminary list of colleges. Attend Spring College Fairs, local College Fairs and College Nights. Compare colleges. Research colleges that have Leaning Disabilities Programs.	Be sure to take courses required for college study.	Make appointments for summer visits and interviews on line.
	Student-Parent-Counselor Conference. Be sure to have the 11th grade Student-Parent Counselor Conference to plan activity for the Summer and Fall.	Select a quality course program for final year in high school.	

June	List colleges to visit. Print out all forms and information needed from college web site.	Take the June SAT. Make arrangements with your counselor if you plan to take the untimed SAT in January.	College applications may be available on line at this time.
SUMMER/JUNIOR YEAR			
July / August	Search college web sites for the most up-to-date information available. Make a few college visits with a tour and information session; begin to note observations; ask questions, listen to questions of others. Compare colleges; take notes, complete worksheet, keep a journal, discuss visits with parents.	Review and prepare for the Fall College Admissions Testing.	Review Applications both printed and on line. Note deadline and requirements. Familiarize yourself with essays and forms. Try one or two trial interviews. Plan Fall visits and make appointments for interviews.

CALENDAR FOR COLLEGE PLANNING
Active College Planning During the High School SENIOR Year

DATE	ACTIVITY	TESTING & COURSES	APPLICATIONS
FALL/SENIOR YEAR			
September – November	Attend Fall College Nights and school visits by college representatives. Make thorough college visits (2-3 days maximum). Attend local and campus Open Houses.	Take November SAT.	Go on campus interview. Begin completing applications on line. Make drafts of your essays. (Have your English teacher read for suggestions.). Seek information about admissions selectivity.
By Thanksgiving	Make a final list of college applications. Review worksheets, review selectivity; consult parents; consult counselor.	Review transcript with counselor.	Complete and submit college applications and essays on line. Notify your counselor when you have done this so your transcripts and letters of recommendation can be sent to the College.
Nov. 1 – Dec. 1	Make college visits before semester ends.		Deadlines for Early Action and Early Decision applications. Give recommendation forms to teachers and others.

By Christmas	End of campus visit program.	Take December SAT or ACT tests. Make arrangements with your counselor if you plan to take the test untimed.	FAF paper worksheets should be available for financial aid but you must apply on line at www.FAFSA.com.
Dec – Jan		Mid-year grade reports sent to colleges.	Mid-year grade reports sent to colleges.
Jan 1 – Feb 1			Check that school forms and recommendations have been sent to colleges. Deadlines for most college applications.
Jan – March			Colleges review applications.
SPRING/SENIOR YEAR			
March 15 – April 15			Notification of decisions on college applications.
April – May			May 1 common reply date. Accept offer of admission. Withdraw other applications.

THE COLLEGE SEARCH

Admissions Process

Search college web sites for information about the colleges you are interested in and print forms (application, dorm/housing, financial aid, etc.) to review before you complete on line.

A source of college web sites is www.collegeboard.com.

Do not submit any forms on line until you print a copy out for someone to check for you. Have your English teacher read your essays for suggestions before you send them to your college choices. Always keep a hard copy of what you send the college.

COMPLETING THE APPLICATION FORM

Most colleges want you to submit your application on line. Submit the Application for Admission and other forms the college or university requires by the requested deadline date. Complete the Checklist for Application Preparation (on page 33) as you gather information about various colleges of your choice and prepare to submit applications.

DISCLOSURE OF LEARNING DISABILITIES

Any college or university that provides a full program for students with learning disabilities will provide an opportunity for students to self-disclose their disability during the application process. An applicant should look for any statement on an admissions application that encourages the applicant to indicate the need for special services or accommodations related to a learning disability. Colleges and universities that request this information are interested in making sure that students who are admitted are provided with appropriate support and accommodations to enhance their educational experience at the institution.

Please note: By law, students are not required to disclose any disability to the college or university. This is an individual decision for each student and should be discussed with parents, the school counselor and the special education specialist.

PREPARING AN AUTOBIOGRAPHY

Many colleges that offer programs for students with learning disabilities request a handwritten essay with autobiographical information in order to get a better picture of you as a person. Even if the college of your choice does not request this information in essay form, it is a good idea for you, at this time, to gather your thoughts about yourself. This will prove helpful to you in a future interview situation.

The best way to approach this task is to assume that you are being asked the question – a favorite one of interviewers – "What can you tell me about yourself?" Assuming that this is your objective, construct an outline which, if followed, would best fulfill your interests, your goal, your accomplishments, etc.

SUGGESTED TOPICS FOR DISCUSSIONS

The following topics should be touched upon in an autobiography. It is not necessary to deal with these in the order they are listed. There are some topics which you may or may not wish to cover, or need to cover. Keep in mind that your objective is to come up with as good a picture of yourself as you possibly can. Try to be interesting, avoid rambling, and do not be afraid to be creative. Since this is a written picture of you, the way in which you present it is extremely important. Well-written sentences, proper spelling and organization will present you in a positive light. These topics are:

1. Describe a pressing problem you have had to face in your life and how you dealt with it. What self-control were you able to exert? What did you learn from the experience? Describe the problems you faced being a student with learning disabilities and how you have learned to compensate.

2. Describe a personal experience in which you showed qualities of leadership. What happened that made you feel influential?

3. Describe something you have done that has given you satisfaction.

4. How do you see yourself in ten years?

5. Select some school or other experience from which you have derived exceptional profit – describe it, explaining its value to you.

OTHER INFORMATION TO INCLUDE IN AN AUTOBIOGRAPHY

1. Discuss your immediate family background
    a. Brothers and sisters? Parents, guardians
    b. Education and kinds of employment of family members
    c. Special interests
2. In what activities have you been involved in the past five years?
    a. School extra/co-curricular
    b. Work
    c. Community
    d. Church or Temple
    e. Summer program

3. What do you consider your most important achievement to date?
   a. Academic
   b. Personal
   c. Social or Community
4. How do you use your leisure time?
5. What are your plans for the next five years?
   a. Educational
   b. Vocational
   c. Personal
6. What school subjects have you liked best - WHY????
7. How do you see yourself as a person? How does this compare with how you believe others see you?

SAMPLE AUTOBIOGRAPHY #1

Every person is made up of many talents, abilities and traits. I am no different. I have worked hard because determination and the will to achieve are attributes that have always been within me. I have overcome many obstacles and I believe that this has strengthened my ability to succeed in college.

In first grade I had difficulty in learning how to read. I was diagnosed as having a learning disability. Throughout my elementary school years I received extra help. I have spent many hours doing drills, exercises, and attending special classes. When I reached the high school level, I had made great strides and was prepared for high school work.

High school has been, in many ways, a difficult experience as well. It is true that very often once a student is labeled, it is difficult to escape that labeling. Interestingly enough, in English and Social Studies where I was in Regents classes, I was motivated to work harder and consistently achieved commendable grades. If I had been challenged in all my courses, I am confident I would have done well.

Because of the hardships and difficulties I have had to overcome, I truly believe that I can make a positive contribution to your school. The maturity and understanding I have acquired together with my intense desire to succeed have given me the confidence to do well in any field I choose to pursue. I am well aware that the path in front of me is not an easy one, but I eagerly await the challenges of the next four years.

SAMPLE AUTOBIOGRAPHY #2

Attending college means a great deal to me for many reasons. Over the past three years, the Resource Room at my high school has greatly benefited my education. Through the program at your school and my desire for an education, I know that I will be a success. As a member of the student body at a four-year school, I feel that I would be an asset. I understand the importance of a college education and know that, in my case, perseverance is a necessity.

The part-time jobs that I have held since the age of 14 have taught me to be organized, efficient and responsible. In addition, through my years of working, I feel that I have learned the importance of relating to other people. In my opinion, this is a critical factor in everyday living.

Being successful and feeling good about that success is extremely important to me. At your school, I feel that I would have the opportunity to use my abilities. With the reputation that precedes your Learning Disabilities Program and the goals I have set for myself, I will be able to accomplish anything I set out to do. I understand you have a high success rate, and I know I can do well, given the opportunity to join your program.

Unfortunately, my past high school grades were poor due to lack of self-confidence and immaturity. However, thanks to the support of my parents, my school counselor and the Resource Room instructor, I have been motivated to produce better grades during this school year and on SAT re-examination. I realize now the importance of a good college education and want to pursue it.

Because of the hardships and difficulties I have had to overcome, I believe that I can make a positive contribution to your school. The maturity and understanding I have acquired, together with my intense desire to succeed, have given me the confidence to do well in any field I choose to pursue. I have many plans for the future, and I have made many promises I am determined to keep. I know that I will overcome the challenges of the next four years.

Testing Programs

THE ACT

The ACT measures the general educational development of high school students and their ability to complete college-level work. English, mathematics, reading and science tests are multiple choice. The optional writing test indicates skill in planning and writing a short essay.

Accommodations are available for test takers with learning disabilities or attention deficit/hyperactivity disorder. If you currently receive accommodations in school, you must provide documentation to take the ACT tests with accommodations.

There are three ways to take the tests with accommodations.

Center Testing #1 – Tests are completed in the standard amount of time, with accommodations, on a national testing date.

Center Testing #2 – Tests are completed with extended time (50% more than standard) on a paper format on a national testing date.

Special Testing – Tests are given with extended time and alternate formats at a time and date which is not part of the national testing. Special testing is appropriate for students who normally use more than time-and-one-half for tests (or use extra time only on writing tests) in school, or require testing over several days or use test formats other than paper, such as a reader, audiocassette or scribe for essays.

REQUESTS FOR TESTING WITH ACCOMMODATIONS

ACT has outlined the following information for requests for the various types of testing.

Center Testing #1 – Standard Time Testing with Accommodations

To request this form of testing, include all of the following information in a written request with your paper registration folder postmarked by the registration deadline:

- Your name, mailing address, and phone number.
- The test date (month and year) and test option (ACT or ACT Plus Writing) you marked in block M on your registration folder.
- The name, city, state, and 6-digit code for each of the test center choices you marked in block N on your registration folder.
- Explain your disability and clearly state the accommodations you

are requesting; give enough detail so they can make arrangements for you.

- Enclose written documentation from your school describing in detail the accommodations you normally receive in school.
- The name and phone number of a school official familiar with your current testing accommodations.

If necessary, ACT will contact you or your high school for additional information. If accommodations are approved, ACT will then make arrangements for you. In order to provide the approved accommodations, ACT may have to assign you to a different test center rather than your original choice.

Center Testing #2 – Extended Time Testing

To request this type of testing, you and a school official must complete and sign a copy of the Application for ACT Extended Time National Testing. The application explains the eligibility criteria, documentation requirements, and how to request a test date change or reregistration after you have been approved.

Your completed Application for ACT Extended Time National Testing and required documentation must be returned with your paper registration folder postmarked by the registration deadline. If you are approved for extended time national testing, you will be notified on your admission ticket. If you are not approved, you will be notified in writing and assigned to a room with standard time limits.

If you select this form of testing, you must register by paper folder (not via the Web), so that you can provide your current documentation.

If necessary, ACT will contact you or your high school for additional information. If accommodations are approved, ACT will then make arrangements for you. In order to provide the approved accommodations, ACT may have to assign you to a different test center rather than your original choice.

Special Testing

If you wish to request Special Testing, do not complete a registration folder. Instead, you and an official from your school must complete and sign a copy of the Request for ACT Special Testing. The Request for ACT Special Testing explains the eligibility criteria, documentation requirements, dates for scheduling the administration, deadlines for submitting the request, and restrictions on retesting.

Further information about ACT testing for students with disabilities can be found at www.act.org/aap/disab/index.html

THE SAT

The College Board administers the SAT Reasoning Test and SAT Subject Tests. The SAT Reasoning Test measures critical thinking skills – how well you analyze and solve problems – you need for academic success in college. The SAT is taken by high school juniors and seniors.

ACCOMMODATIONS

Students with documented disabilities are able to receive appropriate accommodations on the tests. The accommodations may include differences in (a) manner of presentation: large print, audiocassette, reader; (b) method of response: verbal, dictated to scribe, tape recorder, computer; (c) timing and scheduling: frequent breaks, extended time, multiple days; (d) setting: small group, private room, special lighting or acoustics, adaptive furniture or tools.

ELIGIBILITY

To be eligible for accommodations, you must (a) have a disability that necessitates testing accommodations, (b) have documentation on file at your school that supports your need for the requested accommodations and that meets the College Board Guidelines for Documentation, (c) receive and use the requested accommodations for tests at your school, and (d) complete the Student Eligibility Form.

In the event you do not meet all these requirements, you may still be eligible for accommodations by sending the completed Student Eligibility Form along with documentation of your disability to the College Board.

PROCEDURE

Obtain a Student Eligibility Form and a copy of the Instructions for Completing the Student Eligibility Form from your counseling office. Please note that your school must have an SSD Coordinator's Form on file with the College Board.

FOR FURTHER INFORMATION

For further information or to request the booklet information for Students with Special Needs:

WRITE: College Board Services for Students with Disabilities
PO Box 6226
Princeton, NJ 08541-6226

TELEPHONE: Voice: 1-609-771-7137, TTY: 1-609-882-4118
Monday to Friday: 8:00 to 6:00 p.m. Eastern time

FAX: 1-609-771-7944, **E-MAIL:** ssd@info.collegeboard.org

The College Board recommends that colleges consider your test scores in proper perspective as a part of a larger picture that includes your personal characteristics, background, personal history, and high school performance. Although test scores are close, but not exact, your past academic performance is usually the best single indicator of your academic potential.

If you plan to visit colleges, take along a copy of your score report. It will provide quickly some of the information admissions officers need in order to talk to you about their colleges and their admissions policies.

The Personal Interview

The personal interview gives you an opportunity to express how you deal with your particular disability. Your ability to communicate on this topic is very important. College personnel are interested in your knowledge of your disability. An enthusiastic acknowledgement that you will have to work hard in the college's program to achieve success is something interviewers look for.

Do you know who makes the decision regarding the Program for Students with Learning Disabilities? Is it the Director of Admissions, Director of the Program or both? Try to arrange an interview with the person who makes the decision.

You will naturally want to do all that you can to make a great impression on the interviewer. Interviewers can only know what you tell them about yourself, by the way you look, act, and answer questions. Here is a brief summary of important reminders:

1. Dress neatly, and try to choose clothing that suits the situation.
2. Know the college. This will enable you to ask relevant questions.
3. Be on time and greet the receptionist or the person who will introduce you to the interviewer. Be pleasant. Say your name clearly, and tell this person the name of the interviewer, if you know it.
4. Wait patiently, if the interviewer is not ready for you.
5. Shake hands, if it seems appropriate, when you meet the interviewer. Use a firm handshake but not an overpowering one. You should wait for the interviewer to ask you to sit down.
6. Maintain eye contact with the interviewer during your time together. This is considered to be a sign of honesty and self-confidence. It is better not to wear sunglasses during an interview.
7. Choose your words carefully and avoid slang or other special expressions that the interviewer may dislike or misunderstand.
8. Sit up in your chair. If your posture is good, the interviewer will see that you are alert and interested in what is happening.

9. Control any nervous behavior. Tapping your foot or clicking a ball-point pen, for example, may annoy and distract the interviewer. Refrain from chewing gum or smoking during your interview.

10. Talk about what you do well. Often you will find that you can answer a question by mentioning certain talents, interests, or skills. Mention test scores only if you are asked to do so. If you have done poorly on a test, avoid making excuses for your performance. Deal with it in an honest straightforward fashion.

11. Be calm. Try not to show disappointment or anger if you are not accepted, or if the interviewer does not make a decision immediately.

12. Say "thank you." It is a good idea to drop a note to the interviewer with thanks for the opportunity to discuss your candidacy.

The College Visitation

The best way for you to learn about the educational program, faculty, facilities and atmosphere and spirit of a college is to visit the campus, particularly when the college is in session. Most colleges offer information sessions and campus tours. Sign up on line.

COLLEGE VISITS ENABLE YOU TO:

- Learn what college admission officials expect from a candidate.
- Evaluate the environment of the school (academic, physical and social).
- Observe and talk with students who are attending and with whom you would associate.

WHEN TO MAKE THE VISIT:

It is better to visit when the college is in session, so you will get a picture of the daily college routine. Spring of your junior year and Fall of your senior year are the most appropriate times to make a college visit. Summer provides an excellent opportunity for the entire family to visit. You do not have to apply to a college before you visit it.

WHAT TO LOOK FOR:

- The size of classes and faculty/student ratio
- The library facility
- Strength of department you are likely to select as a major
- How and where the Learning Resource Center is set up
- Composition of the student body
- Attractive dormitories - satisfactory study facilities.
- Dining facility - quality of food

- Campus setting - beauty, orderliness and cleanliness
- What can you do when you want a snack?
- Adequate infirmary - the health service
- Religious facilities
- Facilities for leisure time - cultural programs - athletic facilities available - social life
- Do the college students appear to be happy, lively and friendly?
- What is the attitude of the faculty toward the students?
- Were the students friendly and courteous toward visitors?
- Are students serious and business-like toward their work?

SUGGESTIONS

• Visit college web site to arrange for an interview.

• Ask the guidance secretary for an unofficial copy of your transcript several days before you leave for the interviews.

• Prepare for your visit by referring to the college web site for the most up-to-date information and having questions for your interviewer. In most cases, the purpose of an interview is for you to ask questions about the college and its programs rather than for the college to ask questions about you.

SUMMARY OF IMPORTANT FACTORS

- Work closely with your school counselor

- Complete a comprehensive high school program at the highest level possible

- Develop strong study, social and independent living skills

- Know your high school record – get an unofficial copy of your transcript

- Know your rights – be familiar with the laws
  PL 94 - 142
  Section 504 of the Rehabilitation Act of 1973
  Part B of the Individuals with Disabilities Act
  Americans with Disabilities Act of 1990

- Know your disability – how it affects your learning

- Be able to discuss how you learn

- Be able to talk and write about your disability

- Have the proper documentation available to send to colleges:
  Official High School Transcript
  Complete Psychological Evaluations
  WAIS-R (Wechlser Adult Intelligence Scale)
  Most recent IEP (Individualized Education Plan) with services needed clearly stated
  Letters of Recommendation
  College Admissions Testing Results
  Application on line

- Prepare for contact with the Admissions Office and the Disabled Student Services Office
  Who makes the Admissions decision?

- Take advantage of Summer Programs

- Utilize the services of local government agencies
  Example: New York State – VESID (Vocational and Educational Services for Individuals with Disabilities)

- Utilize the services of the George Washington University HEATH Resource Center, the national clearinghouse on postsecondary education for individuals with disabilities.
  WEB SITE: www.heath.gwu.edu, **PHONE:** 1-800-544-3284,
  E-MAIL: askheath@gwu.edu

- Obtain student membership in Learning Disabilities organizations

MOST IMPORTANT: WHEN CONTACT IS MADE WITH THE COLLEGE MAKE SURE IT IS STUDENT CONTACT NOT PARENT CONTACT. Colleges want to hear from the student not the parent. It communicates student interest, self-reliance and initiative.

Good Luck!

COLLEGE COMPARISON WORKSHEET

Comparative Criteria of Programs for Learning Disabled	COLLEGE A________	COLLEGE B________	COLLEGE C________
BASIC FACTS			
1. Enrollment			
2. Location			
3. Cost			
4. Admission Selectibility			
5. Deadline for Application			
YOUR COLLEGE CRITERIA			
Services Available			
1.			
2.			
3.			
4.			
5.			
6.			
7.			
8.			
9.			
10.			
YOUR EVALUATION OF COLLEGE			
1. Positive Impressions			
2. Negative Impressions			
3. Parent/Counselor Opinion			
4. Your Order of Preference			
5. Your Chances of Admission			

CHECKLIST FOR APPLICATION PREPARATION

YOUR RESPONSIBILITIES	COLLEGE A_______	COLLEGE B_______	COLLEGE C_______
COLLEGE INFORMATION:			
Web address			
Information on line			
Application on line			
Campus Visit Planned on			
Info. Session Scheduled at			
Comparison Worksheet Done			
DEADLINES:			
Application			
Transcript & School Report			
Financial Aid			
Last Test Dates Accepted			
Early Decision/Early Action			
TESTING:			
SAT or ACT Required:			
Untimed SAT-Accepted?			
Test Date Plans			
Last Test Dates Accepted?			
Test Scores Sent from College			
Board or ACT			
Requested on			
INTERVIEW:			
Required?			
Campus Appointment on			
Alumni Interview on			
APPLICATION FORMS:			
Essays Written			
App. Fee mailed/sent online			
Secondary School Report:			
delivered to Counselor on			
mailed on			
1st Recommendation			
delivered on			
mailed on			
2nd Recommendation			
delivered on			
mailed on			
Personal Recommendation			
delivered on			
mailed on			

Four-Year Colleges with Programs for Students with Learning Disabilities

The following four-year colleges have specific programs for students with learning disabilities.

ALABAMA

ALABAMA STATE UNIVERSITY

915 SOUTH JACKSON STREET
MONTGOMERY, ALABAMA 36101-0271
(334) 229-4482 X4894; FAX: (334) 229-6924
E-MAIL: jdarrington@alasu.edu **WEB SITE: www.alasu.edu**

Name of Special Program: Disability Student Services/University Counseling Services
Director: Jessyca McCall Darrington
General Information: Four-Year State University; Enrollment: 5,222; **Tuition:** Residents – $9,594, Non-Residents – $12,498; **Room and Board:** Varies according to accommodations. **Majors:** Full, four-year degree programs, as well as Liberal Studies, in most areas
Special Program: Enrollment in Special Program: 60
Staff: Learning disabilities specialists; peer tutors; content tutors (faculty members)
Program Features: Oral and extended time testing; individual and small group tutoring sessions; limited course load (first year); academic advising for students with learning disabilities; basic study skills; faculty made aware of student's learning disability; developmental program; priority registration; self-advocacy
Entrance Requirements: Documentation of learning disability; learning disabilities specialist report; SAT/ACT untimed scores accepted; teacher evaluations; psychoeducational report (within three years)

AUBURN UNIVERSITY AT MONTGOMERY

P.O. BOX 244023
MONTGOMERY, ALABAMA 36124-4023
(334) 244-3468; FAX: (334) 244-3907
E-MAIL: css@mickey.aum.edu **WEB SITE: www.aum.edu**

Name of Special Program: Center for Special Services (CSS)
Director: Holly Brown
General Information: Four-Year State University; Enrollment: 4,900; **Tuition:** Residents – $113 per credit hour, Non-Residents – $339 per credit hour; **Room and Board:** One bedroom for two students – $1,030 per semester. The University is located on a 500-acre tract approximately seven miles east of downtown Montgomery, Alabama's capital city, between Interstate 85 and Highway 80. The University is on a semester system. **Degrees:** Bachelor's degrees are offered in the School of Business; School of Education; School of Liberal Arts; School of Nursing; School of Sciences.
Special Program: Enrollment in Special Program: 51; Cost: None

Staff: Learning disabilities specialists; peer tutors; special counselors
Program Features: Oral and extended time testing; individual tutoring sessions; basic study skills; tape recorders; taped texts; note-taking assistance – scribes; faculty made aware of student's learning disability; support group
Entrance Requirements: Documentation of learning disability; SAT/ACT untimed scores accepted; testing: WAIS, Woodcock-Johnson-R, psychological report; high school transcript or GED
Special Facilities for: Visual, hearing and physical impairments
College Life: Due to the small size of our institution, all students are able to have a one-on-one relationship with faculty and staff. In addition, the Center for Special Services can offer one-on-one counseling and/or mentoring for students via student peer counselors and staff. Further, all AUM students can receive free tutoring in our Learning Center (math and English) and Instructional Support Lab (sciences)) as well as free counseling at the AUM Counseling Center. These services give our students the extra support they may need for overall academic and personal success.

UNIVERSITY OF ALABAMA
220 RESEARCH DRIVE, BOX 870185
TUSCALOOSA, ALABAMA 35487-0185
(205) 348-4285; FAX: (205) 348-0804
E-MAIL: ods@bama.ua.edu **WEB SITE: www.ods.ua.edu**

Name of Special Program: Office of Disability Services
Director: Judy Thorpe
General Information: Four-Year State University; Enrollment: 18,000; **Tuition:** Residents – $1,778 per semester, Non-Residents – $4,812 per semester; **Room and Board:** $960–1,700 per semester. The University is located in Tuscaloosa, a city of approximately 78,000 residents in the west-central part of the state. University grounds comprise some 878 acres. Campus environment is suburban. **Degrees:** Bachelor's degrees offered in arts and sciences, commerce and business administration, communications, community health sciences, education, engineering, human environment sciences; New College/undergraduate and graduate degrees: social work, library sciences
Staff: Learning disabilities specialists
Program Features: Oral and extended time testing; tape recorders; taped texts; note-taking assistance; assistive technology; use of computer, spellcheck, calculation; reduced distraction testing; reading assistance, academic classroom aids, adaptive computer technology.
Entrance Requirements: Documentation of learning disability; SAT/ACT untimed scores accepted; psychological report

Special Facilities for: Visual, hearing and physical impairments
College Life: Students with disabilities are encouraged to contact ODS during orientation sessions. The Alabama Department of Rehabilitation Services (ADRS) assists eligible students with disabilities in their pursuit of employment goals.

ARIZONA

ARIZONA STATE UNIVERSITY
BOX 873202
TEMPE, ARIZONA 85287
(480) 965-1234, (480) 965-9000 TDD; FAX: (480) 965-0441
E-MAIL: disability-q@asu.edu WEB SITE: www.asu.edu

Name of Special Program: Disability Resource Center (DRC)
Director: Carol Takao
General Information: Four-Year State University; Enrollment: 47,000; **Tuition:** Residents – $4,064, Non-Residents – $12,919; **Room and Board:** $5,700. A suburban campus in a small city, 10 miles from downtown Phoenix; 329 sunny days a year make outdoor recreation a way of life. Friends meet in the Student Recreation Complex to work out, compete in court sports, and swim in the nation's largest collegiate pool. The Pete Dye-designed Karsten golf course, skydiving, snowskiing, water skiing, soccer and mountain climbing are only a few of the activities open to students. **Degrees:** Architecture and environmental design (BSD), landscape architecture (BSLA), urban planning (BSP), business (BS), education (BAE), engineering and applied sciences (BS), agribusiness and environmental resources (BS), Del E. Webb School of Construction (BS), School of Technology (BS), School of Engineering (BSE, BS), fine arts (BA, BFA, BM), liberal arts and sciences (BA, BS), nursing (BSN), public programs (BA, BS), School of Social Work (BSW)
Special Program: Enrollment in Special Program: 325 LD; 220 ADHD; Cost: None
Staff: Learning disabilities specialists
Program Features: Oral and extended time testing; limited course load (first year); note-taking assistance – scribes; taped texts; basic study skills; faculty made aware of student's learning disability (at student's request); access learning; computer lab
Entrance Requirements: Documentation of learning disability (appropriate psychoeducational evaluations that are no more than three years old); SAT/ACT untimed scores accepted; testing: WAIS; psychological report; medical evaluation; measles immunization
Special Facilities for: Visual, hearing, and physical impairments, learning

disabilities, acquired brain injury or other hidden disabilities
College Life: In support of the University goals to dedicate itself to superior instruction, excellent student performance, original research endeavor, scholarly achievement, outstanding public service and economic development, DRS facilitates equal access to educational and co-curricular programs, campus activities, career exploration and employment opportunities for qualified ASU students with disabilities.
Scholarships: See page 424.

UNIVERSITY OF ARIZONA
P.O. BOX 210136, 1010 NORTH HIGHLAND AVENUE
TUCSON, ARIZONA 85721-0136
(520) 621-1427; FAX: (520) 626-3260
E-MAIL: jorgera@u.arizona.edu WEB SITE: www.salt.arizona.edu

Name of Special Program: Strategic Alternative Learning Techniques (SALT) Center
Director: Jeff Orgera
General Information: Four-Year State University; Enrollment: 37,000; **Tuition:** Residents – $4,766, Non-Residents – $14,972; **Room and Board:** $7,850. Urban residential campus located in downtown Tucson, approximately two hours from Phoenix, five hours from the Grand Canyon and 65 miles north of Mexico. Famous for its sunny skies and mild winters. Students create their own communities based on where they choose to live and which of the nearly 300 diverse clubs and organizations they choose to join. The campus offers a full range of social and cultural opportunities. **Degrees:** BA, BS, BFA, BM in art, music, media arts, and theatre arts; BS in geosciences, and speech and hearing sciences. The University offers a wide spectrum of programs in the arts, sciences and professional fields.
Special Program: Enrollment in Special Program: 525 (limited enrollment of 150-200 freshmen per year); Cost: Freshmen and sophomores, $1,900 per semester; juniors and seniors, $800 per semester. The percentage of students with learning disabilities receiving a degree in four years is 60% and in five or more years is 40%.
Staff: Learning disabilities specialists; content tutors; peer tutors; education specialists; writing skills coordinator.
Program Features: Individual and small group tutoring sessions; limited course load (first year is suggested); basic study skills; advocacy; writing labs; education specialists; mentor program; learning strategies; computer lab; assistive technology
Entrance Requirements: Documentation of learning disability; learning disabilities specialist report; handwritten essay (personal letter may be typed); teacher evaluation (two letters of recommendation from two peo-

ple who have worked with the student); testing: WAIS, Woodcock-Johnson, psychological report, achievement and cognitive testing
Special Facilities for: Visual, hearing and physical impairments
College Life: SALT is one of the most competitive and thorough programs of its kind in the United States.
Scholarships: See page 424.

ARKANSAS

UNIVERSITY OF ARKANSAS

GARLAND AVENUE, ARKANSAS UNION 116
FAYETTEVILLE, ARKANSAS 72701
(479) 575-3104, (479) 575-3646 TDD; FAX: (479) 575-7445
E-MAIL: ada@uark.edu **WEB SITE: www.uark.edu**

Name of Special Program: Center for Students with Disabilities
Associate Director: Dr. Linda J. Watts
General Information: Four-Year State University; Enrollment: 14,800; **Tuition:** Residents – $4,590, Non-Residents – $12,724; **Room and Board:** $6,127. Founded in 1871, the 329-acre campus is in a small city 180 miles northwest of Little Rock. **Majors:** Agribusiness/agricultural production, agricultural sciences, architecture, area studies, biology, botany, business/management, chemistry, communications, education, engineering, environmental design, ethnic studies, fine arts, geological/health/life/ physical/social sciences, home economics, languages, law, letters/literature, marketing/distribution, mathematics, medical laboratory technologies, multi/interdisciplinary studies, music, parks and recreation, philosophy, physics, protective services, psychology, public affairs, religion, renewable natural resources, visual/performing arts, vocational home economics, zoology
Special Program: Enrollment in Special Program: 350; Cost: None. *Summer Program:* Academic Support for Achievement: This is a college transition program for high-achieving students with disabilities. This program provides students with a head start at the University of Arkansas. Students, parents, and professionals work together to develop an Individual College Plan. The program culminates with the planning conference at which the student's College Plan is discussed and refined. The student's rights as a college student with a disability are discussed and a schedule of action for the first year at college is developed. The student is linked with tutors, counselors and other resources either on the campus or in the community. Academic Support for Achievement assists students only with the transition to college. (Individual services and accommodations are provided by the Office for Campus Access at the University of Arkansas.) Cost: varies with individual need

Staff: Learning disabilities specialists; school psychology specialists; licensed professional counselors; a wide range of consultants
Academic Support for Achievement Features: Testing, assessment, individual planning related to the transition from high school to college and from college to work
Program Features: Individual accommodation plan dictates auxiliary aids and services provided.
Entrance Requirements: Documentation of a disability; SAT/ACT special condition testing accepted
Special Facilities for: Visual, hearing and physical impairments; housing and transportation for students with physical or sensory disabilities

UNIVERSITY OF THE OZARKS
415 NORTH COLLEGE AVENUE
CLARKSVILLE, ARKANSAS 72830
(479) 979-1403; FAX: (479) 979-1429
E-MAIL: jlc@ozarks.edu **WEB SITE: www.ozarks.edu**

Name of Special Program: Jones Learning Center
Director: Julia Frost
General Information: Four-Year Private University; Enrollment: 700; **Tuition:** $14,470; **Room and Board:** $5,260. Nestled in the scenic Ozark Mountains, 100 miles west of Little Rock, and close to the Arkansas River, the University's rural setting provides numerous activities for the student who loves the outdoors. The University is a liberal arts institution, associated with the Presbyterian Church, which provides excellent professional preparation and a unique study abroad program. Students come from diverse educational, cultural, religious and economic backgrounds. **Majors:** Accounting, art, biology, business administration/education, chemistry, communications, composite sciences, early childhood education, mathematics, middle level education, music, physical education, physics, political science, psychology, religion/philosophy, social sciences, sociology, theatre.
Special Program: Enrollment in Special Program: 75 (limited to 80); Cost: $7,750 per semester. The percentage of students with learning disabilities receiving a degree in five or more years is 50%.
Staff: Learning disabilities specialists; peer tutors; content tutors (staff members)
Program Features: Oral and extended time testing; taped texts; note-taking assistance – scribes; individual and small group tutoring sessions; limited course load (if needed); basic study skills; tape recorders; developmental program; academic advising; faculty made aware of student's learning disability; Kurzweil readers; program coordinators; Dragon Naturally Speaking

Entrance Requirements: Documentation of learning disability; learning disabilities specialist report; SAT or ACT untimed scores accepted; diagnostic testing at University of the Ozarks; teacher evaluation; medical evaluation; handwritten essay; testing: WAIS-III, psychological report; on-campus evaluation and interview
Special Facilities for: Visual, hearing and physical impairments on the campus, not in the program.
College Life: The University of the Ozarks is a beautiful, small campus with excellent facilities where faculty, staff, and students know each other by name. The Jones Learning Center has a 30-year history of success. Each student's program is individualized and extensive support provided based on specific needs. Class size on campus averages 16, and professors work closely with the Learning Center staff to help each student succeed.
Scholarships: See page 424.

CALIFORNIA

BIOLA UNIVERSITY

13800 BIOLA AVENUE
LA MIRADA, CALIFORNIA 90639
(562) 944-0351 X5851, (562) 777-4030 TTY
WEB SITE: www.biola.edu

Name of Special Program: Disability Services
Director: Tim Engle
General Information: Four-Year Private University; Enrollment: 3,000; **Tuition:** $23,782; **Room and Board:** $6,998. A private interdenominational Christian institution with a 95-acre campus in a suburban area 22 miles southeast of Los Angeles. The campus is near Disneyland and Knotts Berry Farm and is one hour from mountains and beaches. **Majors:** Biological science, business, communications and the arts, computer and physical science, education, health professions, social science
Special Program: Enrollment in Special Program: 8–15; Cost: $1,800
Staff: Learning disabilities specialists; peer tutors; content tutors (faculty members)
Program Features: Oral and extended time testing; limited course load (first year); tape recorders; taped texts, individual and small group tutoring sessions; academic advising for students with learning disabilities; basic study skills; faculty made aware of student's learning disability, note-taking assistance – scribes, text help software
Entrance Requirements: Documentation of learning disability; SAT/ACT untimed scores accepted; testing: WAIS, IEP, psychological report
Scholarships: See page 426.

CALIFORNIA POLYTECHNIC STATE UNIVERSITY
STUDENT SERVICES BUILDING 124, ROOM 119
SAN LUIS OBISPO, CALIFORNIA 93407
(805) 756-1395 V/TTY; FAX: (805) 756-5451
WEB SITE: www.calpoly.edu; www.drc.calpoly.edu

Name of Special Program: Disability Resource Center
Director: Trey Duffy
General Information: Four-Year State University; Enrollment: 16,000; **Tuition:** Residents – $1,450 per quarter, Non-Residents – $226 per unit; **Room and Board:** $8,800. Located on the central coast of California midway between Los Angeles and San Francisco, and in the beautiful little mission city of San Luis Obispo. A peaceful place. The mild climate and lovely rural scenery draw students outdoors most of the year. Founded in 1901, the college programs stress fundamental scientific knowledge, and great value is placed on the social sciences, arts and humanities. **Majors:** Aerospace engineering, bioresource and agricultural engineering, agricultural business, agricultural science, agricultural systems management, architecture, animal science, art and design, architectural engineering, biochemistry, biological sciences, business administration, chemistry, child development, city/regional planning, civil/environmental/computer/engineering/sciences, construction management, crop science, dairy science, economics, economics, education, electrical/electronic engineering, English, environmental engineering, environmental and industrial engineering, fruit science, forestry and natural resources, forest science, general engineering, manufacturing engineering, plant protection science, theatre, modern languages and literature, philosophy, graphic communication, history, child development, industrial technology, journalism, landscape architecture, liberal studies, mathematics, mechanical/metallurgical, materials engineering, microbiology, music, natural resources management, nutritional and food sciences, environmental horticulture, kinesiology, physical/political science, physics, poultry industry, psychology, recreation parks and tourism administration, social sciences, software engineering, speech communication, statistics, soil science, theatre
Special Program: Enrollment in Special Program: 260; Cost: None. Services are available year-round.
Staff: Learning disabilities specialists; special counselors
Program Features: Testing accommodations; taped texts; note-taking assistance – scribes; tape recorders; faculty made aware of student's learning disability (at student's request); basic study skills assistance; academic advisement for students with disabilities; disability management; campus and community referrals; DRC provides memorandum they can share with faculty
Entrance Requirements: Documentation of learning disability (recommended within the last three years); learning disabilities specialist report (recom-

mended); SAT/ACT untimed scores accepted; testing: WAIS, achievement tests, SEC, psychological report (recommended). Admission to CalPoly is through regular admissions process. Once admitted, students provide documentation of disability to DRC prior to receiving accommodations.
Special Facilities for: Visual, hearing and physical impairments

CALIFORNIA STATE UNIVERSITY: CHICO
SECOND AND IVY
CHICO, CALIFORNIA 95929-0726
(916) 898-5959 V/TTY; FAX: (916) 898-4411
E-MAIL: dssdept@csuchico.edu WEB SITE: www. csuchico.edu/dss

Name of Special Program: Disability Support Services (DSS)
Director: Billie Jackson
General Information: Four-Year State University; Enrollment: 12,500; **Tuition:** Residents – $1,706, Non-Residents – additional $339 per unit, per semester; **Room and Board:** $8,314. Chico is situated at the foot of the western slope of the Sierra Nevada, 170 miles northeast of San Francisco. Unique to Chico is 2,400-acre municipal Bidwell Park located near the University, an 18-hole golf course, softball diamonds, picnic areas, equestrian, jogging, and hiking trails, and natural swimming holes along big Chico Creek. **Degrees:** Bachelor of Arts, Master of Arts, Bachelor of Science, Master of Science, Bachelor of Fine Arts, Bachelor of Vocational Education
Special Program: Enrollment in Special Program: 400; Cost: None
Staff: Learning disabilities specialists
Program Features: Testing accommodations; tutoring sessions; study skills; note-taking assistance – scribes; tape recorders; taped texts; faculty made aware of student's learning disability; computer lab
Entrance Requirements: Documentation of learning disability; SAT/ACT untimed scores accepted; testing: WAIS, psychological report
College Life: California State University at Chico is a friendly, residential campus.

CALIFORNIA STATE UNIVERSITY: NORTHRIDGE
18111 NORDHOFF STREET
NORTHRIDGE, CALIFORNIA 91330-8264
(818) 677-2684; FAX: (818) 677-4932
E-MAIL: sdr@csun.edu WEB SITE: www.csun.edu

Name of Special Program: Students with Disabilities Resources
Director: Dr. Mary Ann Cummins Prager
General Information: Four-Year State University; Enrollment: 28,000;

Annual Tuition: Residents – $3,042, Non-Residents – $5,506; **Room and Board:** $9,323. Founded in 1956, the San Fernando Valley branch of Los Angeles State College was designated a university in 1972. The campus consists of 350 acres and is located about 21 miles northwest of Los Angeles. **Majors:** Pan-American studies, anthropology, art, biochemistry, biology, business administration, business education, chemistry, child development, communicative disorders, computer science, deaf studies, earth-science, economics, engineering, English, environmental and occupational health, French, geography, geology, German, health science, history, home economics, humanities, journalism, liberal studies, linguistics, mathematics, Chicano-American studies, music, philosophy, nursing, physical education, physics, political science, psychology, radio-television, TV-film, recreation, religious studies, sociology, Spanish, speech communication, theatre arts, urban studies, special majors
Special Program: Enrollment in Special Program: 380; Cost: None
Staff: Learning disabilities specialists; special counselors
Program Features: Oral and extended time testing; note-taking assistance – scribes; academic advising for students with learning disabilities; electronic texts; tape recorders; peer mentoring; assistive technology
Entrance Requirements: No specific items of identification as disabled on application to University
Special Facilities for: Visual, hearing, physical impairments, and mental health disabilities
College Life: The Students with Disabilities Resources office does learning disability testing/assessment of students at no charge.
Scholarships: See page 425.

CALIFORNIA STATE UNIVERSITY: SACRAMENTO

SERVICES TO STUDENTS WITH DISABILITIES
6000 J STREET, LSN-1008
SACRAMENTO, CALIFORNIA 95819-6042
(916) 278-6955, (916) 278-7239 TDD; FAX: (916) 278-7825
E-MAIL: sswd@csus.edu **WEB SITE: www.csus.edu**

Name of Special Program: Services to Students with Disabilities
Acting Co-Directors: Judy Dean and Melissa Repa
General Information: Four-Year State University; Enrollment: 28,500; **Tuition:** Residents – $3,280, Non-Residents – $3,280 plus $339 per unit. **Room and Board:** $6,163. The 282-acre (and growing) campus is in an urban area 90 miles northeast of San Francisco. Special learning facilities include a learning resource center, art gallery, planetarium, radio station, TV station, child care center, and an aquatic center. **Majors:** Biological sci-

ence, business, communications and the arts, computer and physical science, education, special education and vocational rehabilitation, engineering and environmental design, health professions, interior design, and social sciences

Special Program: Enrollment in Special Program; 400; Cost: None. The percentage of students with learning disabilities receiving a degree in four years is 40% and in five or more years is 60%.

Staff: Learning disabilities specialists

Program Features: Oral and extended time testing; individual and small group tutoring sessions; limited course load (first year); basic study skills; note-taking assistance – scribes; taped texts; tape recorders; computer lab; academic advising (related to disability only). The program offers a team-taught course (LD50) that is foundational to college success.

Entrance Requirements: Documentation of learning disability; learning disabilities specialist report; testing: WAIS, IEP (helpful), psychological report, diagnostic testing at California State University: Sacramento (if already enrolled); teacher evaluation, medical evaluation; handwritten essay; assessment must be adult normed

Special Facilities for: Visual, hearing and physical impairments

College Life: The program prides itself on providing students with a comprehensive plan regarding their disability and accommodations. Students are encouraged to have an understanding of their strengths and areas of need, and promote self-advocacy.

SAN DIEGO STATE UNIVERSITY
500 CAMPANILE DRIVE
SAN DIEGO, CALIFORNIA 92182-7417
(619) 594-6473, (619) 594-2929 TDD; FAX: (619) 594-4315
E-MAIL: mbehr@sdsu.edu **WEB SITE: www.sdsu.edu**

Name of Special Program: Learning Disabilities Program

Director: Mary Shojai; *Coordinator:* Margo Behr

General Information: Four-Year State University; Enrollment: 30,000; **Tuition:** Residents – $1,805, Non-Residents – additional $339 per unit; **Room and Board:** $10,093 for nine months. Founded in 1897 for the training of elementary school teachers in what was then the far eastern border of the city. In 1931, the college moved to the seven mission-style buildings of the present campus, surrounding the Main Quad. Today it is a major urban comprehensive institution. **Majors:** Area studies, biology, botany, business/management, chemistry, communications, computer/information sciences, engineering, ethnic studies, fine arts, geological sciences, health sciences, home economics, languages, letters/literature, mathematics, music, philoso-

phy, physical sciences (general), physics, protective services, psychology, public affairs, religion, social sciences, visual/performing arts, zoology
Special Program: Enrollment in Special Program; 1,000–1,150; Cost: None
Staff: Learning disabilities specialists; peer tutors; special counselors
Program Features: Oral and extended time testing; individual and small group tutoring sessions; academic advising; basic study skills; note-taking assistance – scribes; taped texts; tape recorders; faculty made aware of student's learning disability; high tech center
Entrance Requirements: Documentation of learning disability; learning disabilities specialist report; handwritten essay; teacher evaluation; medical evaluation, testing: WAIS-R, IEP, psychological report, Woodcock-Johnson III; diagnostic testing at San Diego State University
Special Facilities for: Visual, hearing and physical impairments

SAN FRANCISCO STATE UNIVERSITY
1600 HOLLOWAY AVENUE
SAN FRANCISCO, CALIFORNIA 94132-4046
(415) 338-2472, (415) 338-2472 TTY; FAX: (415) 338-1041
E-MAIL: dprc@sfsu.edu **WEB SITE: www.sfsu.edu/~dprc**

Name of Special Program: Disability Program's Resource Center
Associate Director: Deidre A. Defreese
General Information: Four-Year State University; Enrollment; 27,000; **Tuition:** Residents – $1,564 per semester, Non-Residents – $1,564 plus $339 per unit per semester; **Room and Board:** $9,570. A two-story brick building on Nob Hill housed San Francisco State Normal School which was established in 1899. In 1921 the school became a State Teachers College and in 1935 the school became San Francisco State College. The college dedicated its 95-acre $12-million campus to the state in October 1954 and became a university in 1961. Today the campus consists of eight schools. **Majors:** Behavioral and social sciences, business, creative arts, education, ethnic studies, health, physical education, recreation-leisure studies, humanities and science
Special Program: Enrollment in Special Program: 400; Cost: None
Staff: Learning disabilities specialists; peer tutors; special counselors
Program Features: Extended time testing; individual and small group tutoring sessions; limited course load; note-taking assistance; tape recorders; taped texts; faculty made aware of student's learning disability (at student's request); drop-in tutoring; use of adaptive equipment during tests (computer with spellcheck, electronic speller, etc.)
Entrance Requirements: Documentation of learning disability; SAT/ACT untimed scores accepted; diagnostic testing (within the last three years)
Special Facilities for: Visual, hearing and physical impairments

STANFORD UNIVERSITY
OFFICE OF ACCESSIBLE EDUCATION
563 SALVATIERRA WALK
STANFORD, CALIFORNIA 94305-3005
(650) 723-1066, (650) 723-1067 TTY; FAX: (650) 725-5301
E-MAIL: info@drc.stanford.edu **WEB SITE: www.stanford.edu**

Name of Special Program: Disability Resource Center
Director: Dr. Joan Bisagno
General Information: Four-Year Private University; Enrollment; 14,000; **Tuition:** $35,994 annually; **Room and Board:** $8,030 per quarter. A 8,200-acre campus near Palo Alto, 30 miles south of San Francisco. **Majors:** African / Afro-American studies, American studies, anthropology, art, biological sciences, chemistry, classics, communications, drama, earth sciences, East Asian studies, economics, engineering, English, languages, history, humanities, international relations, linguistics, mathematics, microbiology, music, philosophy, physics, political science, psychology, public policy, religious studies, sociology, symbolic systems, urban studies, values / technology / science / society
Special Program: Enrollment in Special Program: 320; Cost: None
Staff: Learning disabilities specialist
Program Features: Extended time testing; individual peer tutoring sessions; reduced course load; note-taking assistance – scribes; taped texts; faculty made aware of student's learning disability; support groups; adaptive computer workstation
Entrance Requirements: No special admissions process for students with learning disabilities; documentation of learning disability (helpful); learning disabilities specialist report (after admission to University); SAT / ACT untimed scores accepted
Special Facilities for: Visual, hearing and physical impairments

UNIVERSITY OF CALIFORNIA: BERKELEY
260 CESAR CHAVEZ STUDENT CENTER #4250
BERKELEY, CALIFORNIA 94720-4250
(510) 642-3175 or (510) 642-7333; FAX: (510) 643-9686
E-MAIL: cchiba@berkeley.edu
WEB SITE: www.berkeley.edu or www.dsp.berkeley.edu

Name of Special Program: Disabled Students' Program
Director: Ed Rogers; *Disability Services Coordinator:* Connie Chiba, Ph.D.
General Information: Four-Year State University; Enrollment: 31,000; **Tuition:** Residents – $3,899.75 per semester, Non-Residents – $13,241.75 per semester; **Room and Board:** $11,970 double occupancy. Urban campus in

a small city 10 miles from San Francisco. **Majors:** Agribusiness/agricultural production, agricultural sciences, architecture, area studies, biology, botany, business/management, chemistry, communications, communications technologies, computer/information sciences, engineering, environmental design, ethnic studies, fine arts, geological/health/physical/life/social sciences, languages, law, letters/literature, mathematics, multi/interdisciplinary studies, music, philosophy, physics, psychology, religion, renewable natural resources, visual/performing arts, zoology.
Special Program: Enrollment in Special Program: 147 LD; 105 ADHD; Cost: None
Staff: Learning disabilities specialists
Program Features: Oral and extended time testing; limited course load (first year); note-taking assistance – scribes; tape recorders; taped texts; faculty made aware of student's learning disability (at student's request), academic advising for students with learning disabilities; all accommodations are based on an individualized assessment
Entrance Requirements: Documentation of learning disability; learning disabilities specialist report; SAT/ACT untimed scores accepted
Special Facilities for: Visual, hearing and physical impairments
College Life: Highly qualified staff of learning disabilities specialists provides comprehensive services on an individual basis. Special class, "Understanding Learning Differences," for students with learning disabilities and ADHD.

UNIVERSITY OF CALIFORNIA: SANTA BARBARA
629 EAST VALERIO STREET
SANTA BARBARA, CALIFORNIA 93106-3070
(805) 893-2668; FAX: (805) 893-7127
WEB SITE: www.ucsb.edu/dsp

Name of Special Program: Disabled Students Program
Acting Director: Gary White
General Information: Four-Year State University; Enrollment: 18,000; **Tuition:** Residents – $6,495, Non-Residents – $16,956; **Room and Board:** $9,897. The University of California: Santa Barbara is tucked between the Santa Ynez Mountains and the Pacific Ocean. It is located 100 miles north of Los Angeles near the city of Santa Barbara. **Degrees:** The University awards bachelor's, master's and doctoral degrees. Degrees are offered in the College of Creative Studies, College of Engineering, College of Letters and Science, Graduate Division, School of Environmental Science and Management and Graduate School of Education. Special programs include cooperative education, internships, summer sessions for credit, study abroad and Army ROTC.

Special Program: Enrollment in Special Program: 500; Cost: None
Staff: Learning disabilities specialists; peer tutors provided via Campus Learning Assistance Program
Program Features: Oral and extended time testing; note-taking assistance – scribes; tape recorders; taped texts; basic study skills; academic advising; Kurzweil reader, readers to supplement Recording for the Blind & Dyslexic, Dragon Dictate, Reader's Edge; faculty made aware of student's learning disability
Entrance Requirements: Documentation of learning disability; SAT/ACT untimed scores accepted; testing: WAIS, Woodcock Johnson-R achievement test, Nelson-Denny reading test, psychological report
Special Facilities for: Visual, hearing and physical impairments

UNIVERSITY OF THE PACIFIC
3601 PACIFIC AVENUE, BANNISTER HALL
STOCKTON, CALIFORNIA 95211
(209) 946-2879 V/TDD; FAX: (209) 946-2278
E-MAIL: ssd@pacific.edu **WEB SITE: www.pacific.edu**

Name of Special Program: Office of Services for Students with Disabilities
Coordinator: Daniel Nuss
General Information: Four-Year Private University; Enrollment: 5,000; **Tuition, Room and Board:** $36,150. The University of the Pacific is an independent coeducational institution. The 175-acre campus is in a suburban area 80 miles east of San Francisco and 40 miles south of Sacramento. Special facilities include an educational center, art gallery and radio station. **Majors:** Arts and Sciences, Conservatory of Music, Schools of Business, Education, Engineering, International Studies, Pharmacy, Dentistry (San Francisco), and Law (Sacramento). Advantage Programs for freshmen include students with learning disabilities.
Special Program: Enrollment in Special Program: 125; Cost: None
Staff: Learning disabilities specialists; peer tutors, content tutors (faculty members)
Program Features: Oral and extended time testing; individual and small group tutoring sessions; limited course load (optional); note-taking assistance – scribes; tape recorders; taped texts; basic study skills; developmental program; academic advising; Kurzweil reader; sound-resistant testing booth; faculty made aware of student's learning disability
Entrance Requirements: Documentation of learning disability; handwritten essay; testing: psychological report; diagnostic testing at the University of the Pacific for a fee
Special Facilities for: Visual, hearing and physical impairments
College Life: Small classes and a strong support program lead to success.

COLORADO

UNIVERSITY OF COLORADO: BOULDER

107 UCB
BOULDER, COLORADO 80309-0107
(303) 492-8671; FAX: (303) 492-5601
E-MAIL: dsinfo@colorado.edu
WEB SITE: www.colorado.edu/disabilityservices

Name of Special Program: Academic Access and Resources Program
Coordinator: Cindy Donahue
General Information: Four-Year State University; Enrollment: 29,151; **Annual Tuition:** Residents – $4,446, Non-Residents – $21,900; **Room and Board:** $7,980. The University of Colorado: Boulder is the flagship of the four-campus University of Colorado system. It is located 30 miles from Denver at the base of the Rocky Mountains. It is one of 34 U.S. public research universities invited to join the prestigious Association of American Universities. **Degrees:** Degree programs are offered at five colleges and three schools: Arts and Sciences, Leeds School of Business, School of Education, College of Architecture and Planning, and School of Law, College of Music, School of Journalism and Mass Communication. **Majors:** There are 150 fields of study: 85 at the bachelor's level, 70 at the master's level, and 50 at the doctoral level.
Special Program: Enrollment in Special Program: 242; Cost: None
Staff: Disabilities specialists; peer tutors (available free in the Residence Halls)
Program Features: Accommodations as supported by documentation; extended time testing; individual strategy sessions; academic advising; assistive technology lab; writing lab
Entrance Requirements: Documentation of learning disability; testing: WAIS, psychological report; achievement testing and indication of a significant impairment. Guidelines available at disability services website above.
Special Facilities for: Visual, hearing and physical impairments
College Life: The service delivery model in the Academic Access and Resource Program places an emphasis on strategy development, empowerment, independence and building a network of resources.
Scholarships: See page 425.

UNIVERSITY OF DENVER
LEARNING EFFECTIVENESS PROGRAM
2050 EAST EVANS AVENUE SUITE 30
DENVER, COLORADO 80208
(303) 871-2372; FAX: (303) 871-3939
E-MAIL: LEP-info@du.edu **WEB SITE: www.du.edu/lep**

Name of Special Program: Learning Effectiveness Program (LEP). Students with disabilities not enrolled in LEP are part of the Disability Services Program II (DSP).
Director: Ted May; *Associate Director:* David Luker
General Information: Four-Year Private University; Enrollment: 4,456 undergraduate students; 4,792 graduate students; **Tuition:** $29,628; **Room and Board:** $8,166. Founded in 1864, 12 years before Colorado became a state, the University is located seven miles southeast of downtown Denver. The University consists of 125 acres with 100 buildings. **Majors:** Accounting, animal technology, anthropology, art, art history, Asian studies, biological sciences, business, chemistry and bio-chemistry, classical studies, comparative literature, computer science, decision sciences, communications, digital media studies, economics, education, engineering, English, English/theatre, environmental sciences, European studies, finance, foreign languages, geography, geology, history, hotel, restaurant and tourism management, international studies, Jewish studies, Latin-American studies, management, marketing, mass communications, mathematics, music, philosophy, physics, political science, psychology, public affairs, real estate and construction management, religious studies, Russian area studies, science area, social science area, sociology, speech communication, sports science, wellness and human biology and women's studies
Special Program: Enrollment in Special LEP Program: 194; Cost: $2,700 per year. *Summer Program:* Students enrolled in summer school may participate in the full program for $600.
Staff: Learning disabilities specialists; content tutors; counselors — graduate students and professionals trained in learning disabilities
Program Features: Extended time testing; taped texts; tape recorders; study skills; individual and small group tutoring sessions; limited course load recommended (first quarter/first year); developmental program; cognitive/intracognitive strategies; individual academic plans; writing workshops; career counseling; faculty made aware of student's learning disability (at student's request); computer assistance lab, Kurzweil 3000. It is highly recommended that freshmen and sophomore students participate in the full program. Students commit to the program on a yearly basis and may participate in the program throughout their educational experi-

ence at the University of Denver.
Entrance Requirements: Documentation of learning disability; learning disabilities specialist report; SAT/ACT untimed scores accepted; testing: WAIS, Woodcock-Johnson-R; teacher evaluation. Testing must be no older than three years. Note: Students who qualify for financial aid should include the LEP fee in their statement of need; often the fee for LEP is met with the student's financial aid package.
Special Facilities for: Visual, hearing and physical impairments
College Life: The LEP is a comprehensive learning disability support program offered within a rigorous academic setting. The LEP staff works both individually and collaboratively with motivated students to create academic success. LEP students and the LEP's vision are enthusiastically supported by the University and its trustees. The University admissions process is a separate process from the LEP application process. Students must be admitted to the University before being accepted in the LEP. Both admissions application processes should be started concurrently.

CONNECTICUT

MITCHELL COLLEGE

437 PEQUOT AVENUE
NEW LONDON, CONNECTICUT 06320
(860) 701-7141; FAX: (860) 701-5090
E-MAIL: carnevalej@mitchell.edu **WEB SITE: www.mitchell.edu**

Name of Special Program: Learning Resource Center
Director: Dr. Peter Troiano, *Associate Director:* Joanne Carnevale
General Information: Four-Year Private College; Enrollment: 700; **Annual Tuition:** $18,058; **Room and Board**: $9,652. A 67-acre campus located on the waterfront in New London halfway between Boston and New York. New London is known historically as "The Whaling City." Nearby attractions include the Coast Guard Academy, Connecticut College, Mystic Marine Life Aquarium and Mystic Seaport. **Bachelor Degrees**: Business, criminal justice, early childhood education, human development and family studies, liberal arts, professional studies, psychology, sports management. **Associate Degrees:** Business, computer information systems, criminal justice, early childhood education, graphic design, human development and family studies, human services, liberal arts, physical education, sport management.
Special Program: Enrollment in Special Program: 200 (limited to 200); Cost: $6,000 per year. *Summer Program:* Two courses may be taken for college credit; full Learning Resource Center support is available. Cost: $3,500. Optional

Staff: Learning disabilities specialists; content tutors (faculty members); special counselors. The percentage of students with learning disabilities receiving a degree in two years is 75% and in four or more years is 65%.
Program Features: Oral and extended time testing; individual and small group sessions; basic study skills; limited course load; note-taking assistance – scribes, tape recorders
Entrance Requirements: Documentation of learning disability; learning disabilities specialist report; SAT/ACT untimed scores accepted; teacher evaluation; handwritten essay testing: WAIS, IEP, psychological report
College Life: The Learning Resources Center is an academic support program for students with learning disabilities that is designed to promote successful and independent learning. The program is intensive and individualized, offering up to four hours per week of support with trained specialists who are individually assigned.

SOUTHERN CONNECTICUT STATE UNIVERSITY
ENGLEMAN C105, 501 CRESCENT AVENUE
NEW HAVEN, CONNECTICUT 06515
(203) 392-6828, (203) 392-6131 TTY; FAX: (203) 392-6829
E-MAIL: tuckers@southernct.edu WEB SITE: www.southernct.edu

Name of Special Program: Disability Resource Center
Coordinator: Suzanne Tucker; *Assistant Coordinator:* Debbie Fairchild
General Information: Four-Year State University; Enrollment: 12,158; **Tuition:** Residents – $5,634, Non-Residents – $10,316. **Room and Board**: $7,698. An urban university with two semesters, intersession and summer semesters. Depending upon the planned program, there may be internships, student teaching, etc., required. Each student must complete a required program, pass appropriate exams when stated, i.e., Connecticut Concept Exam for Teachers, and maintain the QPR that their degree program requires. **Majors** include full, four-year degree programs, as well as liberal studies, in most areas.
Special Program: Enrollment in Special Program: 600; Cost: None
Staff: Learning disabilities specialists; peer tutors
Program Features: Extended time testing; individual and small group sessions; basic study skills; limited course load; access to note-taking assistance – scribes, tape recorders, taped texts; faculty made aware of student's learning disability; advisement; support; compensatory/organizational skill training; active reading/advocacy
Entrance Requirements: Documentation of learning disability; SAT untimed scores accepted; medical evaluation; achievement testing; testing: WAIS, psychological report
Special Facilities for: Visual, hearing and physical impairments

UNIVERSITY OF CONNECTICUT
NEAG SCHOOL OF EDUCATION
GENTRY BLDG. ROOM 003
249 GLENBROOK ROAD UNIT 2064
STORRS, CONNECTICUT 06269-2064
(860) 486-0178; FAX: (860) 486-5799
E-MAIL: david.parker@uconn.edu WEB SITE: www.upld.uconn.edu

Name of Special Program: University Program for College Students with Learning Disabilities (UPLD)
Director: David R. Parker, Ph.D.
General Information: Four-Year State University; Enrollment: 25,000; **Tuition:** Residents – $6,096, Non-Residents – $18,600; **Room and Board:** $7,704. Founded in 1881, the University is located on a rural campus in a large town 26 miles from Hartford. **Majors**: Agribusiness/agricultural production, agricultural sciences, area studies, biology, business/management, chemistry, communications, computer/information sciences, crafts/design, education, engineering, fine arts, geological sciences, health/life sciences, home economics, languages, letters/literature, mathematics, medical laboratory technologies, multi/interdisciplinary studies, music, parks and recreation, philosophy, physics, psychology, rehabilitation services, social sciences, visual/performing arts, vocational home economics, zoology
Special Program: Enrollment in Special Program: 140–160; Cost: None
Staff: Learning disabilities specialists
Program Features: Reasonable accommodations determined on a case-by-case basis; taped texts; tape recorders; individual tutoring sessions; limited course load (if appropriate); faculty made aware of student's learning disability through student self-advocacy and verification by program
Entrance Requirements: Admissions process is the same for all students. To verify eligibility for services, students must provide documents once they are admitted. Documentation of learning disability (within the last three years); learning disabilities specialist report which must substantiate the need for accommodation(s); SAT untimed scores accepted; testing: WAIS-R, psychological report (any additional learning disability documentation such as Woodcock-Johnson)
Special Facilities for: Visual, hearing and physical impairments
College Life: Learning Disabilities Support Services emphasis independence and self-determination. Students with learning disabilities are, in general, successful in attaining goals and earning degrees in a wide array of majors to a comparable extent as students without learning disabilities.

DISTRICT OF COLUMBIA

THE AMERICAN UNIVERSITY
4400 MASSACHUSETTS AVE. NORTHWEST
WASHINGTON, DC 20016-8027
(202) 885-3360; FAX: (202) 885-1042
E-MAIL: asc@american.edu **WEB SITE: www.american.edu/asc**

Name of Special Program: Learning Services Program
Director: Nancy Sydnor-Greenberg
General Information: Four-Year Private University; Enrollment: 10,537; **Tuition:** $27,552; **Room:** $7,350, **Board:** $4,220. American University is located in Washington, D.C., in a residential setting. Easy access to public transportation and shuttle bus service. **Majors:** Degree programs in the College of Arts & Sciences, Kogod College of Business, School of Communication, School of International Service, School of Public Affairs and Washington College of Law; opportunities for internships and study abroad
Special Program: Enrollment in Special Program: 15–30 (limited to 30 per year); Cost: $1,000 – one time fee
Staff: Learning disabilities specialists; peer tutors; writing mentor
Program Features: The Learning Services Program is located within the Academic Support Center. The focus of the program is to assist students with learning disabilities with their transition from high school to college during their freshman year. It is a small, mainstream program offering weekly individual meetings with the coordinator of the program throughout the student's first year, additional writing support in the College Writing class, and free course-content tutoring as needed. Students with learning disabilities who are not in the program may receive services through the Academic Support Center (ASC). There is no separate admissions process or fee for using the ASC.
Entrance Requirements: Documentation of learning disability, SAT/ACT (untimed scores accepted); testing: WAIS-III, Woodcock-Johnson III, psychoeducational report
Special Facilities for: Physical and psychological disabilities — handled by Disability Support Services

FLORIDA

BARRY UNIVERSITY
11300 NORTHEAST 2nd AVENUE
MIAMI SHORES, FLORIDA 33161-6695
(305) 899-3461; FAX: (305) 899-3778
E-MAIL: vcastro@mail.barry.edu; **WEB SITE: www.barry.edu**

Name of Special Program: Center for Advanced Learning (CAL)
Director: Vivian Castro

General Information: Four-Year Private University; Enrollment: 9,042; **Annual Tuition:** $24,000; **Room:** $7,850 per year. Barry University is a comprehensive university with its main campus located in Miami Shores, Florida, with other sites throughout Florida. The University attracts a diverse student body, including traditional and non-traditional students from a variety of geographic, ethnic, religious and socio-economic backgrounds who are committed to taking full advantage of the opportunities provided for learning and personal growth. **Degrees:** Barry University offers more than 60 undergraduate degree programs, and 50 graduate programs including dual degree options, specialist's degrees and 10 doctoral degrees, including one of seven in podiatric medicine nationally.
Special Program: Enrollment in Special Program: limited to 45; Cost: $2,150 per semester. All services are available to bilingual and graduate students. The CAL Program runs during the summer session. The percentage of students with learning disabilities who receive a degree in four years is 35% and in five or more years is 65%.
Staff: Learning disabilities specialists; content tutors (faculty members); special counselors
Program Features: Oral and extended time testing; individual and small group tutoring sessions; limited course load (first year); basic study skills; academic advising for students with learning disabilities; tape recorders; taped texts; faculty made aware of student's learning disability
Entrance Requirements: Documentation of learning disability; learning disabilities specialist report; handwritten essay; SAT / ACT untimed scores accepted; testing: WAIS, IEP, psychological report
Special Facilities for: Visual, hearing and physical impairments
College Life: Barry University is committed to offering students small class sizes, individualized support, and a nurturing environment.

BEACON COLLEGE
105 EAST MAIN STREET
LEESBURG, FLORIDA 34748
(352) 787-7660; FAX: (352) 787-0721
E-MAIL: admissions@beaconcollege.edu
WEB SITE: www.beaconcollege.edu

Beacon College is a special mission college, solely for students with learning disabilities.
President: Deborah Brodbeck; *Director of Admissions:* Carolyn Scott
General Information: Two- and Four-Year Private College (exclusively for students with language-based learning disabilities and ADHD). The college is located in the small community of Leesburg, Florida, about one hour from Orlando. Enrollment: 100; **Annual Tuition:** $22,700; **Room:** $4,000. **Board:**

$2,860. Beacon College offers students the opportunity to earn an associate in arts degree or a bachelor of arts degree in liberal studies or human services, credit-bearing courses in field placement, work experience and career guidance. In addition to the fall and spring terms, students can also register for a summer term course which includes a trip abroad linking cultural experience with academics. **Majors:** BA and AA in human services, liberal studies and computer information systems. Minors in art, education, history and psychology. *Summer Program:* The summer term is a combination of a mini master program on campus and a cultural studies program abroad. The cultural studies program enables currently enrolled students the opportunity to combine academics such as art, history, music, and literature with travel opportunities. The Summer 2006 trip included stops in Italy and Greece. Approximate cost: $1,600 (does not include travel arrangements)
Staff: Learning disabilities specialists; content tutors (faculty members); special counselors
Program Features: Oral and extended time testing; individual and small group tutoring sessions; limited course load (first year); academic advising; basic study skills; note-taking assistance – scribes; tape recorders; taped texts; developmental program (reading, writing, math); faculty made aware of student's learning disability; college strategies courses; college success courses; academic mentoring program focuses on self-awareness and strategies for learning with individual mentoring sessions weekly
Entrance Requirements: Application (fee – $50); autobiographical statement; most recent educational evaluation (an adult measure within three to five years), including a diagnosis of learning disability or AD/HD; official high school transcript; any official college transcripts (for transferring students); references; health form; campus visit; testing: Wechsler scales (WAIS-III are preferred) with full scale, cluster, and sub-test scores included; Woodcock Johnson cognitive assessments with an age or grade equivalence in reading, writing or mathematics
Special Facilities: There is limited access to historic buildings on campus for students with physical disabilities.
College Life: The Office of Student Services is committed to providing non-academic, student support services and activities that contribute to the cultural, social, intellectual, moral, and physical development of the Beacon College students. The Office of Student Services provides a wide variety of activities throughout the year to promote student development, campus and community involvement, and to increase faculty, staff, and student interaction. In order to produce well-rounded individuals, the Office of Student Services staff is committed to providing out-of-classroom experiences to enhance the environment in which students learn and to promote student growth and development in all areas of the student's life.

FLORIDA A & M UNIVERSITY

667 ARDELIA COURT
TALLAHASSEE, FLORIDA 32307
(850) 599-3180; FAX: (850) 561-2513
E-MAIL: nholmes@famu.edu **WEB SITE: www.famu.edu**

Name of Special Program: Learning Development and Evaluation Center
Director: Nathaniel Holmes, Ph.D.
General Information: Four-Year State University; Enrollment: 11,956; **Tuition:** Residents – $98.66 per credit, Non-Residents – $498.29 per credit; **Room and Board:** $1,380 depending on housing and meal plan. A predominantly black, post-secondary institution of higher education located in Tallahassee, an urban/suburban community. Special attractions are Wakulla Springs National Park, Springtime Tallahassee and close proximity to the Gulf of Mexico. University renowned for its band, College of Pharmacy, School of Architecture, School of Business and the number of Merit scholars. FAMU is a general-purpose institution with curricula offerings in most of the arts and sciences, business, and education at the baccalaureate level and some graduate and Ph.D. degree programs. **Majors:** Agriculture, biological science, communications and the arts, computer and physical science, education, engineering and environmental design, health professions, social science
Special Program: Enrollment in Special Program: 200; Cost: None. *Summer Program:* The summer transition program for high school and first-time college students with a learning disability provides intense instruction in study skills, memory skills, mathematics, reading improvement and socialization. The transition program serves as a feeder for students with a learning disability who intend to pursue post-secondary education. Cost: $1,500. Mandatory
Staff: Learning disabilities specialists; content tutors; peer tutors; special counselors
Program Features: Oral and extended time testing; basic study skills; note-taking assistance – scribes; tape recorders; taped texts; developmental program; technology component; special exam preparation
Entrance Requirements: Documentation of learning disability; handwritten essay; SAT/ACT untimed scores accepted; teacher evaluations; summer transition program; testing: IEP, psychological report
Special Facilities for: Visual, hearing and physical impairments
Scholarships: See page 426.

FLORIDA ATLANTIC UNIVERSITY
777 GLADES ROAD, SU 133, PO BOX 3091
BOCA RATON, FLORIDA 33431
(561) 297-3880, (561) 297-0358 TTY; FAX: (561) 297-2184
E-MAIL: nrokos@fau.edu **WEB SITE: www.osd.fau.edu**

Name of Special Program: Office for Students with Disabilities
Director: Nicole Rokos
General Information: Four-Year State University; Enrollment: 25,000; **Annual Tuition** Residents – $3,300, Non-Residents – $546.36 per credit hour; **Room and Board:** $8,280. A suburban campus located in a small city 15 miles from Fort Lauderdale and 25 miles from West Palm Beach. **Majors:** Botany, business/management, chemistry, communications, computer/information sciences, education (special and teacher), engineering, fine arts, geological sciences, health sciences, languages, letters/literature, life sciences (specialized), mathematics, medical laboratory technologies, multi/interdisciplinary studies, music, philosophy, physics, protective services, psychology, public affairs, social sciences, visual/performing arts, zoology
Special Program: Enrollment in Special Program: 50–80 (limited to 80 students; Cost: $35 per credit hour
Staff: Learning disabilities specialists; special counselors
Program Features: Oral and extended time testing; note-taking assistance – scribes; tape recorders; taped texts; limited course load (first year); academic advising for students with learning disabilities; basic study skills; faculty made aware of student's learning disability (at student's request); strategies group tutoring; assistive technology lab.
Entrance Requirements: Documentation of learning disability; SAT/ACT untimed scores accepted; a completed application for support services through the OSD; testing: WAIS, psychological report
Special Facilities for: Visual, hearing and physical impairments
College Life: The staff at Florida Atlantic University is eager to give personalized assistance including training in the use of assistive technology to students with disabilities.
Scholarships: See page 426.

LYNN UNIVERSITY
3601 NORTH MILITARY TRAIL
BOCA RATON, FLORIDA 33431-5598
(561) 237-7064; FAX: (561) 237-7873
WEB SITE: www.lynn.edu/institute

Name of Special Program: The Comprehensive Support Program
Dean, Institute for Achievement and Learning: Dr. Marsha Glines
General Information: Four-Year Private University; Enrollment: 2,600; **Tuition:** $26,200; **Room and Board:** $9,650. Lynn University is located in a suburban area on a 123-acre campus. It is midway between Fort Lauderdale and Palm Beach. Students come from 35 states, and 41 foreign countries. **Majors:** Business, hospitality, communications, education, art and design, behavioral and environmental science
Special Program: Enrollment in Special Program: 290; Cost $4,075 per semester
Staff: Learning disabilities specialists; content tutors (faculty members); special counselors
Program Features: Extended time testing; basic study skills; individual and small group tutoring sessions; limited course load (first year); academic advising for students with learning disabilities; developmental program; faculty made aware of student's learning disability; Kurzweil reader, Dragon Speak Software
Entrance Requirements: Documentation of learning disability; current (within three to five years) psychoeducational evaluation; SAT/ACT untimed scores accepted; teacher evaluation; handwritten essay; testing: WAIS, psychological report
Special Facilities for: Visual, hearing and physical impairments

ST. PETERSBURG COLLEGE
6605 5th AVENUE, NORTH
ST. PETERSBURG, FLORIDA 33733-3489
(727) 341-4758; FAX: (727) 341-4770
E-MAIL: Giar.Linda@spcollege.edu WEB SITE: www.spcollege.edu

Name of Special Program: Office of Services for Students with Disabilities (OSSD)
Learning Specialist: Dr. Linda Giar
General Information: Four- and Two-Year Private College; Enrollment: 3,800; **Tuition:** Residents – $61.11 per credit hour, Non-Residents – $241.05 per credit hour; **Room and Board:** No college housing available. Saint Petersburg/Gibbs, is one of the campuses in a multi-campus system near the Gulf of Mexico. Other campuses are in Clearwater, Seminole Pinellas Park

and Tarpon Springs. **Degrees:** AA, AS, vocational and certificate programs, bachelor's degrees in dental hygiene, education, international business, nursing, orthotics and prosthetics, paralegal studies, public safety administration, technology management, veterinary technology
Special Program: Enrollment in Special Program: 885; Cost: None
Staff: Learning disabilities specialists; content tutors (faculty members); special counselors
Program Features: Oral and extended time testing; individual and small group tutoring sessions; tape recorders; note-taking assistance – scribes; faculty made aware of student's learning disability (at student's request); taped texts; academic advising for students with learning disabilities
Entrance Requirements: Documentation of learning disability; learning disabilities specialist report (psychologist); SAT/ACT untimed scores accepted; testing: WAIS, psychological report
Special Facilities for: Visual, hearing and physical impairments
Scholarships: See page 427.

GEORGIA

BRENAU UNIVERSITY WOMEN'S COLLEGE

ONE CENTENNIAL CIRCLE
GAINESVILLE, GEORGIA 30506
(770) 534-6134; FAX: (770) 297-5883
E-MAIL: vyamilkoski@lib.brenau.edu
WEB SITE: www.brenau.edu/learningcenter

Name of Special Program: Brenau Learning Center
Director: Dr. Vincent Yamilkoski
General Information: Four-Year Private College; Enrollment: 650; **Annual Tuition:** $16,440; **Room and Board:** $8,550. Brenau University is located in Northeast Georgia near Atlanta and the Blue Ridge Mountains. Lake Sydney Lanier provides the area with many water-related recreational activities. A site that was used for Olympic rowing is still used today by rowing clubs. Within an hour's drive from the campus, there are numerous universities, cultural, social and sporting events. **Majors:** The Women's College is one division of the University and is a liberal arts college with a variety of high-quality degree programs in the following areas: early childhood/middle grades, special education, psychology, human resources management; business administration in accounting, corporate communications, management and marketing; mass communication with concentrations in journalism, broadcasting, public relations and corporate communications; occupational therapy, nursing, biology (science) and environmental science; dance pedagogy, dance education and dance per-

formance; art education, arts management, commercial art, studio art, interior design and fashion merchandising; theatre, musical theatre, music performance, music education; English, history/political science, international studies, legal studies and conflict resolution
Special Program: Enrollment in Special Programs: 40; Cost: $900 per tutored course ($3,000 maximum per semester). There is no fee for the other services of the program and students do not need to receive tutoring to be in the program and to utilize the services. A majority of students have one to two tutors each semester. *Summer Program:* The Learning Center program operates each semester of the school year, including the summer, with the same services. Summer tutoring fees are $450 per tutored course. There are some summer residential (housing) scholarships available that include paid campus work positions for full-time students.
Staff: Learning disabilities specialists; content tutors
Program Features: Oral and extended time testing; basic study skills; developmental program; individual tutoring sessions; limited course load (first year); academic advising for students with learning disabilities; note-taking assistance – scribes; faculty made aware of student's learning disability; taped texts; tape recorders; various assistive technology
Entrance Requirements: Documentation of learning disability; learning disabilities specialist report; SAT/ACT untimed scores accepted; testing: WAIS, psychological report; achievement scores in reading and math
College Life: The Women's College has the tradition of a strong sorority system as well as numerous organizations for independent students. First-year students live in freshman housing. Students receive a strong orientation and advising program from faculty and student peer advisors in the course, "Freshman Year Experience." Brenau has athletic teams in tennis, soccer, volleyball, cross country and softball. Brenau is a terrific college for students with learning disabilities. Students have all the advantages of a small liberal arts college, smaller classes with faculty focused on students' success. Additionally, the Learning Center provides students with structure and support to be successful.

GEORGIA COLLEGE AND STATE UNIVERSITY
130 LANIER HALL CAMPUS BOX 04
MILLEDGEVILLE, GEORGIA 31061
(478) 445-5931; FAX: (478) 445-2962
E-MAIL: helenhill@gcsu.edu **WEB SITE: www.gcsu.edu**

Name of Special Program: Office of Disabled Student Support Services
Director: Dr. Helen T. Hill
General Information: Four-Year State College; Enrollment: 5,000; **Tuition:** Residents – $3,404, Non-Residents – $13,616; **Room:** $3,690; **Board:** $3,188.

Georgia College, a senior college of the University System of Georgia, is a comprehensive coeducational, residential institution. Additional campuses are located in Macon with centers located in Warner Robins. Milledgeville is less than a dozen miles from the geographic center of Georgia and is the county seat of Baldwin County. It is approximately 100 miles from Augusta, Albany, Atlanta, and Columbus and 30 miles from Macon. The town, which is the antebellum capital of Georgia, has a population of 20,000 and is a center of history and culture. Located on the fall line in a setting of rolling hills and recreational lakes, Milledgeville's natural beauty is among its most appealing assets. **Degrees:** Bachelor of Arts, Business Administration, General Studies, Music, Music Education, Music Therapy, Science, Science in Logistics Systems, Science in Nursing
Special Program: Enrollment in Special Program: 80: Cost: None. The percentage of students with learning disabilities earning a degree in five or more years is 60%.
Staff: Learning disabilities specialists; peer tutors; special counselors
Program Features: Oral and extended time testing; taped texts; basic study skills; limited course load (first year); academic advising for students with learning disabilities; note-taking assistance – scribes; developmental program; faculty made aware of student's learning disability
Entrance Requirements: Documentation of learning disability; learning disabilities specialist report; SAT/ACT untimed scores accepted; testing: WAIS, psychological report
Special Facilities for: Visual, hearing and physical impairments
College Life: Small college, compact campus, and a caring faculty.

GEORGIA STATE UNIVERSITY
152 SPARKS HALL
ATLANTA, GEORGIA 30303-3038
(404) 651-3357; FAX: (404) 651-4281
E-MAIL: oeomjf@langate.gsu.edu **WEB SITE: www.gsu.edu**

Name of Special Program: Student Support Services
Director: Dr. Joy Bailey
General Information: Four-Year State University; Enrollment: 23,375; **Tuition:** Residents – $2,409 per semester, Non-Residents – $8,248 per semester; **Room and Board:** $4,195 per semester for four- to six-bedroom apartments. Georgia State University is an urban campus located in downtown Atlanta. The university location gives students direct access to many of Atlanta's attractions, including CNN Center, Underground Atlanta, the World of Coca-Cola Museum and the Martin Luther King Museum. **Majors:** *College of Arts and Sciences:* Anthropology, art education, art studio, biological sciences, chemistry, classics, computer science, economics,

English, film and video, French, geography, geology, German, history, interdisciplinary studies, journalism, mathematics, music (music industry), philosophy, physics, political science, psychology, religious studies, secondary education, sociology, Spanish, speech, theater. *College of Business Administration:* Accounting, actuarial science, computer information systems, decision sciences, economics - BBA, finance, management, marketing, real estate, risk management, and insurance. *College of Education:* Dance, early childhood education, exercise science, health and physical education, human resource development, middle childhood education, recreation (vocational education). *College of Health Sciences:* Medical technology, nursing, nutrition and dietetics, physical therapy, respiratory therapy. *School of Policy Studies:* Criminal justice, hospitality administration, social work, urban studies, aviation administration, community planning and development, gerontology, human resources, urban government administration, urbanology, volunteer agency administration.

Special Program: Enrollment in Special Program: 200 (limited to 200); Cost: None

Staff: Learning disabilities specialists; peer tutors; special counselors; content tutors (faculty members); graduate students and / or learning disabilities coaches

Program Features: Oral and extended time testing; taped texts; basic study skills; developmental program; tape recorders; individual and small group tutoring sessions; limited course load (first year); academic advising for students with learning disabilities; advocacy; referral for note-taking assistance; faculty made aware of student's learning disability; two-hour non-credit course in personal and academic development for students with learning disabilities

Entrance Requirements: Documentation of learning disability; SAT / ACT untimed scores accepted; certificate of immunization, diploma or GED (proof); intake information

Special Facilities for: Visual, hearing and physical impairments

College Life: Georgia State University has many offices to help students with disabilities. In addition to Student Support Services, there is an Office of Disability Services and Counseling Center. Academic assistance and learning support programs all work together to help students with accommodations, academic and personal concerns.

UNIVERSITY OF GEORGIA
114 CLARK HOWELL HALL
ATHENS, GEORGIA 30602
(706) 542-8719; FAX: (706) 542-8778
E-MAIL: dshimket@uga.edu **WEB SITE: www.dissvcs.uga.edu**

Name of Program: Disability Resource Center
Director: Dr. Karen Kalivoda; *Intake Specialist:* Diane Shimkets
General Information: Four-Year State University; Enrollment: 30,000 **Tuition:** Residents – $4,624, Non-Residents – $16,848; **Room and Board:** $6,376. A suburban campus in a small city 70 miles northeast of Atlanta. Special studies include internships, cooperatives, study abroad, and national exchange. **Majors:** Agribusiness, agricultural education, agriscience and environmental systems, anthropology, art, biological sciences, chemistry, child and family development, classical culture, communication sciences and disorders, literature, consumer foods, dance, economics, environmental forestry, genetics, geography, geology, health science, history, horticulture, international business, landscape architecture, management, marketing, mathematics, microbiology, music, political science, real estate, physics, social work, special education, telecommunication arts, religion, women's studies
Special Program: Enrollment in Special Program: 250; Cost: $300 for evaluation, no cost for services. *Summer Program:* Students admitted under special criteria for learning disabilities are admitted as regular students to the summer quarter. The Disability Resource Center offers special activities to orient freshmen to campus and academic life.
Staff: Learning disabilities specialists; special counselors
Program Features: Oral and extended time testing; individual and small group sessions; limited course load; tape recorders; note-taking assistance – scribes; taped texts; basic study skills; academic advising for students with learning disabilities; individual and group therapy; student advocacy group; computer lab
Entrance Requirements: SAT / ACT untimed scores accepted; diagnostic testing at University of Georgia or submitted documentation which meets state criteria for students with learning disabilities
Special Facilities for: Visual, hearing and physical impairments, through the Office for Students with Disabilities
College Life: Well-staffed, hospitable center, which is centrally located on large, interesting campus. Program has strong administrative support from university. Wide range of services, consumer driven.
Scholarships: See page 427.

HAWAII

UNIVERSITY OF HAWAII AT MANOA
STUDENT SERVICES CENTER 013
2600 CAMPUS ROAD
HONOLULU, HAWAII 96822
(808) 956-7511 V/TTY
E-MAIL: kokua@hawaii.edu **WEB SITE: www.hawaii.edu**

Name of Special Program: KOKUA Program
Director: Ann Ito
General Information: Four-Year State University; Enrollment: 20,000; **Tuition:** Residents – $1,344 per semester, Non-Residents – $5,976 per semester; **Room and Board:** $8,050. An urban setting within the city of Honolulu, adjacent to the world-renowned Waikiki Beach. A heavy commuter college. Environment is multicultural with a relatively high cost of living. **Majors:** Approximately 86 undergraduate degree programs from accountancy to zoology.
Special Program: Enrollment in Special Program: 125–150; Cost: None
Staff: Learning resource specialist; peer tutors; special counselors
Program Features: Testing accommodations (according to individual need); note-taking assistance – scribes; tape recorders; taped texts; faculty made aware of student's learning disability
Entrance Requirements: Documentation of learning disability
Special Facilities for: Visual, hearing and physical impairments

IDAHO

BOISE STATE UNIVERSITY
1885 UNIVERSITY DRIVE
BOISE, IDAHO 83725
(208) 426-3583; FAX: (208) 426-2310
E-MAIL: gmartin@boisestate.edu **WEB SITE: www.boisestate.edu**

Name of Special Program: Student Success Program (SSP)
Director: Gregory Martinez
General Information: Four-Year State University; Enrollment: 15,000; **Tuition:** Residents – $4,154, Non-Residents – $11,932; **Room and Board:** $5,778. An urban campus in a small city located in the commercial, financial, health care and governmental center of Idaho. **Majors:** Students may choose their majors in any one of seven colleges: arts and sciences, business, education, health science, social sciences and public affairs, technology, graduate or two schools: School of Engineering Technology and School of Applied Technology

Special Program: Enrollment in Special Program: 28 (limited to 40); Cost: None
Staff: Learning disabilities specialists; peer tutors; special counselors; content tutors (faculty members)
Program Features: Oral and extended time testing; individual tutoring sessions; limited course load (first year); academic advising; note-taking assistance – scribes; tape recorders; taped texts; basic study skills; developmental program; faculty made aware of student's learning disability
Entrance Requirements: Documentation of learning disability
Special Facilities for: Visual, hearing and physical impairments

UNIVERSITY OF IDAHO
IDAHO COMMONS ROOM 306
P.O. BOX 442537
MOSCOW, IDAHO 83844-2537
(208) 885-6307, 1-888-884-3246; FAX: (208) 885-9404
E-MAIL: dss@uidaho.edu **WEB SITE: www.uidaho.edu**

Name of Special Program: Disability Support Services
Director: Gloria R. Jensen; *Learning Disabilities Specialist:* Rosie Pavlov
General Information: Four-Year State University; Enrollment: 7,107; **Tuition:** Residents – $2,100, Non-Residents – $6,900 per semester; **Room and Board:** $4,935. The University of Idaho is located in the Northern Idaho Panhandle surrounded by Palouse Hills and access to mountains and lakes of North Idaho, 90 miles southeast of Spokane, Washington. **Majors:** There are nine colleges: Science, Agricultural and Life Sciences, Business and Economics, Education, Engineering, Graduate Studies, Law, Letters, Arts and Social Sciences, and Natural Resources.
Special Program: Enrollment in Special Program: 145; Cost: None
Staff: Learning disabilities specialists; special counselors
Program Features: Oral and extended time testing; individual tutoring sessions; limited academic advising; note-taking assistance – scribes; tape recorders; taped texts; faculty made aware of student's learning disability
Entrance Requirements: Documentation of learning disability; learning disabilities specialist report; diagnostic testing at University of Idaho
Special Facilities for: Visual, hearing and physical impairments
College Life: Our program offers testing accommodations, note taking, and alternate text. We refer students with learning disabilities, ADD or ADHD to Student Support Services for learning strategies and academic coaching.

ILLINOIS

DE PAUL UNIVERSITY

2320 NORTH KENMORE AVENUE SAC 220
CHICAGO, ILLINOIS 60614
(773) 325-1677; FAX: (773) 325-4673
E-MAIL: plusinfo@depaul.edu
WEB SITE: http://studentaffairs.depaul.edu/plus

Name of Special Program: Productive Learning Strategies (PLuS) Program
Director: Stamatios Miras
General Information: Four-Year Private University; Enrollment: 17,000; **Tuition:** $22,365; **Room and Board:** $6,939–8,637. A private urban university located in the city of Chicago. It offers a wide variety of degrees and it operates on a quarter system (10 weeks of classes – 1 week of finals). It is the largest Catholic university in the nation. It offers 130 different programs in Liberal Arts and Sciences, College of Commerce, College of Law, Computer Science and Information Systems, School of Music, and the Theatre School, all within one mile of Lake Michigan, Lincoln Park Zoo and Chicago's famous skyline. *The De Paul Bridge Program:* this year-round university-wide program (separate from the PLuS program) is offered for potential De Paul freshmen who do not necessarily have learning disabilities. It is designed to provide extensive support services to students who will receive intensive language and mathematics instruction, assistance in developing study and organizational skills, orientation to and experience in utilizing De Paul's resources and exposure to academic and career opportunities.
Degrees: Liberal arts and sciences, commerce, music, theatre, law, School for New Learning, education
Special Program: Enrollment in Special Program: 145; Cost: $1,800 only if student has weekly meetings with learning disabilities specialist.
Staff: Learning disabilities specialists
Program Features: Oral and extended time testing; individual tutoring sessions; note-taking assistance; taped texts; tape recording lectures; faculty made aware of student's learning disability; advocacy; priority registration; students can meet with learning disabilities specialists for one or two hours per week to work on organization skills, time management, reading and writing strategies
Entrance Requirements: Must be admitted to De Paul University prior to admission to PLuS; documentation of learning disability; learning disabilities specialist report; SAT/ACT untimed scores accepted; testing: WAIS, psychological report
College Life: De Paul's PLuS Program continues to assist students in achieving their academic goals. Many students came to the program who have been unsuccessful elsewhere but graduate from De Paul University with the help of PLuS.

ILLINOIS STATE UNIVERSITY
350 FELL HALL, CAMPUS BOX 1290
NORMAL, ILLINOIS 61790-1290
(309) 438-5853, (309) 438-8620 TTY; FAX: (309) 438-7713
E-MAIL: ableisu@ilstu.edu **WEB SITE: www.ilstu.edu**

Name of Special Program: Disability Concerns
Director: Ann M. Caldwell
General Information: Four-Year State University; Enrollment: 20,000; **Tuition:** Residents – $4,020, Non-Residents – $7,365; **Room and Board:** $6,578. Illinois State University was founded in 1857 as the state's first public university to offer education programs to meet the demand for teachers. The campus is tree-shaded and consists of 850 acres near the geographic center of the state. **Majors**: Illinois State University has one of the largest undergraduate programs in Illinois with 34 academic departments organized into six colleges: Colleges of Applied Science and Technology, Arts and Sciences, Business, Education, Fine Arts and Nursing
Special Program: Enrollment in Special Program: 150; Cost: None
Staff: Learning disabilities specialists
Program Features: Oral and extended time testing; individual tutoring sessions; note-taking assistance – scribes; taped texts; academic advising; faculty made aware of student's learning disability (at student's request); conferences with learning disabilities specialist; adaptive computers; advocacy; separate test rooms
Entrance Requirements: Documentation of learning disability; SAT/ACT untimed scores accepted; testing: WAIS, IEP, psychological report
Special Facilities for: Visual, hearing, health and physical impairments
College Life: Disability Concerns considers the student with a learning disability as a person first. Services provided to students are individualized to meet the student's needs. Students have the opportunity to work closely with a case coordinator to learn the best methods for utilizing accommodations to develop academic skills.

NATIONAL LOUIS UNIVERSITY
2840 SHERIDAN ROAD
EVANSTON, ILLINOIS 60201
(847) 475-1100 X2357
E-MAIL: jpiper@nl.edu **WEB SITE: www.nl.edu**

Name of Special Program: Center for Academic Development
Coordinator: Jadwiga Piper
General Information: Four-Year Private University; Enrollment: 5,000; **Tuition:** $9,000; **Room and Board:** $4,000. National Louis University, for-

merly known as National College of Education, located at its main campus in Evanston in 1926. Other campuses are in Chicago and the western suburbs. **Majors:** Allied health, business/management, computer/information studies, human services, education (general and teacher), psychology, liberal arts, sports management

Special Program: Enrollment in Special Program: 5; Cost: None. *Summer Program:* Two-week program for students with learning disabilities who are already admitted to the university and need help with study skills, tutoring and adjustment to college life in general. Cost: $50

Staff: Learning disabilities specialists; content tutors (faculty members); peer tutors

Program Features: Oral and extended time testing; individual and small group tutoring sessions; basic study skills; limited course load (first year); note-taking assistance – scribes; tape recorders; taped texts; developmental program; academic advising for students with learning disabilities; faculty made aware of student's learning disability; two hours/week/course tutoring for students with documented learning disabilities

Entrance Requirements: Documentation of learning disability; learning disabilities specialist report; SAT/ACT untimed scores accepted; teacher evaluation; testing: WAIS, psychological report, diagnostic testing at National Louis University

Special Facilities for: Visual and hearing impairments

ROOSEVELT UNIVERSITY
430 SOUTH MICHIGAN AVENUE
CHICAGO, ILLINOIS 60605-1394
(312) 341-3810; FAX: (312) 341-2471
E-MAIL: nlitke@roosevelt.edu **WEB SITE: www.roosevelt.edu**

Name of Special Program: Learning and Support Services Program (LSSP)
Director: Nancy Litke
General Information: Four-Year Private University; Enrollment: 7,000; **Tuition:** $7,657; **Room and Board:** $10,366. Urban university located in downtown Chicago near convenient modes of transportation. The Albert A. Robin campus is located at 1651 McConnor Parkway, Schaumburg, IL 60173. **Majors:** Actuarial science, African/African-American studies, allied health programs, American studies, laboratory science, biology, cartography, chemistry, computing/information science, economics, electronics engineering technology, English, geography, geology, history, industrial engineering, international studies, interior design, Jewish studies, journalism, labor relations, languages, literature, liberal studies, mathematical sciences, music, philosophy, physical education and science, physics,

political science, post-baccalaureate programs in pre-medicine, pre-legal, pre-pharmacy, pre-professional health sciences, psychology, public administration, social sciences, sociology, urban environmental studies, visual and performing arts, art, dance, speech communications, broadcasting, theatre, women's studies
Special Program: Enrollment in Special Program: 18; Cost: $1,000 per semester.
Staff: Learning disabilities specialists; special counselors
Program Features: Oral and extended time testing; taped texts; limited course load (first year); individual and small group tutoring sessions; tape recorders; basic study skills; academic advising for students with learning disabilities; faculty made aware of student's learning disability; one-on-one tutoring with learning disabilities specialists
Entrance Requirements: Documentation of learning disability; ACT untimed scores accepted; testing: WAIS, SEC, psychological report; handwritten essay
Special Facilities for: Visual, hearing and physical impairments
College Life: Our one-on-one support program combined with small classes and an excellent caring faculty make Roosevelt an excellent choice for students with learning disabilities.

SOUTHERN ILLINOIS UNIVERSITY AT CARBONDALE
CLINICAL CENTER ACHIEVE PROGRAM

CARBONDALE, ILLINOIS 62901-4615
(618) 453-2595; FAX: (618) 453-3711
E-MAIL: achieve@siu.edu **WEB SITE: www.siu.edu/~achieve**

Name of Special Program: Clinical Center Achieve Program
Coordinator: Sally DeDecker
General Information: Four-Year State University; Enrollment: 24,000; **Tuition:** Residents – $3,316, Non-Residents – $6,801; **Room and Board:** $5,582. **Annual Fees:** $650. A rural campus in a large town located 100 miles southeast of St. Louis. **Majors:** Agribusiness/agricultural production, agricultural sciences, biology, botany, business/management, chemistry, civil technologies, communications, computer/information sciences, crafts/design, education (special and teacher), engineering/technologies, environmental design, fine arts, geological sciences, health sciences, home economics, industrial production, languages, law, letters/literature, marketing/distribution, mathematics, multi/interdisciplinary studies, music, parks and recreation, philosophy, physics, protective services, psychology, public affairs, rehabilitation services, religion, renewable natural resources, social sciences, theology, visual/performing arts, vocational home economics, zoology

Special Program: Enrollment in Special Program: 130 (limited to 50 new students each year); Cost: $2,800 per semester
Staff: Learning disabilities specialists; peer tutors
Program Features: Oral and extended time testing; taped texts; individual and small group tutoring sessions; limited course load (first year); note-taking assistance – scribes; basic study skills; developmental program; academic advising for students with learning disabilities; faculty made aware of student's learning disability; developmental writing course; math remediation, supervision, organizational training
Entrance Requirements: Documentation of learning disability; learning disabilities report; ACT untimed scores accepted; testing: WAIS, psychological report, diagnostic testing at Southern Illinois University at Carbondale; completion of application forms
Special Facilities for: Visual, hearing and physical impairments through Disabled Student Services
College Life: The Achieve program is especially attractive because of the program's comprehensive services, high staff-to-student ratio, and very competitive cost. Southern Illinois University at Carbondale offers over 140 different degrees and is a nationally ranked educational and research institution. In the midst of the Shawnee National Forest, the college setting is beautiful.
Scholarship: See page 427.

INDIANA

PURDUE UNIVERSITY

YOUNG HALL ROOM 830, 302 WOOD STREET
WEST LAFAYETTE, INDIANA 47907
(765) 494-1247; FAX: (765) 496-3759
E-MAIL: csdunning@purdue.edu **WEB SITE: www.purdue.edu**

Name of Special Program: Adaptive Programs
Coordinator: Carole Dunning
General Information: Four-Year State University; Enrollment: 36,000; **Tuition:** Residents – $6,458, Non-Residents – $19,824; **Room and Board:** $6,640. Purdue University is located in a suburban/rural setting two hours from Chicago and one hour from Indianapolis. Special features are study abroad programs, internships and co-op experiences. Purdue is considered one of the "Big 10" schools. **Majors:** Aeronautics/astronautics, agriculture, School of Agriculture – department of agricultural engineering, chemical, civil and land surveying engineering; School of Engineering – division of construction engineering and management, consumer/family sciences, electrical/computer engineering, education, forestry/freshman engineering, health sciences, liberal arts, physical/art education, health, kinesiology and leisure

accepted each year); Cost: First-year students, $1,838 per semester; Upperclassmen, $1,575 per semester
Staff: Learning disabilities specialists; peer tutors
Program Features: Oral and extended time testing; individual and small group tutoring sessions; limited course load (optional first year); note-taking assistance; taped texts; academic advising; weekly meetings; strategies class (first year students); assistive technology; computer lab; faculty made aware of student's learning disability (at student's request)
Entrance Requirements: High school transcript; handwritten essay; on-campus interview, SAT/ACT scores (untimed accepted); WAIS (or other intelligence test) report and achievement testing/report to document learning disability. Deadline is November 15.

MORNINGSIDE COLLEGE
1501 MORNINGSIDE AVENUE
SIOUX CITY, IOWA 51106
(712) 274-5191, 1-800-831-0806 X5191; FAX: (712) 274-5101
E-MAIL: tennapel@morningside.edu
WEB SITE: www.morningside.edu

Name of Special Program: Focus Program
Director: Karmen Ten Napel
General Information: Four-Year Private College; Enrollment: 950; **Tuition:** $17,170; **Room and Board:** $5,624. Morningside College, is a private, four-year liberal arts institution affiliated with the United Methodist Church. Morningside's 41-acre campus is in a scenic, secure residential area of Sioux City (population 125,000). **Majors:** Art, biology and chemistry, business administration and economics, education, English, history and political science, mass communication, mathematical sciences and physics/engineering, modern languages, music, nursing education, philosophy, pre-professional programs, psychology, religious studies, theatre.
Special Program: Enrollment in Special Program: 20 (limited to 35 new students accepted each year); Cost: $2,800 freshman year; $1,600 subsequent years.
Staff: Learning disabilities specialists; peer tutors; content tutors (faculty members); special counselors
Program Features: Oral and extended time testing; individual and small group tutoring sessions; note-taking assistance – scribes; taped texts; tape recorders; academic advising for students with learning disabilities; faculty made aware of student's learning disability; basic study skills; departmental program; WYNN software
Entrance Requirements: Documentation of learning disability; ACT untimed scores accepted; teacher evaluation.

College Life: A friendly, safe campus with small class sizes and individualized services to support student needs. Understanding and outgoing faculty and staff who want to help students succeed.
Scholarships: See page 428.

SAINT AMBROSE UNIVERSITY
518 WEST LOCUST STREET
DAVENPORT, IOWA 52803
(563) 333-6275 V/TTY; FAX: (563) 333-6243
E-MAIL: SaddlerRyanC@sau.edu **WEB SITE: www.sau.edu**

Name of Special Program: Services for Students with Disabilities
Director: Ryan Saddler
General Information: Four-Year Private University; Enrollment: 3,500; **Annual Tuition:** $19,460; **Room and Board:** $7,560. St. Ambrose is a Catholic University located in Davenport, Iowa, one of the Quad Cities which line the shores of an east-west stretch of the Mississippi River joining eastern Iowa and western Illinois. **Degrees:** Bachelor of Applied Management Technology, Bachelor of Arts, Bachelor of Arts in Special Studies, Business Administration, Bachelor of Elected Studies, Bachelor of Music Education, Bachelor of Science, Bachelor of Science in Industrial Engineering, Bachelor of Science in Nursing
Special Program: Enrollment in Special Program: 100; Cost: None. *Summer Program:* A four-week summer program is designed to give students with learning disabilities a head start on developing skills for a successful college career. A three-credit course is included. Cost: $2,700
Staff: Learning disabilities specialists; special counselors; peer tutors
Program Features: Oral and extended time testing; individual tutoring sessions; note-taking assistance – scribes: tape recorders; taped texts; basic study skills; academic advising for students with learning disabilities; developmental program; faculty made aware of student's learning disability
Entrance Requirements: Documentation of learning disability; SAT / ACT untimed scores accepted; testing: WAIS-R, psychological report
Special Facilities for: Visual, hearing, and physical impairments
College Life: St. Ambrose University offers a caring environment for students with learning disabilities where they can benefit from small classes, a faculty knowledgeable about learning disabilities and a focus on individual student needs.

KENTUCKY

EASTERN KENTUCKY UNIVERSITY
521 LANCASTER AVENUE, TURLEY HOUSE 1
RICHMOND, KENTUCKY 40475-3136
(859) 622-1500 V/TDD; FAX: (859) 622-6395
E-MAIL: disbellu@acs.eku.edu
WEB SITE: www.eku.edu/student services

Name of Special Program: Project SUCCESS
Project SUCCESS Director: Teresa Belluscio (859) 622-2933
General Information: Four-Year State University; Enrollment: 15,700; **Tuition:** Residents – $2,596, Non-Residents – $7,269; **Room and Board:** $1,356 double per year, $2,112 single per year. Situated near the heart of the Bluegrass, Richmond is served by a network of major highways which makes Eastern easily accessible from all parts of Kentucky and surrounding states. In and around Richmond are many areas of historic and scenic interest. Boonesborough State Park, birthplace of Kentucky, is located 12 miles to the north. The city of Lexington is approximately 25 miles from campus. **Degrees:** Eastern Kentucky University offers six certificate programs, eight preprofessional programs, 20 associate degree programs, 82 bachelor's degree programs, 27 master's programs, six specialist's degree programs, and a joint doctoral program.
Special Program: Enrollment in Special Program: 50, limited to 50; Cost: None. *Summer Program:* Project SUCCESS conducts a Summer Transition Program. The program is geared towards high school juniors and seniors with learning disabilities who desire to transition from secondary to postsecondary education. Attendance is approximately 40 people. First 40 receive stipend, others pay fee of $40.
Staff: Learning disabilities specialist; coordinators; peer tutors; note takers
Program Features: Oral and extended time testing; taped texts; limited course load (first year); note-taking assistance – scribes; basic study skills; tape recorders; individual tutoring sessions; developmental program; academic advising for students with learning disabilities; faculty made aware of student's learning disability; word processors
Entrance Requirements: Documentation of learning disability; ACT untimed scores accepted; two letters of recommendation; personal interview; testing: WAIS, psychological report; diagnostic testing at Eastern Kentucky University
Special Facilities for: Visual, hearing, and physical impairments
College Life: Project SUCCESS is a comprehensive program for students with learning disabilities. Individualized tutoring within a framework of support services provides the key for students' success in the program.
Scholarships: See page 428.

THOMAS MORE COLLEGE
333 THOMAS MORE PARKWAY
CRESTVIEW HILLS, KENTUCKY 41017
(859) 341-3521; FAX: (859) 344-3342
E-MAIL: barb.davis@thomasmore.edu
WEB SITE: www.thomasmore.edu

Name of Special Program: Student Services/Students with Disabilities
Coordinator: Barbara S. Davis
General Information; Four-Year Private College; Enrollment: 1,400; **Tuition:** $9,750 per semester; **Room and Board:** $3,125 per semester (double room and 19-meal plan); a Catholic College in a suburban area, with access to rural urban areas, across the Ohio River from Cincinnati, Ohio. **Majors:** Accounting, art, biology, business administration, chemistry, computer information systems, computer science, drama, economics, education, English, history, international studies, mathematics, medical technology, nursing, philosophy, physics, psychology, sociology, communication, theology, criminal justice
Special Program: Enrollment in Special Program: 50; Cost: None
Staff: Learning disabilities specialists; peer tutors
Program Features: Oral and extended time testing; individual and small group tutoring sessions; limited course load (first year); academic advising; note-taking assistance – scribes; taped texts; tape recorders; basic study skills; developmental program; faculty made aware of student's learning disability; study skills class paired with world history class; word processors available
Entrance Requirements: Documentation of learning disability; SAT/ACT untimed scores accepted; testing: WAIS, psychological report
College Life: Small, Catholic, liberal arts college with caring staff and advisors. Needed accommodations are met, and staff works one-on-one with students within a positive environment.

LOUISIANA

LOUISIANA COLLEGE
1140 COLLEGE DRIVE, BOX 545
PINEVILLE, LOUISIANA 71360
(318) 487-7629; FAX: (318) 487-7285
E-MAIL: matthews@lacollege. edu **WEB SITE: www.lacollege.edu**

Name of Special Program: Program to Assist Student Success (PASS)
Director: Betty P. Matthews
General Information: Four-Year Private College; Enrollment: 1,135;

Tuition: Residents – $9,650; **Room:** $1,860 per year, **Board:** $1,172 with unlimited meal plan per semester. The Louisiana College campus is located in central Louisiana on an 81-acre tract covered by native pines, oaks, and a variety of flowering trees and shrubs. Beautifully landscaped walks and gardens are adjacent to academic facilities designed to compliment the natural setting. The architectural style of the college's first buildings is epitomized in Alexandria Hall, whose columns are symbols of Louisiana College to generations of students. The building is listed on the National Register of Historic Places. The campus is three to four hours from historic New Orleans. Recreational activities include water-skiing, sailing, and boating. **Majors:** Art, biology, business administration, chemistry, physics, communication arts, education, English, journalism, and languages, health and physical education, history and political science, mathematics, music, nursing, psychology, religion and philosophy, sociology and social work, art education, biology education, English education, French, French education, music education, science, social studies education, graphic design, pre-law, pre-medicine

Special Program: Enrollment in Special Program: 40, limited to students with identified disabilities: Cost in addition to tuition and fees: $450–850 (various levels). *Summer Program:* The summer session consists of two five-week sessions. Many types of assistance for students with identified disabilities are available. Cost: $60 per semester hour

Staff: Learning disabilities specialists; peer tutors; content tutors (faculty members); special counselors

Program Features: Oral and extended time testing; taped texts; limited course load (if needed); note-taking assistance; basic study skills; tape recorders; individual and small group tutoring sessions; academic advising for students with learning disabilities; developmental program (for math); faculty made aware of student's learning disability

Entrance Requirements: In addition to general college entrance criteria, documentation of learning disability; SAT / ACT untimed scores accepted; disability evaluation; handwritten essay

Special Facilities for: Visual, hearing and physical impairments

College Life: The comprehensiveness of PASS appeals to students with special needs. Students experience the cooperative, helpful faculty, supportive administration and staff and an excellent staff for PASS. Louisiana College has a superior academic reputation. A very high value is placed on a degree from Louisiana College. PASS facilitates a student's success by meeting an individual's specific needs. Small classes, personal attention, and a beautiful, friendly campus create an optimum environment for learning.

McNEESE STATE UNIVERSITY
4205 RYAN STREET
P.O. BOX 92904
LAKE CHARLES, LOUISIANA 70609-2687
(337) 475-5916; FAX: (337) 475-5878
WEB SITE: www.mcneese.edu

Name of Special Program: Office of Services for Students with Disabilities
Director: Tim Delaney
General Information: Four-Year State University; Enrollment: 7,795; **Tuition:** Residents – $1,602 per semester, Non-Residents – $4,150 per semester; **Room and Board:** $1,272 semi-private per semester, $1,432 per semester for a private room. The main campus consists of 92 acres located in the growing city of Lake Charles. The urban university setting is located between Houston, Texas, and New Orleans, Louisiana. **Majors:** Accounting, finance, business administration, management, marketing, mathematics, computer science, statistics, physics, chemistry, education, health and human performance, psychology, education, engineering, liberal studies, languages, communications, music, nursing, agriculture, pre-veterinary medicine, biological / environmental sciences, family / consumer sciences. Associate degrees are also offered in nursing, office administration, word processing, computer technology, paralegal studies, general studies, petroleum services technology
Special Program: Enrollment in Special Program; 70; Cost: None
Staff: Learning disabilities specialists
Program Features: Oral and extended time testing; note-taking assistance – scribes; tape recorders; small group tutoring sessions; academic advising for students with learning disabilities; faculty made aware of student's learning disability (at student's request)
Entrance Requirements: Documentation of learning disability; ACT untimed scores accepted.
Special Facilities for: Visual, hearing, and physical impairments
College Life: Services for students with disabilities provides not only assistance and accommodations according to the individual needs of the student, but attempts to regard the total person and provide a relaxed, supportive setting.

NICHOLLS STATE UNIVERSITY
LOUISIANA CENTER FOR DYSLEXIA AND RELATED LEARNING DISORDERS
906 EAST FIRST STREET, P.O. BOX 2050
THIBODAUX, LOUISIANA 70310
(985) 448-4214; FAX: (985) 448-4423
E-MAIL: karen.chauvin@nicholls.edu
WEB SITE: www.nicholls.edu/dyslexia

Name of Special Program: Louisiana Dyslexia Center
Director: Karen Chauvin (985) 448-4897
General Information: Four-Year State University; Enrollment: 7,300; **Tuition:** Residents – $1,729.25 per semester, Non-Residents – $4,453.25 per semester; **Room and Board:** $2,820. The University is located in a small town one hour from New Orleans. **Degrees:** BA, BS, AA, self-designed majors, certificates and academic minors
Special Program: Enrollment: 120; Cost: $375 per semester
Staff: Learning disabilities specialists; special counselors
Program Features: Oral and extended time testing; individual and small group tutoring sessions; limited course load; academic advising for students with learning disabilities; taped texts; tape recorders; basic study skills; remedial reading, English and math and college algebra classes designated for students with dyslexia; assistance in scheduling and registration, copier available; faculty made aware of student's learning disability (at student's request)
Entrance Requirements: Documentation of learning disability (within three years); untimed ACT; testing: WAIS, psychological report; diagnostic testing at Nicholls State University

MAINE

UNITY COLLEGE
QUAKER HILL ROAD, RR 78, P.O. BOX 1
UNITY, MAINE 04988-9502
(207) 948-3131 X263; FAX: (207) 948-5626
E-MAIL: jhoran@unity.edu **WEB SITE: www.unity.edu**

Name of Special Program: Learning Resource Center
Director: James J. Horan
General Information: Four-Year Private College; Enrollment: 550; **Annual Tuition:** $16,740; **Room and Board:** $6,630. A small independent, coeducational liberal arts college with an emphasis on natural resource management. The campus is on 185 acres of fields and woodlands overlooking

Lake Winecook and the village of Unity, Maine, 200 miles north of Boston, 40 miles from Augusta and Bangor and 25 miles from Waterville and Penobscot Bay. Strong internship and cooperative education element. **Degrees:** Associate of Arts, liberal studies, fine arts. Associate of Science, Associate of Applied Science, forest management technology. Baccalaureate programs include Bachelor of Arts, interdisciplinary studies and pre-law. Bachelor of Science includes environmental sciences (self-designed), aquaculture, conservation, law enforcement, ecology, fisheries, wildlife. social sciences include environmental education, environmental policy, park management, outdoor recreation (administrative and leadership)
Special Program: Enrollment in Special Program: 50–60; Cost: None
Summer Program: The Summer Institute of Unity College is a four-week program with credit and non-credit courses, instruction in study skills and individualized tutorial assistance: basic writing, basic mathematics, introduction to computers and introduction to science. Cost: $1,295
Staff: Learning disabilities specialists; peer tutors; special counselors; content tutors (faculty members)
Program Features: Oral and extended time testing; taped texts; limited course load (first year); note-taking assistance – scribes; basic study skills (available, not required); tape recorders; individual and small group tutoring sessions; developmental program; faculty made aware of student's learning disability (at student's request)
Entrance Requirements: Documentation of learning disability; learning disabilities specialist report; teacher evaluation; handwritten essay; interview (if possible); testing: WAIS
Special Facilities for: Physical impairments
Scholarships: See page 429.

MARYLAND

FROSTBURG STATE UNIVERSITY

150 PULLEN HALL
FROSTBURG, MARYLAND 21532-1099
(301) 687-4483; FAX: (301) 687-4671
E-MAIL: lpullen@frostburg.edu
WEB SITE: www.frostburg.edu/clife/dss

Name of Special Program: Disability Support Services
Director: Leroy Pullen
General Information: Four-Year State University; Enrollment: 4,800; **Annual Tuition:** Residents – $5,000, Non-Residents – $14,050; **Room and Board:** $6,382. A rural campus in a small town, 10 miles from Cumberland, 150 miles west of Baltimore and Washington, D.C., and 100 miles south of

Pittsburgh. **Majors:** Biology, business/management, chemistry, computer/information sciences, education, environmental design, fine arts, health sciences, languages, law, letters/literature, life sciences, mathematics, multi/interdisciplinary studies, music, parks and recreation, philosophy, physical sciences, physics, psychology, public affairs, renewable natural resources, social sciences, visual/performing arts, zoology
Special Program: Enrollment in Special Program: 240; Cost: None
Staff: Learning disabilities specialists; content tutors; peer tutors; special counselors for academic issues; math/writing lab
Program Features: Oral and extended time testing; individual and small group tutoring sessions; limited course load; academic advising for students with learning disabilities; note-taking assistance – scribes; tape recorders; taped texts; basic study skills; developmental program; faculty made aware of student's learning disability (at student's request)
Entrance Requirements: Documentation of learning disability; SAT/ACT untimed scores accepted; some diagnostic testing at Frostburg State University; testing: WAIS, IEP, psychological report
Special Facilities for: Visual, hearing and physical impairments
Scholarships: See page 430.

McDANIEL COLLEGE
STUDENT ACADEMIC SUPPORT SERVICES
2 COLLEGE HILL
WESTMINSTER, MARYLAND 21158
(410) 857-2504; FAX: (410) 386-4617
E-MAIL: sass@mcdaniel.edu **WEB SITE: www.mcdaniel.edu**

Name of Special Program: Academic Skills Program
Director: Kevin Selby; *Co-Director:* Susan Dorsey
General Information: Four-Year Private College; Enrollment: 1,610; **Annual Tuition:** $26,980; **Room:** $5,800; **Board:** $2,810. A 160-acre campus located in rural Western Maryland, 45 minutes from Baltimore and one hour from Washington, D.C. The college is centered in the liberal arts and features study abroad. **Majors:** American studies, art, biology, business administration, chemistry, communication, economics, English, foreign languages, history, mathematics, music, philosophy, physical education, physics, political science, psychobiology, psychology, religious studies, social work, sociology, Spanish, theatre arts. Dual majors available; student-designed majors, pre-engineering, pre-forestry, pre-professional programs for the health professions, pre-law studies, pre-museum studies, pre-occupation therapy, pre-physical therapy, teacher certification, military science

Special Program: Enrollment in Special Program: 150. Cost: $1,500 per year. The percentage of students receiving degrees within four years is 85% and in five or more years 15%.
Staff: Learning disabilities specialists; content tutors in math (faculty members); graduate assistants; peer tutors as needed.
Program Features: Extended time testing; individual and small group tutoring sessions; note-taking assistance – scribes; tape recorders; taped texts; basic study skills; faculty made aware of student's learning disability; academic advising for students with learning disabilities; computer with speech input; enrollment in freshman non-credit course, "Your College Experience;" specialized career development information for juniors and seniors; supervised study lab with access to computers, evening supervised study sessions; advanced training in use of assistive technology (Kurzweil 3000, Inspiration, Text Help, RFB recorders) available for additional fee of $500.
Entrance Requirements: Documentation of learning disability; SAT untimed scores accepted; testing: WAIS; psychoeducational evaluation must be current (within three years)
Special Facilities for: Visual, hearing and physical impairments; interpreters available for deaf students
College Life: McDaniel College has private school perks such as small classes and accessible faculty. We have a global attitude regarding academics and course offerings.

MASSACHUSETTS

AMERICAN INTERNATIONAL COLLEGE

1000 STATE STREET, BOX 50
SPRINGFIELD, MASSACHUSETTS 01109
(413) 205-3426, 1-800-242-3142; FAX: (413) 737-2803
E-MAIL: sls@aic.edu **WEB SITE: www.aic.edu**

Name of Special Program: Supportive Learning Services Program
Director: Mary Saltus
General Information: Four-Year Private College; Enrollment: 1,200; **Annual Tuition:** $20,990; **Room and Board:** $9,270. An urban campus in a small city three miles from downtown Springfield. Special attractions are: Basketball Hall of Fame, Mount Tom. Member of Cooperating Colleges of Greater Springfield. Majors: Biology, biochemistry, business/management, chemistry, communication, computer/information sciences, education (special and teacher), English, health sciences, history, medical technology/nursing/physical therapy, public administration, languages, pre-

law, mathematics, criminal justice, psychology, political science, sociology, occupational therapy
Special Program: Enrollment in Special Program: 100; limited enrollment of 35 freshmen per year; Cost: $4,000 per year
Staff: Learning disabilities specialists
Program Features: Oral and extended time testing; individual tutoring sessions; limited course load; tape recorders; taped texts; study skills; faculty made aware of student's learning disability; test scanner readers (reading system that works in conjunction with computer)
Entrance Requirements: Documentation of learning disability; learning disabilities specialist report; SAT/ACT untimed scores accepted; teacher evaluations; regular admissions requirement; personal interview; testing: WAIS, SEC, psychological report
Limited Facilities for: Visual, hearing and physical impairments

BOSTON UNIVERSITY
19 DEERFIELD STREET
BOSTON, MASSACHUSETTS 02215
(617) 353-3658 V/TTY; FAX: (617) 353-9646
E-MAIL: lwolf@bu.edu or access@bu.edu
WEB SITE: www.bu.edu/disability

Name of Special Program: Learning Disabilities Services (LDS)
Clinical Director: Lorraine Wolf, Ph.D.
General Information: Four-Year Private University; Enrollment: 30,000; **Annual Tuition:** $33,330; **Room and Board**: $9,680–12,110. Boston University is an independent, coeducational, nonsectarian center of higher education and research. It is the third largest independent institution of higher education in the United States. The 71-acre urban campus is in the heart of the historic Back Bay section of Boston, convenient to all major cultural recreational facilities. **Degree Programs and Majors:** Boston University has 15 schools and colleges, 11 offering undergraduate degrees.
Special Program: Enrollment in Special Program: 550; Cost: $1,600 per semester for learning disability strategy tutoring. *Summer Program:* To assist students with their transition to college, LDS offers a unique summer program designed specifically for incoming freshman with disabilities. ENTRY! provides an opportunity for entering students to develop the skills necessary to reach their fullest potential in college. Students move into their assigned dormitory one week early to participate in daily learning strategies seminars, workshops and recreational activities. A special workshop is also offered to assist parents of students enrolled in ENTRY! with this important transition. Personalized support continues through

the academic semester.
Staff: Coordinator of LDS; learning disabilities specialists; clinical director; learning disabilities strategy tutors
Program Features: Access to academic accommodations; counseling and support; access to assistive technology; skills and strategies workshop series; workshops for academic and study strategies; note-taking; time management; self-advocacy; fee-based program offering weekly one-to-one tutoring with a professional learning disabilities strategy tutor
Entrance Requirements: Documentation of learning disability and learning disabilities specialist report (within three years) which should include IQ test and comprehensive testing of academic achievement; medical diagnosis; recommendations for accommodations/services
Scholarships: See page 430.

CURRY COLLEGE

1071 BLUE HILL AVENUE
MILTON, MASSACHUSETTS 02186-2395
(617) 333-2270; FAX: (617) 333-2018
E-MAIL: Ijiri@curry.edu **WEB SITE: www.curry.edu**

Name of Special Program: Program for Advancement of Learning (PAL)
Director: Dr. Lisa Ijiri
General Information: Four-Year Private College; Enrollment: 1,600; **Tuition:** $23,400; **Room and Board:** $9,640 (flexible meal plan). Curry College has a beautiful, wooded campus just seven miles from Boston. **Majors:** Biology, business management, chemistry, communications, education, English, nursing, philosophy, physics, politics and history, psychology, sociology, visual arts, environmental science, criminal justice
Special Program: Enrollment in Special Program: freshmen 165, total 400; Cost: $4,500. *Summer Program:* The Program for Advancement of Learning (PAL) begins with Summer PAL which runs for three weeks in June or July. Students deepen their understanding of themselves, how they learn and how to monitor their own learning. They develop knowledge that leads to greater competence, effectiveness and independence as a learner. Cost: $2,700. Optional
Staff: Learning disabilities specialists; special counselors; content tutors (faculty members)
Program Features: Oral and extended time testing; individual and small group tutoring sessions; limited course load (first year); tape recorders; taped texts: basic study skills; academic advising for students with learning disabilities; counseling; computer facility; faculty made aware of student's learning disability

Entrance Requirements: Documentation of learning disability; learning disabilities specialist report; SAT/ACT untimed scores accepted; teacher evaluation, supplementary application; testing: WAIS-R, IEP, psychological report
Special Facilities for: Visual, hearing and physical impairments
College Life: PAL's 31-year history has led to a strong supportive community on campus where learners of all styles are appreciated and encouraged. With approximately one third of the student body participating in PAL, students benefit from both the sense of community with other students with learning disabilities and also experience the challenge of learning in a mainstream environment.
Scholarships: See page 430.

FITCHBURG STATE COLLEGE
160 PEARL STREET
FITCHBURG, MASSACHUSETTS 01420
(978) 665-3427; FAX: (978) 665-4799
E-MAIL: dstevenson@fsc.edu **WEB SITE: www.fsc.edu**

Name of Special Program: Disability Services
Director: Dawn Stevenson
General Information: Four-Year State College; Enrollment: 5,117; **Annual Tuition:** Residents – $5,056, Non-Residents – $11,136; **Room and Board:** $5,120. A suburban college only 40 miles west of Boston and 22 miles north of Worcester, Massachusetts, and within 10 minutes from fabulous skiing. Two-semester plan, liberal arts college with unparalleled preprofessional programs, internships and exchange programs. **Degrees:** Bachelor's degrees: accounting, biology, bio/education, business, clinical lab science, clinical chemistry, communications, computer systems, criminal justice, education, economics, English, environmental science, exercise science, fitness management, general systems, geography, graphic design, history, human services, industrial technology, management, marketing, mathematics, medical technology, microbiology, nursing, photography technology, political science, professional writing, psychology, sociology, theater, TV/film production
Special Program: Enrollment in Special Program: 200; Cost: None
Staff: Learning disabilities specialists; peer tutors; special counselors
Program Features: Oral and extended time testing; individual and small group tutoring sessions; limited course load (any year, is optional); note-taking assistance – scribes; tape recorders; taped texts; basic study skills; academic advising for students with learning disabilities; adaptive technology lab; leadership program; peer mentor program; student group; international exchange program

Entrance Requirements: Documentation of learning disability; SAT untimed scores accepted (not required if submitted documentation); testing: psychological report
Special Facilities for: Visual, hearing, and physical impairments
Scholarships: See page 431.

MOUNT IDA COLLEGE
777 DEDHAM STREET
NEWTON CENTRE, MASSACHUSETTS 02459
(617) 928-4648; FAX: (617) 928-4507
E-MAIL: jmehler@mountida.edu **WEB SITE: www.mountida.edu**

Name of Special Program: Learning Opportunities Program (LOP)
Director: Jill Mehler
General Information: Four-Year Private College; Enrollment: 1,100; **Tuition:** $19,800; **Room and Board:** $10,225. Two-plus-two college, suburban campus eight miles from downtown Boston. Liberal education coupled with action-career-orientated curriculum, internships, opportunities to study abroad at Regents College, London, England. **Majors:** Animal sciences – veterinary and equine studies; business – management, hotel, marketing, travel and tourism, computers; design and merchandising – fashion, graphic, interior; technical – electricity; education – child study, teacher certification, liberal arts; communication; criminal justice; human services; public administration; paralegal studies; funeral service – bereavement counseling; science and allied health – dental assistant, occupational therapy assistant, optician, exercise; health and fitness; sports management; pre-engineering. BA degrees in criminal investigation and business economics. Associate degrees and certificates.
Special Program: Enrollment in Special Program: 80–110; Cost: $2,995
Staff: Learning disabilities specialists; professional tutors; peer tutors
Program Features: Oral and extended time testing; individual tutoring sessions; limited course load; tape recorders; taped texts; basic study skills; academic assistance for students with learning disabilities; faculty made aware of student's learning disability (student's self-disclosure with accommodation form). Students in the LOP are enrolled in a regular academic major and take a full course load (15 credits a semester, depending on the major unless they choose to do otherwise). The Horizon Program offers all services in the LOP Program with an additional 1/2 hour of coaching, a reduced course load, a supplemental support class each semester and appropriate classroom accommodations where indicated by a documented learning disability.
Entrance Requirements: Documentation of learning disability; learning

disabilities report; handwritten essay (optional); interview recommended; any other documentation useful; testing: WAIS-R, IEP
College Life: Students in both programs are fully integrated members of the college community with all the opportunities and responsibilities of any Mount Ida student. After the freshman year in either program, students have the choice of one or two academic coaching sessions per week, depending on their perceived need and past performance, or they can choose to leave the program.

NORTHEASTERN UNIVERSITY
DISABILITY RESOURCE CENTER
360 HUNTINGTON AVENUE, 20 DODGE HALL
BOSTON, MASSACHUSETTS 02115
(617) 373-2675, (617) 373-2730 TTY; FAX: (617) 373-7800
E-MAIL: d.auerbach@neu.edu
WEB SITE: www.disabilityresourcecenter.neu.edu

Name of Special Program: Learning Disabilities Program
Service Coordinator: Debbi Auerbach
General Information: Five-Year Private Co-op University; Enrollment: 20,000; **Tuition:** $28,400; **Room and Board:** $7,000. Founded in 1898. An urban campus in downtown Boston which includes a Museum of Fine Art and the Hatch Schell Museum of Sciences. **Majors:** College of Arts and Sciences: BA, BS, and BS in Education. College of Pharmacy and Health Sciences: AS, BS, AS and BS in Dental Hygiene. College of Business Administration: BS in Business, and BS in International Business. College of Computer Science: BS and BA. College of Criminal Justice: BS. College of Engineering: BS in Chemical Engineering, Civil Engineering, Electrical Engineering, Industrial Engineering, Mechanical Engineering and MS in Electrical Engineering, Industrial Engineering, Mechanical Engineering. College of Nursing: BS in School of Engineering Technology: BS in College of Human Development Professions: BS in Education, and Recreation and Leisure Studies
Special Program: There is a general LD/ADHD Program with unlimited enrollment and a special LD/ADHD program with limited enrollment. Enrollment: general program, 300; enrollment in special program, limited to 35. Cost: $1,400 per quarter
Staff: Learning disabilities specialists; peer tutors; content tutors (faculty members)
Program Features: Extended time testing; taped texts; note-taking assistance – scribes; tape recorders; individual tutoring sessions; limited course load; developmental program; academic advising for students with learn-

ing disabilities; faculty made aware of student's learning disability; adaptive equipment
Entrance Requirements: SAT/ACT untimed scores accepted; testing: WAIS, psychological report
Special Facilities for: Visual, hearing and physical impairments

SPRINGFIELD COLLEGE
263 ALDEN STREET
SPRINGFIELD, MASSACHUSETTS 01109
(413) 748-3768, (413) 748-3390 TTD; FAX: (413) 748-3937
E-MAIL: ddickens@spfldcol.edu **WEB SITE: www.spfldcol.edu**

Name of Special Program: Student Support Services
Director: Deb Dickens
General Information: Four-Year Private College; Enrollment: 2,516; **Tuition:** $21,595; **Room and Board:** $7,770. The College is located in the geographical center of the city of Springfield, Massachusetts, on the shores of Lake Massasoit. The setting provides students with an attractive New England atmosphere in which to study, but at the same time makes possible a healthy sampling of social and cultural events associated with an urban setting. **Degrees:** Bachelor of Arts (BA), Bachelor of Science (BS) and Bachelor of Physical Education (BPE)
Special Program: Enrollment in Special Program: 100; Cost: None
Staff: Learning disabilities specialists; peer tutors; content tutors (faculty members)
Program Features: Extended time testing; taped texts; note-taking assistance – scribes; tape recorders; individual small group tutoring sessions; limited course load (first year); academic advising for students with learning disabilities
Entrance Requirements: Documentation of learning disability; SAT untimed scores accepted; medical evaluation; testing: WAIS, IEP, psychological report
Special Facilities for: Visual, hearing and physical impairments

UNIVERSITY OF MASSACHUSETTS: AMHERST
231 WHITMORE BLDG.
AMHERST, MASSACHUSETTS 01003-0620
(413) 545-0892 V/TTY; FAX: (413) 577-0122
E-MAIL: ds@educ.umass.edu **WEB SITE: www.umass.edu/disability**

Name of Special Program: Disability Services
Director: Madeline L. Peters

General Information: Four-Year State University; Enrollment: 20,000; **Tuition, Room, Board, and Fees:** Residents – $8,292 per semester, Non-Residents – $13,153 per semester. The University of Massachusetts is the public university of the Commonwealth of Massachusetts, and was founded in 1863. Situated in the lovely Connecticut River Valley, the University joins four nearby colleges – Amherst, Hampshire, Smith and Mount Holyoke (the Five Colleges) – in a rich tradition of learning and cultural activity. **Majors:** 130 undergraduate majors in the following areas of study: College of Arts and Sciences, School of Education, College of Engineering, College of Food and Natural Resources, School of Management, School of Nursing, School of Physical Education, School of Public Health
Special Program: Enrollment in Special Program: 800; Cost: None
Staff: Professional staff are specialists in the field of disability, i.e., learning disabilities, attention deficit disorder
Program Features: Extended time on assignments and tests; modified exams, note takers, reduced course loads, proctored exams, books-on-tapes, academic assistants, classroom assistants, adaptive computing and advocacy within the University community
Entrance Requirements: Documentation of disability; neuropsychological reports, psychological reports, medical reports, and audiological reports; diagnostic testing at University of Massachusetts: Amherst
Special Facilities for: Visual, hearing and physical impairments
College Life: Well-established, well-staffed program, widespread support among instructional staff and faculty.

MICHIGAN

ALMA COLLEGE
CENTER FOR STUDENT DEVELOPMENT & DISABILITY SERVICES
HAMILTON COMMONS, LOWER LEVEL
ALMA, MICHIGAN 48801
(989) 463-7225; FAX: (989) 463-7353
E-MAIL: chase@alma.edu **WEB SITE: www.alma.edu**

Name of Special Program: Center for Student Development
Director: Dr. Patricia Chase, *Assistant Director:* Janet Tissue
General Information: Four-Year Private College; Enrollment: 1,550; **Tuition:** $22,170; **Room and Board:** $7,774. Founded more than 110 years ago, Alma College is a Phi Beta Kappa institution and ranks in the top 7% of liberal arts colleges nationally. The 100-acre campus is in Alma, Michigan (population 10,000), located one hour north of Michigan's capital, Lansing, and less than three hours away from both beaches and snow skiing. **Majors:** 40 academic and preprofessional programs and majors are

offered besides unusual courses such as scene design and lighting, physiology of aging, environmental studies, gerontology, peacemaking and conflict resolution, public health and women's studies.
Special Program: Enrollment in Special Program: 25; Cost: None
Staff: Learning disabilities specialists; peer tutors; special counselors
Program Features: Oral and extended time testing; individual and small group tutoring sessions; note-taking assistance – scribes; limited course load (first year); tape recorders; taped texts; basic study skills; developmental program; faculty made aware of student's learning disability; personal and career counseling
Entrance Requirements: Documentation of learning disability; learning disabilities specialist report; SAT / ACT untimed scores accepted

NORTHERN MICHIGAN UNIVERSITY
3302 HEDGCOCK
MARQUETTE, MICHIGAN 49855
(906) 227-1550; FAX: (906) 227-1510
E-MAIL: phollida@nmu.edu **WEB SITE: www.nmu.edu**

Name of Special Program: Student Support Services
Director: Peter J. Holliday
General Information: Four-Year State University; Enrollment: 8,000; **Tuition:** Residents – $2,796 per semester for 16 credit hours, Non-Residents – $4,764 per semester for 16 credit hours; **Room and Board:** $6,874 per year. Northern Michigan University is located in the heart of Michigan's Upper Peninsula, an area of unsurpassed beauty and recreational opportunities. Marquette, on the south shore of Lake Superior, is the largest city in the Upper Peninsula. **Majors:** Area studies, business, communications, computer science, crafts and design, education, engineering, environmental control, health sciences, humanities, languages, preprofessional, sciences, social sciences, visual and performing arts, vocational
Special Program: Enrollment in Special Program: 80; Cost: None
Staff: Learning disabilities specialists; peer tutors; content tutors (faculty members); special counselors
Program Features: Oral and extended time testing; individual and small group tutoring sessions; note-taking assistance – scribes; tape recorders, taped texts; basic study skills; developmental program
Entrance Requirements: Documentation of learning disability; ACT untimed scores accepted; testing: WAIS, psychological report
Special Facilities for: Visual, hearing and physical impairments

WAYNE STATE UNIVERSITY
5155 GULLEN MALL, 1600 UGL
DETROIT, MICHIGAN 48202
(313) 577-1851, (313) 577-3365 TTY; FAX: (313) 577-4898
WEB SITE: www.eas.wayne.edu

Name of Special Program: Educational Accessibility Services
Director: Jan Collins-Eaglin
General Information: Four-Year State University; Enrollment: over 30,000; **Tuition:** Residents – $3,194.70 for 15 credit hours, Non-Residents – $6,860.70 for 15 credit hours; **Room:** On-campus apartments; fee varies. The main campus is located in the heart of Detroit, largely bounded by York Street on the north, Woodward Avenue on the east, Forest Avenue on the south and Trumbull Avenue on the west. The major classrooms, laboratory, library and other academic buildings are located on the east side of the Lodge Expressway while the athletic and recreational facilities are mostly on the west side of the Expressway. **Majors:** The University offers over 4,800 courses, 377 major subject areas, 143 master's programs, and 23 specialist programs. It is a national research university and an urban teaching institution.
Special Program: Enrollment in Special Program: 40; Cost: None
Staff: Learning disabilities specialists; program specialists
Program Features: Oral and extended time testing; individual and small group tutoring sessions; faculty made aware of student's learning disability (at student's request); personal/career counseling; word processors; spellcheckers; recorded text books; note takers; tutoring
Entrance Requirements: Documentation of learning disability; SAT/ACT untimed scores accepted
Special Facilities for: Visual, hearing and physical impairments; psychological, temporary; all types
Scholarships: See page 431.

MINNESOTA

AUGSBURG COLLEGE
2211 RIVERSIDE AVENUE, CB #57
MINNEAPOLIS, MINNESOTA 55454
(612) 330-1053, (612) 330-1748 TDD; FAX: (612) 330-1137
E-MAIL: class@augsburg.edu
WEB SITE: www.augsburg.edu/classprogram

Name of Special Program: Center for Learning and Adaptive Student Services (CLASS)
Disability Specialist: Anne Lynch (612) 330-1217, lyncha@augsburg.edu

General Information: Four-Year Private College; Enrollment: 3,375; **Tuition:** $21,958; **Room and Board:** $8,000 (varies). The 23-acre campus, affiliated with the Evangelical Lutheran Church in America, is in a residential area of downtown Minneapolis. Special learning facilities include a learning resource center, art gallery, radio station and TV studio. **Majors:** Area studies, biology, business/management, chemistry, communications, computer/information sciences, education, fine arts, languages, letters/literature, mathematics, multi/interdisciplinary studies, music, philosophy, physics, psychology, physician's assistant, religion, social sciences, social work, visual/performing arts; Master of Arts in leadership, teaching and social work
Special Program: Enrollment in Special Program: 160; Cost: None
Staff: Learning disabilities specialists; accommodation specialist; licensed psychologist; peer tutors
Program Features: Oral and extended time testing; note-taking assistance – scribes; individual and small group tutoring sessions; basic study skills; limited course load (first year); tape recorders; taped texts; academic advising for students with learning disabilities; faculty made aware of student's learning disability by student; computer lab; adaptive technology
Entrance Requirements: Documentation of learning disability; learning disabilities report; interview with specialist; SAT or ACT untimed scores accepted; personal essay; interview with specialist (all documentation within the last three years recommended); testing: WAIS, IEP, Woodcock-Johnson, tests of memory and processing, psychological report
Special Facilities for: Visual, hearing and physical impairments; campus is very accessible and includes a skyway/elevator/tunnel system that connects most major buildings
College Life: Program model stressing the development of student independence and self-advocacy. Low faculty-to-student ratio, and receptive faculty willing to work with students with disabilities. The college mission is to develop leaders by providing an education based on liberal arts and shaped by faith in a diverse campus community.
Scholarships: See page 432.

BETHEL UNIVERSITY
3900 BETHEL DRIVE
ST. PAUL, MINNESOTA 55112
(651) 635-8759; FAX: (651) 635-8880
E-MAIL: K-mcgillivray@bethel.edu WEB SITE: www.bethel.edu

Name of Special Program: Office of Disability Services
Director: Kathleen J. McGillivray
General Information: Four-Year Private University; Enrollment: 2,700;

Annual Tuition: $22,590; **Room:** $4,260; **Board:** $2,880. The University is located in a suburban area near the Mall of America in St. Paul, Minnesota. **Majors:** Approximately 52 undergraduate degree programs from art to youth ministries
Special Program: Enrollment in Special Program: 30; Cost: None
Staff: Learning disabilities specialists; content tutors (faculty members); peer tutors; special counselors
Program Features: Oral and extended time testing; individual and small group tutoring sessions; tape recorders; limited course load (first year); basic study skills; note-taking assistance – scribes; taped texts; faculty made aware of student's learning disability; academic advising for students with learning disabilities
Entrance Requirements: Documentation of learning disability; learning disabilities specialist report; ACT untimed scores accepted
Special Facilities for: Visual, hearing and physical impairments
College Life: The faculty focus is on teaching and learning rather than research. There is a low faculty-to-student ratio, individualized service and accommodations.

SOUTHWEST MINNESOTA STATE UNIVERSITY
1501 STATE STREET
MARSHALL, MINNESOTA 56258
(507) 537-6169; FAX: (507) 537-6027
E-MAIL: leach@southwestmsu.edu
WEB SITE: www.southwestmsu.edu

Name of Special Program: Learning Resources, TRIO Program
Director: Marilyn M. Leach
General Information: Four-Year State University; Enrollment: 3,000; **Tuition:** $3,120 per semester; **Room and Board:** $2,680 per semester. The 216-acre campus is in a large town, 90 miles from Sioux Falls, South Dakota, and 150 miles from Minneapolis-St. Paul. Special learning facilities include an art gallery, natural history museum, planetarium, radio station and TV station. **Majors:** Agribusiness / agricultural production, biology, business / management, business / office, chemistry, communications and the arts, computer / information sciences, education, engineering and environmental design, fine arts, health sciences, literature, marketing, mathematics, multi / interdisciplinary studies, music, physical / social sciences, psychology, visual and performing arts; Global Studies for lower division students (General Studies courses clustered with common theme; voyage to a different environment, some United States, some abroad); graduate programs in education and business management

Special Program: Enrollment in Special Program: 80; Cost: None
Staff: Learning disabilities specialists; content tutors (faculty members); peer tutors; special counselors
Program Features: Oral and extended time testing; individual and small group tutoring sessions; tape recorders; limited course load (first year); basic study skills; note-taking assistance – scribes; taped texts; developmental program; faculty made aware of student's learning disability (at student's request); student organization and mentors; academic advising
Entrance Requirements: Documentation of learning disability; ACT untimed scores accepted; diagnostic testing at Southwest Minnesota University (preferred prior to admittance); fulfillment of university admissions criteria including college prep courses; testing: WAIS, WCJ-R
Special Facilities for: Visual, hearing and physical impairments
Scholarships: See page 432.

UNIVERSITY OF MINNESOTA: TWIN CITIES
200 OAK STREET SE, SUITE 180
MINNEAPOLIS, MINNESOTA 55455
(612) 626-1333 V/TTY; FAX: (612) 626-9654
E-MAIL: ds@umn.edu **WEB SITE: www.umn.edu/tc**

Name of Program: Disability Services Program
Director: Roberta "Bobbi" Cordano, J.D.
General Information: Four-Year State University; Enrollment: 45,000; **Tuition:** Residents – $3,794 per semester, Non-Residents – $9,609 per semester; **Room:** $2,282 per semester, **Board:** $1,447, 19-meal plan per semester. The University of Minnesota is located in the Twin Cities of Minneapolis and St. Paul. The research and scholarship of world-class professors have earned the University of Minnesota international recognition and top national rankings. **Majors:** From astrophysics to family social science, from plant biology to art and music, from urban forestry to international relations, from pre-med to pre-law, about 150 undergraduate majors to choose from or design your own degree program
Special Program: Enrollment in Special Program: 300; Cost: None
Staff: Learning disabilities specialists
Program Features: Extended time testing; taped texts; academic advising for students with learning disabilities; tape recorders; limited course load; note-taking assistance – scribes; faculty made aware of student's learning disability; disability-specific support groups
Entrance Requirements: Documentation of learning disability; SAT/ACT untimed scores accepted. Admission to University of Minnesota: Twin Cities and acceptance in Disability Services Program are two separate processes.

Special Facilities for: Visual, hearing and physical impairments
College Life: There are many choices for majors and over 200 student organizations. Students work with one of three learning disabilities specialists. Accommodations are individually determined.

MISSOURI

EVANGEL UNIVERSITY

1111 NORTH GLENSTONE
SPRINGFIELD, MISSOURI 65802
(417) 865-2815 X7983; FAX: (417) 865-1574
E-MAIL: rogersl@evangel.edu **WEB SITE: www.evangel.edu**

Name of Program: Academic Support Center
Director: Dr. Laynah J. Rogers
General Information: Four-Year Private College; Enrollment: 2,000; **Tuition:** $6,380 per semester; **Room and Board:** $2,435 per semester. Suburban college in a medium-sized city, 40 miles from Branson, Missouri. Evangel is a private college of arts/sciences under the auspices of the Assemblies of God. Students applying must have a minister's reference attesting to their religious faith. Special features include an active chapel program and ministry activities, as well as other types of outreach programs. **Majors:** Business, humanities, psychology, social work, criminal justice, teacher education, music, social sciences, sciences, computer science, bible, communication, sociology
Special Program: Enrollment in Special Program: 25; Cost: None
Staff: Learning disabilities specialists; peer tutors; special counselors
Program Features: Oral and extended time testing; individual and small group tutoring sessions; limited course load (first year); taped texts; tape recorders; basic study skills; developmental program; academic advising for students with learning disabilities; faculty made aware of student's learning disability
Entrance Requirements: Documentation of learning disability; learning disabilities specialist report; SAT/ACT untimed scores accepted; diagnostic testing at Evangel University; teacher evaluation, medical evaluation, handwritten essay; testing: WAIS, IEP, psychological report
Special Facilities for: Visual, hearing and physical impairments
College Life: Students with learning disabilities know faculty are supportive and understanding.

KANSAS CITY ART INSTITUTE
4415 WARWICK BOULEVARD
KANSAS CITY, MISSOURI 64111
(816) 802-3371; FAX: (816) 802-3480
E-MAIL: bburgard@kcai.edu or arc@kcai.edu
WEB SITE: www.kcai.edu

Name of Special Program: Academic Resource Center
Director: Bambi Burgard, Ph.D.
General Information: Four-Year Private Art Institute; Enrollment: 550; **Tuition:** $14,000; **Room and Board:** $8,000. The Kansas City Art Institute is an urban and design college, nestled on a small 15-acre campus adjacent to the Nelson/Atkins Museum of Art and Sculpture Garden and the Kemper Museum of Contemporary Art. **Majors:** Bachelor of Fine Arts degree program within which a comprehensive liberal arts program complements an emphasis in art history, ceramics, creative writing, design/illustration, fiber, painting/printmaking, photography/new media or sculpture
Special Program: Enrollment in Special Program: 25; Cost: None. The percentage of students with learning disabilities receiving a degree in four years is 90%.
Staff: Learning disabilities specialists; peer tutors
Program Features: Oral and extended time testing, individual and small group tutoring sessions; limited course load (first year); academic advising for students with learning disabilities; basic study skills; faculty made aware of student's learning disability
Entrance Requirements: Documentation of learning disability; SAT/ACT untimed scores accepted; testing: IEP, psychological report
College Life: The Kansas City Art Institute offers an intimate educational setting where open communication among faculty, student, and support staff is the norm. We strive to meet students' individual educational needs.

MISSOURI STATE UNIVERSITY
901 SOUTH NATIONAL, PROFESSIONAL BLDG. RM. 275
SPRINGFIELD, MISSOURI 65805-0088
(417) 836-4787; FAX: (417) 836-6372
E-MAIL: douglasgere@missouristate.edu
WEB SITE: www.missouristate.edu.edu

Name of Special Program: Project Success/Learning Diagnostic Clinic
Project Success Coordinator: Douglas Gere; *Learning Diagnostic Clinic Director:* Dr. Steve Capps – stevecapps@missouristate.edu
General Information: Four-Year State University; Enrollment: 18,000; **Tuition:** Residents – $2,076 for 12 credit hours, Non-Residents – $4,044 for

12 credit hours; **Room and Board:** $1,500, approximately. Founded in 1905, the main campus is located on 225 acres in a residential area of Springfield, Missouri, which is only 33 miles north of Branson, Missouri, and surrounded by several beautiful lakes and the hills of the Ozarks. **Degrees:** Arts and letters, education and psychology, health and applied sciences, humanities, social sciences, science and mathematics

Special Program: Enrollment in Special Program: 50; Cost: Level I services – none; Level II services – $1,300 per semester

Staff: Learning disabilities specialists; peer tutors; special counselors

Program Features: Oral and extended time testing, individual tutoring sessions; limited course load (first year); basic study skills; developmental program; faculty made aware of student's learning disability; books on tape; remedial math; developmental writing workshop and writing lab

Entrance Requirements: Documentation of learning disability; learning disabilities specialist report; SAT / ACT untimed scores accepted; testing: WAIS, SEC, psychological report, diagnostic testing at Missouri State University; teacher evaluation; medical evaluation; handwritten essay

Special Facilities for: Visual, hearing and physical impairments through a separate campus office

WESTMINSTER COLLEGE
501 WESTMINSTER AVENUE
FULTON, MISSOURI 65251-1299
(573) 592-5304; FAX: (573) 592-5180
E-MAIL: ottingh@westminster-mo.edu **WEB SITE: www.wcmo.edu**

Name of Special Program: Learning Disabilities Program

Director: Henry F. Ottinger

General Information: Four-Year Private College; Enrollment: 850; **Annual Tuition:** $14,600; **Room and Board:** $6,140. Fulton, Missouri, is a small town with a population of 11,000. The nearest metropolitan area is St. Louis, 100 miles from Fulton. Westminster is a liberal arts institution offering a strong internship program, plus excellent placement into the job market or graduate school. Special programs are United Nations, Washington Semester, Chicago Urban Studies Program, Study Abroad with the Institute of European Studies and the Institute of Asian Studies. **Majors:** Accounting, business administration, economics, anthropology, history, international studies, philosophy, political science, psychology, religion, sociology, art, theatre, education (special, secondary), biology, chemistry, mathematics, physics, English, French, Spanish

Special Program: Enrollment in Special Program: 30, limited to 12–14 each fall; Cost: $1,500 per semester for freshmen; $750 per semester for others

Staff: Learning disabilities specialists; peer tutors; content tutors (faculty members)
Program Features: Oral and extended time testing; taped texts; note-taking assistance – scribes; limited course load (first year); tape recorders; basic study skills; individual tutoring sessions; developmental writing class; faculty made aware of student's learning disability
Entrance Requirements: Documentation of learning disability; learning disabilities specialist report; handwritten essay; teacher evaluation; on-campus visit and testing; SAT or ACT untimed scores essential; testing: WAIS, psychoeducational evaluation

MONTANA

ROCKY MOUNTAIN COLLEGE

1511 POLY DRIVE
BILLINGS, MONTANA 59102-1796
(406) 657-1128, 1-800-877-8259; FAX: (406) 259-9751
E-MAIL: vandykj@rocky.edu or sas@rocky.edu
WEB SITE: www.rocky.edu

Name of Special Program: Services for Academic Success (SAS)
Director: Dr. Jane Van Dyk
General Information: Four-Year Private College; Enrollment: 850; **Tuition:** $14,500; **Room:** $1,200 per semester; **Board:** $1,214 per semester. Rocky Mountain College is a small private college, located on 60 park-like acres in a residential section of Billings, Montana's largest city. Billings is a regional hub, a cultural, medical, and entertainment center with museums, art galleries, and theaters. There is easy access to outdoor areas like the Absaroka-Beartooth Wilderness for skiing and hiking, the Yellowstone River, Yellowstone Park and Little Bison Natural Monument. **Majors:** Traditional liberal arts majors such as English, psychology, art, history and music, also business and education. Degrees offered in unique programs include aviation, physician's assistant, environmental science, and equestrian studies. Associate of Arts degrees and certificates in several programs.
Special Program: Enrollment in Special Program: 25; Cost: None
Staff: Learning disabilities specialist; peer tutors; special counselors; content tutors (faculty members)
Program Features: Oral and extended time testing; individual and small group tutoring sessions; limited course load (first year); basic study skills; note-taking assistance – scribes; tape recorders; taped texts; developmental program; academic advising for students with learning disabilities; supplemental instruction; faculty made aware of student's learning disability
Entrance Requirements: SAT / ACT untimed scores accepted; high school

diploma or GED, minimum CPA of 2.5; ACT of 21 or SAT of 1,000; documentation of learning disability
College Life: The small size of the college is one of the reasons why Rocky Mountain College is a "learning disabled friendly" college. The average class size is 14 students. Rocky's caring faculty demonstrate daily that students come first. The college also has an excellent support program that offers services tailored to the individual student's needs.
Scholarships: See page 432.

NEBRASKA

UNION COLLEGE

3800 SOUTH 48th STREET
LINCOLN, NEBRASKA 68506
(402) 486-2506; FAX: (402) 486-2895
E-MAIL: tlc@ucollege.edu **WEB SITE: www.ucollege.edu**

Name of Special Program: Teaching Learning Center
Director: Debbie Forshee-Sweeney, deforshe@ucollege.edu
General Information: Four-Year Private College; Enrollment: 950; **Annual Tuition:** $14,790; **Room and Board:** $4,948. Union College is affiliated with the Seventh-Day Adventist Church. It is situated on a 26-acre campus in a suburban area five miles southeast of Lincoln and about 50 miles from Omaha. Graduate programs in nursing and education are offered on campus through affiliations with Andrews University in Michigan and LaSierra University in California. **Degrees:** Union College offers approximately 50 degrees in six divisions: Business and Computer Science, Fine Arts, Health Sciences, Human Development, Religion and Science and Math.
Special Program: Enrollment in Special Program: 70; Cost: $575 per semester
Staff: Learning disabilities advisors; peer tutors
Program Features: Oral and extended time testing; individual and small group tutoring sessions; limited course load (first year); basic study skills; note-taking assistance – scribes; tape recorders; taped texts; developmental program; academic advising for students with learning disabilities; faculty made aware of student's learning disability; assistive technology; academic coaching
Entrance Requirements: Documentation of learning disability; SAT/ACT untimed scores accepted; diagnostic testing at Union College.
Special Facilities for: Limited visual, hearing and physical impairments
College Life: Union's campus size is a definite plus. Faculty get to know the students very well and take a personal interest in the success of each student. Faculty are easily accessible to students who need additional help.

NEVADA

UNIVERSITY OF NEVADA: LAS VEGAS

4505 MARYLAND PARKWAY, BOX 453013
LAS VEGAS, NEVADA 89154-3013
(702) 895-0866, (702) 895-0652 TDD; FAX: (702) 895-0651
E-MAIL: drc@ccmail.nevada.edu or clark.hochstetler@unlv.edu
WEB SITE: www.unlv.edu

Name of Special Program: Learning Abilities Program
Coordinator: Clark Hochstetler
General Information: Four-Year State University; Enrollment: 20,000; **Tuition:** Residents – $105.25 per credit, Non-Residents – $105.25 plus $4,955.50 per semester; **Room and Board:** $4,428.50 per semester. A 335-acre campus located in metropolitan Las Vegas. Within a 30-mile radius of the university lies the shores of Lake Mead, Hoover Dam, the Colorado River recreation area, snow skiing and hiking trails of 12,000-foot Mount Charleston and a panorama of redrock mountains and eroded sandstone landscapes. **Majors:** Business and communications, economics, education, engineering, fine arts, health sciences, hotel administration, human performance and development, liberal arts, and science and mathematics
Special Program: Enrollment in Special Program: 50; Cost: None if admitted to the University; $150 testing fee if not admitted. Learning Abilities Program services continue through the summer.
Staff: Learning disabilities specialists; special counselors; reading center and clinic staff; graduate assistants
Program Features: Extended time testing; taped texts; tutoring sessions; limited course load (suggested for first year); basic study skills; tape recorders; use of computers/word processing for class assignments; advisement; optional liaison with instructors
Entrance Requirements: Documentation of learning disability and learning disabilities specialist report (if available); SAT/ACT untimed scores accepted; diagnostic testing at University of Nevada: Las Vegas; personal interview; regular admissions requirements (or may go through alternate criteria if not accepted)
Special Facilities for: Visual, hearing and physical impairments

UNIVERSITY OF NEVADA: RENO
DISABILITY RESOURCE CENTER 078
107 THOMPSON STUDENT SERVICES CENTER
RENO, NEVADA 89557-0072
(702) 784-6000; FAX: (702) 784-1353
E-MAIL: mzabel@unr.edu **WEB SITE: www.unr.edu**

Name of Special Program: Disability Resource Center
Director: Mary Zabel
General Information: Four-Year State University; Enrollment: 15,534; **Tuition:** Residents – $109.25 per credit, Non-Residents – $109.25 plus $4,955.50 per semester; **Room:** $4,400–5,590 double occupancy per year. **Board:** $2,799-3,799 per year. The 200-acre main campus is located minutes from downtown Reno. It features traditional buildings, a tree-lined quadrangle and Manzanita Lake. The University has 10 schools and colleges and offers graduate as well as baccalaureate degrees. **Majors:** Agribusiness/agricultural production and sciences, biology, botany, business/management, chemistry, communications, computer/information sciences, education, engineering, environmental design, fine arts, geological sciences, health sciences, home economics, languages, law, letters/literature, marketing/distribution, mathematics, music, philosophy, physical sciences, physics, protective services, psychology, public affairs, renewable natural resources, social sciences, vocational home economics, zoology
Special Program: Enrollment in Special Program: 130; Cost: None
Staff: Learning disabilities specialists; peer tutors, special counselors (student support services project)
Program Features: Alternative time testing; individual and small group tutoring sessions; limited course load (first year); academic advising for students with learning disabilities; basic study skills; tape recorders; taped texts; note-taking assistance – scribes; faculty made aware of student's learning disability; special mathematics course taught over two semesters rather than one semester. The University of Nevada has a written policy dealing with students with learning disabilities.
Entrance Requirements: Documentation of learning disability; learning disabilities specialist report; SAT/ACT untimed scores accepted; testing: WAIS, psychological report
Special Facilities for: Visual, hearing and physical impairments
Scholarships: See page 433.

NEW JERSEY

FAIRLEIGH DICKINSON UNIVERSITY – METROPOLITAN CAMPUS
1000 RIVER ROAD, TEANECK, NEW JERSEY 07666
(201) 692-2716 (Metropolitan Campus)
COLLEGE AT FLORHAM CAMPUS
285 MADISON AVENUE, MADISON, NJ 07940)
(973) 443-8981
WEB SITE: www.fdu.edu

Name of Special Program: Regional Center for College Students with Learning Disabilities
Directors of Regional Center: Dr. Mary L. Farrell (University Director), Vincent Varrassi (Metropolitan Campus Director); Paul Vico (College at Florham Campus Director)
General Information: Four-Year Private University; Enrollment: 6,134; **Tuition:** $22,604; **Room and Board:** $10,066. Fairleigh Dickinson has two campuses in the United States, and one in England. The Metropolitan Campus is so close to New York City that students can take advantage of many of the Big Apple's countless cultural, career and recreational resources. The College at Florham in Madison, New Jersey is located on 177 acres and was formerly the country estate of Florence Vanderbilt and Hamilton Twombly. Wroxton College is located in the heart of rural England near Banbury, between Oxford and Stratford-upon-Avon. It is a one-hour train ride from London. **Degrees:** Baccalaureate programs in liberal arts, general studies, health-related professions, business administration, engineering, engineering technology, sciences, combined programs, two-year associate programs
Special Program: Enrollment in Special Program: 150, limited to 25 per year per campus; Cost: None. The percentage of students with learning disabilities receiving a degree in four years is 50% and in five or more years is 50%.
Staff: Learning disabilities specialists; special counselors.
Program Features: Oral and extended time testing; small group tutoring sessions; limited course load (first year); academic advising for students with learning disabilities; taped texts; tape recorders; basic study skills; faculty made aware of student's learning disability; "A Course for Success" – two-semester required course, focusing on time management, reading comprehension and test preparation and exploring topics such as stress reduction and self-advocacy
Entrance Requirements: Documentation of learning disability; learning disabilities specialist report; SAT/ACT untimed scores accepted; teacher evaluation; handwritten essay; testing: WAIS, IEP, psychological report
Special Dorm Rooms for: Physical impairments

GEORGIAN COURT UNIVERSITY
900 LAKEWOOD AVENUE
LAKEWOOD, NEW JERSEY 08701-2697
(732) 364-2200 X2659; FAX: (732) 987-2026
E-MAIL: cohenp@georgian.edu WEB SITE: www.georgian.edu

Name of Special Program: The Learning Center (TLC)
Director: Patricia A. Cohen
General Information: Four-Year Private College; Enrollment: 2,976; **Tuition:** $19,612; **Room and Board:** Approximately $9,800. A suburban campus in a large town, 60 miles south of New York City and 60 miles east of Philadelphia. Liberal arts college for women during the day with a coeducational evening division. **Degrees:** BA, BS, BSW, BFA; **Majors:** Computer information systems; computer science, fine arts, graphic design/illustration, communications
Special Program: Enrollment in Special Program: 40; Cost: $2,400 per year. The percentage of students with learning disabilities receiving degrees in two years is 90% and in four years is 10%.
Staff: Learning disabilities specialists; content tutors; special counselors
Program Features: Oral and extended time testing; individual and small group tutoring sessions; note-taking assistance – scribes; tape recorders; taped texts; basic study skills; developmental program; faculty made aware of student's learning disability; academic advising for students with learning disabilities; comprehensive care of a multitude of needs
Entrance Requirements: Documentation of learning disability; SAT/ACT untimed scores accepted; diagnostic testing at Georgian Court University; testing: WAIS, IEP
Special Facilities for: Visual and hearing impairments. Campus is barrier-free and can accommodate physical impairments.

NEW JERSEY CITY UNIVERSITY
2039 KENNEDY MEMORIAL BOULEVARD
JERSEY CITY, NEW JERSEY 07305-1597
(201) 200-2091; FAX: (201) 200-3083
E-MAIL: projmentor@njcu.edu WEB SITE: www.njcu.edu

Name of Special Program: Project Mentor, Regional Center for Students with Learning Disabilities
Director: Jennifer Aitken
General Information: Four-Year State University; Enrollment: 10,000; **Tuition:** Residents – $7,040, Non-Residents – $10,359; **Room and Board:** $6,586. An urban campus in a small city within minutes of the New York metropolitan area. **Majors:** Art, biology, chemistry, computer science, eco-

nomics, English, geoscience, history, math, media arts, music, dance, theatre, philosophy, psychology, physics, political science, sociology, Spanish, early childhood education, elementary and secondary education, special education, multicultural education, business, criminal justice, fire science, health science. More than 25 undergraduate degree programs are offered. Graduate programs and teacher certification programs are also offered.
Special Program: Enrollment in Special Program: 100; Cost: None. *Summer Program:* A four-week summer orientation program, which prepares students for success in an academic setting, is available to incoming freshmen students who are eligible. If a Project Mentor student participates in the summer orientation program, he/she will be expected to pay tuition and fees for any college level course for which he/she is registered. In addition, residential students participating in the summer orientation program are required to pay the cost of room and board during their summer stay. Writing in response to assigned and self-chosen readings, editing, computer applications, and mathematics instruction form the foundation of the summer curriculum. Placement testing and advising registration for the fall semester also take place.
Staff: Learning disabilities specialists; content tutors (faculty members)
Program Features: Oral and extended time testing; small group tutoring sessions; limited course load (first year); academic advising for students with learning disabilities; basic study skills; faculty made aware of student's learning disability; training in assistive technology; faculty mentor assignments; advisement; priority registration; special tutorials; learning strategy workshops; counseling and advocacy services
Entrance Requirements: Documentation of learning disability; learning disabilities specialist report; SAT/ACT untimed scores accepted; teacher evaluation; testing: WAIS, IEP, psychological report; handwritten essay
Special Facilities for: Visual, hearing and physical impairments through the Office of Specialized Services

NEW YORK

ADELPHI UNIVERSITY

BOX 701, ONE SOUTH AVENUE
GARDEN CITY, NEW YORK 11530-0701
(516) 877-4710, 1-800-ADELPHI; FAX: (516) 877-4711
E-MAIL: ldprogram@adelphi.edu WEB SITE: www.adelphi.edu

Name of Special Program: Learning Disabilities Program
Assistant Dean and Director: Susan Spencer
General Information: Four-Year Private University; Enrollment: 3,746; **Annual Tuition:** $20,900; **Room and Board:** $8,500. A suburban campus on 75 acres within 40 minutes of New York City. It is easily reached by car or

Long Island Railroad and is 30 minutes from Jones Beach. **Degrees:** BA, BS, BBA, BFA, BS Ed, liberal arts, business, nursing, education, social work
Special Program: Enrollment in Special Program: 125; Cost: $4,840 per year. *Summer Program:* A five-week diagnostic/experiential program. Students earn seven credits while receiving academic and counseling support from professional staff. Cost: $1,200 plus tuition, room and board
Staff: Learning disabilities specialists; special counselors; clinical social workers
Program Features: Oral and extended time testing; individual counseling sessions; limited course load (first year); academic advising for students with learning disabilities; note-taking assistance – scribes; taped texts; tape recorders; faculty made aware of student's learning disability; basic skills; counseling
Entrance Requirements: Documentation of learning disability; learning disabilities specialist report; teacher evaluation; medical evaluation; testing: WAIS, IEP, psychological report
College Life: Structured and individualized support prepares students for academics at the college level and for life in the real world. Excellent record with ADHD.

CANISIUS COLLEGE
2001 MAIN STREET
BUFFALO, NEW YORK 14208
(716) 888-3748; FAX: (716) 888-3747
E-MAIL: dobies@canisius.edu **WEB SITE: www.canisius.edu**

Name of Special Program: Disability Support Services
Director: Anne-Marie Dobies
General Information: Four-Year Private College; Enrollment: 5,100; **Annual Tuition:** $23,930; **Room:** $5,620-7,780. **Board**: $2,450-3,860. Founded in 1870 by the Jesuits (Society of Jesus), Canisius College is a Roman Catholic, liberal arts, private, four-year educational institution. It is located in a residential neighborhood in the northcentral section of Buffalo, New York. This urban campus sits on 36 acres of land which house academic buildings and state-of-the-art residential facilities. Canisius is within a 30-minute drive to Niagara Falls. The college has a Division I sports program. **Majors:** Canisius offers more than 1000 courses in over 70 distinct majors and special programs — education, business, liberal arts, biological science, communications and the arts, computer and physical science, education, engineering and environmental design, health professions, social science
Special Program: Enrollment in Special Program: 86; Cost: None

Staff: Learning disabilities specialists; content tutors (faculty members); peer tutors
Program Features: Oral and extended time testing; individual and small group tutoring sessions; limited course load (first year); academic advising for students with learning disabilities; taped texts, note-taking assistance – scribes; developmental program; faculty made aware of student's learning disability
Entrance Requirements: Documentation of learning disability; testing: psychological report
Special Facilities for: Visual, hearing and physical impairments
College Life: Canisius College is a small Jesuit college that offers small class sizes and an excellent professor/student ratio, and a personal approach to an educational experience.

CONCORDIA COLLEGE

171 WHITE PLAINS ROAD
BRONXVILLE, NEW YORK 10708
(914) 337-9300 X2361
E-MAIL: ghg@concordia-ny.edu **WEB SITE: www.concordia-ny.edu**

Name of Special Program: The Concordia Connection
Director: Dr. George Groth
General Information: Four-Year Private College; Enrollment: 640; **Annual Tuition:** $20,700; **Room and Board:** $8,230. Concordia College is a liberal arts institution supported by the Lutheran Church - Missouri Synod. It is nestled in the affluent village of Bronxville, 30 minutes from New York City. **Majors:** Behavioral science, biology, business administration, business education, business "plus," education (elementary and secondary), English, environmental science, history, interdisciplinary studies, international studies, mathematics, music (applied, church, general), music education, religious studies, social work. Programs: pre-law, pre-med, pre-physical therapy, pre-seminary, New York State Teacher Certification, Lutheran Teacher's Diploma
Special Program: Enrollment in Special Program: 22 (limited to 30 students); Cost: $5,000 per year. *Summer Program:* A three-day intensive workshop focusing on study skills and basic college orientation is provided prior to regular freshman orientation. Cost: None. The percentage of students with learning disabilities receiving a degree in four years is 70% and five or more years is 30%, depending on major.
Staff: Learning disabilities specialists; content tutors (faculty members); peer tutors; special counselors; school psychologist
Program Features: Oral and extended time testing; individual and small

group tutoring sessions; limited course load (first year); academic advising; tape recorders; taped texts (requires advanced notice); basic study skills; faculty made aware of student's learning disability; counseling
Entrance Requirements: Documentation of learning disability; learning disabilities specialist report; SAT or ACT untimed scores accepted; handwritten essay; testing: WAIS, IEP, psychological report
College Life: The college offers a caring, nurturing atmosphere with a dedicated staff and supportive peers.

HOFSTRA UNIVERSITY
130 HOFSTRA UNIVERSITY
HEMPSTEAD, NEW YORK 11549-1300
(516) 463-5038; FAX: (516) 463-4049
E-MAIL: PALS@hofstra.edu **WEB SITE: www.hofstra.edu**

Name of Special Program: Program for Academic Learning Skills (PALS)
Director: Linda Damotta – (516) 463-5059
General Information: Four-Year Private University; Enrollment: 14,000; **Annual Tuition:** $23,800; **Room and Board:** $9,350. Located in Nassau County, Long Island, 25 miles east of Manhattan. Founded in 1935, Hofstra was Long Island's first coeducational college. **Degrees:** Offered in 90 areas of study within the College of Liberal Arts and Sciences, New College, School of Business, School of Education, School of Law, School for University Studies, and University College for Continuing Education.
Special Program: Enrollment in Special Program: 140 (limited to 45 freshmen per year); Cost: $5,500 for one year only
Staff: Learning disabilities specialists; special counselors
Program Features: Oral and extended time testing; tape recorders; taped texts; note-taking assistance – scribes; individual tutoring sessions; basic study skills; special computer equipment; faculty made aware of student's learning disability
Entrance Requirements: Documentation of learning disability; learning disabilities specialist report; SAT or ACT untimed scores accepted; testing: WAIS, psychological report
Special Facilities for: Visual, hearing and physical impairments
Scholarships: See page 433.

IONA COLLEGE
715 NORTH AVENUE
NEW ROCHELLE, NEW YORK 10801-1890
(914) 633-2159; FAX: (914) 633-2174
E-MAIL: lrobertello@iona.edu **WEB SITE: www.iona.edu**

Name of Special Program: College Assistance Program (CAP)
Director: Linda Refsland
General Information: Four-Year Private College; Enrollment: 3,000; **Tuition:** $21,518; **Room and Board:** $10,000. The campus is situated in the Beechmont section of New Rochelle, a city of 72,000 people, located on the Long Island Sound, in Westchester County, New York. New Rochelle offers the sophistication of an established suburb, as well as easy access to New York City by automobile or public transportation. Iona College draws inspiration from the theological and philosophical bases characterizing the Judeo-Christian tradition. **Majors:** Liberal Arts and Science: area studies, biology, biochemistry, chemistry, communication arts, computer application and information systems, computer electronics science, computer and information sciences, computer science, criminal justice, ecology, economics, elementary education, English, French, history, interdisciplinary science, international studies, Italian, mathematics, medical technology, philosophy, physics, political science, psychology, religious studies, social work, sociology, Spanish, speech and dramatic arts, urban studies; Business Administration: accounting, business administration, finance, international business, management, management information systems, marketing, production and operation management
Special Program: Enrollment in Special Program: 70 maximum (limited to 20 for each fall semester); Cost: $1,300 per semester. *Summer Program:* A 12-day, 9 AM to 3 PM, college transition program covering many study skills, including research paper writing, lecture note-taking, text reading and note-taking, stress management, learning style awareness, self-advocacy and training. Cost: $750
Staff: Learning disabilities specialists; special counselor
Program Features: Freshman summer transition program (limited to incoming CAP Iona freshmen); supplementary academic planning and advising, including matching student and instructor styles; priority registration; career and personal counseling; two hours per week of scheduled individual skill-based tutoring with a professional learning specialist; opportunities for additional tutoring; group study sessions; study skills workshops; testing accommodations; special equipment; self-advocacy training.
Entrance Requirements: A complete interpretive report based on a psychological evaluation completed within the last two years, including the WAIS-III subtest scores and a comprehensive description of the learning

disability, and recommendations for instruction and accommodation; achievement test scores; a letter of recommendation from the high school resource room teacher; student must meet general college requirements.
College Life: CAP is committed to developing academic independence; fostering personal growth; encouraging community participation.

JOHN JAY COLLEGE OF CRIMINAL JUSTICE
CITY UNIVERSITY OF NEW YORK
445 WEST 59th STREET
NEW YORK, NEW YORK 10019
(212) 237-8185; FAX: (212) 237-8282
WEB SITE: www.jjay.cuny.edu

Name of Special Program: Accessibility Programs for Students with Disabilities
Director: Farris Forsythe
General Information: Four-Year City College; Enrollment 11,000; **Tuition:** Residents – $2,000 per semester, Non-Residents – $360 per credit; **Room and Board:** No college housing available. An urban liberal arts college of the City University of New York, John Jay has an international reputation for excellence in criminal justice and public safety education. Internships and cooperative plans are encouraged and are available to students in good academic standing. **Majors:** BA and BS degrees in criminal justice/administration, criminology, government, judicial studies, public administration, legal studies, fire/forensic science, forensic psychology, security management, computer information systems. AS degrees in correction administration, police science and security management. Certificate programs in dispute resolution and alcohol and substance abuse studies.
Special Program: Enrollment in Special Program: 150; Cost: None
Staff: Learning disabilities specialists; content tutors (faculty members); peer tutors; special counselors
Program Features: Oral and extended time testing; individual and small group tutoring sessions; limited course load (first year); basic study skills; tape recorders; taped texts; note-taking assistance – scribes; developmental program; faculty made aware of student's learning disability with student's permission; Reader's Edge
Entrance Requirements: Documentation of learning disability; learning disabilities specialist report; diagnostic testing at John Jay College; testing: WAIS, IEP, psychological report; medical evaluation; handwritten essay
Special Facilities for: Visual, hearing and physical impairments
College Life: While the program stresses individualized accomplishments for students, personal development is just as important. Support groups are available for students with learning disabilities. An active student orga-

nization called "Able Forces" helps students develop leadership skills, political lobbying and generally focuses on self-esteem development.
Scholarships: See page 434.

LONG ISLAND UNIVERSITY/ C.W. POST CAMPUS
720 NORTHERN BLVD.
BROOKVILLE, NEW YORK 11548
(516) 299-3057; FAX: (516) 299-2126
E-MAIL: susan.rock@liu.edu **WEB SITE: www.liu.edu**

Name of Special Program: Academic Resource Center
Director: Susan Rock; *Associate Director:* Cynthia D'Arpiro
General Information: Four-Year Private University; Enrollment: 8,624; **Tuition:** $22,100; **Room and Board:** $8,700 (includes meal plan). The C.W. Post 307-acre tree-lined campus is located on Long Island's famed Gold Coast, a historic suburban community that has been the subject of popular novels and major motion pictures. Modern buildings and magnificent historic mansions, formal gardens, sprawling lawns, and nature trails shape the campus. **Majors:** C.W. Post offers a comprehensive range of undergraduate programs in accounting, business, computer science, education, health professions and nursing, liberal arts and sciences, library and information science, public service, and the visual and performing arts.
Special Program: Enrollment in Special Program: 130 (limited to 130); Cost: $1,600 per semester
Staff: Learning disabilities specialists; special counselors.
Program Features: Oral and extended time testing; taped texts; note-taking assistance – scribes; tape recorders; limited course load (first year); individual and small group tutoring sessions; academic advising for students with learning disabilities; basic study skills; faculty made aware of student's learning disability; text-to-speech and speech-to-text computers; assistive technology
Entrance Requirements: Students must be accepted by the university first; then they can apply to the Academic Resource Center. Documentation of learning disability; handwritten essay; testing: WAIS, IEP, psychological report
Special Facilities for: Visual, hearing and physically impairments
College Life: Small classes and individual attention.
Scholarships: See page 434.

MANHATTAN COLLEGE
4513 MANHATTAN COLLEGE PARKWAY
RIVERDALE, NEW YORK 10471
(718) 862-7885, (718) 862-8000 TDD; FAX: (718) 862-7821
WEB SITE: www.manhattan.edu

Name of Special Program: Specialized Resource Center
Director: Dr. Ross Pollack
General Information: Four-Year Private College; Enrollment: 3,400; **Tuition:** $20,350; **Room and Board:** $9,000. Located between suburban Westchester County and the heart of New York City, the 31-acre campus provides a safe environment among tree-lined streets in the Fieldstone neighborhood of Riverdale. Midtown New York City is just 10 miles from campus where students find world-class museums, Broadway, music, galleries, athletic events, Greenwich Village, Fifth Avenue shops, and Wall Street. **Degrees:** arts, business, education, engineering, science
Special Program: Enrollment in Special Program: 50; Cost: None. *Summer Program:* Summer sessions overlap so that the student garners three credits while building a sense of collegiate life.
Staff: Learning disabilities specialists; peer tutors; content tutors (faculty members); special counselors
Program Features: Priority registration; alternative testing environment; readers; note-taking assistance – scribes; adaptive technology; books on tape; liaison with faculty and other college departments
Entrance Requirements: Documentation of learning disability; learning disabilities specialist report; SAT untimed scores accepted; testing: WAIS, IEP, psychological report
Special Facilities for: Visual, hearing and physical impairments

MANHATTANVILLE COLLEGE
2900 PURCHASE STREET
PURCHASE, NEW YORK 10577
(914) 323-5313
E-MAIL: help@mville.edu **WEB SITE: www.mville.edu**

Name of Special Program: Higher Education Learning Program (HELP)
Coordinator: Eleanor Schwartz
General Information: Four-Year Private College; Enrollment: 1,500; **Tuition:** $35,000; **Room and Board:** $8,320. Manhattanville College is a four-year, private, independent, coeducational, liberal arts college. The 100-acre, suburban campus is located approximately 30 minutes north of New York City in Westchester County at the Connecticut border. The school operates on a two-semester per year calendar. **Majors:** Bachelor of

Arts: art, art history, Asian studies, biology, chemistry, computer science, dance, theatre, economics, English, French, history, international studies, management, mathematics, music/management, philosophy, physics, political science, pre-law, pre-medicine, psychology, religion, sociology, Spanish. Interdisciplinary Areas: American studies, classical civilization, environmental/German/medieval/Renaissance/Russian area studies, women's studies **Degrees:** Fine arts, music, certification in elementary, secondary, special education and English as a second language
Special Program: Enrollment in Special Program: 34; Cost: $3,600 per year
Staff: Learning disabilities specialists
Program Features: Oral and extended time testing; limited course load (first year); basic study skills; individual and small group tutoring sessions; tape recorders; taped texts; note-taking assistance; faculty made aware of student's learning disability (at student's request); distraction-free testing environment; spellcheckers; priority registration; learning strategies; substitutions for math courses; study labs; counseling services; internship programs; academic advising for students with learning disabilities
Entrance Requirements: Must meet College Admissions requirements

MARIST COLLEGE
3399 NORTH ROAD
POUGHKEEPSIE, NEW YORK 12601-1387
(845) 575-3274; FAX: (845) 575-3011
E-MAIL: specserv@marist.edu **WEB SITE: www.marist.edu**

Name of Special Program: Learning Disabilities Support Program
Coordinator of Office of Special Services: Gale Canale
General Information: Four-Year Private College; Enrollment: 3,500; **Tuition:** $22,066; **Room and Board:** $10,740. Marist College is situated on the Hudson River along Route 9, the major north-south route east of the Hudson. Located within two hours of Albany or New York City by railroad, bus, or car. Known for its internships, work-study programs, and travel and study abroad program. **Majors:** Biology, business/management, chemistry, communications, computer/information sciences, fine arts, health sciences, languages, law, letters/literature, life sciences, marketing/distribution, mathematics, medical laboratory technologies, protective services, psychology, public affairs, social sciences, environmental science
Special Program: Enrollment in Special Program: 80; Cost: $3,000 per year
Staff: Learning disabilities specialists; peer tutors; special counselors
Program Features: Wide range of testing accommodations; taped texts; note-taking assistance – scribes; limited course load (first year); tape recorders; individual tutoring sessions; basic study skills; adaptive equip-

ment; special advisement/career counseling/planning; faculty made aware of learning disability (at student's request)
Entrance Requirements: Documentation of learning disability; learning disabilities specialist report; essay; teacher evaluation; interview (by invitation); academic achievement scores in reading, math and written expression; testing: WAIS (with sub-test scores and narrative), psychological report
Special Facilities for: Visual, hearing and physical impairments

MARYMOUNT MANHATTAN COLLEGE
221 EAST 71st STREET
NEW YORK, NEW YORK 10021
(212) 774-0724; FAX: (212) 517-0419
E-MAIL: jbonomo@mmm.edu
WEB SITE: www.marymount.mmm.edu

Name of Special Program: Program for Academic Access for Students with Learning Disabilities
Director: Dr. Ann Jablon; *Assistant Director*: Dr. Jacquelyn Bonomo
General Information: Four-Year Private College; Enrollment: 2,100; **Tuition:** $18,748; **Room and Board:** $12,090 per year. An urban campus on the Upper East Side in New York City, with strong liberal arts along with outstanding programs in theater, dance and communication arts and traditional disciplines, operating on a semester calendar. **Majors:** Art, accounting, biology, business/management, communication arts, dance, English, history, international studies, liberal arts, psychology, political science, sociology, visual/performing arts, speech/language, pathology/audiology, education (minor)
Special Program: Separate admissions process for applicants with learning disabilities in addition to the Marymount Manhattan College application. A minimum of two consecutive semesters participation in the program is required. Enrollment in Special Program: 30 (limited to 30); Cost: $2,000 per semester. *Summer Program:* Individual tutoring is recommended and arranged by the program to strengthen preparation for the first year. The percentage of students with learning disabilities receiving a degree in four years is 85%.
Staff: Learning disabilities specialists.
Program Features: Oral and extended time testing; limited course load; individual and small group tutoring sessions; taped texts (available from Recording for the Blind & Dyslexic); tape recorders; basic study skills; note-taking assistance – scribes; faculty made aware of student's learning disability; academic advising for students with learning disabilities; developmental program; Kurzweil reading station; coaching; individual tutoring by learn-

ing specialists two hours a week; workshops sponsored by the program
Entrance Requirements: Documentation of learning disability; learning disabilities specialist report; SAT/ACT untimed scores accepted; letters of reference; essay on academic and career goals; testing: WAIS, psychological report, psychoeducational reports with diagnosis records and recommendations (complete and current within three years)
Special Facilities for: Visual, hearing and physically impairments
College Life: The Access Program offers assistance by learning specialists who have worked with young adults with learning disabilities for many years. Their tutoring is informed by clear understanding of the strengths and weaknesses of their clients as reflected in their diagnostic reports and their functioning in the tutorial partnership. On an ongoing basis, learning specialists discuss underlying learning issues with students and help set goals for improvement. The program also provides coaching for students with ADD in areas of time-management, organizational strategies, goal-setting and self-monitoring.

MERCY COLLEGE: DOBBS FERRY CAMPUS
555 BROADWAY
DOBBS FERRY, NEW YORK 10522
(914) 674-7324
E-MAIL: TRich@mercy.edu **WEB SITE: www.mercy.edu**

Name of Special Program: STAR Program
Director: Terry Rich, Associate Dean for Student Affairs (914) 674-7218
General Information: Four-Year Private College; Enrollment: 2,000; **Tuition:** $6,185 per semester for 12–18 credits; **Room and Board:** $3,400 to $3,800 per semester. The college setting is suburban and located on the Hudson River, 45 minutes from New York City by train or car. **Majors:** General accounting, management accounting, public accounting, behavioral science, biology, business administration, computer information systems, computer science, criminal justice, English, government, history, hotel/restaurant management, journalism, media, mathematics, medical technology, music, nursing, paralegal studies, pre-chiropractic, pre-pharmacy, psychology, public safety, social work, sociology, Spanish, speech, therapeutic recreation, veterinary technology, pre-occupational/pre-physical therapy.
Special Program: Enrollment in STAR Program: 50; Cost: $1,250 per semester. *Summer Program:* A pre-college seminar is held for students in the STAR Program. Cost: $700
Staff: Learning disabilities specialists; content tutors; special counselors
Program Features: Oral and extended time testing; limited course load

(first year); note-taking assistance – scribes; tape recorders; taped texts; basic study skills; developmental program; faculty made aware of student's learning disability; sessions held by licensed professionals in learning disabilities; special academic advising; special counseling; special seminar that meets twice weekly to discuss disability issues
Entrance Requirements: Documentation of learning disability; learning disabilities specialist report; teacher evaluation; SAT untimed scores accepted; testing: WAIS, psychological report

MOLLOY COLLEGE
1000 HEMPSTEAD AVENUE
ROCKVILLE CENTRE, NEW YORK 11570-1199
(516) 678-5000 X6381
E-MAIL: bmerola@molloy.edu **WEB SITE: www.molloy.edu**

Name of Special Program: Disability Support Services/Success Through Expanded Education Program (DSS/STEEP)
Coordinator: Barbara Merola
General Information: Four-Year Private College; Enrollment: 3,100 **Tuition:** $8,280 per semester. **Room and Board:** No college housing available. Molloy College, affiliated with the Catholic Church is primarily a commuter college. The college is located on a 25-acre campus in Rockville Centre, Long Island, 30 minutes from the heart of New York City. **Degrees:** Business management, sociology, English, nursing, biology, psychology, music, interdisciplinary studies, computer science, music therapy, cardiorespiratory science, education, criminal justice, environmental studies. *Graduate Programs*: Nursing, education, social work, business.
Special Program: Enrollment in Special Program: 75; Cost: None
Staff: Learning disabilities specialists; peer tutors; content tutors (faculty members); special counselors
Program Features: Extended time testing; individual and small group tutoring sessions; limited course load (first year if needed); note-taking assistance – scribes; tape recorders; basic study skills; developmental program; academic advising for students with learning disabilities; faculty made aware of student's learning disability
Entrance Requirements: Recent comprehensive documentation of learning disability; SAT/ACT untimed scores accepted; testing: WAIS, IEP, psychological report, psychoeducational report
Special Facilities for: Visual, hearing and physical impairments
College Life: Molloy College is a small individualized institution.

NEW YORK INSTITUTE OF TECHNOLOGY
300 CARLETON AVENUE, INDEPENDENCE HALL
P.O. BOX 9029
CENTRAL ISLIP, NEW YORK 11722-9029
(631) 348-3354 or 1-800-345-NYIT
WEB SITE: www.nyit.edu

Name of Special Program: Vocational Independence Program
Director: David Finkelstein
General Information: Four-Year Private Institution; Enrollment: 10,000; **Tuition, Room and Board:** $36,380; **Room and Board:** $8,464. The Vocational Independence Program at New York Institute of Technology is on a suburban campus in a small town, 40 miles east of New York City and accessible to all modes of transportation.
Special Program: The Vocational Independence Program is a three-year certificate program with its own curriculum geared specifically to the needs of students with learning disabilities. Major areas of study include career skills, independent living skills, social skills and academics. Career offerings include retail, hospitality services, clerical skills, culinary arts, child care and automotive repairs. The program maintains its own dormitory and specialized staff. Students also have the option to earn credits toward a degree at New York Institute of Technology. Enrollment in Special Program: 86. *College Degree Prep Program:* Track II (tutoring to become degree students); Cost: None. *Summer Program:* "Introduction to Independence" is a seven-week co-educational summer program for young adults with learning disabilities, between 16 and 20 years of age, who are considering post-secondary options. "I to I" provides educational, vocational, social and recreational programming designed to prepare the student for a successful transition to campus life, independent living and the work environment. The Program features a four-day trip to a place such as Montreal, Quebec, Niagara Falls, Toronto, Williamsburg, Virginia, and Virginia Beach in the final week, and a mid-summer Parents' Weekend includes a workshop on post-secondary options. Cost: $8,495
Staff: Certified learning disabilities specialists; content tutors (faculty members); special counselors
Program Features: Oral and extended time testing; individual and small group tutoring sessions; tape recorders; basic study skills courses; faculty made aware of student's learning disability
Entrance Requirements: Handwritten essay; personal interview; documentation of learning disability; testing: WAIS, TAT, psychological report
Special Facilities for: Visual impairments

NEW YORK UNIVERSITY
240 GREENE STREET, 2nd FLOOR
NEW YORK, NEW YORK 10012
(212) 998-4979; FAX: (212) 995-4114
E-MAIL: lc83@nyu.edu **WEB SITE: www.nyu.edu/osl/csd**

Name of Special Program: Henry and Lucy Moses Center for Students with Disabilities
Coordinator: Lakshmi Clark
General Information: Four-Year Private University; Enrollment: 51,901; **Tuition:** $34,780; **Room and Board:** $11,390 per academic year. A 29-acre urban campus located in the heart of Greenwich Village, Manhattan. **Degrees:** Over 175 majors and areas of concentration including agriculture, biological science, business, communications and the arts, computer and physical science, education, health professions, social science
Special Program: Enrollment in Special Program: 312; Cost: None. *Summer Program:* "Transitioning to College for Students with Learning Disabilities" workshop is offered in summer and fall.
Staff: Learning disabilities specialists
Program Features: Oral and extended time testing; taped texts (through Recording for the Blind & Dyslexic); individual and small group tutoring sessions; limited course load (first year); tape recorders; basic study skills; weekly support group; faculty made aware of student's learning disability (at student's request)
Entrance Requirements: Documentation of learning disability; SAT untimed scores accepted; diagnostic testing at New York University; medical evaluation; testing: WAIS-III, psychological report
Special Facilities for: Visual, hearing and physical impairments
College Life: New York University Center for Students with Disabilities offers comprehensive services to eligible students.
Scholarships: See page 434.

ROCHESTER INSTITUTE OF TECHNOLOGY
LEARNING SUPPORT SERVICES
LEARNING DEVELOPMENT CTR., EASTMAN BLDG. (01-2355)
ONE LOMB MEMORIAL DRIVE
ROCHESTER, NEW YORK 14623
(716) 475-5296; FAX: (716) 475-5832
E-MAIL: lafldc@rit.edu **WEB SITE: www.rit.edu/sa/ldc**

Name of Special Program: Learning Support Services (LSS/LDC)
Chair: Lisa Fraser
General Information: Four-Year Private College; Enrollment: 14,100; **Annual Tuition:** $24,000; **Room:** $8,750. A suburban campus five miles

from downtown Rochester. **Majors:** Allied health, biology, business/management, chemistry, civil technologies, communications technologies, computer/ information sciences, crafts/design, diagnostic/treatment services, engineering and technologies, environmental control technologies, environmental design, fine arts, health sciences, home economics, industrial production, law, letters/literature, life sciences, marketing/distribution, mathematics, medical laboratory technologies, physics, precision production, protective services, public affairs, science technologies, social sciences, visual performing arts, vocational home economics
Special Program: Enrollment: 80; Structured Monitoring Cost: Level 1 – $440 per quarter; Level II – $880 per quarter; Level III – $950 per quarter
Staff: Learning disabilities specialists; peer tutors
Program Features: Extended time testing, taped texts, note-taking assistance – scribes, limited course loads, basic study skills courses, tape recorders, individual and small group tutoring sessions, developmental program, academic advising for students with learning disabilities, faculty made aware of student's learning disability. Structured monitoring is a fee-based coaching relationship between the student and a learning support specialist that focuses on organizational skills, study strategies, and advocacy skills in a college-level academic environment. Students may decide whether to use the service daily, twice a week, or once a week.
Entrance Requirements: Documentation of learning disability on official letterhead; SAT/ACT untimed scores accepted; testing: WAIS, psychological report
Special Facilities for: Visual, hearing and physical impairments
College Life: The Learning Development Center houses LSS (Learning Support Services), structured monitoring, the Office of Special Services, disability services, academic accommodations, math and writing labs, reading and study skills specialists.
Scholarships: See page 435.

SAINT THOMAS AQUINAS COLLEGE
125 ROUTE 340
SPARKILL, NEW YORK 10976
(845) 398-4230; FAX: (845) 398-4229
E-MAIL: pathways@stac.edu **WEB SITE: www.stac.edu**

Name of Special Program: Pathways
Director: Dr. Richard F. Heath
General Information: Four-Year Private College; Enrollment: 2,200; **Annual Tuition:** $16,200; **Room:** $4,640; **Board:** $1,030–3,950. The school is located on a 43-acre suburban campus, 16 miles north of New York City. The college calendar operates on a semester basis. Courses are also offered

during three summer sessions and one winter intersession. NCAA Division II athletics; Honors Program; graduate programs; independent study; study abroad; cooperative (dual degree) programs (engineering, physical therapy, chiropractic, podiatry). **Degrees:** BS, BA, and BS Ed. **Majors:** Art, art therapy, graphic design, communications arts (general journalism), English, romance languages, Spanish, philosophy, religious studies, mathematics (pure, applied, actual science), biology, chemistry, natural sciences, medical technology, computer and information science, criminal justice, history, psychology, recreation and leisure studies (therapeutic recreation, sports management, leisure management), social sciences, accounting, business administration, finance, marketing, education (childhood, childhood/special, adolescence), liberal arts and sciences.

Special Program: Separate admissions process for applicants with learning disabilities. Enrollment in Special Program: 75 (limited to 78); Cost: $3,400.

Summer Program: All incoming Pathways freshmen are required to attend a four-day, three-night summer program prior to the first semester. The goals are to learn the specific needs of each student, to begin preparing individuals for the academic rigors of higher education and to build a sense of trust and community within the group. The program integrates the first part of a three-credit course called Studies in Culture whose topic may vary from year to year. This aspect of the program continues into the fall semester. The summer program, which includes both field trips and classroom lectures, fosters a sense of community among the students through shared activities, while building their self-confidence and comfort within the college setting. Cost: $550–650. The percentage of students with learning disabilities receiving a degree in four or more years is 81%.

Staff: Learning disabilities specialists; content tutors; peer tutors; professional mentors.

Program Features: Oral and extended time testing; individual and small group tutoring sessions; academic advising for students with learning disabilities; faculty made aware of student's learning disability (at student's request); note-taking assistance–scribes; tape recorders; basic study skills

Entrance Requirements: Documentation of learning disability; learning disabilities specialist report; SAT/ACT untimed scores accepted; diagnostic testing at St. Thomas Aquinas College; handwritten essay; testing: WAIS (must include sub-test scores), IEP, psychological report

Special Facilities for: Visual, hearing and physical impairments

College Life: Pathways, formerly known as the STAC Exchange, is one of the oldest college support programs in the nation. The focus is individualized and interpersonal. Services are provided by professional mentors with college degrees. Twice weekly, each student meets one-to-one with his/her mentor; additional mentoring is available and encouraged.

Scholarships: See page 435.

NORTH CAROLINA

APPALACHIAN STATE UNIVERSITY

LAP – D. D. DOUGHERTY HALL
BOONE, NORTH CAROLINA 28608
(828) 262-2291; FAX: (828) 262-6834
WEB SITE: www.appstate.edu

Name of Special Program: Learning Disability Program
Coordinator: Suzanne T. Wehner
General Information: Four-Year State University; Enrollment: 14,343; **Annual Tuition, Fees, Room and Board:** Residents – $8,093, Non-Residents – $17,835. Founded in 1899, the university is located on a 75-acre main campus and a 180-acre west campus in a small town 120 miles from Charlotte in the heart of the Blue Ridge Mountains. **Majors:** Biology, business / management, business / office, chemistry, communications, computer / information sciences, crafts / design, education, education administration, environmental design, fine arts, geological sciences, health sciences, home economics, industrial production, languages, law, letters / literature, library / archival sciences, marketing / distribution, mathematics, multi / interdisciplinary studies, music, parks and recreation, philosophy, physics, precision production, protective services, psychology, public affairs, religion, social sciences, visual / performing arts, vocational home economics
Special Program: Enrollment in Special Program: 395; Cost: None
Staff: Learning disabilities specialist; peer tutors; content tutors; graduate assistants
Program Features: Oral and extended time testing; assistance with taped texts; note-taking assistance – scribes; individual and small group tutoring sessions; limited course load (as needed); tape recorders; basic study skills; academic advising for students with learning disabilities; faculty made aware of student's learning disability
Entrance Requirements: Documentation of learning disability (after admission); SAT untimed scores accepted
Special Facilities for: Visual, hearing and physical impairments on a limited basis. Mountainous terrain is challenging for mobility impairments.

UNIVERSITY OF NORTH CAROLINA AT CHAPEL HILL
BANK OF AMERICA BUILDING
137 EAST FRANKLIN STREET – STE 602 CB #3447
CHAPEL HILL, NORTH CAROLINA 27514-3447
(919) 962-7227; FAX: (919) 962-3674
E-MAIL: jane_benson@unc.edu or tmaitlan@email.unc.edu
WEB SITE: www.unc.edu/depts/lds

Name of Special Program: Learning Disabilities Services
Director: Jane Benson; *Assistant Director and Learning Disabilities/ADHD Specialist:* Theresa Laurie Maitland
General Information: Four-Year State University; Enrollment: 24,211; **Tuition:** Residents – $2,516, Non-Residents – $9,840 per semester; **Room and Board:** $6,000 per year. Founded in 1789, the university is on a suburban campus in a small city 30 miles west of Raleigh, two and a half hours to coast/beaches and three hours to mountains. **Majors:** Accounting, administration of criminal justice, African/Afro-American/American studies, anthropology, applied science, art history, Asian studies, astronomy, biology, bio-statistics, business/management, chemistry, classics, communications, dental hygiene, dramatic arts, economics, education, environmental science, engineering, geography, geology, health behavior, education, health policy/administration, history, journalism, languages, letters/literature, linguistics, mathematics, medical technology, music, nursing, parks, recreation, philosophy, physical/social sciences, physics, psychology, rehabilitation services, religion
Special Program: Enrollment in Special Program: 301; Cost: None. *Summer Orientation:* Testing accommodations are provided for the Foreign Language Placement test during summer orientation for entering freshmen and transfer students who qualify for these accommodations. Accommodations for LD/ADHD students are determined on a case-by-case basis depending upon documentation, the same as during regular college sessions.
Staff: Learning disabilities/ADHD specialists; accommodations special project manager; math and foreign language tutors (graduate students)
Program Features: Services are available to work on disability awareness, self-advocacy, learning strategy instruction in reading, written language, time management, test preparation, test taking and problem solving. Coaching services are available to help ADHD students deal with the serious time and task management problems that students may experience in college. Accommodations are determined on a case-by-case basis depending upon documentation. These include extended time (50%), separate administration for students diagnosed as ADHD, a reader and/or a scribe for exams, note takers, books on tape, tutors for math and foreign language, limited courseload, priority registration. There is an annual semi-

nar for the community on topics of interest regarding post-secondary programming for students with LD and ADHD as well as an annual banquet for students, parents, faculty and staff.
Entrance Requirements: Documentation of learning disability, attention deficit disorder or traumatic brain injury; SAT/ACT untimed scores accepted; medical evaluation (if appropriate – ADD/ADHD); regular admissions required; diagnostic testing at University of North Carolina at Chapel Hill; testing: WAIS, SEC, psychological report; achievement test (Woodcock-Johnson preferred)
Special Facilities for: Visual and hearing impairments
College Life: Well-trained staff who provide individual strategy instruction and coaching services to ADHD students, in addition to accommodations, as part of a comprehensive program.

UNIVERSITY OF NORTH CAROLINA AT WILMINGTON
601 SOUTH COLLEGE ROAD
WILMINGTON, NORTH CAROLINA 28403-4297
(910) 962-7555, (910) 962-3853 TDD; FAX: (910) 962-7556
E-MAIL: turner_m@uncw.edu
WEB SITE: www.uncw.edu/stuaff/disability

Name of Special Program: Disability Services
Director: Margaret Turner, Ph.D.
General Information: Four-Year State University; Enrollment: 11,000; **Tuition:** Residents – $2,080 per semester, Non-Residents – $7,048 per semester; **Room and Board:** $2,000 per semester. A suburban campus in a small city 125 miles from Raleigh. **Majors:** Biology, business/management, chemistry, computer/information sciences, education, fine arts, geological sciences, health sciences, languages, letters/literature, life sciences, mathematics, parks and recreation, philosophy, physics, psychology, religion, social sciences
Special Program: Cost: None
Staff: Learning disabilities specialist; peer tutors
Program Features: Oral and extended time testing; individual and small group tutoring sessions; note-taking assistance – scribes; faculty made aware of student's learning disability
Entrance Requirements: Documentation of learning disability; learning disabilities specialist report; SAT/ACT untimed scores accepted; meet admissions criteria; medical evaluation, testing: SEC, WAIS-R, psychological report, Woodcock-Johnson-R (within three years)
Special Facilities for: Visual, hearing and physical impairments

WINGATE UNIVERSITY
ACADEMIC RESOURCE CENTER, CAMPUS BOX 3068
WINGATE, NORTH CAROLINA 28174
(704) 233-8265, 8269 or 1-800-755-5550; FAX: (704) 233-8192
E-MAIL: stedje@wingate.edu
WEB SITE: www.wingate.edu/arc/mainpage.htm

Name of Special Program: Academic Resource Center – Learning Disabilities Support Program
Coordinator: Linda Stedje-Larsen
General Information: Four-Year Private University; Enrollment: 1,200; **Annual Tuition, Room and Board:** $24,400. The campus is located in a rural community, 30 miles from Charlotte. Founded in 1896, Wingate is a liberal arts college with internships, international study-tour programs and travel programs. **Majors:** American studies, athletic training, art, biology, business administration, chemistry, communications, computer information systems, economics, education, English, history, human services, mathematics, music, parks and recreation administration, psychology, physical education, religious studies, sociology, Spanish, pre-professional programs – law, medicine, pharmacy, engineering
Special Program: Enrollment in Special Program: 80; Cost: None
Staff: Learning disabilities specialist; peer tutors
Program Features: Individual and small group tutoring; co-advising with coordinator; priority registration; assistance with self-advocacy skills; testing accommodations; reduced course load; note-taking assistance; ordering of taped texts
Entrance Requirements: Documentation of learning disability; SAT / ACT untimed scores accepted; psychoeducational evaluation including scores of achievement and aptitude tests; interview deadline August 1st

NORTH DAKOTA

NORTH DAKOTA STATE UNIVERSITY
212 CERES HALL
FARGO, NORTH DAKOTA 58105
(701) 231-7198; FAX: (701) 231-8756
WEB SITE: www.ndsu.nodak.edu/counseling/disability.shtml

Name of Special Program: Disability Services
Coordinator: Bunnie Johnson-Messelt
General Information: Four-Year State University; Enrollment: 9,700; **Annual Tuition, Room and Board:** Residents – $11,232, Non-Residents – $19,205. An urban campus located in southeastern North Dakota in a small

city. Population is approximately 100,000 along with twin city of Moorhead, Minnesota. **Majors:** Agribusiness/agricultural production sciences, architecture, biology, botany, business/management, chemistry, communications, computer/information sciences, construction trades, education, engineering, environmental design, health sciences, home economics, languages, letters/literature, mathematics, medical laboratory technologies, multi/interdisciplinary studies, music, parks and recreation, physical sciences, physics, psychology, social sciences, visual/performing arts, vocational home economics, zoology

Special Program: Enrollment in Special Program: 180; Cost: None

Staff: Learning disabilities specialist; peer tutors; special counselors; accommodations coordinator; assistive technology coordinator.

Program Features: Oral and extended time testing in some cases; taped texts; note-taking assistance – scribes; basic study skills; individual and small group tutoring sessions; tape recorders; faculty made aware of student's learning disability; support group; assistive technology which includes a computer installed with an external Dectalk voice synthesizer, IBM screen reader as well as training on power secretary computer

Entrance Requirements: Documentation of learning disability; ACT untimed scores accepted; testing: WAIS, SEC

Special Facilities for: Visual, hearing and physical impairments

College Life: Experienced, dedicated, "student friendly" staff who have a good relationship with university faculty and staff. Exciting new assistive technology program.

OHIO

COLLEGE OF MOUNT ST. JOSEPH

5701 DELHI ROAD
CINCINNATI, OHIO 45233-1670
(513) 244-4623; FAX: (513) 244-4222
E-MAIL: jane_pohlman@mail.msj.edu **WEB SITE: www.msj.edu**

Name of Special Program: Project EXCEL

Director: Jane Pohlman

General Information: Four-Year Private College; Enrollment: 2,600; **Tuition:** $9,825 per semester; **Room and Board:** $3,850 per semester, semi-private. The college was built in 1962 and overlooks the Ohio River, approximately seven miles from the downtown area. A Catholic liberal arts college sponsored by the Sisters of Charity, offering 44 undergraduate majors with more than 70 areas of concentration. **Majors:** Accounting, art, fine arts, biology, business administration, chemistry, communication/ arts, computer information systems, education, English, gerontological

studies, health and physical education history, human services, humanities, liberal arts, liberal studies, management communication, management of nursing services, mathematics, mathematics computer science, music, natural science, nursing, paralegal, physical therapy, psychology, recreational therapy, religious studies, sociology, special education, women's studies
Special Program: Enrollment in Special Program: 100; Cost: $765–1,530 per semester
Staff: Learning disabilities specialist; special counselors; professional content tutors
Program Features: Oral and extended time testing; writing lab; individual and small group tutoring sessions; limited course load (first year); note-taking assistance – scribes; tape recorders; taped texts; assistive technology; basic study skills; academic advising for students with learning disabilities; faculty made aware of student's learning disability; computers for testing.
Entrance Requirements: Documentation of learning disability; verification of learning disability (a psychoeducational evaluation administered within three years of application for admission); SAT / ACT untimed scores accepted; Project EXCEL application; letters of recommendation; testing: preferably WAIS III, standardized tests of academic achievement and cognitive processing (e.g., perception, integration, memory, attention)

MUSKINGUM COLLEGE
MONTGOMERY HALL
NEW CONCORD, OHIO 43762-1199
(740) 826-8280; FAX: (740) 826-8404
E-MAIL: ehenry@muskingum.edu WEB SITE: www.muskingum.edu

Name of Special Program: PLUS Program
Director: Eileen Henry, Ed.D.
General Information: Four-Year Private College; Enrollment: 1,500; **Annual Tuition, Room and Board:** $24,000. A rural setting along Interstate 70, one hour east of Columbus, two hours southwest of Pittsburgh, and two and one half hours south of Cleveland. The college was founded in 1837 and is affiliated with the Presbyterian Church. **Majors:** Accounting, art, biology, business, chemistry, Christian education, computer science, earth science, economics, elementary education, English, French, geology, German, history, mathematics, music, philosophy, physical education, physics, political science, psychology, religion, religious philosophy, sociology, Spanish, speech communication, theatre, American studies, early childhood, environmental science, humanities, international affairs, international business, neuroscience, public affairs, self-designed, secondary education, special education certifications, pre-professional – dentistry,

law, medical technology, medicine, physical therapy, veterinary medicine
Special Program: Enrollment in Special Program: 150; Cost: $4,850 per year (full program), $2,425 per year (maintenance). *Summer Program:* Two-week residential program consisting of non-credit expository course, writing, speech. Experiences are similar to the college semester with weekend field trips and many social activities. Cost: FIRST STEP $1,500. Optional. The percentage of students with learning disabilities receiving a degree in five or more years is 58%.
Staff: Learning disabilities specialists; special counselors
Program Features: Oral and double-time testing; readers; note-taking assistance – scribes; taped texts; tape recorders; individual and small group tutoring sessions; limited course load (first year); academic advising for students with learning disabilities; faculty made aware of student's learning disability; basic study skills; priority registration.
Entrance Requirements: Documentation of learning disability; SAT/ACT untimed scores accepted; personal interview for invited students and parents; testing: aptitude and achievement, psychological report
College Life: Small caring environment with a professionally staffed program which has been in operation since 1982.

OBERLIN COLLEGE
PETERS HALL 5B
50 NORTH PROFESSOR STREET
OBERLIN, OHIO 44074-1091
(440) 775-8467; FAX: (440) 775-5589
E-MAIL: jane.boomer@oberlin.edu **WEB SITE: www.oberlin.edu**

Name of Special Program: OBIE (Overcoming Barriers in Education)
Coordinator: Jane Boomer
General Information: Four-Year Private College; Enrollment: 2,800; **Annual Tuition:** $34,220; **Room and Board:** $9,200. A rural campus in a small town, 34 miles from Cleveland, Ohio. Founded in 1833. **Majors:** Biology, chemistry, communications, computer/information sciences, education, ethnic studies, fine arts, geological sciences, languages, law, letters/literature, mathematics, music, philosophy, physics, psychology, religion, social sciences, classics, multi-disciplinary studies
Special Program: Enrollment in Special Program: 112; Cost: None
Staff: Learning disabilities specialists; content tutors (faculty members); peer tutors; special counselors
Program Features: Oral and extended time testing; individual and small group tutoring sessions; limited course load (first year); basic study skills; note-taking assistance – scribes; tape recorders; taped texts; developmen-

tal program (reading skills); faculty made aware of student's learning disability; academic advising for students with learning disabilities; adaptive technology center; special therapy
Entrance Requirements: Documentation of learning disability; SAT untimed scores accepted; medical evaluation; handwritten essay; diagnostic testing at Oberlin College; testing: WAIS, IEP, psychological report
Special Facilities for: Visual, hearing and physical impairments

OREGON

EASTERN OREGON STATE UNIVERSITY

ONE UNIVERSITY BOULEVARD
LA GRANDE, OREGON 97850-2899
(541) 962-3672, 1-800-452-8639; FAX: (541) 962-3820
E-MAIL: parnson@eou.edu
WEB SITE: www.eou.edu/disability_services.html

Name of Special Program: Disability Services Program
Coordinator: Patricia Arnson
General Information: Four-Year State University; Enrollment: 2,000; **Tuition:** $1,593–2,175 for 12–18 credit hours per semester; **Room and Board:** $8,000. A rural campus in the scenic Grande Ronde Valley of Oregon and the only university located along the Oregon Trail. Located 260 miles east of Portland and 174 miles northwest of Boise, Idaho, Eastern Oregon State University has been ranked as one of the top four Western public liberal arts colleges by *U.S. News and World Report*. **Majors:** *Baccalaureate Degrees:* agricultural business management, agricultural / resource economics, anthropology / sociology, art, biology, business administration, business / economics, chemistry, computer science / multimedia studies, crop and soil science, English / writing, fire services administration, history, liberal studies, multidisciplinary studies, mathematics, music, philosophy, politics, economics, physics, physical education and health, psychology, rangeland resources, and theater. *Pre-Professional Programs*: engineering, home economics, law, medical technology, dentistry, dental hygiene, fisheries / wildlife, forestry, medicine, nursing, optometry, pharmacy, physical therapy, veterinary medicine. *Associate of Arts Degrees:* general studies
Special Program: Enrollment in Special Program: 125; Cost: None. The percentage of students with learning disabilities receiving a degree in two years is 42%, in four years is 13% and in five or more years is 40%. In the summer, individual accommodations in the form of tutoring, note taking, readers, extended test time and books on tape are available. The Learning Center and Computer Lab are open and available for student use, seven days a week, during the summer academic sessions.

Staff: Learning disabilities specialists; peer tutors; special counselors; content tutors (faculty members)
Program Features: Oral and extended time testing; individual and small group tutoring sessions; basic study skills; tape recorders; taped texts; note-taking assistance – scribes; academic advising for students with learning disabilities; developmental programs; faculty made aware of student's learning disability
Entrance Requirements: Documentation of learning disability; learning disabilities specialist report
Special Facilities for: Visual, hearing and physical impairments
College Life: Eastern Oregon University is well-known as a student-centered university. The University places the interests of all its students — both traditional and non-traditional — at the forefront of its curriculum, student services, and extracurricular activities. An exceptional faculty, small class sizes, attractive facilities, and individual opportunities for student success are highlights of the college experience at Eastern Oregon State University.

PENNSYLVANIA

COLLEGE MISERICORDIA

301 LAKE STREET
DALLAS, PENNSYLVANIA 18612
(570) 674-6347; FAX: (570) 675-2441
E-MAIL: jrogan@misericordia.edu WEB SITE: www.misericordia.edu

Name of Special Program: The Alternative Learners Project (ALP)
Director: Joseph Rogan, Ed.D.
General Information: Four-Year Private College; Enrollment: 1,700; **Tuition:** $9,900 per semester; **Room and Board:** $4,370 per semester. A suburban campus nine miles northwest of Wilkes-Barre, 20 miles southwest of Scranton, affiliated with the Roman Catholic Church and founded in 1924. **Majors:** Biology, business/management, computer/information sciences, diagnostic/treatment services, education, health/social sciences, law, letters/literature, marketing/distribution, mathematics, medical laboratory technologies, multi/interdisciplinary studies, music, occupational/physical therapy, public affairs, rehabilitation service
Special Program: Enrollment in Special Program: 50; Cost: $500 per semester
Staff: Learning disabilities specialists; peer tutors; special counselors
Program Features: Oral and extended time testing; tape recorders; note-taking assistance – scribes; individual tutoring sessions; limited course load (first year); taped texts; Kansas learning strategies; faculty made aware of student's learning disability; calculators; talking calculators; writing/editing assistance; Kurzweil personal reader; Franklin spell-

checkers; each student assigned a Program Coordinator who meets weekly or more often with student; specialized career counseling
Entrance Requirements: Documentation of learning disability; psychoeducational report; SAT/ACT untimed scores accepted; teacher evaluation; interview; testing: WAIS, psychological report
Special Facilities for: Visual, hearing and physical impairments via Office of the Dean of Students

DUQUESNE UNIVERSITY
ADMINISTRATION BUILDING
600 FORBES AVENUE
PITTSBURGH, PENNSYLVANIA 15282-0206
(412) 396-6661; FAX: (412) 396-5466
E-MAIL: griggs@duq.edu
WEB SITE: www.duq.edu; www.lsc.duq.edu

Name of Special Program: Michael P. Weber Learning Skills Center
Director: Judith R. Griggs, Ph.D.
General Information: Four-Year Private University; Enrollment: 10,000; **Tuition:** $550 per credit; **Room and Board:** $8,120 academic year. Duquesne University is located in downtown Pittsburgh, convenient to all attractions, which include Mellon Arena, Point State Park, Heinz Field, and area suburbs. **Majors:** Liberal arts, natural and environmental sciences, pharmacy, nursing, health sciences, education, business and music.
Special Program: Enrollment in Special Program: varies; Cost: None. *Summer Program:* The program consists of a five-week pre-college experience. Students are assessed by way of diagnostic testing; they participate in developmental and/or remedial courses prior to matriculating into college. Students are then monitored by counselors throughout the school year to assist in their area of need. The program is ongoing during the academic year; it is not limited to those students who have a learning disability. Various outreach programs also have been instituted, such as Project for Academic Coaching through Tutoring (PACT), and Outreach Opportunity for marginally Performing Students (OOPS). Cost: $717
Staff: Learning disabilities specialists; content tutors (faculty members); peer tutors; special counselors
Program Features: Oral and extended time testing; individual and small group tutoring sessions; limited course load; academic advising for students with learning disabilities; note-taking assistance – scribes; use of tape recorders; tape texts; basic study skills; developmental program; faculty made aware of student's learning disability; workshops; two-year academic retention

Entrance Requirements: Documentation of learning disability; SAT/ACT untimed scores accepted; diagnostic testing at Duquesne University; grade reports
Special Facilities for: Physical impairments
College Life: After receiving diagnostic testing, the student is followed throughout his/her college experience. In addition to on-going tutoring, the student receives counseling services, which include personal, career and academic advisement, social adjustment and financial aid. The student is covered under academic retention for a period of two years.

EDINBORO UNIVERSITY OF PENNSYLVANIA
OFFICE FOR STUDENTS WITH DISABILITIES
SHAFER HALL
EDINBORO, PENNSYLVANIA 16444
(814) 732-2462 V/TDD; FAX: (814) 732-2866
E-MAIL: mcconnell@edinboro.edu or strosser@edinboro.edu
WEB SITE: www.edinboro.edu

Name of Special Program: Office for Students with Disabilities (OSD) – Learning Disabilities Program
Director: Robert McConnell, Ed.D.
General Information: Two- and Four-Year State University; Enrollment: 8,045; **Annual Tuition:** Residents – $4,917, Non-Residents – $9,814; **Room and Board:** $5,518. The college consists of 585 acres and 40 buildings. There is a five-acre lake, open fields and woods. **Majors:** Anthropology, art history, biology, Black studies/social science, communications, drama, earth sciences, English/literature/writing, environmental studies, languages, geography, history, humanities, mathematics, music, natural sciences and mathematics, philosophy, physics, political science, engineering, pre-law, psychology, social science, specialized studies, applied media arts, crafts, economics, geology, industrial biochemistry, industrial trades leadership, physics, pre-professional studies, education, criminal justice, business administration, computer science, health and physical education, school dental hygiene, medical technology, nuclear medicine technology, nursing, nutrition, social work
Special Program: Enrollment in Special Program: 250; Cost: $306.19-876.37 per semester (subject to change)
Staff: Learning disabilities specialists; peer mentors
Program Features: Extended time testing; mentoring sessions; limited course load; taped texts; faculty made aware of student's learning disability (at student's request); adaptive computer lab; private testing areas; readers; scribes
Entrance Requirements: Recent documentation of learning disability;

SAT / ACT untimed scores accepted; testing: WAIS, diagnostic achievement
Special Facilities for: Visual, hearing and physical impairments
College Life: Edinboro University of Pennsylvania is attractive to students with learning disabilities because of the strong support services offered. In addition to testing and classroom accommodations, students work one-on-one with trained peer mentors on their study, learning and organizational skills. These services help the students to compensate for their learning disability.

GANNON UNIVERSITY
UNIVERSITY SQUARE
ERIE, PENNSYLVANIA 16541-0001
(814) 871-5326; FAX: (814) 871-5657
E-MAIL: lowrey001@gannon.edu
WEB SITE: www.gannon.edu/departmental/psld

Name of Special Program: Program for Students with Learning Disabilities (PSLD)
Director: Sr. Joyce Lowrey
General Information: Four-Year Private College; Enrollment: 3,400; **Tuition:** $19,500; **Room and Board:** $7,790. Gannon University is a Catholic liberal arts institution adjacent to the downtown business district, Bayfront and Lake Erie. **Degrees:** Bachelor degree programs are offered in business administration, humanities, science and engineering, education, and health sciences
Special Program: Enrollment in Special Program: 60, limited to 10–15 new students depending on openings within that year; Cost: $600
Staff: Learning disabilities specialist; content tutors (faculty members)
Program Features: Oral and extended time testing; individual and small group tutoring sessions; limited course load (first year); tape recorders; taped texts; basic study skills; academic advising; faculty made aware of student's learning disability; advocacy seminars; Kurzweil reader; small computer lab
Entrance Requirements: Documentation of learning disability; SAT / ACT untimed scores accepted; testing: WAIS, psychological report; handwritten essay; three letters of recommendation
Special Facilities for: Physical impairments

KING'S COLLEGE
133 NORTH RIVER STREET
WILKES-BARRE, PENNSYLVANIA 18711
(717) 826-5800; FAX: (717) 825-9049
E-MAIL: jaburke@kings.edu **WEB SITE: www.kings.edu**

Name of Special Program: Academic Skills Center – First Year Academic Studies Program (FASP)
Director: Jacintha Burke
General Information: Four-Year Private College; Enrollment: 1,815; **Tuition:** $22,800; **Room and Board:** $8,590. King's College is a Catholic college founded in 1946 by the Holy Cross Fathers. King's proximity to the Pocono Mountains offers the recreational activities of several major ski resorts and state parks plus a triple A baseball team and a semi-pro basketball team. Downtown Wilkes-Barre is just two blocks from campus and features shops, restaurants, and the F.M. Kirby Center of the Performing Arts. **Majors:** Accounting, biology, business administration, chemistry, clinical lab science, communications, computers and information systems, computer science, criminal justice, economics, elementary and secondary education, English, finance, French, gerontology, health care administration, history, human resources management, international business, marketing, mathematics, management information systems, philosophy, physician assistant, physics, political science, psychology, sociology, Spanish, theatre, theology, general science, and legal assistant
Special Program: Enrollment in Special Program: 50; Cost: $1,800 per semester. *Summer Program:* Optional college entry program includes small classes, core requirements, tutoring, and provides orientation to college living and learning.
Staff: Learning disabilities specialists; content tutors (faculty members); peer tutors
Program Features: Oral and extended time testing; individual and small group tutoring sessions; limited course load (first year); academic advising for students with learning disabilities; note-taking assistance – scribes; tape recorders; taped texts; basic study skills; developmental program; faculty made aware of student's learning disability. FASP recognizes that the first year of college is a year of transition for students with learning disabilities. The need for independence and self-confidence must be balanced with the development of successful strategies for learning and self-advocacy. To facilitate this transition, the First Year Academic Studies Program enrolls students in regular Core classes at the college, but supports each class with a structured, supplementary program of course-specific learning strategies.
Entrance Requirements: Documentation of learning disability; learning

disabilities specialist report; SAT untimed scores accepted; teacher evaluation; testing: WAIS, IEP, psychological report
Special Facilities for: Visual, hearing and physical impairments
College Life: A self-contained urban campus with small class size, King's offers students a culture class option to meet foreign language requirements. College life offers opportunities for students to participate in student life and student government.

MERCYHURST COLLEGE
501 EAST 38th STREET
ERIE, PENNSYLVANIA 16546-0001
(814) 824-2450, 1-800-825-1926 X2450
E-MAIL: drogers@mercyhurst.edu WEB SITE: www.mercyhurst.edu

Name of Special Program: Learning Differences Program
Director: Dianne D. Rogers
General Information: Four-Year Private College; Enrollment: 3,900; **Annual Tuition, Room and Board:** $28,633. Mercyhurst College is a Catholic liberal arts institution which is located on a beautiful site overlooking the city of Erie and Lake Erie. The suburban campus of 85 acres is just minutes away from downtown. **Degrees:** Bachelor of Arts; Bachelor of Science; Bachelor of Music; Associate of Arts; Associate of Science
Special Program: Enrollment in Special Program: 71; Cost: Fee varies, maximum $1,500 per year. *Summer Program:* A three-week, all-day program required for incoming students. Students earn three credits toward graduation. Cost: $1,700 approximately
Staff: Learning disabilities specialists; peer tutors; special counselors
Program Features: Oral and extended time testing; individual and small group tutoring sessions; limited course load; note-taking assistance – scribes; tape recorders; taped texts; basic study skills; developmental program; faculty made aware of student's learning disability; Kurzweil personal reader
Entrance Requirements: Documentation of learning disability; SAT/ACT untimed scores accepted; testing: WAIS, IEP, psychological report
College Life: Attending to the special needs of diverse learners is a large component of the mission of Mercyhurst College. Students find compassionate and knowledgeable individuals who can help them in the transitions they face at college. Two levels of service are available — a less structured program that provides accommodations that comply with Section 504 requirements and the structured program that offers accommodations that go beyond what is required by law.
Special Facilities for: Visual and hearing impairments

RHODE ISLAND

SALVE REGINA UNIVERSITY

100 OCHRE POINT AVENUE
NEWPORT, RHODE ISLAND 02840
(401) 341-2228 or 1-800-321-7124; FAX: (401) 848-2823
E-MAIL: Theo.Greenblatt@salve.edu WEB SITE: www.salve.edu

Name of Special Program: Academic Development Center
Director: Theo Greenblatt
General Information: Four-Year Private University; Enrollment: 3,000; **Annual Tuition:** $24,976; **Room and Board:** $9,800. Salve Regina University has a spectacular campus located in historic Newport, Rhode Island. It is 30 minutes from Providence and 90 minutes from Boston. Experiences for field learning, study abroad and internships are available. **Majors:** Accounting, administration of justice, American studies, art, biology and biomedical sciences, business administration, chemistry, cytotechnology, early childhood education, economics, elementary education, English, French, history, information systems science, mathematical sciences, medical technology, music, nursing, philosophy, politics, pre-law, pre-med, psychology, religious studies, secondary education, social work, sociology, Spanish, special education, theatre arts
Special Program: Enrollment in Special Program: 100–150; Cost: None
Staff: Learning disabilities specialists; peer tutors
Program Features: Oral and extended time testing; limited course load (first year); tape recorders; taped texts; note-taking assistance – scribes; academic advising for students with learning disabilities; faculty made aware of student's learning disability
Entrance Requirements: SAT / ACT untimed scores accepted
Special Facilities for: Visual, hearing and physical impairments
College Life: Salve Regina University is a community that provides individual attention to help students reach their full potential.

SOUTH CAROLINA

LIMESTONE COLLEGE

1115 COLLEGE DRIVE
GAFFNEY, SOUTH CAROLINA 29340
(864) 489-8377; FAX: (864) 487-8706
E-MAIL: kkearse@limestone.edu
WEB SITE: www.limestone.edu/prospect/pals.htm

Name of Special Program: Program for Alternative Learning Styles (PALS)
Director: Karen W. Kearse
General Information: Four-Year Private College; Enrollment: 600; **Annual**

Tuition: $14,040; **Room and Board:** $5,800. Limestone College is located in the Piedmont section of the state, a populous area with diversified industrial and agricultural interests. The well-known resort areas of the Blue Ridge Mountains, the Smoky Mountains, and the beaches of the Atlantic coast are accessible for weekend visits. In the immediate area, facilities are available for all water sports, horseback riding, golf and tennis. **Majors:** Art education/studio, counseling/human services, elementary education, English, history, liberal studies, music, psychology, social studies, social work, biology, chemistry, business/accounting, computer science, economics, general business, management, marketing, computer science, mathematics, physical education

Special Program: Enrollment in Special Program: 30; Cost: $3,000 for first year. Fee is reduced by 50% in the following years for students who meet GPA requirements.

Staff: Learning disabilities specialists; content tutors (faculty members); peer tutors; special counselors

Program Features: Oral and extended time testing, individual tutoring sessions; limited course load (first year); academic advising for students with learning disabilities; note-taking assistance – scribes; tape recorders; taped texts; developmental program; basic study skills; faculty are made aware of student's learning disability and are given suggestions as to ways to help students be successful; follow-up with faculty

Entrance Requirements: Documentation of learning disability; SAT/ACT untimed scores accepted; testing: WAIS, IEP, psychological report

College Life: Our program has several built-in accountability measures that help keep students focused, learning, growing and achieving success in college and preparing for their careers.

TENNESSEE

LEE UNIVERSITY

1120 NORTH OCOEE STREET
CLEVELAND, TENNESSEE 37311
(423) 614-8181; FAX: (423) 614-8179
E-MAIL: ggallaher@leeuniversity.edu
WEB SITE: www.leeuniversity.edu

Name of Special Program: Academic Support

Director: Gayle Gallaher, Ph.D.

General Information: Four-Year Private University; Enrollment 3,800; **Tuition:** $5,099 per semester; **Room:** $1,265, **Board:** $1,140. Lee University has a lovely campus on the edge of the charming town of Cleveland, Tennessee. Lee is 30 miles from Cherokee National Forest, the site of the

1996 Summer White Water Olympics, 30 miles from Chattanooga and 2 hours from Atlanta. **Majors:** A total of 28 majors in 56 programs of study range from the latest computer training to traditional studies such as teacher education. To ensure these programs are appropriate for today, the university stays in constant touch with changing trends and developments in the career world.
Special Program: Enrollment in Special Program: 150; Cost: None
Staff: Learning disabilities specialists; peer tutors; special counselors
Program Features: Oral and extended time testing, individual and small group tutoring sessions; limited course load (first year); academic advising for students with learning disabilities; note-taking assistance – scribes; tape recorders; taped texts; developmental program; basic study skills; faculty are made aware of student's learning disability (at student's request)
Entrance Requirements: Documentation of learning disability; SAT/ACT untimed scores accepted
Special Facilities for: Physical impairments
College Life: Students with learning disabilities are treated with respect and support. Students are loved and encouraged to reach their goals.

THE UNIVERSITY OF MEMPHIS
110 WILDER TOWER
MEMPHIS, TENNESSEE 38152-3520
(901) 678-2880 V/TTY; FAX: (901) 678-3070
E-MAIL: stepaske@memphis.edu **WEB SITE: www.memphis.edu**

Name of Special Program: Student Disability Services
Director: Susan TePaske; *Learning Disabilities Coordinator:* Dr. Joey Ciavarella
General Information: Four-Year State University; Enrollment 20,000; **Tuition and Fees:** Residents – $2,628 per semester, Non-Residents – $7,861 per semester; **Room:** $950–1,900 per semester; **Board:** $1,700 for meal plan. The University of Memphis has a 1,159 acre campus in an urban area. Special learning facilities include a learning resource center, an art gallery, a radio and TV station, an earthquake research center, a center for electronic microscopy, Chucalissa Indian Village and Museum and a speech and hearing center. **Majors:** Area studies, anthropology, accounting, biology, business/management, business/finance, chemistry, communications, computer/information sciences, crafts/design, education, engineering, fine arts, geological sciences, health sciences, home economics, languages, law, letters/literature, life sciences, mathematics, multi/interdisciplinary studies, music, philosophy, physical sciences, physics, criminology and criminal justice, psychology, public affairs, social sciences, visu-

al/performing arts, vocational home economics, nursing, physical education, exercise science, recreation
Special Program: Enrollment in Special Program: 475; Cost: None
Staff: Learning disabilities specialists; peer tutors; special counselors; content tutors (peer and professional)
Program Features: Oral and extended time testing; individual and small group tutoring sessions; limited course load; academic advising for students with learning disabilities; note-taking assistance – scribes; tape recorders; taped texts; basic study skills; developmental program; faculty make aware of student's learning disability; reading machines, adaptive software and computers
Entrance Requirements: Documentation of learning disability; handwritten essay; SAT/ACT untimed scores accepted; teacher evaluation; medical evaluation; testing: WAIS, psychological report, Woodcock-Johnson
Special Facilities for: Visual, hearing and physical impairments

TEXAS

ABILENE CHRISTIAN UNIVERSITY

1600 CAMPUS COURT, BOX 29204
ABILENE, TEXAS 79699-9204
(325) 674-2667; FAX: (325) 674-6847
E-MAIL: bradshawg@acu.edu **WEB SITE: www.acu.edu**

Name of Special Program: Alpha Academic Services
Director: Dr. Gloria Bradshaw
General Information: Four-Year Private University; Enrollment: 4,500; **Tuition**: $16,330; **Room and Board:** $6,120. Abilene Christian University is located in west Texas in a rural area known as the "Big Country." The Fort Worth/Dallas metroplex is 150 miles east on Interstate 20. The university is affiliated with Churches of Christ. It was founded in 1906 as Childers Classical Institute. In addition to regular fall and spring semester courses, short courses are offered in January and May. **Degrees:** Bachelor's degrees in biological and physical science, education, English, foreign languages, social sciences, communication arts, journalism/mass communication, business, Biblical studies, ministry
Special Program: Enrollment in Special Program: 100, limited to 125; Cost: None. Counseling, tutoring and disability accommodations are available in summer sessions during July and August.
Staff: Learning disabilities specialists; peer tutors; special counselors; content tutors (professional staff)
Program Features: Oral and extended time testing; individual and small group tutoring sessions; note-taking assistance – scribes; tape recorders;

basic study skills; faculty made aware of student's learning disability (at student's request); developmental courses; counseling — academic, personal, career, financial aid
Entrance Requirements: Documentation of learning disability; SAT untimed scores accepted; handwritten essay: family income information; testing: WAIS, IEP, psychological report
Special Facilities for: Visual, hearing and physical impairments
College Life: Abilene Christian University's mission as a university involves helping students develop to their full potential. Faculty and staff are supportive and caring. Each student's needs are considered on an individual basis.

SCHREINER UNIVERSITY
CAMPUS BOX 6209
KERRVILLE, TEXAS 78028
(830) 792-7256, 1-800-343-4919
WEB SITE: www.schreiner.edu

Name of Special Program: Learning Support Services Program
Director: Jude Gallik, Ph.D.
General Information: Four-Year Private College; Enrollment: 700; **Tuition:** $7,740 per semester; **Room and Board:** $4,525 per semester. A Presbyterian-related college in the heart of the Texas Hill country on the Guadalupe River. Located a scenic one hour drive from San Antonio, Kerrville is noted for its mild year-round weather, its clear, clean air and its panoramic rolling hills. **Degree Programs:** Liberal arts, science, education, health and physical education, psychology, business, history, art
Special Program: Enrollment in Special Program: 70–85; Cost: $5,980 per year
Staff: Learning disabilities specialists; adult tutors; special counselors
Program Features: Oral and extended time testing; individual and small group tutoring sessions; limited course load (first year); recorded texts; basic study skills; faculty made aware of student's learning disability; developmental classes
Entrance Requirements: Documentation of learning disability; SAT/ACT untimed scores accepted; medical evaluation; interview with learning support services director and staff; testing: WAIS, individual achievement tests, psychological report
Scholarships: See page 438.

TEXAS STATE UNIVERSITY
601 UNIVERSITY DRIVE
SUITE 5-5.1 LBJ STUDENT CENTER
SAN MARCOS, TEXAS 78666-4616
(512) 245-3451 V/TTY; FAX: (512) 245-3452
E-MAIL: disability-services@txstate.edu
WEB SITE: www.ods.txstate.edu

Name of Special Program: Office of Disability Services
Director: Tina Schultz
General Information: Four-Year State University; Enrollment: 24,980; **Tuition:** Residents – $2,349 for 12 hours per semester, Non-Residents – $5,649 for 12 hours per semester; **Room and Board:** $1,233–2,721. Southwest Texas State University is located in San Marcos, a hill country community, halfway between Austin and San Antonio. Its location on the banks of the San Marcos River provides recreational and leisure activities for students throughout the year. **Majors**: Applied arts and sciences, agriculture, anthropology, applied sociology, art, biology, business administration, chemistry, communication disorders, computer science, criminal justice, economics, English, exercise and sports science, fine arts, French, geography, German, health information management/wellness promotion/professions, history, home economics, international studies, mass communication, mathematics, medical technology, music, philosophy, physics, physical therapy, political science, psychology, sociology, recreational administration, respiratory care, Spanish, speech communication, technology, theater arts
Special Program: Enrollment in Special Program: 285; Cost: None
Staff: Learning disabilities specialists; physical disability specialist; interpreters
Program Features: Oral and extended time testing; note-taking assistance – scribes; taped texts; basic study skills; faculty made aware of student's learning disability; computer with voice recognition
Entrance Requirements: SAT/ACT untimed scores accepted
Special Facilities for: Visual, hearing and physical impairments

UNIVERSITY OF TEXAS AT SAN ANTONIO
6900 NORTH LOOP 1604 WEST
SAN ANTONIO, TEXAS 78249
(210) 458-4157; FAX: (210) 458-4980
E-MAIL: Lorraine.Harrison@utsa.edu **WEB SITE: www.utsa.edu**

Name of Special Program: Disability Services
Director: Lorraine Harrison
General Information: Four-Year State University; Enrollment: 24,665;

Tuition: Residents – $3,093 for 12 hours per semester, Non-Residents – $5,932 for 12 hours per semester; **Room:** $2,724. The University of Texas at San Antonio is located in the northwest quadrant of Bexar County, 16 miles from downtown San Antonio. It has been identified as the state's fastest growing university. **Majors:** Accounting, American studies, anthropology, architecture, art, biology, chemistry, civil/electrical/mechanical engineering, clinical laboratory sciences, computer science, criminal justice, economics, English, finance, French, geography, geology, German, health, history, humanities, information systems, interdisciplinary studies, interior design, occupational/physical therapy, kinesiology, management, marketing, mathematics, Mexican-American studies, multi/disciplinary science, music, nursing, personnel/human resources management, philosophy, physics, political science, psychology, sociology, Spanish
Special Program: Enrollment in Special Program: 65; Cost: None
Staff: Learning disabilities specialists
Program Features: Extended time testing; small group tutoring sessions; limited course load (first year); note-taking assistance – scribes; tape recorders; taped texts; faculty made aware of student's learning disability; adaptive computer technology; support group; advocacy
Entrance Requirements: Documentation of learning disability; SAT/ACT untimed scores accepted
Special Facilities for: Visual, hearing and physical impairments

UTAH

SOUTHERN UTAH UNIVERSITY
351 UNIVERSITY BLVD.
CEDAR CITY, UTAH 84720
(435) 865-8022; FAX: (435) 865-8235
E-MAIL: alldredge@suu.edu
WEB SITE: www.suu.edu/ss/support/disability

Name of Special Program: Student Support Center/Disability Support Center
Director: Carmen R. Alldredge
General Information: Four-Year State University; Enrollment: 6,048; **Tuition:** Residents – $1,782.25 per semester, Non-Residents – $5,301.25 per semester; **Room and Board:** $4,154. Southern Utah University is in a rural setting, one-and-a-half hours from St. George and 5 hours from Salt Lake City. Cedar City has the Shakespearean Festival and Utah Summer Games in the warm months. Brianhead is one hour away. Cedar City is three hours from Las Vegas and two hours away from Zion's Park and Bryce Canyon. **Majors:** Bachelor of Arts and Bachelor of Science offered with 64

majors, numerous associate degrees and certificates
Special Program: Enrollment in Special Program: Unlimited; Cost: None
Staff: Learning disabilities specialists; peer tutors; content tutors (faculty members); special counselors
Program Features: Extended time testing; small group tutoring sessions; limited course load; academic advising; note-taking assistance – scribes; tape recorders; taped texts; basic study skills; developmental program; faculty made aware of student's learning disability; involvement with different student committees and clubs
Entrance Requirements: Documentation of learning disability; learning disabilities specialist report; SAT/ACT untimed scores accepted; teacher evaluation; testing: WAIS, IEP, psychological report; diagnostic testing at Southern Utah University
Special Facilities for: Visual, hearing and physical impairments
College Life: The Disability Office at Southern Utah University prides itself on one-on-one counseling, a good relationship between the department and faculty members, and good rapport with students.
Scholarships: See page 438.

UNIVERSITY OF UTAH
CENTER FOR DISABILITY SERVICES
162 UNION BUILDING
200 SOUTH CENTRAL CAMPUS DRIVE
SALT LAKE CITY, UTAH 84112-9107
(801) 581-5020 V/TDD; FAX: (801) 581-5487
E-MAIL: info@disability.utah.edu
WEB SITE: www.utah.edu or www.disability.utah.edu

Name of Special Program: Center for Disability Services
Director: Joe Pete Wilson
General Information: Four-Year State University; Enrollment: 28,000; **Tuition:** Residents – $2,331 for 15 credit hours, Non-Residents – $7,296 for 15 credit hours; **Room:** $2,000. University of Utah is a suburban campus in a small city, 14 blocks from downtown. Attractions include the State Arboretum, and the Utah Museums of Fine Arts and Natural History. **Majors:** Area studies, biology, business/management, chemistry, communications, education, engineering, environmental design, fine arts, geological sciences, health sciences, home economics, languages, letters/literature, mathematics, medical laboratory technologies, multi/interdisciplinary studies, music, parks and recreation, philosophy, physical sciences, physics, psychology, rehabilitation services, social sciences, visual/performing arts

Special Program: Enrollment in Special Program: 700; Cost: None
Staff: Learning disabilities specialists; peer tutors; content counselors
Program Features: Extended time testing; limited course load; basic study skills; note-taking assistance – scribes; tape recorders; taped texts; faculty made aware of student's learning disability; basic study skills; scanning and reading technology
Entrance Requirements: Documentation of learning disability; SAT/ACT untimed scores accepted; testing; WAIS, psychological report
Special Facilities for: Visual, hearing, and physical impairments
College Life: The University of Utah has an open and accommodating attitude toward students with disabilities.
Scholarships: See page 438.

UTAH VALLEY STATE COLLEGE
800 WEST UNIVERSITY PARKWAY, MAIL STOP 190
OREM, UTAH 84058-5999
(801) 863-8747; FAX: (801) 863-8377
E-MAIL: millersh@uvsc.edu or asd@uvsc.edu
WEB SITE: www.uvsc.edu

Name of Special Program: Accessibility Services Department
Director: Sherine A. Miller
General Information: Four-Year State College; Enrollment: 23,000; **Tuition:** Residents – $1,654 per semester, Non-Residents – $5,169 per semester; **Room and Board:** No college housing available. Utah Valley State College is located in a suburban area on a 200-acre campus with easy access to Salt Lake City. **Majors:** Accounting, automotive/aviation technology, business administration/ commerce/management, carpentry, child care/family studies, commercial art, computer information systems, construction management/technologies, drafting and design, education, electrical and electronics technologies, pre-engineering sequence, finance/banking, fire science, graphic arts, hospitality services, hotel and restaurant management, human services, international business, legal secretarial studies, legal studies, liberal arts/general studies, machine and tool technologies, marketing/retailing/merchandising, medical secretarial studies, practical nursing, radiological technology, retail management, secretarial studies/office management, transportation technologies, welding technology
Special Program: Enrollment in Special Program: 750; Cost: None
Staff: Learning disabilities specialists.
Program Features: Oral and extended time testing; limited course load; basic study skills; tape recorders; taped texts; developmental program; faculty made aware of student's learning disability; academic advising

Entrance Requirements: Documentation of learning disability; learning disabilities specialist report; open enrollment
Special Facilities for: Visual, hearing and physical impairments
College Life: At Utah Valley State College, approximately one out of every ten students has an identified disability. Students with disabilities seek to be educated at Utah Valley State College partially as a result of the College's facility accessibility, quality of accommodative services, open door admission and competitive tuition.
Scholarships: See page 439.

VERMONT

COLLEGE OF SAINT JOSEPH

71 CLEMENT ROAD
RUTLAND, VERMONT 05701
(802) 773-5900 X3239; FAX: (802) 773-5900, X268
E-MAIL: cgillam@csj.edu **WEB SITE: www.csj.edu**

***Name of Special Program*:** Project Success
Director: Charlotte R. Gillam
General Information: Four-Year Private College: Enrollment: 538; **Annual Tuition:** $14,650; **Room and Board:** $7,150. The College of Saint Joseph is a small, Catholic, liberal arts college located on a compact and easily accessible campus nestled within 99 wooded acres of college-owned land on the outskirts of the city of Rutland, Vermont's second largest city. The campus is easily reached via interstate highway, plane, train and bus. Montreal, Albany, Boston, Hartford and New York City are all within easy driving distance. In the college's own backyard there is some of the best skiing in the east. Killington and Pico are within a 15-minute drive and five other major ski areas are within a 60-minute drive. Lake Champlain, Bomoseen, and Saint Catherine, the Appalachian Trail and Long Trail and some of the most beautiful state forests offer exceptional year-round recreational opportunities. **Degrees:** Associate of Arts in liberal studies; Associate of Science in accounting, business management, computer information systems; Bachelor of Arts or Bachelor of Science in accounting, information systems, education, English history, human services, journalism, liberal studies, political science, pre-law, psychology, resort and recreation management
Special Program: Enrollment in Special Program: 24; Cost: None
Staff: Learning disabilities specialist; peer tutors; content tutors (faculty members); special counselors
Program Features: Oral and extended time testing; limited course load (first year); basic study skills; individual and small group tutoring sessions; note-taking assistance – scribes; tape recorders; taped texts; devel-

opmental program; credit courses in reading; critical thinking and study skills; faculty made aware of student's learning disability.
Entrance Requirements: Documentation of learning disability; SAT untimed scores accepted; medical evaluation; handwritten essay; diagnostic testing at the College of Saint Joseph; testing: WAIS, IEP, psychological report
Special Facilities for: Visual, hearing and physical impairments.
College Life: The student-to-faculty ratio of 14:1 with classes averaging 15 students and an exceptional student support services program combine to create a supportive family atmosphere and learning environment in which the individual is valued by students and faculty alike.

JOHNSON STATE COLLEGE
DEWEY CAMPUS CENTER, 337 COLLEGE HILL
JOHNSON, VERMONT 05656
(802) 635-1259, (802) 635-1456 TTY; FAX: (802) 635-1454
E-MAIL: duranled@jsc.vsc.edu or maddenk@jsc.vsc.edu
WEB SITE: www.jsc.vsc.edu

Name of Special Program: Academic Support Services
Acting Director: Karen Madden, Ph.D.; *Learning Specialist*: Dian Duranleau
General Information: Four-Year State College; Enrollment: 1,759; **Annual Tuition:** Residents – $13,300; Non-Residents – $28,652, NEBHE – $19,968; **Room and Board:** $13,884. Johnson State College is located in the heart of one of Vermont's most scenic areas, within a half-hour of Stowe and Smuggler's Notch ski areas. On top of a hill, with 360 degree views of the Green Mountains, Johnson State has vast opportunities for hiking, canoeing, bicycling and downhill/cross-county skiing. The village of Johnson is home to the Vermont Studio Center, which attracts numerous national and international artists and writers. **Degrees**: Associate of Arts; Associate of Science; BA, BFA, BS, Certificates; Teacher Licensure; MA in Counseling, Education, MFA in Studio Arts; External Degree Programs
Special Program: Enrollment in Special Program: 114; Cost: None
Staff: Learning disabilities specialist; peer tutors; content tutors (faculty members); special counselors
Program Features: Oral and extended time testing; individual and small group tutoring sessions; limited course load (first year); academic advising for students with learning disabilities; note-taking assistance – scribes; taped texts; tape recorders, basic study skills; faculty made aware of student's learning disability; exams administered in reduced distraction environment; course substitution for math disability; assistive technology available
Entrance Requirements: Documentation of learning disability; learning

disabilities specialist report; SAT/ACT untimed scores accepted; testing: WAIS, IEP, psychological report
Special Facilities for: Visual, hearing and physical impairments
College Life: Johnson State College has a long-standing tradition of providing accommodations and services in an environment friendly to students with disabilities. Its Academic Support Services program is one of the oldest and most respected in the state, staffed by experienced, caring professionals. Assistive technology is available to help students with learning disabilities.

SOUTHERN VERMONT COLLEGE
982 MANSION DRIVE
BENNINGTON, VERMONT 05201-6002
(802) 447-6360; FAX: (802) 447-4695
E-MAIL: dlindenberg@svc.edu **WEB SITE: www.svc.edu**

Name of Special Program: Learning Differences Support Program (LDSP)
Coordinator: David Lindenberg
General Information: Four-Year Private College; Enrollment: 600; **Annual Tuition, Room and Board:** $22,450. Founded in 1926, the campus consists of 371 acres and is located on the eastern slope of Mt. Anthony, commanding a picturesque view of the entire valley below. Bennington is an historic New England town located in the heart of the Green Mountains. It is in prime ski country with innumerable opportunities for outdoor recreation, one hour drive from Albany and three and a half hour drive from Boston or New York City. **Majors**: Accounting, business, business administration, child development, communications, criminal justice, English/communications, environmental studies, hospitality/resort management, human services, liberal arts leading to secondary education licensure, liberal arts, liberal arts/management nursing, psychology, social work
Special Program: Enrollment in Special Program: 70–80; Cost: None
Staff: Learning disabilities specialist; peer tutors; content tutors (faculty members); special counselors
Program Features: Extended time testing; individual tutoring sessions; limited course load (first year); note-taking assistance – scribes; academic advising for students with learning disabilities; faculty made aware of student's learning disability (at student's request); taped texts; Recording for the Blind & Dyslexic; tape recorders; basic study skills; Kurzweil reader; Dragon Dictate
Entrance Requirements: Documentation of learning disability; learning disabilities specialist report; SAT/ACT untimed scores accepted; testing:

WAIS, IEP, psychological report; placement tests (untimed)
Special Facilities for: Visual, hearing and physical impairments
College Life: The Learning Differences Support Program of Southern Vermont College offers a highly supportive environment for students with special educational needs. Students who participate in the program are offered a wide range of support services tailored to their individual needs.

UNIVERSITY OF VERMONT
A170 LIVING/LEARNING CENTER
BURLINGTON, VERMONT 05405-0386
(802) 656-7753; FAX: (802) 656-0739
E-MAIL: access@uvm.edu **WEB SITE: www.uvm.edu/access**

Name of Special Program: ACCESS / Academic Support Programs
Director: Margaret Ottinger (802) 656-7853
General Information: Four-Year State University; Enrollment: 7,500; **Annual Tuition, Room and Board:** Residents – $18,966, Non-Residents – $33,950. Located on an urban campus in Burlington, a small city of 40,000 people on the shores of Lake Champlain in northwestern Vermont, near the Green Mountains of Vermont and the Adirondack Mountains of New York State. **Majors**: The university is composed of eight divisions: Colleges of Arts and Engineering and Mathematics, Agriculture and Life Sciences, Sciences, Education and Social Services, and Schools of Business, Natural Resources, Allied Health Sciences and Nursing; over 100 majors, including English, psychology, political science, language, civil and mechanical engineering, computer science, accounting, marketing, natural resources, environmental studies, education, sciences, merchandising, design, nursing / physical therapy, interdisciplinary major in environmental studies
Special Program: Enrollment in Special Program: 200. Cost: None
Staff: Learning disabilities specialists; peer tutors; content tutors (faculty members); special counselors
Program Features: Assistance with academic and programmatic accommodations; disability-related advising; referral to content tutors; study skills tutors, writing tutors, and supplemental instruction; one-credit college success strategies course; faculty consultation; adaptive technology lab; Exam Proctoring Center
Entrance Requirements: Documentation of learning disability; learning disabilities specialist report (voluntary); SAT untimed scores accepted; teacher evaluation; cognitive achievement testing; current psychoeducational report (within past three years) that includes achievement and intelligence testing (including test scores) and a clear diagnosis. Report must

describe the degree to which learning is impacted.
Special Facilities for: Visual, hearing and physical impairments. Students with all types of disabilities may seek services at ACCESS.

VIRGINIA

VIRGINIA INTERMONT COLLEGE

1013 MOORE STREET
BRISTOL, VIRGINIA 24202-4298
(276) 466-7905; FAX: (276) 645-6493
E-MAIL: tdobbins@vic.edu **WEB SITE: www.vic.edu**

Name of Special Program: Student Support Services
Director: Talmage Dobbins
General Information: Four-Year Private College; Enrollment: 1,146; **Tuition, Room and Board:** $23,940. Virginia Intermont College is located in Bristol, a small city on Virginia/Tennessee state line with a view of the Holston Mountain range. The school is a comprehensive college and is affiliated with the Baptist General Association of Virginia. **Majors:** Art, biology, business, computer information management, criminal justice, culinary arts, dance, dietetics, English, equine studies, history, interdisciplinary studies, legal studies, liberal arts, performing arts, photography and digital imaging, physical education, political science, psychology, public policy administration, religious studies, social work, sport management, theatre
Special Program: Enrollment in Special Program: 31; Cost: None
Staff: Learning disabilities specialist; peer tutors; counselors.
Program Features: Oral and extended time testing; individual and small group tutoring sessions; limited course load; basic study skills; tape recorders; taped texts; note-taking assistance – scribes; faculty made aware of student's learning disability (at student's request); academic advising for students with learning disabilities; computer optical scanner with voice synthesizer for reading texts aloud
Entrance Requirements: Documentation of learning disability required for special program features; SAT/ACT untimed scores accepted; testing: WAIS, IEP, psychological report
College Life: Specialty majors and small student-faculty ratio combined with a strong support program for providing academic accommodations make Virginia Intermont particularly attractive to students with special needs.

WEST VIRGINIA

DAVIS AND ELKINS COLLEGE

100 CAMPUS DRIVE
ELKINS, WEST VIRGINIA 26241-3996
(304) 637-1270; FAX: (304) 637-1413
E-MAIL: sneedd@davisandelkins.edu
WEB SITE: www.davisandelkins.edu

Name of Special Program: Supported Learning Program
Director: David Sneed, Vice President for Student Life, Dean of Students
General Information: Four-Year Private College; Enrollment: 700; **Tuition:** $17,210, **Room and Board:** $6,300 (double). Located in the center of a major rural outdoor recreation area which offers many activities, the college is within a day's drive of most metropolitan areas of the east, south and midwest. **Majors:** Accounting, biology/environmental science, business administration, computer science, chemistry, communication, economics, education, English, foreign languages, health, history, management, marketing, mathematics, nursing, political science, psychology and human services, physical education, recreation management and tourism, religion and philosophy, sociology, hospitality management, criminology, cooperative programs and pre-professional programs; green studies minor
Special Program: Enrollment in Special Program: 35; Cost; $2,700
Staff: Learning disabilities specialist; peer tutors
Program Features: Oral and extended time testing; individual and small group tutoring sessions; limited course load (first year); basic study skills; tape recorders; taped texts; note-taking assistance – scribes (when possible); faculty made aware of student's learning disability; academic advising for students with learning disabilities; lab with assistive technology; supplemental instruction in math; study groups
Entrance Requirements: Documentation of learning disability; learning disabilities specialist report; SAT/ACT untimed scores accepted; teacher evaluation; handwritten essay; interview highly recommended; testing: WAIS, IEP, psychological report
College Life: In our small, rural setting, students have access to many types of support services and faculty members. Because of the program's longevity, it operates seamlessly and strives to support students while fostering their independence.

MARSHALL UNIVERSITY
520 18th STREET, MYERS HALL
HUNTINGTON, WEST VIRGINIA 25755
(304) 696-6252; FAX: (304) 696-3231
E-MAIL: guyerb@marshall.edu **WEB SITE: www.marshall.edu**

Name of Special Program: Higher Education for Learning Problems (H.E.L.P.)
Director: Dr. Barbara P. Guyer; *Assistant Director:* Lynne Weston
General Information: Four-Year State University; Enrollment: 16,000; **Tuition:** Residents – $1,909, Non-Residents – $5,064; **Room and Board:** $1,296 per semester. Located on the Ohio River one hour from Charleston, West Virginia. **Majors:** The university consists of eleven colleges: Business, Education, Fine Arts, Information Technology and Engineering, Journalism, Liberal Arts, Science, Community College, Graduate School, School of Medicine, School of Nursing. Professional, technical and industrial career studies are offered as well as independent studies, internships, field experiences and the Yeager Scholarship Program.
Special Program: Enrollment in Special Program: 200; Cost; Residents – $275 per semester hour, Non-Residents – $475 per semester hour. *Summer Program:* The H.E.L.P. Program offers a five-week summer session. Students attend a class in the morning and then receive tutoring in the afternoon. Along with course subject tutoring, there is work on study skills, note-taking and test-taking skills and remediation. Cost: Residents – $1,000, Non-Residents – $2,200
Staff: Learning disabilities specialist; content tutors; graduate students
Program Features: Oral and extended time testing; individual tutoring sessions; basic study skills; tape recorders; taped texts; developmental program; faculty made aware of student's learning disability; remediation in reading/spelling/written language; math medical H.E.L.P., a remedial program for medical students with learning disabilities
Entrance Requirements: Documentation of learning disability and/or ADD; learning disabilities specialist report; handwritten essay; SAT/ACT untimed scores accepted; interview; two references; testing: WAIS-III, individually administered achievement test
College Life: Marshall University has a very accessible campus with reasonable class size. The H.E.L.P. Program is structured and comprehensive with a dedicated, educated staff.
Scholarships: See page 440.

WEST VIRGINIA WESLEYAN COLLEGE
59 COLLEGE AVENUE
BUCKHANNON, WEST VIRGINIA 26201-2995
(304) 473-8563; FAX: (304) 473-8497
E-MAIL: kuba_s@wvwc.edu or belknap_r@wvwc.edu
WEB SITE: www.wvwc.edu/stu/sass

Name of Special Program: Student Academic Support Services
Director: Shawn Kuba
General Information: Four-Year Private College; Enrollment: 18,200; **Tuition, Room and Board:** $26,880. Founded in 1890, affiliated with the United Methodist Church. A rural campus in a small town, near Morgantown and Charleston and 135 miles from Pittsburgh, Pennsylvania. Several attractions are ski resorts, state parks, white rafting on New River, and a national forest. Semester and May term offer international travel plus special courses. **Degrees:** Bachelor of Arts, Bachelor of Science, Bachelor of Music Education and Master of Business Administration.
Special Program: Enrollment in Special Program: 100–120; Cost: None
Staff: Learning disabilities specialist; peer tutors; special counselors
Program Features: Oral and extended time testing; distraction-reduced testing environment and scribes if appropriate; walk-in tutoring program certified by the College Reading and Learning Association; individual and small group tutoring sessions; limited course load; academic advising; tape recorders; taped texts; note-taking assistance – scribes; basic study skills; college strategies class; Lindamood-Bell Reading Program offered on a fee-for-services basis; Assistive Instructional Technology Lab offers Kurzweil 3000 scanner and reader; Dragon Professional *Naturally Speaking* (voice-activated software); programs designed to assess learning styles, build vocabulary, improve reading rate and comprehension and enhance math skills
Entrance Requirements: Documentation of learning disability; SAT/ACT untimed scores accepted; teacher evaluation; testing: WAIS-III, IEP, Woodcock-Johnson Standard Achievement Battery
Special Facilities for: Visual, hearing and physical impairments when appropriate to the needs of the student.
College Life: West Virginia Wesleyan College offers comprehensive services including a certified tutoring program and a clinical reading program. Wesleyan's staff is responsive to the needs and concerns of the students enrolled in the program, and the faculty is accessible and cooperative in helping students with disabilities achieve their academic goals. Wesleyan's campus life offers opportunities for personal development on many levels.
Scholarships: See page 440.

WISCONSIN

UNIVERSITY OF WISCONSIN: LACROSSE

1725 STATE STREET
LACROSSE, WISCONSIN 54601
(608) 785-6900; FAX: (608) 785-6910
E-MAIL: ability@uwlax.edu/drs **WEB SITE: www.uwlax.edu**

Name of Special Program: Disability Resource Services
Director: June Reinert, reinert.june@uwlax.edu
General Information: Four-Year State University; Enrollment: 8,750; **Tuition:** Residents – $5,225, Non-Residents – $15,271; **Room:** $2,720; **Board:** $2,100. The university is located on an urban campus in a medium-sized city between the bluffs of Wisconsin and Minnesota. **Majors:** Accounting, archaeology, art, athletic training emphasis, biology, business/management, chemistry, communications, computer sciences, education, English, finance, French, geography, German, history, health sciences, international business, international studies, marketing, mathematics, medical technology, music, nuclear medicine technology, philosophy, physical education, physical therapy, physics, psychology, political science, social sciences, sociology, Spanish, visual/performing arts, women's studies
Special Program: Enrollment in Special Program: 400; Cost: None
Staff: Learning disabilities specialists
Program Features: Oral and extended time testing; note-taking assistance – scribes; academic advising for students with learning disabilities; faculty made aware of student's learning disability; taped texts; tape recorders.
Entrance Requirements: Documentation of learning disability; learning disabilities specialist report (within past three years); testing: WAIS, psychological report; Woodcock-Johnson
Special Facilities for: Visual, hearing and physical impairments
College Life: The University of Wisconsin: LaCrosse is proud of its excellent advising.

UNIVERSITY OF WISCONSIN: MILWAUKEE

P.O. BOX 413, STUDENT ACCESSIBILITY CENTER
MILWAUKEE, WISCONSIN 53211
(414) 229-6239; FAX: (414) 229-2237
E-MAIL: lauriep@uwm.edu **WEB SITE: www.uwm.edu**

Name of Special Program: Learning Disabilities Program
Director: Laurie Petersen
General Information: Four-Year State University; Enrollment: 19,223; **Annual Tuition:** Residents – $6,630, Non-Residents – $16,232; **Room:** $2,200, **Board:** $3,594 and up depending on meal plan. The University of

Wisconsin: Milwaukee (UWM) is a large urban university located within blocks of Lake Michigan in an attractive residential area of Milwaukee. UWM operates on a semester basis with a three-week winter term called "UWinteri M" available to interested students. UWM is also considered a commuter campus to the nearly 10,000 students within the greater Milwaukee area. The University offers an honor program, Division I athletics, intramurals, study abroad programs, internships and many other opportunities. **Majors:** UWM offers more than 120 undergraduate majors and sub-majors, 47 master's degrees and 17 doctoral degrees. The University has 11 colleges and schools that offer both undergraduate and graduate programs: School of Allied Health Professions, School of Architecture and Urban Planning, School of the Arts, School of Business Administration, School of Education, College of Engineering and Applied Science, School of Library and Information Science, College of Letters and Science, School of Nursing, and School of Social Welfare.

Special Program: Enrollment in Special Program: 230; Cost: None. At UWM the majority of students with learning disabilities earn a degree in six years.

Staff: Learning disabilities specialists; peer tutors

Program Features: Oral and extended time testing; individual and small group tutoring sessions (referred); limited course load; basic study skills; note-taking assistance – scribes; taped texts; developmental program; faculty made aware of student's learning disability (at student's request); assistive technology; computer lab; monitoring

Entrance Requirements: Documentation of learning disability; learning disabilities specialist report; ACT untimed scores accepted; teacher evaluation; personal interview; testing: WAIS, psychological report; Woodcock-Johnson-Revised; achievement tests. Students can also apply to UWM through the Academic Opportunity Center (AOC), an alternative admission program which offers courses in basic skills and intensive advising. Students will need to take the AOC placement tests including the University's math and English and the Nelson Denny reading tests. Accommodations can be requested for the placement tests and for ADHD students who need comprehensive psychoeducational assessment.

Special Facilities for: Visual, hearing and physical impairments and other disabilities.

College Life: Learning Disabilities Program works closely with students with learning disabilities and ADHD to ensure equal access to programs and activities within the University. Students are known on a first name basis and have a strong connection to the program and the campus community.

UNIVERSITY OF WISCONSIN: OSHKOSH
800 ALGOMA BLVD.
OSHKOSH, WISCONSIN 54901-8662
(920) 424-1033; FAX: (920) 424-0858
E-MAIL: kitz@uwosh.edu
WEB SITE: www.uwosh.edu/organizations/success

Name of Special Program: Project Success
Director: William Kitz
General Information: Four-Year State University; Enrollment 11,000; **Annual Tuition:** Residents – $6,600, Non-Residents – $16,232; **Room and Board:** $3,570 per semester. A suburban campus in a small city, 80 miles from Milwaukee. Founded in 1871. **Majors:** Biology, business/management, chemistry, communications, computer/information sciences, education, fine arts, geological sciences, health sciences, languages, law, letters/literature, library/archival sciences, mathematics, music, philosophy, physical sciences, physics, protective services, psychology, public affairs, religion, social sciences, visual/performing arts.
Special Program: Enrollment in Special Program; 290; Cost: None. *Summer Program:* An eight-week Language Remedial Program includes reading, spelling, writing and algebra.
Staff: Learning disabilities specialists; peer tutors; special counselors
Program Features: Untimed private testing (Spanish classes specifically designed for dyslexic students); individual and small group tutoring sessions; academic advising for students with learning disabilities; faculty made aware of student's learning disability; total language remediation
Entrance Requirements: Documentation of learning disability; testing at University of Wisconsin: Oshkosh; personal on-campus interview and assessment; handwritten essay
Special Facilities for: Visual, hearing and physical impairments
College Life: Project Success is a unique remediation program that teaches students to have phonemic awareness and ability to execute phonemic segmentation to read and spell words rather than just an assistance program.

UNIVERSITY OF WISCONSIN: WHITEWATER
800 WEST MAIN STREET, ROSEMAN 2021
WHITEWATER, WISCONSIN 53190
(262) 472-4788; FAX: (262) 472-5210
E-MAIL: assist@uww.edu **WEB SITE: www.uww.edu**

Name of Special Program: Project ASSIST
Director: Nancy Amacher (262) 472-5239, amachern@uww.edu; *Assistant Director:* Jamie Leurquin (262) 472-4788, leurquij@uww.edu

General Information: Four-Year State University; Enrollment: 11,000; **Tuition Room and Board:** Residents – $4,920 per semester, Non-Residents – $8,657 per semester. The University of Wisconsin: Whitewater is a 400-acre campus centrally located near major cities of Madison and Milwaukee, and Chicago, Illinois. **Majors:** Teacher education, business administration, liberal arts, the arts, and pre-professional studies, nationally ranked business and education program
Special Program: Enrollment in Special Program: 225; Cost: $750–1,350 per semester, depending on the amount of one-on-one requirements. *Summer Program:* Project ASSIST offers a four-week intensive high school-to-college transition for incoming freshmen with learning disabilities. The program is a three-credit study skills course, including individual tutoring, academic advising, assessment of needs, advocacy skill instruction, strategy instruction, social activities, orientation to campus services. Cost: Residents – $1,700, Non-Residents – $2,900, includes tuition, room, board and Project Assist fee. The percentage of students with learning disabilities receiving a degree in four years is 14%, and in five or more years is 41%.
Staff: Learning disabilities specialists; peer tutors
Program Features: Oral and extended time testing; individual tutoring sessions; limited course load (first year); note-taking assistance – scribes; tape recorders; taped texts; basic study skills; academic advising for students with learning disabilities; developmental program; computer lab exclusive to students in program
Entrance Requirements: Documentation of learning disability; learning disabilities specialist report; ACT untimed scores accepted; teacher evaluation; testing: WAIS, IEP, psychological report
Special Facilities for: Visual, hearing and physical impairments

WYOMING

UNIVERSITY OF WYOMING
DISABILITY SUPPORT SERVICES
BOX 82071
LARAMIE, WYOMING 82071-3808
(307) 766-6189; FAX: (307) 766-4010
E-MAIL: udss@uwyo.edu or cfprimus@uwyo.edu
WEB SITE: www.uwyo.edu

Name of Special Program: University Disability Support Services (UDSS)
Associate Director: Chris Primus
General Information: Four-Year State University; Enrollment: 10,000; **Tuition:** Residents – $1,498.35, Non-Residents – $4,665; **Room and Board:** $3,086 annually. The university is located on a 785-acre campus in a small

town 128 miles north of Denver, Colorado. Special learning facilities include a learning resource center, art gallery, natural history museum, planetarium, radio station, television station and American Heritage Center. **Bachelor Degrees:** Agriculture, biological science, business, communications and the arts, computer and physical science, education, engineering and environmental design, health professions, social science
Special Program: Enrollment in Special Program: 75; Cost: None
Staff: Learning disabilities specialists; peer tutors
Program Features: Oral and extended time testing; individual and small group tutoring sessions; limited course load; tape recorders; taped texts; note-taking assistance – scribes; academic advising for students with learning disabilities; faculty made aware of student's learning disability; adapted computers; voice synthesizers, screen readers
Entrance Requirements: Documentation of learning disability; SAT/ACT untimed scores accepted. Report needs to include current information on educational impact of disability and services provided to date.
Special Facilities for: Visual, hearing and physical impairments
College Life: Small campus, friendly atmosphere and knowledgeable, flexible faculty.

CANADA

UNIVERSITY OF OTTAWA

85 UNIVERSITY, ROOM 339
P.O. BOX 450 STN A
OTTAWA, ONTARIO K1N-6N5
(613) 562-5976, (613) 564-8105 V/TDD; FAX: (613) 562-5159
E-MAIL: yruel@uottawa.ca **WEB SITE: www.uottawa.ca**

Name of Special Program: Center for Special Services (CSS)
Coordinator: Yolane Ruel
General Information: Four-Year Provincial University; Enrollment: 25,000; **Tuition:** Residents – $4,500 Canadian, Non-Residents – $10,000 Canadian; **Board:** $2,300. The University of Ottawa is in an urban setting. It is a world leader in research. The university is bilingual. **Bachelor Degrees**: law, arts, medicine, social sciences, engineering, sciences, graduate studies, education, health sciences, administration
Special Program: Enrollment in Special Program: 240; Cost: None. Separate admission process in both education and law faculties.
Staff: Learning disabilities specialists; tutors
Program Features: Oral and extended time testing; individual and small group tutoring sessions; limited course load (first year); tape recorders; taped texts; basic study skills; developmental program; note-taking assis-

tance – scribes; faculty made aware of student's learning disability; access to computers, reading and writing specialist
Entrance Requirements: Documentation of learning disability; learning disabilities specialist report; medical evaluation
Special Facilities for: Visual, hearing and physical impairments
Scholarships: See page 440.

Two-Year Colleges with Programs for Students with Learning Disabilities

The following two-year colleges have specific programs for students with learning disabilities.

CALIFORNIA

ALLAN HANCOCK COLLEGE

800 SOUTH COLLEGE DRIVE, LAP Bldg. I
SANTA MARIA, CALIFORNIA 93454-6399
(805) 922-6966 X3274; FAX: (805) 928-7905
WEB SITE: www.hancockcollege.edu

Name of Special Program: Learning Assistance Program
Director: Mark Malangko
General Information: Two-Year Community College; Enrollment 10,000; **Tuition:** Residents – $26 per unit, Non-Residents – $149 per unit; **Room and Board:** No college housing available. The Santa Maria Valley is located mid-way between Los Angeles and San Francisco on the central coast of California. The primary economic base of the area is farming, oil fields and Vandenberg Air Force Base. **Majors:** Accounting, administration of justice, applied design/media, architectural drafting, art, automotive technology, biology, business management, chemistry, computer business, cosmetology, dance, dental assisting, early childhood studies, electronics technology, engineering, fire technology, graphic communication, international studies, liberal arts, machine technology, medical assisting, music, nursing, physics, social sciences, welding technology
Special Program: Enrollment in Special Program: 252; Cost: None. The percentage of students with learning disabilities receiving a degree in two years is 15%, in four years is 10% and in five or more years is 3%.
Staff: Learning disabilities specialists; special counselors; high-tech specialists (faculty members)
Program Features: Oral and extended time testing; taped texts; note-taking assistance – scribes; limited course load (first year); tape recorders; individual and small group tutoring sessions; academic advising for students with learning disabilities; faculty made aware of student's learning disability (at student's request)
Entrance Requirements: Documentation of learning disability; learning disabilities specialist report; diagnostic testing at Allan Hancock College; testing: WAIS
Special Facilities for: Visual, hearing and physical impairments
College Life: Our program, and the college in general, offers very high-quality programs and services. We pay close attention to the individualized needs of our students in a mainstream setting emphasizing self-advocacy and advanced uses of technology.

ANTELOPE VALLEY COLLEGE
3041 WEST AVENUE K
LANCASTER, CALIFORNIA 93536-5426
(661) 722-6300 X6162; FAX: (661) 722-6361
E-MAIL: dgreenleaf@avc.edu **WEB SITE: www.avc.edu**

Name of Special Program: Learning Disabilities Program
Director: Louis Lucero; *Learning Disabilities Specialist:* David Greenleaf
General Information: Two-Year Community College; Enrollment: 6,290; **Tuition:** Residents – $26 per credit per semester, Non-Residents – $141 plus $26 per credit per semester; **Room and Board:** No college housing available. A suburban campus, 60 miles from Los Angeles in a high desert community. **Majors:** Allied health, business education, fine arts, family and consumer education, language arts, mathematics/science, physical education/health education/intercollegiate athletics, social sciences, technical education
Special Program: Enrollment in Special Program: 250; Cost: None
Staff: Learning disabilities specialists; peer tutors
Program Features: Oral and extended time testing; taped texts; note-taking assistance – scribes; basic study skills; tape recorders; individual and small group tutoring sessions; limited course load (first year); developmental program; faculty made aware of student's learning disability
Entrance Requirements: Documentation of learning disabilities; learning disabilities specialist report; diagnostic testing at Antelope Valley College; testing: WAIS, IEP, psychological report
Special Facilities for: Visual, hearing and physical impairments

BAKERSFIELD COLLEGE
1801 PANORAMA DRIVE
BAKERSFIELD, CALIFORNIA 93305
(661) 395-4557 or (661) 395-4334
E-MAIL: jkirst@bakersfieldcollege.edu
WEB SITE: www.bakersfieldcollege.edu

Name of Special Program: Learning Disabilities Program/Supportive Services
Learning Disabilities Coordinator: Joyce Kirst
General Information: Two-Year Community College; Enrollment: 15,000; **Tuition:** Residents – $26 per unit, Non-Residents – $167 per unit; **Room and Board:** No college housing available. Bakersfield College is located in an urban area on a 175-acre campus. **Majors:** Agribusiness/agricultural production, agricultural sciences, allied health, architecture, biology, botany, business/management, business/office, chemistry, communica-

tions, communications technologies, computer/information sciences, construction trades, crafts/design, diagnostic/treatment services, engineering technologies, environmental design, geological sciences, health sciences, home economics, industrial production, languages, law letters/literature, mathematics, mechanical/electromechanical technologies, multi/interdisciplinary studies, music, park and recreation, philosophy, physics, precision production, protective services, psychology, renewable natural resources, science technologies, social sciences, visual-performing arts, vocational home economics
Special Program: Enrollment in Special Program: 260; Cost: None
Staff: Learning disabilities specialists; peer tutors; special counselors; content tutors (faculty members for writing skills)
Program Features: Extended time testing; taped texts; note-taking assistance – scribes; basic study skills; tape recorders; individual and small group tutoring sessions; learning strategies instruction; assistive computers; spellcheckers, calculators
Entrance Requirements: Diagnostic testing at Bakersfield College or prior learning disabilities diagnostic tests
Special Facilities for: Visual, hearing and physical impairments
College Life: Bakersfield College's mission includes preparing students for transfer to four-year institutions, developing vocational and technical skills, fostering basic skills, general education knowledge, critical thinking, and an interest in lifelong learning.

BARSTOW COMMUNITY COLLEGE
2700 BARSTOW ROAD
BARSTOW, CALIFORNIA 92311
(760) 252-2411; FAX: (760) 252-1875
E-MAIL: pdedios@barstow.edu **WEB SITE: www.barstow.edu**

Name of Special Program: Disabled Students Programs and Services
Dean of Student Services: Paul R. de Dios
General Information: Two-Year Community College; Enrollment: 2,900; **Tuition:** Residents – $26 per unit, Non-Residents – $141 plus $26 per unit; **Room and Board:** No college housing available. Located 90 miles east of Los Angeles in the heart of Southern California. A community college offering Associate of Arts and Sciences degree and certificate programs in all major vocations and transfer programs to four-year colleges and universities. **Majors:** Business and vocational technology, humanities, natural science and social sciences
Special Program: Enrollment in Special Program: 80; Cost: None
Staff: Learning disabilities specialists; peer tutors; special counselors; content tutors (faculty members)

Program Features: Oral and extended time testing; individual and small group tutoring sessions; basic study skills; note-taking assistance – scribes; tape recorders; developmental program; high-tech center; faculty made aware of student's learning disability
Entrance Requirements: Documentation of learning disability; learning disabilities specialist report; medical evaluation; diagnostic testing at Barstow Community College; testing: SEC
Special Facilities for: Visual, hearing and physical impairments
Scholarships: See page 441.

BUTTE COMMUNITY COLLEGE
3536 BUTTE CAMPUS DRIVE
OROVILLE, CALIFORNIA 95965
(916) 895-2455; FAX: (916) 895-2235
E-MAIL: thorsellsu@butte.cc.ca.us **WEB SITE: www.butte.edu**

Name of Special Program: Disabled Student Programs and Services (DSP&S)
Coordinator: Richard L. Dunn; *Learning Disabilities Specialist:* Susan Thorsell
General Information: Two-Year Community College; Enrollment: 15,200; **Tuition:** Residents – $26 per unit for 6 units and fees – $175 full-time student, Non-Residents – $1,102 for 6 units and fees; **Room and Board:** No college housing available. A rural campus in a large town, 100 miles north of Sacramento. **Majors:** Agribusiness/agricultural production, agricultural sciences, allied health, business/management, business/office, civil technologies, communications, crafts/design, diagnostic/treatment services, education, engineering technologies, environmental control technologies, fine arts, health sciences, home economics, industrial production, marketing/distribution, mathematics, mechanical/electromechanical technologies, multi/interdisciplinary studies, parks and recreation, physical sciences, precision production, protective services, renewable natural resources, social sciences, visual/performing arts, vocational home economics, tourism and travel, computer-assisted drafting (CAD), police academy, fire science academy, early childhood education, CNA, LVN, RN
Special Program: Enrollment in Special Program: 250; Cost: None
Staff: Learning disabilities specialists; peer tutors; special counselors
Program Features: Oral and extended time testing; basic study skills; tape recorders; spellcheckers; individual and small group tutoring sessions; essay test scribes; developmental program; faculty made aware of student's learning disability (at student's request); computer instructional lab; Kurzweil personal readers and Kurzweil 3000 for reading/taping textbooks.

Entrance Requirements: Documentation of learning disability; learning disabilities specialist report; diagnostic testing at Butte Community College; testing: WAIS, Woodcock-Johnson; California Community College Eligibility Assessment
Special Facilities for: Visual, hearing and physical impairments
Scholarships: See page 441.

CABRILLO COLLEGE
6500 SOQUEL DRIVE
APTOS, CALIFORNIA 95003
(831) 479-6220 X6563
E-MAIL: saderouc@cabrillo.edu **WEB SITE: www.cabrillo.edu**

Name of Special Program: Learning Skills Program
Learning Disabilities Specialist: Sara DeRouchey
General Information: Two-Year Community College; Enrollment: 7,800; **Tuition:** Residents – $234 per 12 units, Non-Residents – $2,142 per 12 units, International Students – $2,142 per 12 units; **Room and Board:** No college housing available. Located on hills overlooking Monterey Bay in Aptos, small coastal community situated near the center of Santa Cruz County. A spectacular coastline, accessible beaches and wooded mountains, all within a short distance of San Francisco and San Jose, have made Santa Cruz County an important vacation and recreation area. Cabrillo provides two-year academic programs for students planning to transfer to four-year colleges or universities and one- and two-year vocational programs which prepare students for employment upon leaving the college. **Degrees and Programs:** Associate in Science, Associate in Arts. Occupational programs are offered. Cabrillo offers a study-travel program which includes a semester abroad and short-term study-travel programs taught off-campus within a specific environment.
Special Program: Enrollment in Special Program: 450; Cost: None
Staff: Learning disabilities specialists; special counselors
Program Features: Extended time testing; taped texts; note-taking assistance – scribes; tape recorders; small group tutoring sessions; limited course load; adaptive word processing; study skills; computer lab; faculty made aware of student's learning disability
Entrance Requirements: Documentation of learning disability or diagnostic testing at Cabrillo College; California Community College Eligibility Assessment

CAÑADA COLLEGE
4200 FARM HILL BLVD.
REDWOOD CITY, CALIFORNIA 94116
(650) 306-3259, (650) 306-3161 TDD; FAX: (650) 306-3185
E-MAIL: blokr@smccd.net WEB SITE: www.canadacollege.net

Name of Special Program: Disabled Students Programs and Services
Director: Regina Blok
General Information: Two-Year Community College; Enrollment: 5,273; **Tuition:** Residents – $26 per unit, Non-Residents – $170 per unit; **Room and Board:** No college housing available. A suburban campus in a small city, 20 miles south of San Francisco. **Majors:** Allied health, architecture, biology, botany, business/management, business/office, chemistry, computer/information sciences, diagnostic/treatment services, education, engineering, engineering technologies, environmental design, fine arts, library/archival sciences, life sciences, marketing/distribution, mathematics, multi/interdisciplinary studies, music, parks and recreation, philosophy, physical sciences, physics, protective services, psychology, public affairs, science technologies, social sciences, visual/performing arts, vocational home economics
Special Program: Enrollment in Special Program: 75; Cost: None
Staff: Learning disabilities specialists; content tutors (faculty members)
Program Features: Oral and extended time testing, taped texts; basic study skills; small group tutoring sessions; note-taking assistance – scribes; faculty made aware of student's learning disability; E-Text; Jaws; Dragon Dictate
Entrance Requirements: Learning disabled evaluation to meet California Community College standards
Special Facilities for: Visual, hearing and physical impairments

CERRITOS COLLEGE
11110 ALONDRA BLVD.
NORWALK, CALIFORNIA 90650-6203
(310) 860-2451 X2335
E-MAIL: aspetrino@cerritos.edu WEB SITE: www.cerritos.edu

Name of Special Program: Instructional Support Center
Director: Albert A. Spetrino, Jr.
General Information: Two-Year Community College; Enrollment: 21,000; **Tuition:** Residents – $26 per unit, Non-Residents – $175 per unit, International Students – $189 per unit; **Room and Board:** No college housing available. A suburban campus in a small city, 15 miles east of Los Angeles. Founded in 1955. **Majors:** Agricultural sciences, allied health,

architecture, biology, botany, business/management, business/office, chemistry, communications, computer/information sciences, education, engineering technologies, environmental design, ethnic studies, geological sciences, health sciences, home economics, industrial production, languages, law, letters/literature, marketing/distribution, mathematics, mechanical/electromechanical technologies, mechanics/repairers, multi/interdisciplinary studies, music, parks and recreation, philosophy, physics, precision production, protective services, psychology, rehabilitation services, renewable natural resources, social sciences, visual performing arts, vocational home economics, zoology
Special Program: Enrollment in Special Program: 180; Cost: None
Staff: Learning disabilities specialists; content tutors (faculty members); peer tutors; special counselors
Program Features: Oral and extended time testing; taped texts; note-taking assistance – scribes; basic study skills (non-credit); tape recorders; individual and small group tutoring sessions; limited course load (first year); basic classes in reading, mathematics, English, spelling, writing; faculty made aware of student's learning disability (at student's request); developmental program
Entrance Requirements: Documentation of learning disability; California Community College Eligibility Assessment; learning disabilities specialist report; diagnostic testing at Cerritos College; SEC; teacher evaluation; ability to mainstream in reasonable time frame
Special Facilities for: Visual, hearing and physical impairments

CHAFFEY COMMUNITY COLLEGE
5885 HAVEN AVENUE
RANCHO CUCAMONGA, CALIFORNIA 91737
(909) 941-2336
WEB SITE: www.chaffey.edu

Name of Special Program: Learning Resource Program
Coordinator: Will Carrick
General Information: Two-Year Community College; Enrollment: 14,000; **Tuition:** Residents – $26 per unit, Non-Residents – $155 per unit; **Room and Board:** No college housing available. A suburban campus in a small city, 50 miles east of Los Angeles. Founded in 1883. **Majors:** Allied health, biology, business/management, business/office, chemistry, communications, computer/information sciences, crafts/design, diagnostic/treatment services, education, engineering and technologies, environmental design, fine arts, geological sciences, health sciences, home economics, languages, law, letters/literature, marketing/distribution, mathematics, mechanical/electromechanical technologies, mechanics/repairers, multi/interdisciplinary

studies, music, philosophy, physics, precision production, protective services, psychology, public affairs, religion, science technologies, social sciences, visual/performing arts, vocational home economics, zoology
Special Program: Enrollment in Special Program: 400; Cost: None
Staff: Learning disabilities specialists; content tutors (faculty member); special counselors
Program Features: Oral and extended time testing; individual and small group tutoring sessions; limited course load (first year); basic study skills; note-taking assistance – scribes; developmental program; faculty made aware of student's learning disability; basic skill courses in reading, math, spelling and language
Entrance Requirements: Documentation of learning disability according to California Community College Eligibility Assessment; testing: SEC
Special Facilities for: Visual, hearing and physical impairments

CITRUS COLLEGE
1000 WEST FOOTHILL BLVD.
GLENDORA, CALIFORNIA 91740-1899
626) 963-5323 V/TDD
WEB SITE: www.citruscollege.edu

Name of Special Program: Disabled Student Programs and Services (DSP&S)
Counselor: Dr. Stephanie Lee
General Information: Two-Year Community College; Enrollment: 7,350; **Tuition:** Residents – $26 per unit, Non-Residents – $143 plus $26 per unit, International – $169 plus $26 per unit; **Room and Board:** No college housing available. A suburban campus in a large town, 39 miles from Los Angeles. Founded in 1915. **Majors:** Allied health, biology, botany, business/management, business/office, chemistry, civil technologies, communications, computer/information sciences, engineering and technologies, fine arts, health sciences, languages, law, letters/literature, library/archival sciences, life sciences, mathematics, mechanical/electromechanical technologies, mechanics/repairers, multi/interdisciplinary studies, music, physical sciences, physics, precision production, protective services, psychology, public affairs, social sciences, zoology
Special Program: Enrollment in Special Program: 200; Cost: None
Staff: Learning disabilities specialist; peer tutors; special counselors
Program Features: Oral and extended time testing; note-taking assistance – scribes; individual and small group tutoring sessions; limited course load; tape recorders; taped texts; basic study skills; developmental program; faculty made aware of student's learning disability; computer technology

Entrance Requirements: Documentation of learning disability
Special Facilities for: Visual, hearing and physical impairments

COLLEGE OF ALAMEDA
555 ATLANTIC AVENUE
ALAMEDA, CALIFORNIA 94501
(510) 748-2388, 748-2328
WEB SITE: www.alameda.peralta.edu

Name of Special Program: Learning Disabilities Program
Director: Judy Merrill
General Information: Two-Year Community College; Enrollment: 5,088; **Tuition**: Residents – $26 per unit, Non-Residents – $145 per unit; **Room and Board:** No college housing available. College of Alameda is situated on a 62-acre campus with easy access to San Francisco in a small city adjacent to Oakland. **Degrees:** Terminal Associates, Transfer Associates, and Certificates
Special Program: Enrollment in Special Program: 121; Cost: None
Staff: Learning disabilities specialists; special counselors
Program Features: Oral and extended time testing; individual tutoring sessions; limited course load (first year); basic study skills; note-taking assistance – scribes; tape recorders; taped texts; faculty made aware of student's learning disability; adapted computer learning center; computer-assisted instruction
Entrance Requirements: Documentation of learning disability (if available); testing: WAIS-R (if available); Woodcock-Johnson-R psychoeducational battery, Parts I and II; California Community College Eligibility Assessment
Special Facilities for: Visual, hearing and physical impairments

COLLEGE OF SAN MATEO
1700 WEST HILLSDALE BLVD.
SAN MATEO, CALIFORNIA 94402-3784
(650) 574-6433; FAX: (650) 358-6803
E-MAIL: paparelli@smccd.net
WEB SITE: www.collegeofsanmateo.edu

Name of Special Program: Assessment Center / Special Programs and Services
Learning Disability Specialist: Marie Paparelli
General Information: Two-Year Community College; Enrollment: 10,750; **Tuition:** Residents – $26 per unit, Non-Residents – $157 per unit; **Room and Board:** No college housing available. A suburban campus situated on 153 acres in the San Mateo Hills in a small city, 15 miles south of San Francisco.

Majors: Administration of justice, aeronautics, banking and finance, building inspection, business operations/management, office administration, medical assisting, medical transcription, business information processing, computer/information science, cosmetologist, drafting technology, electronics technology, fire science, health care, horticulture, interior design, machine tool technology, merchandising, nursing, nutrition and foods, real estate, technical art/graphics, transportation, welding technology
Special Program: Enrollment in Special Program: 130; Cost: None
Staff: Learning disabilities specialists; peer tutors; special counselors
Program Features: Oral and extended time testing; individual and small group tutoring sessions; basic study skills; note-taking assistance – scribes; tape recorders; taped texts; faculty made aware of student's learning disability; high-tech center for computer adaptive assistance – word processing programs
Entrance Requirements: Documentation of learning disability; learning disabilities specialist report; diagnostic testing at College of San Mateo; testing: WAIS, IEP, psychological report. All learning disability services are provided when California Community College Eligibility Assessment is applied.
Special Facilities for: Visual, hearing and physical impairments
Scholarships: See page 441.

COLLEGE OF THE CANYONS
26455 ROCKWELL CANYON ROAD
SANTA CLARITA, CALIFORNIA 91355-1899
(661) 362-3341
WEB SITE: www.canyons.edu

Name of Special Program: Disabled Student Programs and Services
Director: Dr. Jane A. Feuerhelm
General Information: Two-Year Community College; Enrollment: 7,200; **Tuition:** Residents – $26 per unit, Non-Residents – $157 per unit; **Room and Board:** No college housing available. A suburban campus in a large town, 40 miles north of Los Angeles. **Majors:** Allied health, biology, business/management, business/office, communications, computer/information sciences, education, engineering technologies, geological sciences, health sciences, industrial production, languages, letters/literature, mathematics, mechanical/electromechanical technologies, multi/interdisciplinary studies, music, physical sciences, precision production, protective services, psychology, science technologies, social sciences, visual/performing arts, vocational home economics
Staff: Learning disabilities specialists; content tutors (faculty members); peer tutors, special counselors; high-tech computer-assisted instruction specialist

Program Features: Extended time testing; small group tutoring sessions; basic study skills; note-taking assistance – scribes; tape recorders; taped texts; faculty made aware of student's learning disability; adaptive computer technology
Entrance Requirements: Documentation of learning disability; learning disabilities specialist report; eligibility testing at College of the Canyons, including cognitive and achievement assessment
Scholarships: See page 442.

COLLEGE OF THE DESERT
43-500 MONTEREY AVENUE
PALM DESERT, CALIFORNIA 92260
(760) 773-2534; FAX: (760) 776-0198
E-MAIL: moneill@collegeofthedesert.edu
WEB SITE: www.collegeofthedesert.edu

Name of Special Program: Disabled Student Programs and Services (DSP&S)
Director: Michael O'Neill
General Information: Two-Year Community College; Enrollment: 4,510; **Tuition:** Residents – $26.25 per unit, Non-Residents – $167.25 per unit, International Students – $182.25 per unit. **Room and Board:** No college housing available. The College of the Desert campus consists of nine buildings on a 160-acre site at Monterey Avenue and Fred Waring Drive in Palm Desert. The College is located in the Coachella Valley near Palm Springs (10 miles), 90 miles from Los Angeles and 120 miles from San Diego, in a suburban/rural area, a major golf area with over 120 golf courses and a winter resort. **Majors:** Administration of justice, agriculture, air conditioning/HVAC, architecture/environmental design, art, automotive technology, business and hospitality industries, communication, culinary arts, developmental education (GED), digital design and production, drafting/CAD, fire technology, foreign language, health, physical education and recreation, health sciences, human services, liberal arts, liberal studies, mathematics, music, nutrition care, dietetic technician, science, biological, chemical and physical, social science, theatre arts
Special Program: Enrollment in special program: 125; Cost: None. The percentage of students with learning disabilities receiving a degree in two years is 40%.
Staff: Learning disabilities specialists; peer tutors; special counselors
Program Features: Oral and extended time testing; individual and small group tutoring sessions; basic study skills; note-taking assistance – scribes; tape recorders; taped texts; academic advising for students with learning

disabilities; faculty made aware of student's learning disability; E-text
Entrance Requirements: Documentation of learning disability; learning disabilities specialist report; diagnostic testing at College of the Desert
Special Facilities for: Visual, hearing and physical impairments
College Life: The primary mission of the College of the Desert is to provide a comprehensive, student-centered community college education and to prepare students for transfer programs that assure their access to upper-division education at public and private universities.

COLLEGE OF THE REDWOODS
7351 TOMPKINS HILL ROAD
EUREKA, CALIFORNIA 95501
(707) 445-6812
WEB SITE: www.redwoods.cc.ca.us

Name of Special Program: Disabled Student Programs and Services (DSP&S)
Director: Sonja Roseth
General Information: Two-Year Community College; Enrollment: 4,400; **Tuition:** Residents – $26 per unit, Non-Residents – $133 plus $26 per unit per semester; **Room and Board:** No college housing available. College of the Redwoods is located on a 323-acre campus just south of the city of Eureka, and on a second campus on the Mendocino Coast in Fort Bragg. **Degrees:** Associate in Arts, Associate in Arts in Transfer Studies, Associate in Science, Certificates of Achievement and Certificates of Completion
Special Program: Enrollment in Special Program: 100; Cost: None
Staff: Learning disabilities specialists; content tutors (faculty members); special counselors; adapted computer technology specialist; acquired brain injuries specialist
Program Features: Oral and extended time testing; individual and small group tutoring sessions; note-taking assistance – scribes; tape recorders; taped texts; basic study skills; faculty made aware of student's learning disability; high-tech center for disabled – remedial computer programs; word processing classes
Entrance Requirements: Documentation of learning disability; diagnostic testing at College of the Redwoods; testing: Woodcock-Johnson and WAIS-R raw scores (within the last three years)
Special Facilities for: Visual, hearing, physical impairments and acquired brain injuries

COLLEGE OF THE SEQUOIAS
915 SOUTH MOONEY BLVD.
VISALIA, CALIFORNIA 93277
(559) 730-3805; FAX: (559) 730-3803
E-MAIL: davidm@cos.edu **WEB SITE: www.cos.edu**

Name of Special Program: Disability Resource Center
Director: David J. Maciel
General Information: Two-Year Community College; Enrollment: 11,169; **Tuition:** Residents – $26 per unit, Non-Residents – $163 per unit; **Room and Board:** Off-campus housing only. A suburban campus in a small city, 40 miles south of Fresno, one hour's drive from the mountains on the east, two hours from the ocean on the west. It is known as the Gateway to the Sequoias. **Majors:** Agribusiness/agricultural production, agricultural sciences, allied health, architecture, biology, business/management, business/office, chemistry, communications, communications technologies, construction trades, education, engineering technologies, environmental control technologies, health sciences, home economics, industrial production, languages, law, marketing/distribution, mathematics, mechanical/electromechanical technologies, mechanics/repairers, multi/interdisciplinary studies, music, parks and recreation, physical sciences, precision production, protective services, public affairs, science technologies, social sciences
Special Program: Enrollment in Special Program: 800; Cost: None. The percentage of students with learning disabilities receiving degrees in two years is 10%, four years is 75%, and in five or more years is 15%.
Staff: Learning disabilities specialists; peer tutors; special counselors
Program Features: Oral and extended time testing; individual and small group tutoring sessions; limited course load; academic advising for students with learning disabilities, note-taking assistance – scribes; tape recorders; taped texts; basic study skills; faculty made aware of student's learning disability
Entrance Requirements: Documentation of learning disability; diagnostic testing at College of the Sequoias; testing: WAIS, IEP, Woodcock-Johnson; high school grades or equivalency - specific criteria for eligibility
Special Facilities for: Visual, hearing and physical impairments

COLLEGE OF THE SISKIYOUS
800 COLLEGE AVENUE
WEED, CALIFORNIA 96094
(530) 938-5884; FAX: (530) 938-5227
E-MAIL: cordoba@siskiyous.edu **WEB SITE: www.siskiyous.edu**

Name of Special Program: Learning Disabilities Program
Director: Marlys Cordoba
General Information: Two-Year Community College; Enrollment: 2,000; **Tuition:** Residents – $26 per unit; Non-Residents – $200 per unit; **Room and Board:** $2,196 per semester for 7-day food plan; $1,986 per semester for 5-day food plan. Founded in 1957, a rural campus, 270 miles north of Sacramento, located at the base of 14,000 foot Mount Shasta and 40 miles south of the Oregon border on Interstate 5. **Majors:** Agricultural sciences, allied health, biology, business/management/office, communications, computer/information sciences, education, engineering and technologies, fine arts, health sciences, home economics, languages, law, letters/literature, mathematics, mechanical/electromechanical technologies, mechanics/repairers, multi/interdisciplinary studies, music, physical sciences, precision production, protective services, renewable natural resources, science technologies, social sciences, visual/performing arts
Special Program: Enrollment in Special Program: 105; Cost: None
Staff: Learning disabilities specialists; peer tutors; special counselors
Program Features: Oral and extended time testing; individual and small group tutoring sessions; limited course load (first year); academic advising for students with learning disabilities; note-taking assistance – scribes; taped texts; tape recorders; basic study skills; developmental program; faculty made aware of student's learning disability; high-tech lab
Entrance Requirements: Diagnostic testing at College of the Siskiyous; testing: WAIS, IEP, Woodcock Johnson III
Special Facilities for: Visual, hearing and physical impairments
College Life: We are a small college in a small community. Classes are small with personal teacher interaction.

COLUMBIA COLLEGE
11600 COLUMBIA COLLEGE DRIVE
SONORA, CALIFORNIA 95370-8582
(209) 588-5130; FAX: (209) 588-5330
E-MAIL: cordovam@yosemite.cc.ca.us
WEB SITE: www.columbia.yosemite.edu

Name of Special Program: Disabled Student Programs and Services
Director: Mario Cordova, Ph.D.

General Information: Two-Year Community College; Enrollment: 3,300; **Tuition:** Residents – $26 per unit, Non-Residents – $186 per unit; **Room and Board:** No college housing available. Located in the foothills of the Sierra Nevada Mountains, approximately 150 miles east of San Francisco. The campus is in a rural setting, surrounded by oaks and evergreens, three miles from the historical state park of Columbia and seven miles from the gold town of Sonora. A semester campus offering classes for transfer to the four-year schools, vocational degrees and certificate programs. **Majors:** Fine arts, health and physical education, language/arts, liberal studies, mathematics, music, social science, automotive technology, business, child development, computer science, fire technology, forestry technology, hospitality management, natural resources, office occupations, science
Special Program: Enrollment in Special Program: 79; Cost: None
Staff: Learning disabilities specialist; peer tutors; special counselor; content tutors (faculty members)
Program Features: Oral and extended time testing; note-taking assistance – scribes; basic study skills; tape recorders; taped texts; small group tutoring sessions; limited course load (first year); faculty made aware of student's learning disability; high-tech equipment
Entrance Requirements: Documentation of learning disability (helpful); learning disabilities specialist report (helpful); diagnostic testing at Columbia College; medical evaluation (ADD); testing: WAIS, Woodcock-Johnson-R
Special Facilities for: Visual, hearing and physical impairments
Scholarships: See page 442.

CONTRA COSTA COMMUNITY COLLEGE

2600 MISSION BELL DRIVE
SAN PABLO, CALIFORNIA 94806
(510) 235-7800 X7220
WEB SITE: www.contracosta.cc.ca.us

Name of Special Program: Disabled Students Programs and Services
***Learning Disability Specialist*:** Alissa Scanlin
General Information: Two-Year Community College; Enrollment: 4,383; **Tuition:** Residents – $26 per unit, Non-Residents – $157 per unit, International Students – $164 per unit; **Room and Board:** No college housing available. An urban campus in a large town, 20 miles northeast of San Francisco and eight miles from University of California: Berkeley. **Majors:** Art, architecture, biological sciences, administration of justice, business, culinary arts, dental assistant, geography, history, liberal studies, math, English, nursing, automotives, electronics, physical education, welding,

early childhood education, psychology, sociology, computer science, office information, appliance repair, Hispanic studies, Spanish, general studies – transfer, architecture, engineering, biotechnology
Special Program: Enrollment in Special Program: 400-600; Cost: None
Staff: Learning disabilities specialists; peer tutors; special counselors; content tutors (faculty members); high-tech specialist
Program Features: Oral and extended time testing; classes: spelling, math, writing, reading, computer technology; basic study skills; note-taking assistance – scribes; tape recorders; taped texts; developmental program; faculty made aware of student's learning disability
Entrance Requirements: Documentation of learning disability; learning disabilities specialist report; testing: WAIS, IEP; medical evaluation; California Community College Eligibility Assessment
Special Facilities for: Visual, hearing and physical impairments

CRAFTON HILLS COLLEGE
11711 SAND CANYON ROAD
YUCAIPA, CALIFORNIA 92399
(909) 389-3578; FAX: (909) 794-3684
WEB SITE: www.craftonhills.edu

Name of Special Program: Disabled Students Services
General Information: Two-Year Community College; Enrollment: 3,000; **Tuition:** Residents – $26 per unit, Non-Residents – $177 per unit; **Room and Board:** No college housing available. A rural/suburban campus 50 miles from Los Angeles in the foothills of the San Bernadino Mountains. Also 50 miles from Palm Springs and the Pacific Ocean. Part of the San Bernadino Community College District. Boasts of skiing and water sports. **Majors:** Allied health, business management, business/office, child development, communications technologies, computer/information sciences, emergency medical/paramedics, fine arts, fire science, marketing/distribution, multi/interdisciplinary studies, music, protective services, science technologies, visual/performing arts
Special Program: Enrollment in Special Program: 100; Cost: None
Staff: Learning disabilities specialists; peer tutors; special counselors; content tutors
Program Features: Oral and extended time testing; taped texts; note-taking assistance – scribes; tape recorders; basic study skills; individual and small group tutoring sessions; limited course load (first year); developmental program; academic advising for students with learning disabilities; faculty made aware of student's learning disability
Entrance Requirements: Testing provided at Crafton Hills College; prior

assessment information used if it includes WAIS-R, Woodcock-Johnson psychoeducational battery; must meet California Community College Eligibility Assessment requirements for learning disabilities services
Special Facilities for: Visual, hearing and physical impairments

CUESTA COLLEGE
HIGHWAY 1, P.O. BOX 8106
SAN LUIS OBISPO, CALIFORNIA 93403-8106
(805) 546-3100 X3148; FAX: (805) 546-3930
E-MAIL: pschwab@cuesta.edu **WEB SITE: www.cuesta.edu**

Name of Special Program: Disabled Students Programs and Services
Director: Patrick Schwab, Ed.D.
General Information: Two-Year Community College; Enrollment: 7,000; **Tuition:** Residents – $26 per unit, Non-Residents – $157 per unit; **Room and Board:** No college housing available. Cuesta College is located in the Chorro Valley between the cities of San Luis Obispo and Morro Bay on State Highway 1. The College has a permanent campus on 150 district-owned acres, leased facilities on adjacent California National Guard property and a 75-acre field campus. **Majors:** Biological sciences, business education, engineering and technology, fine arts, human development, language arts, nursing and allied health, occupational education courses, physical education, physical science / mathematics
Special Program: Enrollment in Special Program: 585; Cost: None
Staff: Learning disabilities specialists; peer tutors; special counselors; adapted technology specialists
Program Features: Oral and extended time testing; taped texts; note-taking assistance – scribes; tape recorders; basic study skills; individual and small group tutoring sessions; limited course load (first year available); developmental program; faculty made aware of student's learning disability; Kurzweil readers, computers, personal and career counseling; high-tech center
Entrance Requirements: Meet entrance requirements to college; documentation of learning disability; 18 years or older for learning disability program
Special Facilities for: Visual, hearing and physical impairments

CUYAMACA COLLEGE
900 RANCHO SAN DIEGO PARKWAY
EL CAJON, CALIFORNIA 92019-4304
(619) 660-4386, (619) 660-4239 TTY; FAX: (619) 660-4399
E-MAIL: poppy.bush@gcccd.net WEB SITE: www.cuyamaca.edu

Name of Special Program: Disabled Student Programs and Services (DSP&S)
Student Services Specialist: Poppy Bush (619) 660-4533
General Information: Two-Year Community College; Enrollment 4,799; **Tuition:** Residents – $26 per unit, Non-Residents – $157 per unit; **Room and Board:** No college housing available. A suburban campus in a suburban area 18 miles east of San Diego. Assets include beautiful weather and sunny beaches. **Majors:** Accounting, art, automotive technology, biological sciences, business, chemistry, child development, computer information systems, drafting technology, elementary education, engineering, English, entrepreneurship, environmental technology, graphic design, history, liberal arts, management, ornamental horticulture, paralegal studies, physical science, physics, real estate, speech communication, supervision, surveying
Special Program: Enrollment in Special Program: 175; Cost: None. *Summer Program:* The summer learning disability program includes educational assessment to determine eligibility for services and tutoring in basic skills.
Staff: Learning disabilities specialists; peer tutors; special counselors
Program Features: Oral and extended time testing; taped texts; note-taking assistance – scribes; tape recorders; individual and small group tutoring sessions; basic study skills; faculty made aware of student's learning disability; specialized reading course; DSP&S high-tech center
Entrance Requirements: Documentation of learning disability; learning disabilities specialist report; medical evaluation; diagnostic testing at Cuyamaca College; testing: WAIS-R or Woodcock-Johnson-R, IEP
Special Facilities for: Visual, hearing and physical impairments
College Life: Cuyamaca College is attractive to students with learning disabilities because of its suburban location and size. Our relatively small size creates an ease of access to our department. In addition, there is a sense of camaraderie between the faculty, staff and students which makes for a less stressful learning atmosphere.

CYPRESS COLLEGE — ROOSEVELT CENTER
9200 VALLEY VIEW
CYPRESS, CALIFORNIA 90630-5897
(714) 484-7104 X104; FAX: (714) 826-4042
WEB SITE: www.cypresscollege.edu

Name of Special Program: Disabled Student Programs and Services
Director: Kimberly Bartlett, Ph.D.
General Information: Two-Year Community College; Enrollment: 15,000; **Tuition:** Residents – $18 per unit, Non-Residents – $134 plus $18 per unit, International Students – $154 plus $18 per unit; **Room and Board:** No college housing available. An urban campus in a small city, 30 miles from Los Angeles. Founded in 1966. **Majors:** Allied health, area studies, biology, business/management, business/office, chemistry, communications and technologies, computer/information sciences, crafts/design, diagnostic/treatment services, education, engineering and technologies, fine arts, geological sciences, health sciences, languages, law, letters/literature, marketing/distribution, mathematics, mechanical/electromechanical technologies, mechanics/repairers, multi/interdisciplinary studies, music, parks and recreation, philosophy, physics, psychology, public affairs, rehabilitation services, social sciences, transportation, visual/performing arts, mortuary science
Special Program: Enrollment in Special Program: 125; Cost: Tuition cost for 1/2 unit of course credit
Staff: Learning disabilities specialists; peer tutors; special counselors
Program Features: Oral and extended time testing; individual and small group tutoring sessions; tape recorders; taped texts; basic study skills; note-taking assistance – scribes; faculty made aware of student's learning disability (at student's request/with signed release only); adapted computer technology
Entrance Requirements: Documentation of learning disability; learning disabilities specialist report; medical evaluation (for verification of severe head trauma/acquired brain injury); diagnostic testing at Cypress College; testing: WAIS-R, Woodcock-Johnson-R, WRAT-R, SEC
Special Facilities for: Visual, hearing and physical impairments
Scholarships: See page 442.

DE ANZA COLLEGE
21250 STEVENS CREEK BLVD.
CUPERTINO, CALIFORNIA 95014
(408) 864-5678; FAX: (408) 864-5492
E-MAIL: waathiqpauline@deanza.edu
WEB SITE: www.deanza.edu

Name of Special Program: Educational Diagnostic Center
Director: Pauline Waathiq
General Information: Two-Year Community College; Enrollment: 22,770; **Tuition:** Residents – $72 per unit, Non-Residents – approximately $110 per unit; **Room and Board:** No college housing available. De Anza College is located on a 112-acre campus in the heart of the Silicon Valley, about 15 miles north of San Jose. De Anza, through its distinctive architecture, harmonizes with the surrounding community, creating a natural, restful campus atmosphere conducive to study. The buildings are a blending of Spanish and modern architecture with adobe-like walls and red tile roofs. Architectural accent points are expressed in buildings such as Flint Center (a 2,570-seat auditorium), an Olympic aquatics complex, a 5,000-seat Outdoor Events Area, the 200-seat Minolta Planetarium and three-story Advanced Technology Center. **Majors:** Accounting, administration of justice, art, automotive technician / technology, business administration / management, child development, computer information systems, electronic publishing, engineering / environmental / fabrication technology, film / television, intercultural studies, liberal arts, manufacturing / design technology, marketing / materials management, medical / therapist assistant, music, nursing, paralegal studies, photography, physical education, purchasing, speech / technical communications
Special Program: Enrollment in Special Program: 500; Cost: None
Staff: Learning disabilities specialists; content tutors (faculty members); special counselors
Program Features: Oral and extended time testing; small group tutoring sessions; academic advising for students with learning disabilities; tape recorders; basic study skills; developmental program; faculty made aware of student's learning disability; special high-tech lab with adaptive equipment such as voice command
Entrance Requirements: Documentation of learning disability or learning disabilities specialist report or diagnostic testing at De Anza College; medical evaluation; testing: WAIS III
Special Facilities for: Visual, hearing and physical impairments
College Life: The college offers variety in curriculum as well as life experiences. It is a bustling campus with interesting activities offered daily.
Scholarships: See page 442.

EVERGREEN VALLEY COLLEGE
3095 YERBA BUENA ROAD
SAN JOSE, CALIFORNIA 95135
(408) 274-7900, (408) 238-8722 TDD
E-MAIL: bonnie.clark@evc.edu **WEB SITE: www.evc.edu**

Name of Special Program: Disabled Student Programs
Learning Disabilities Specialist: Bonnie Clark
General Information: Two-Year Community College; Enrollment: 6,000; **Tuition:** Residents – $26 per unit, Non-Residents – $177 per unit; **Room and Board:** No college housing available. Located in the southeast corner of San Jose in a suburban area which was once surrounded by cherry / apricot orchards. **Academic and Vocational Programs:** The college offers the first two years of a transfer curriculum to four-year colleges and universities. The college also offers vocational / technical certificates and degrees in auto technology, computer-aided drafting design and design, business information systems, computer information systems, administration of justice, legal assistance, nursing, and engineering technology, legal assistant, and accounting
Special Program: Enrollment in Special Program: 75; Cost: None
Staff: Learning disabilities specialists; special counselors
Program Features: Oral and extended time testing; individual and small group tutoring sessions; tape recorders; taped texts; limited course load (first year); basic study skills; note-taking assistance – scribes; developmental program; faculty made aware of student's learning disability (at student's request); learning strategies
Entrance Requirements: Documentation of learning disability; learning disabilities specialist report; diagnostic testing at Evergreen Valley College
Special Facilities for: Visual, hearing and physical impairments

FEATHER RIVER COLLEGE
570 GOLDEN EAGLE AVENUE
QUINCY, CALIFORNIA 95971
(530) 283-0202 X247; FAX: (530) 283-3757
E-MAIL: trose-boehme@frc.edu **WEB SITE: www.frc.edu**

Name of Special Program: Disabled Student Programs and Services (DSPS), Workability III
Coordinator DSPS: Terrie Rose-Boehme; *Sr. Program Specialist:* Karen Paiva; *Educational Psychologist:* Larry Holcomb, Ed.D.
General Information: Two-Year Community College; Enrollment: 500-1,000; **Tuition:** Residents – $26 per unit, Non-Residents – $180 per unit (3.5 or more units); **Room and Board:** College apartments available. Located in

Quincy approximately 100 miles north of Reno, Nevada. A rural isolated campus in a beautiful setting. **Academic and Vocational Programs:** The semester system at Feather River offers unique programs such as Watershed Management, Pack Station Management and Recreation Leadership. The Forestry Program offers a unique opportunity to use what is learned in the classroom in the 'lab' of the surrounding national forests. The college itself is a wildlife preserve including a virgin forest and the remains of an Indian settlement.
Special Program: Enrollment in Special Program: 75–100; Cost: None
Staff: Learning disabilities specialists; peer tutors; Workability Program specialists; special counselors; instructional aides
Program Features: Oral and extended time testing; individual tutoring sessions; academic advising for students with learning disabilities; note-taking assistance – scribes; taped texts; tape recorders; faculty made aware of student's learning disability (at student's request); high-tech center / instructional media lab; Learning Skills Program provides instruction in basic academic and study skills, Workability Program
Entrance Requirements: Documentation of learning disability; diagnostic testing at Feather River Community College; teacher evaluation; testing: IEP, psychological report or Department of Rehabilitation document
College Life: Beautiful rural setting where students can get individualized help from faculty and staff

FOOTHILL COLLEGE

12345 EL MONTE ROAD
LOS ALTOS HILLS, CALIFORNIA 94022-4599
(650) 949-7038; FAX: (415) 941-3767
E-MAIL: DobbinsMargo@foothill.edu
WEB SITE: www.foothill.edu

Name of Special Program: Student Tutorial Evaluation Program (STEP)
Director: Margo Dobbins
General Information: Two-Year State College; Enrollment: 13,800; **Tuition:** Residents – $17 per unit, Non-Residents – $118 per unit, International Students – $129 per unit; **Room and Board:** No college housing available. A suburban campus in a small city, approximately 35 miles south of San Francisco, and 15 miles north of San Jose. Founded in 1958. **Majors:** Accounting, anthropology, art, aviation technology, biological sciences, business international studies, chemistry, child development, classics, communications arts and new media careers, computer / information sciences, creative writing, dramas, economics, engineering, English, geography, geology, German, history, individual studies, Japanese, liberal arts,

linguistics, mathematics, multicultural studies, music, ornamental horticulture, philosophy, physical education, physics, political science, psychology, pre-law, radio broadcasting, sociology, Spanish, speech-communication, theater technology, women's studies
Special Program: Enrollment in Special Program: 115; Cost: None
Staff: Learning disabilities specialists; peer tutors; special counselors
Program Features: Oral and extended time testing; individual and small group tutoring sessions; note-taking assistance – scribes; tape recorders; basic study skills; academic advising for students with learning disabilities; faculty made aware of student's learning disability
Entrance Requirements: Documentation of learning disability; diagnostic testing at Foothill College required by California Chancellor's Office
Special Facilities for: Visual, hearing and physical impairments

GAVILAN COLLEGE
5055 SANTA TERESA BLVD.
GILROY, CALIFORNIA 95020
(408) 847-1400
E-MAIL: ealster@gavilan.edu or mfriedman@gavilan.edu
WEB SITE: www.gavilan.edu

Name of Special Program: Learning Skills Program
Directors: Elaine Alster and Mark Friedman
General Information: Two-Year Community College; Enrollment: 4,100; **Tuition:** Residents – $26 per unit, Non-Residents and International Students – $174 per unit; **Room and Board**: No college housing available. A suburban campus, 40 miles south of San Jose, and 30 minutes from Pacific Ocean beaches. **Degrees and Vocational Programs:** Gavilan has an early start semester, liberal arts and vocational degrees. Associate degrees offered in most academic disciplines and vocational certificates in cosmetology, business, auto, aviation maintenance, nursing
Special Program: Enrollment in Special Program: 100; Cost: None
Staff: Learning disabilities specialists; peer tutors; instructional assistants
Program Features: Oral and extended time testing; note-taking assistance – scribes; basic study skills courses; individual and small group tutoring sessions; tape recorders; taped texts; faculty made aware of student's learning disability. Learning Skills Lab is open part time in the summer for continuing students and is staffed with one instructional aide.
Entrance Requirements: Diagnostic testing at Gavilan College
Special Facilities for: Visual, hearing and physical impairments

GROSSMONT COLLEGE
8800 GROSSMONT COLLEGE DRIVE
EL CAJON, CALIFORNIA 92020-1799
(619) 644-7112; FAX: (619) 644-7980
E-MAIL: Jane.Nolan@gcccd.net
WEB SITE: www.grossmont.edu/dsps

Name of Special Program: Disabled Student Services – Learning Development Center
Learning Disabilities Specialist: Jane Nolan
General Information: Two-Year Community College; Enrollment 11,800; **Tuition:** Residents – $26 per unit, Non-Residents – $151 per unit; **Room and Board:** No college housing available. Grossmont College is located on 135 acres. The open landscape and tree-rich campus create a pleasant atmosphere for learning and academic excellence. **Majors:** Accounting, administration of justice, art, biological sciences, business office technology, child development, computer science information systems, cross-cultural studies, economics, marketing, music, nursing, philosophy, political science, speech, telecommunications, theatre arts
Special Program: Enrollment in Special Program: 230; Cost: None
Staff: Learning disabilities specialists; peer tutors; special counselors
Program Features: Oral and extended time testing, note-taking assistance – scribes; tape recorders; taped texts; small group tutoring sessions; developmental program; academic advising for students with learning disabilities; faculty made aware of student's learning disability; assistive technology center. In the summer, learning disabilities assessment, test accommodations, registration assistance, NCR paper and tape recorder loans, assistive technology, and access to taped texts are available.
Entrance Requirements: Documentation of learning disability; testing at Grossmont College: WAIS-R, Woodcock-Johnson-R
Special Facilities for: Visual, hearing and physical impairments, psychologically disabled, head injured, speech/language disabled and health impaired
College Life: The Learning Disabilities Program at Grossmont College was among the first to be developed at the post-secondary level in California. Full and comprehensive services, frequent student contact with supportive specialists and aides, and faculty liaisons and in-servicing are highlights of the program.
Scholarships: See page 443.

HARTNELL COLLEGE
156 HOMESTEAD AVENUE
SALINAS, CALIFORNIA 93901
(831) 755-6760, (831) 770-6199 TDD
E-MAIL: wdavis@hartnell.edu **WEB SITE: www.hartnell.edu**

Name of Special Program: Disabled Students Programs and Services (DSP&S)
Coordinator: Wayne Davis
General Information: Two-Year Community College; Enrollment 2,800; **Tuition**: Residents – $26 per unit, Non-Residents – $157 per unit; **Room and Board:** No college housing available. A suburban campus, 100 miles from San Francisco. Nearby tourist attractions includes Monterey Bay, Big Sur, Carmel, Pebble Beach, Boronda Adobe and Monterey Bay Aquarium. **Degrees:** The college offers multiple AA and AS degrees. It offers a condensed but comprehensive program for summer with the same classes as those taught during the regular academic year. Vocational certificates are also available.
Special Program: Enrollment in Special Program: 913; Cost: None
Staff: Learning disabilities specialists; special counselors
Program Features: Oral and extended time testing; note-taking assistance – scribes; taped texts; faculty made aware of student's learning disability; testing in distraction-free environment
Entrance Requirements: Documentation of learning disability; learning disabilities report; handwritten essay; diagnostic testing at Hartnell College; testing: WAIS, SEC, psychological report, Woodcock-Johnson
Special Facilities for: Visual, hearing and physical impairments

IMPERIAL VALLEY COLLEGE
BOX 158, 380 EAST ATEN ROAD
IMPERIAL, CALIFORNIA 92251
(760) 352-8320 X311; FAX: (760) 355-6107
E-MAIL: ted.ceasar@imperial.edu **WEB SITE: www.imperial.edu**

Name of Special Program: Disabled Student Programs and Services (DSP&S)
Director: Ted Ceasar
General Information: Two-Year Community College; Enrollment: 2,800; **Tuition:** Residents – $26 per unit, Non-Residents – $177 per unit; **Room and Board:** No college housing available. A rural setting 93 miles east of San Diego. Founded in 1922. **Majors:** Agricultural business/sciences, banking, business management/office, computer/information sciences, correctional science, education, engineering, English, fine arts, fire science, graphic arts, health sciences, humanities, journalism, languages, letters/literature, marketing/distribution, mathematics, mechanical/electromechan-

ical technologies, mechanics/repairers, multi/interdisciplinary studies, music, nursing, parks and recreation, physical education, psychology, public affairs, social sciences, water treatment technology, welding technology
Special Program: Enrollment in Special Program: 383; Cost: None
Staff: Learning disabilities specialists; peer tutors; special counselors
Program Features: Oral and extended time testing; individual and small group tutoring sessions; limited course load (first year); note-taking assistance – scribes; tape recorders; taped texts; basic study skills; developmental program; faculty made aware of student's learning disability
Entrance Requirements: Documentation of learning disability; learning disability specialist report; handwritten essay; testing: WAIS, psychological report
Special Facilities for: Visual, hearing and physical impairments

IRVINE VALLEY COLLEGE
5500 IRVINE CENTER DRIVE
IRVINE, CALIFORNIA 92720
(949) 451-5630; FAX: (949) 451-5270
E-MAIL: czucker@ivc.edu **WEB SITE: www.ivc.edu**

Name of Special Program: Disabled Students Programs and Services (DSP&S)
Program Specialist: Connie Zucker (949) 451-5678
General Information: Two-Year Community College; Enrollment: 11,500; **Tuition:** Residents – $26 per unit, Non-Residents – $177 per unit; **Room and Board:** No college housing available. A community college with a rural atmosphere in an urban area. The campus consists of 100 acres, much of it still in orange groves, and has many cultural activities; near beaches and mountains. **Majors:** Administration of justice, anthropology, psychology, sociology, humanities, literature, economics, history, accounting, real estate, business, computers, French, Spanish, art, marketing, office management, life fitness certificate
Special Program: Enrollment in Special Program: 160; Cost: None
Staff: Learning disabilities specialists; peer tutors; special counselors
Program Features: Oral and extended time testing; individual and small group tutoring sessions; note-taking assistance – scribes; tape recorders; taped texts; basic study skills; faculty made aware of student's learning disability; priority registration; Challenger's Club
Entrance Requirements: Documentation of learning disability; learning disabilities specialist report; diagnostic testing at Irvine Valley College: WAIS-R, Woodcock-Johnson-R I, II, primary degrees of reading power (DRP) and standard progressive matrices-secondary

Special Facilities for: Visual, hearing and physical impairments
College Life: Irvine Valley College has small classes and a very accessible campus with a caring staff.
Scholarships: See page 443.

LASSEN COMMUNITY COLLEGE
P.O. BOX 3000, HIGHWAY 139
SUSANVILLE, CALIFORNIA 96130
(530) 257-6181 X8914; FAX: (530) 251-8863
E-MAIL: sbeckwith@lassencollege.edu
WEB SITE: www.lassencollege.edu

Name of Special Program: Learning Disabilities Department
Coordinator: Sandy Beckwith, X8035
General Information: Two-Year Community College; Enrollment: 2,489; **Tuition:** Residents – $26 per unit, Non-Residents – $209 per unit; **Room and Board:** $5,564 per year. A rural campus in a small town, 84 miles north of Reno, Nevada, in northeastern California. The good neighbor fees are $42 per unit. Founded in 1925. **Majors:** Administration of justice, agriculture, automotive technology, business, computer information systems, construction technology, correctional science, cosmetology, early childhood education, gunsmithing, human services, journalism, power generation technology, vocational nursing, welding technology, art, liberal arts, math/science, physical education, university studies
Special Program: Enrollment in Special Program: 77; Cost: None
Staff: Learning disabilities specialists; content tutors (faculty members); peer tutors; special counselors
Program Features: Oral and extended time testing; tape recorders; taped texts; basic study skills (non-credit); developmental program; individual and small group tutoring sessions; computers for word processing; academic advising for students with learning disabilities; faculty made aware of student's learning disability
Entrance Requirements: Documentation of learning disability; learning disabilities specialist report; diagnostic testing at Lassen Community College
Special Facilities for: Visual, hearing, and physical impairments

LONG BEACH CITY COLLEGE
4901 EAST CARSON STREET
LONG BEACH, CALIFORNIA 90808
(562) 938-4558; FAX: (562) 938-3921
E-MAIL: mmatsui@lbcc.edu **WEB SITE: www.lbcc.edu**

Name of Special Program: Learning Disabilities Program
Coordinator: Mark Matsui
General Information: Two-Year Community College: Enrollment: 20,000; **Tuition:** Residents – $26 per unit, Non-Residents – $132 per unit; **Room and Board:** No college housing available. Urban campus in a city in the metropolitan Los Angeles area. Founded in 1927. **Majors:** Allied health, biology, business/management, business/office, communications technologies, diagnostic/treatment services, fine arts, health sciences, home economics, languages, letters/literature, marketing/distribution, mathematics, mechanical/electromechanical technologies, mechanics/repairers, multi/interdisciplinary studies, music, physical sciences, precision production, science technologies, social sciences, transportation, visual/performing arts, vocational home economics
Special Program: Enrollment in Special Program: 100; Cost: None
Staff: Learning disabilities specialists; content tutors; peer tutors; special counselors
Program Features: Oral and extended time testing; individual tutoring sessions; limited course load (first year); tape recorders; taped texts; basic study skills; developmental program; faculty made aware of student's learning disability; special assessment and verification report; special classroom accommodations; test proctoring
Entrance Requirements: Documentation of learning disability; learning disabilities specialist report; diagnostic testing at Long Beach City College; testing: Woodcock-Johnson psychoeducational battery, WAIS-III
Special Facilities for: Visual, hearing and physical impairments

LOS ANGELES CITY COLLEGE
855 NORTH VERMONT AVENUE
LOS ANGELES, CALIFORNIA 90029
(323) 953-4000 X2273; FAX: (323) 953-4013
E-MAIL: matransb@lacitycollege.edu
WEB SITE: www.lacitycollege.edu

Name of Special Program: Office of Special Services/Learning Disabilities Program
Directors: Susan Matranga and Andrea Smith
General Information: Two-Year Community College; Enrollment: 16,000;

Tuition: Residents – $26 per unit, Non-Residents – $154 per unit, International Students – $164 per unit; **Room and Board:** No college housing available. Located on 40 acres in the heart of Hollywood. The college provides a range of specialized programs as well as a strong liberal arts transfer education. Student body is multicultural, multilingual and multigenerational, reflecting the diverse mid-city neighborhoods. **Majors:** Chicano studies, human services, Asian studies, radiology, radio-television, cinema, theatre academy, pre-law, accounting, dental technology, computer technology, languages (Japanese, Italian, Spanish, Hebrew, Korean, Portuguese, German, French, Filipino, Chinese), child development, art, photography, mathematics, English, office administration, music

Special Program: Enrollment in Special Program: 250; Cost: None

Staff: Learning disabilities specialists; peer tutors; special counselors

Program Features: Oral and extended time testing; individual tutoring sessions; limited course load; basic study skills; tape recorders; taped texts; note-taking assistance – scribes; faculty made aware of student's learning disability

Entrance Requirements: Documentation of learning disability or diagnostic testing at Los Angeles City College; testing: WAIS-III, Woodcock-Johnson-R, psychological report

Special Facilities for: Visual, hearing and physical impairments

Scholarships: See page 444.

LOS ANGELES MISSION COLLEGE
13356 ELDRIDGE AVENUE
SYLMAR, CALIFORNIA 91342-3245
(818) 364-7734, (818) 364-7861 TTD; (818) 364-7734
E-MAIL: rick_j._scuderi@laccd.cc.ca.us
WEB SITE: www.lamission.edu

Name of Special Program: Disabled Student Programs and Services

Director: Dr. Richard Scuderi

General Information: Two-Year Community College; Enrollment: 4,065; **Tuition:** Residents – $26 per unit, Non-Residents – $159 per unit, International Students – $175 per unit; **Room and Board:** No college housing available. A suburban campus in a large town, 20 miles from Los Angeles. **Majors:** Area studies, biology, business/management, business/office, chemistry, communications, culinary arts institute, education, environmental design, home economics, languages, letters/literature, mathematics, mechanical/electromechanical technologies, multi/interdisciplinary studies, music, physical sciences, psychology, social sciences, visual/performing arts, vocational home economics

Special Program: Enrollment in Special Program: 340; Cost: None
Staff: Learning disabilities specialists; peer tutors; special counselors
Program Features: Oral and extended time testing; taped texts; tape recorders; note-taking assistance – scribes; basic study skills; developmental program; individual and small group tutoring sessions; faculty made aware of student's learning disability (at student's request)
Entrance Requirements: Documentation of learning disability; learning disabilities specialist report; diagnostic testing at Los Angeles Mission College; California Community College Eligibility Assessment; testing: WAIS, SEC, psychological report
Special Facilities for: Visual, hearing and physical impairments

LOS ANGELES PIERCE COLLEGE
6201 WINNETKA AVENUE
WOODLAND HILLS, CALIFORNIA 91371
(818) 719-6430, (818) 710-4220 TTY; FAX: (818) 710-4219
E-MAIL: phoenid@piercecollege.edu
WEB SITE: www.piercecollege.edu

Name of Special Program: Disabled Students Program
Director: Norm Crozer
General Information: Two-Year Community College; Enrollment: 15,780; **Tuition:** Residents – $26 per unit, Non-Residents – $154 per unit, International Students – $190 per unit; **Room and Board:** No college housing available. An urban/rural setting northwest of metropolitan Los Angeles. **Degrees:** AA or AS in typical curriculum
Special Program: Enrollment in Special Program: 250; Cost: None
Staff: Learning disabilities specialists; peer tutors; special counselors; content tutors (faculty members)
Program Features: Oral and extended time testing; taped texts; note-taking assistance – scribes; tape recorders; basic study skills; individual and small group tutoring sessions; limited course load (first year); developmental program; academic advising for students with learning disabilities; faculty made aware of student's learning disability; ABI emphasis
Entrance Requirements: Documentation of learning disability; learning disabilities specialist report, SAT / ACT untimed scores accepted; diagnostic testing at Los Angeles Pierce College; medical evaluation; testing: WAIS, IEP, psychological report
Special Facilities for: Visual, hearing and physical impairments and acquired brain injuries
College Life: Excellent assessment, counseling and tutorial assistance with liaison to mainstream courses

MERRITT COLLEGE
12500 CAMPUS DRIVE
OAKLAND, CALIFORNIA 94619
(510) 531-4911; FAX: (510) 434-3888
WEB SITE: www.merritt.peralta.edu

Name of Special Program: Disabled Student Programs and Services
Coordinator: Cristina Tessot (510) 436-2516; *Learning Specialist:* Barbara Dimopoulos
General Information: Two-Year Community College; Enrollment: 6,600; **Tuition:** Residents – $26 per unit, Non-Residents – $170 per unit; **Room and Board:** No college housing available. A tranquil urban 130-acre campus with easy access to San Francisco. **Programs and Majors:** Transfer programs, vocational programs, particularly computer science, nursing and radiologic technology
Special Program: Enrollment in Special Program: 350; Cost: None
Staff: Learning disabilities specialists; peer tutors; special counselors; content tutors (faculty members)
Program Features: Oral and extended time testing; taped texts; tape recorders; note-taking assistance – scribes; basic study skills; individual tutoring sessions; academic advising for students with learning disabilities; special classes in spelling, reading, writing, mathematics; career planning; faculty made aware of student's learning disability; adapted computer learning center and classes in word processing; testing accommodations
Entrance Requirements: Documentation of learning disability; learning disabilities specialist report; diagnostic testing at Merritt College; teacher evaluation; medical evaluation; testing: WAIS, IEP, psychological report
Special Facilities for: Visual, hearing and physical impairments and acquired brain injuries

MODESTO JUNIOR COLLEGE
435 COLLEGE AVENUE
MODESTO, CALIFORNIA 95350-9977
(209) 575-6181; FAX: (209) 575-6666
WEB SITE: www.mjc.edu

Name of Special Program: Learning Disabilities Program
Director: Alysa Pearson
General Information: Two-Year Community College; Enrollment: 16,855; **Tuition:** Residents – $26 per unit, Non-Residents – $160 per unit; **Room and Board**: No college housing available. A suburban campus in a small city, 90 miles from San Francisco. Founded in 1921. Yosemite National Park is only a short drive to the east. **Majors:** Administration of justice,

agriculture, agricultural technology, arts, humanities and communication, behavioral and social sciences, biological sciences, business, engineering, mathematics and physical sciences, health occupations, home economics, literature and language arts, physical education, recreation and health education, trade and technical
Special Program: Enrollment in Special Program: 250; Cost: None
Staff: Learning disabilities specialists; special counselors; instructional assistants
Program Features: Oral and extended time testing; taped texts; note-taking assistance – scribes; basic study skills; tape recorders; small group tutoring sessions; limited course load (first year); academic advising for students with learning disabilities; faculty made aware of student's learning disability; assistance with transferring to other institutions; strategies instruction; high-tech computer center
Entrance Requirements: Diagnostic testing at Modesto Junior College; California Community College Eligibility Assessment; testing: WAIS, IEP, psychological report
Special Facilities for: Visual, hearing and physical impairments

MONTEREY PENINSULA COLLEGE
980 FREMONT BLVD.
MONTEREY, CALIFORNIA 93940-4799
(831) 646-4000
WEB SITE: www.mpc.edu

Name of Special Program: Learning Skills Program
Director: Susan Osorino
General Information: Two-Year Community College; Enrollment: 6,205; **Tuition:** Residents – $26 per unit, Non-Residents – $160 per unit; **Room and Board:** No college housing available. A suburban campus in a large town, 120 miles from San Francisco. Founded in 1947. **Majors:** Agricultural sciences, allied health, business/management, business/office, computer/information sciences, environmental design, health sciences, home economics, mechanical/electromechanical technologies, mechanics/repairers, multi/interdisciplinary studies, music, precision production, protective services, public affairs, visual/performing arts
Special Program: Enrollment in Special Program: 350, Cost: None
Staff: Learning disabilities specialist; content tutors (faculty members); peer tutors; special counselors
Program Features: Oral and extended time testing, taped texts; note-taking assistance – scribes; basic study skills; developmental program; tape

recorders; individual and small group tutoring sessions; limited course load (first year); faculty made aware of student's learning disability; computers
Entrance Requirements: Documentation of learning disability; learning disabilities specialist report; diagnostic testing at Monterey Peninsula College
Special Facilities for: Visual, hearing and physical impairments

MOORPARK COLLEGE
7075 CAMPUS ROAD
MOORPARK, CALIFORNIA 93021-1695
(805) 378-1461; FAX: (805) 378-1594
E-MAIL: pewins@vcccd.net WEB SITE: www.moorpark.cc.ca.us

Name of Special Program: ACCESS (Accessibility Coordination Center and Educational Support Services)
Coordinator: Patricia Ewins
General Information: Two-Year Community College; Enrollment: 13,000; **Tuition:** Residents – $26 per unit, Non-Residents – $163 per unit; **Room and Board:** No college housing available. Located 50 miles from Los Angeles on a 121-acre campus in Ventura County. **Programs and Majors:** Associate of Arts degree, Associate of Science degree, Certificates of Achievement for vocational courses. All majors are commonly available and special programs are exotic animal training, radiologic technology, nursing education and radio-television.
Special Program: Enrollment in Special Program: 400; Cost: None
Staff: Learning disabilities specialists; psychologist; academic counselor; high-tech center specialist; peer tutors
Program Features: Oral and extended time testing; basic study skills; individual and small group tutoring sessions; limited course load (first year); note-taking assistance – scribes; taped texts; tape recorders; academic advising for students with learning disabilities; faculty made aware of student's learning disabilities (at student's request); assistive technology lab
Entrance Requirements: Documentation of learning disability; learning disabilities specialist report; testing: WAIS, IEP, psychological report; diagnostic testing at Moorpark College; medical evaluation
Special Facilities for: Visually, hearing and physically impaired
Scholarships: See page 444.

MT. SAN ANTONIO COLLEGE
1100 NORTH GRAND AVENUE
WALNUT, CALIFORNIA 91789
(909) 594-5611 X4290
E-MAIL: ghanson@mtsac.edu **WEB SITE: www.mtsac.edu**

Name of Special Program: Disabled Student Programs and Services
Director: Grace T. Hanson
General Information: Two-Year Community College; Enrollment: 33,000; **Tuition:** Residents – $26 per unit, Non-Residents – $168 per unit, International Students – $183 per unit plus $30 application fee. **Room and Board:** No college housing available. A 421-acre suburban campus 20 miles east of Los Angeles. **Majors:** Advertising, agriculture, air-conditioning/refrigeration, air traffic control/traffic management, airframe/powerplant maintenance, drafting, business, commercial flight, computer science, construction inspection, early childhood education, fashion merchandise, forestry, electronics, interior design, interpreting for the deaf, machine tool technology, metallurgy, photography, plastics technology, radio and television broadcasting, allied health, water technology, welding supervision, certificates and associate's degrees in science and arts
Special Program: Enrollment in Special Program: 546; Cost: $3.00 lab fee. In the summer adaptive learning lab is available for basic skills building. Cost: $18 per unit (if required)
Staff: Learning disabilities specialists; peer tutors; special counselors
Program Features: Limited course load (first year); tape recorders; taped texts and taped exams; academic advising for students with learning disabilities; adaptive learning lab, laptop computer, Franklin spellers, specialized software; tutorial support for math and English; on-site counselor/psychologist; assessment of learning disabilities
Entrance Requirements: Documentation of learning disability; medical evaluation
Special Facilities for: Visual, hearing, speech and physical impairments; psychologically disabled; acquired brain injuries

MT. SAN JACINTO COLLEGE
SAN JACINTO CAMPUS
1499 NORTH STATE STREET
SAN JACINTO, CALIFORNIA 92583-2399
(909) 487-6752 X1524
E-MAIL: mcvetko@msjc.edu **WEB SITE: www.msjc.edu/lsp**

Name of Special Program: Learning Skills Program
Director: Dr. Marlene Cvetko

General Information: Two-Year Community College; Enrollment: 12,735; **Tuition:** Residents – $26 per unit, Non-Residents – $163 per unit; **Room and Board:** No college housing available. San Jacinto's 180-acre campus is located in a rural, farm community, one hour's drive from Disneyland, Palm Springs, and the Pacific Ocean beaches. The Menifee Valley campus is located at 28237 La Piedra Road, Menifee, California; (951) 672-6752 X2719. The Learning Skills Program Director is Dr. James Decker, jdecker@msjc.edu. **Majors:** Administration of justice, anthropology, art, auto body, auto mechanics, biological sciences, business, chemical dependency, chemistry, computer information science, early childhood studies, economics, electronics, drafting, English, fire science, foreign languages, forestry, geography, health and nutrition, history, management supervision, mathematics, music, nuclear service technology, nursing, philosophy, photography, physical education, physics and astronomy, political science, psychology, real estate, sociology, speech, theater arts
Special Program: Services are available at both campuses. Cost: None
Staff: Learning disabilities specialists; content tutors (staff members); special counselors
Program Features: Oral and extended time testing; individual tutoring sessions; taped texts; note-taking assistance – scribes; limited course load (first year); tape recorders; academic advising for students with learning disabilities; faculty made aware of student's learning disability (at student's request); small group instruction in study skills, phonics, English and math; assistive tech lab
Entrance Requirements: Documentation of learning disability; learning disabilities specialist report (not required but helpful); diagnostic testing at Mt. San Jacinto College; testing: WAIS, IEP, psychological report
Special Facilities for: Visual, hearing and physical impairments
College Life: Mt. San Jacinto has a comprehensive Learning Skills Program that builds community, supports academic programs and fosters independence.

NAPA VALLEY COLLEGE
2277 NAPA-VALLEJO HIGHWAY
NAPA, CALIFORNIA 94558
(707) 253-3284; (707) 259-8044
E-MAIL: rscott@napavalley.edu **WEB SITE: www.napavalley.edu**

Name of Special Program: Diagnostic Learning Services
Director: Rebecca Scott
General Information: Two-Year Community College; Enrollment: 5,950; **Tuition:** Residents – $26 per unit, Non-Residents – $149 per unit; **Room**

and Board: No college housing available. A 188-acre campus in a suburban area, situated on a lovely tree-lined campus with easy access to San Francisco. **Majors:** Natural science, social and behavioral science, humanities and fine arts, general education/breadth requirements, transfer in a special major, general studies, accounting, administration of justice, agricultural science, nursing, biomedical electronics technology, clerical studies, communications/CATV technology, computer studies, drafting technology, early childhood education, electronics technology, fire science, machine tool technology, management and supervision, marketing, photography technology, psychiatric technician, real estate, respiratory therapy, secretarial sciences, word processing, telecommunications technology, vocational nursing, welding technology

Special Program: Enrollment in Special Program: 100 per semester; Cost: None

Staff: Learning disabilities specialists; content tutors (faculty members); peer tutors; special counselors

Program Features: Oral and extended time testing; individual and small group tutoring sessions; limited course load (first year); academic advising for students with learning disabilities; note-taking assistance – scribes; taped texts; basic study skills; tape recorders; faculty made aware of student's learning disability (at student's request); developmental program

Entrance Requirements: Diagnostic testing at Napa Valley College; students must qualify for special accommodations based on criteria set by the Chancellor's Office for California Community Colleges. This testing is done for Napa Valley College students by the Diagnostic Learning Services. Previous diagnostic testing completed at another California Community College within the last three years is also accepted.

Special Facilities for: Visual, hearing and physical impairments

ORANGE COAST COLLEGE

P.O. BOX 5005, 2701 FAIRVIEW ROAD
COSTA MESA, CALIFORNIA 92628-5005
(714) 432-5535; FAX: (714) 432-5557
WEB SITE: www.orangecoastcollege.edu

Name of Special Program: Learning Disabilities Program

Director: Dr. Kenneth K. Ortiz

General Information: Two-Year Community College; Enrollment: 20,017; **Tuition:** Residents – $26 per unit, Non-Residents – $182 per unit; **Room and Board:** No college housing available. A 200-acre suburban campus 40 miles from Los Angeles. **Majors:** Food service/hotel management, heating and air conditioning, interior design, machine technology, marketing,

medical assisting, medical transcription, music, neurodiagnostic technology, nutrition care, nutrition education, ornamental horticulture, photography, radiography, radiologic technology, respiratory care, welding technology, coaching school athletic teams, computer information systems, home economics, home management, religious studies, writing program, accounting, administrative services, airframe/powerplant technology, airline travel careers, animal science, architectural/construction technology, aviation and space, cardiovascular technology, textiles, commercial art, computer/graphics information systems, culinary arts, dental assisting-registered, dental technology, diagnostic medical sonography, dietetic technology, display and visual presentation, drafting technology, early childhood education, electrocardiography technician, electronics technology, emergency medical services, energy engineering, fashion merchandising, film/video, fitness specialist
Special Program: Enrollment in Special Program: 360; Cost: None
Staff: Learning disabilities specialists; peer tutors; special counselors
Program Features: Individual and small group tutoring sessions; basic study skills; note-taking assistance – scribes; tape recorders; academic advising for students with learning disabilities; faculty made aware of student's learning disability
Entrance Requirements: Documentation of learning disability; learning disabilities specialist report; testing: WAIS, IEP, psychological report
Special Facilities for: Visually, hearing and physically impaired
College Life: The Orange Coast College Learning Center is designed to assist students who have been identified as having a learning disability and who demonstrate specific learning problems in the academic skill areas of reading, writing, spelling and mathematics.
Scholarships: See page 444.

OXNARD COLLEGE
4000 SOUTH ROSE AVENUE
OXNARD, CALIFORNIA 93033-6699
(805) 986-5830, (805) 488-8022 TTY; FAX: (805) 986-5928
WEB SITE: www.oxnardcollege.edu

Name of Special Program: Educational Assistance Center
Coordinator: Leo Orange
General Information: Two-Year Community College; Enrollment: 6,000; **Tuition:** Residents – $26 per unit, Non-Residents – $155 per unit; **Room and Board:** No college housing available. A 119-acre campus in a semi-urban setting, situated between Los Angeles and Santa Barbara just off the Pacific Coast Highway. **Majors:** Business management, communications

(television/journalism/public relations), mathematics, art (two- and three-dimensional), electronics, dental hygiene, legal assisting, hotel and restaurant management, fire technology, air conditioning/refrigeration, child development, fitness management, information processing, automotive technology, diesel mechanics, auto body painting and repair, alcohol/drug studies, applied electronics, travel and tourism
Special Program: Enrollment in Special Program: 80; Cost: None. The High-Tech Center for the Disabled provides all support services, adaptive physical education and basic skills instruction throughout the year including the summer session. Cost: regular tuition and fees
Staff: Learning disabilities specialists; content tutors (faculty members); special counselors
Program Features: Oral and extended time testing; individual and small group tutoring sessions; limited course load (first year); academic advising for students with learning disabilities; tape recorders; basic study skills; note-taking assistance – scribes; developmental program; faculty made aware of student's learning disability; priority registration; High-Tech Center for the Disabled; voice recognition, optical character recognition; job development and placement
Entrance Requirements: Documentation of disability; learning disability testing within two years; processing deficit; diagnostic testing at Oxnard College; teacher evaluation; testing: WAIS, IEP
Special Facilities for: Visual, hearing and physical impairments
College Life: Highly personalized, individualized contact with staff, open faculty and staff, accessible campus, adapted physical education, excellent interpretation of sign language for deaf students.
Scholarships: See page 445.

PORTERVILLE COLLEGE
100 EAST COLLEGE
PORTERVILLE, CALIFORNIA 93257
(209) 791-2326; FAX: (209) 784-4779
WEB SITE: www.portervillecollege.edu

Name of Special Program: Learning Disabilities Program
Director: Diane Allen
General Information: Two-Year Community College; Enrollment: 4,600; **Tuition:** Residents – $26 per unit, Non-Residents – $149 per unit; **Room and Board:** No college housing available. A 60-acre rural campus located three hours from Los Angeles. Founded in 1927. **Majors:** Business administration, art, automotive mechanic, building trades, business, child development, drafting, English, liberal arts, photography, real estate, social sci-

ence, welding, criminology, information systems, office technology, psychiatric technician, vocational nurse
Special Program: Enrollment in Special Program: 104; Cost: None
Staff: Learning disabilities specialists; peer tutors; special counselors
Program Features: Oral and extended time testing; individual and small group tutoring sessions; limited course load; basic study skills; note-taking assistance – scribes; tape recorders; taped texts; faculty made aware of student's learning disability
Entrance Requirements: Learning disabilities specialist report; California Community College Eligibility Assessment; diagnostic testing at Porterville College; testing: SEC
Special Facilities for: Visual, hearing and physical impairments

SACRAMENTO CITY COLLEGE
3835 FREEPORT BLVD., ROOM A2
SACRAMENTO, CALIFORNIA 95822-1386
(916) 558-2665, (916) 558-2545; FAX: (916) 558-2670
E-MAIL: schafer@scc.losrios.edu WEB SITE: www.scc.losrios.edu

Name of Special Program: Learning (dis)Abilities Program
Coordinator: Dr. Ann Schafer
General Information: Two-Year Community College; Enrollment 15,700; **Tuition:** Residents – $26 per unit, Non-Residents – $177 per unit, International Students – $193 per unit; **Room and Board:** No on-site college housing available. A 60-acre urban campus located near downtown Sacramento, close to Lake Tahoe, Reno, Nevada, and San Francisco. Also located near California State University, Sacramento and California State University, Davis. **Majors:** Accounting, administration of justice, aeronautics, bookkeeping/office management, computer information science, cosmetology, dental assisting, early childhood education, electronics technology, engineering design technology, family and consumer science, gerontology, graphic communication, instructional assisting, journalism, library technology, management, marketing, mechanical/electrical technology, metals industry technology, music, nursing/vocational nursing, office information systems, railroad operations, real estate, recreational vehicle service technician, surveying (geomatics), workplace communication
Special Program: Enrollment in Special Program: 384; Cost: $13
Staff: Learning disabilities specialists; peer tutors; content tutors (faculty members); special counselors
Program Features: Oral and extended time testing; distraction-reduced environment; individual tutoring sessions; limited course load; academic advising for students with learning disabilities; note-taking assistance –

scribes; taped texts; tape recorders; faculty made aware of student's learning disability; basic skills classes in math and English; special classes in reading, spelling, and math testing; high-tech center; adaptive computer technology available
Entrance Requirements: Documentation of learning disability; testing: diagnostic testing at Sacramento City College using six-step California Community College guidelines
Special Facilities for: Visual, hearing and physical impairments (on campus but not through Learning (dis)Abilities program)
College Life: Sacramento City College supports students with learning disabilities in reaching their academic goals, strengthening and developing their skills and provides opportunities that maximize the potential of each student.
Scholarships: See page 445.

SAN BERNARDINO VALLEY COLLEGE
701 SOUTH MOUNT VERNON AVENUE
SAN BERNARDINO, CALIFORNIA 92410
(909) 384-8668 X1163; FAX: (909) 384-9072
WEB SITE: www.valleycollege.edu

Name of Special Program: Disabled Student Programs and Services
Director: Rebeccah K. Warren-Marlatt
General Information: Two-Year Community College; Enrollment 11,500; **Tuition:** Residents – $26 per unit, Non-Residents – $145 per unit; **Room and Board:** No college housing available. The Valley College campus, located midway between the central business districts of San Bernardino and Colton, has expanded from its original 30 acres to 85. A four-building campus has grown to one of 18 major buildings, grouped conveniently around a central quadrangle and mall, giving easy access to numerous special purpose classrooms, lecture halls, laboratories, studios, shops and practice rooms. **Majors and Degree Programs:** Associate of Arts degree programs in accounting, administration of justice, aeronautics, architecture, art, automotive technology, astronomy, biology, business administration, chemistry, child development, communications/broadcasting, computer science/systems, electricity/electronics, engineering and drafting technology, family/consumer science, geography, geology, human services, inspection technology, legal administration, liberal arts, library technology, machinist technology, management information systems, mathematics, music, nursing, office information systems, pharmacy technology, physical education and athletics, physics, police science, psychiatric technology, real estate, refrigeration and air conditioning, restaurant, water

supply engineering, welding. Vocational certificate programs are also available.

Special Program: Enrollment in Special Program: 124; Cost: None
Staff: Learning disabilities specialist; peer tutors
Program Features: Oral and extended time testing; individual and small group tutoring sessions; note-taking assistance – scribes; tape recorders; taped texts; limited course load; academic advising for students with learning disabilities; faculty made aware of student's learning disability; development program limited to English, math and reading; basic study skills
Entrance Requirements: Documentation of learning disability; learning disabilities specialist report; diagnostic testing at San Bernardino Valley College; testing: WAIS-R or WAIS-III, IEP, psychological report
Special Facilities for: Visual, hearing and physical impairments
College Life: San Bernardino Valley College has an excellent high-tech center with a reading machine, speech output system and speech input systems. The faculty is committed to teaching students with a variety of learning styles and backgrounds.

SAN DIEGO CITY COLLEGE
1313 PARK BLVD.
SAN DIEGO, CALIFORNIA 92101
(619) 388-3513, (619) 388-3313 TTY
E-MAIL: bmason@sdccd.net **WEB SITE: www.sdcity.edu**

Name of Special Program: Disability Support Program and Services (DSPS)
Director: Barbara Mason
General Information: Two-Year Community College; Enrollment: 14,541; **Tuition:** Residents – $26 per unit, Non-Residents – $160 per unit; **Room and Board:** No college housing available. A 56-acre campus in an urban setting with access to San Diego Zoo, Sea World, Seaport Village and Old Town. **Majors:** Vocational and technical (automotive, printing, cosmetology, refrigeration, electronics, environmental control, machine, plastics and manufacturing technology), creative arts, radio and television, behavioral sciences, physical sciences, nursing, commercial and fine arts, liberal arts, business, computer and information sciences
Special Program: Enrollment in Special Program: 126; Cost: None. All program features and services except Basic Skills classes are available during the summer sessions.
Staff: Learning disabilities specialists; content tutors; peer tutors; special counselors; technology specialist
Program Features: Oral and extended time testing; individual tutoring

sessions; limited course loads; basic study skills; note-taking assistance - scribes; tape recorders; taped texts; faculty made aware of student's learning disability (at student's request); test proctoring
Entrance Requirements: Documentation of learning disability; diagnostic testing at San Diego City College; California Community College Eligibility Assessment; testing: WAIS-II, Woodcock-Johnson-III psychoeducational battery
Special Facilities for: Visual, hearing and physical impairments, DDL, ABI, LD, mobility, psychological

SAN DIEGO MESA COLLEGE

7250 MESA COLLEGE DRIVE
SAN DIEGO, CALIFORNIA 92111
(619) 388-2780, (619) 388-2974 TTY; FAX: (619) 388-2460
E-MAIL: gconrad@sdccd.edu **WEB SITE: www.sdmesa.edu**

Name of Special Program: Disabled Students Programs and Services (DSP&S)
Coordinator: Gail Conrad
General Information: Two-Year Community College; Enrollment: 25,000; **Tuition:** Residents – $26 per unit; **Room and Board:** No college housing available. A 104-acre campus in a suburban area. **Majors:** Accounting, American sign language/interpreting, animal health technology, anthropology, apprenticeship, architecture, art/fine arts, aviation, biology, Black studies, building construction technology, business administration and management, Chicano studies, child development, computer and information sciences, consumer and nutrition studies, dramatic arts, English, engineering, escrow, fashion, fitness specialist, food service occupations, foreign languages, hotel-motel management, interior design, liberal arts, marketing, mathematics, medical assisting, medical record technology, music, nursery and landscape technology, nutrition, office information systems, physical education, physical sciences, physical therapist assistant, psychology, political science, radiologic technology, real estate, registered dental assistant, selected studies, social sciences, sociology, speech communications, travel and tourism, water/waste water technology
Special Program: Enrollment in Special Program: 30; Cost: Based on unit value. *Summer Program:* The Disabled Student Programs and Services Department offers tutoring and software instructional services through the High-Tech Lab for all summer sessions.
Staff: Learning disabilities specialists; peer tutors; special counselor
Program Features: Oral and extended time testing; taped texts; note-taking assistance – scribes; tape recorders; individual and small group tutor-

ing sessions; faculty made aware of student's learning disability (at student's request)
Entrance Requirements: Documentation of learning disability; diagnostic testing at San Diego Mesa Community College
Special Facilities for: Visual, hearing and physical impairments

SAN JOSE CITY COLLEGE
2100 MOORPARK
SAN JOSE, CALIFORNIA 95128
(408) 288-3746, (408) 294-3447 TTY
WEB SITE: www.sjcc.edu

Name of Special Program: Disabled Students Program and Services (DSP&S)
Learning Disabilities Specialists: Donna Wirt, Patty Blankenship
General Information: Two-Year Community College; Enrollment: 8,435; **Tuition:** Residents – $26 per unit, Non-Residents – $175 per unit; **Room and Board:** No college housing available. An urban campus in a very large city, 55 miles south of San Francisco. Founded in 1921. **Majors:** Allied health, biology, business/management, business/office, chemistry, communications technologies, computer/information sciences, construction trades, crafts/design, education, engineering technologies, fine arts, languages, letters/literature, marketing/distribution, mathematics, mechanical/electromechanical technologies, mechanics/repairers, multi/ interdisciplinary studies, music, parks and recreation, physical sciences, physics, precision production, protective services, psychology, public affairs, science technologies, social sciences, visual/performing arts
Special Program: Enrollment in Special Program: 50–60; Cost: None
Staff: Learning disabilities specialists; special counselors; instructional aides
Program Features: Oral and extended time testing; limited individual tutoring sessions; small group remedial classes; tape recorders; taped texts; basic study skills; faculty made aware of student's learning disability; diagnostic assessment; support in regular classes; enlarged print books for visually impaired
Entrance Requirements: Handwritten essay; learning disabilities specialist current report; diagnostic testing at San Jose City College; educational contract; testing: Woodcock-Johnson psychoeducational battery; SEC
Special Facilities for: Visual, hearing and physical impairments

SANTA ANA COLLEGE
1530 WEST 17th STREET
SANTA ANA, CALIFORNIA 92706
(714) 564-6260; FAX: (714) 285-9619
E-MAIL: choo_brooke@sac.edu or kobane_mary@sac.edu
WEB SITE: www.sac.edu

Name of Special Program: Learning Disabilities Program
Instructors: Brooke Choo, Mary Kobane
General Information: Two-Year Community College; Enrollment 22,000; **Tuition:** Residents – $26 per unit, Non-Residents – $159 per unit; **Room and Board:** No college housing available. An urban campus 40 miles from Los Angeles, 10 miles from Disneyland. Founded in 1915. **Majors:** Science and technology, applied arts and sciences, performing and fine arts, business, humanities, social sciences and others
Special Program: Enrollment in Special Program: 340; Cost: None. *Summer Program:* Six week program; Cost: None
Staff: Learning disabilities specialists; special counselors; peer tutors
Program Features: Oral and extended time testing; individual and small group tutoring sessions; basic study skills; note-taking assistance – scribes; tape recorders; taped texts; academic advising for students with learning disabilities; faculty made aware of student's learning disability; assistive computer center; special classes; adapted physical education
Entrance Requirements: Documentation of learning disability; diagnostic testing at Santa Ana College; teacher evaluation; California Community College Eligibility Assessment; testing: WAIS, IEP, psychological report
Special Facilities for: Visually, hearing and physical impairments; psychologically disabled students; acquired brain injuries; developmentally delayed learners
Scholarships: See page 445.

SANTA BARBARA CITY COLLEGE
721 CLIFF DRIVE
SANTA BARBARA, CALIFORNIA 93109-2394
(805) 965-0581 X2364, (805) 962-4084 TTY
E-MAIL: dspshelp@sbcc.edu **WEB SITE: www.sbcc.edu**

Name of Special Program: Disabled Student Programs and Services (DSPS)
Director: Dr. Janet Shapiro
General Information: Two-Year Community College; Enrollment: 12,000; **Tuition:** Residents – $26 per unit, Non-Residents – $149 per unit, International Students – $155 per unit; **Room and Board:** No college housing available. A 65-acre suburban campus in a small city, 90 miles north of

Los Angeles. Founded in 1908. **Majors:** Agricultural sciences, allied health, biology, botany, business/management, business/office, chemistry, civil technologies, communications, computer/information sciences, crafts/design, cosmetology, diving (marine), earth science, economics, emergency medicine, English, environmental horticulture, French, geography, German, graphic design, hotel, restaurant culinary, physical education, engineering technologies, ethnic studies, fine arts, health sciences, languages, law, letters/literature, life sciences, marketing/distribution, mathematics, mechanical/electromechanical technologies, mechanics/repairers, multi/interdisciplinary studies, music, parks and recreation, philosophy, physical sciences, physics, precision production, protective services, psychology, social sciences, visual/performing arts
Special Program: Enrollment in Special Program: 600; Cost: None
Staff: Learning disabilities specialists; strategies tutors for regular college classes; job placement counselor; learning disabilities counselors; trained tutors for learning disabilities classes
Program Features: Extended time testing; note-taking assistance; taped texts; word processing facilities; assistive technology resource center; small group tutoring sessions; option of limited course load; diagnostic testing; faculty made aware of student's learning disability; electronic text reader; learning disabilities classes open door policy
Entrance Requirements: English and math placement tests for Santa Barbara City College; verification of disability and functional limitations in an educational setting
Special Facilities for: College provides access for all populations with disabilities.
Scholarships: See page 446.

SANTA MONICA COLLEGE

1900 PICO BLVD.
SANTA MONICA, CALIFORNIA 90405
(310) 434-4684; FAX: (310) 434-3694
E-MAIL: marcopulos_george@smc.edu WEB SITE: www.smc.edu

Name of Special Program: Learning Disabilities Program
Director: George Marcopulos
General Information: Two-Year Community College; Enrollment: 24,000; **Tuition:** Residents – $26 per unit, Non-Residents – $181 per unit, International Students – $206 per unit; **Room and Board:** No college housing available. Santa Monica College is located close to Los Angeles in Santa Monica, California, one mile from the Pacific Ocean. **Associate Degrees:** Accounting, administration of justice, architecture, art, auto-

body repair, automotive technology, broadcasting, business administration, Chicano studies, child development, cinema, computer information systems, construction technology, cosmetology, dance, electronics, ethnic studies, fashion merchandising, fire science, graphic design, interior design, journalism, liberal arts, management, merchandising, music, nursing, office information systems, photography, physical education, printing, real estate and escrow, recreation leadership, respiratory therapy, general science, speech theatre arts, welding

Special Program: Enrollment in Special Program: 300; Cost: None. *Summer Program:* Assessment workshop to determine eligibility for learning disabilities program.

Staff: Learning disabilities specialists; peer tutors; special counselors; instructional assistants

Program Features: Oral and extended time testing, individual and small group tutoring sessions; basic study skills are offered by English and math department; (remedial) development classes; limited course load; academic advising for students with learning disabilities; faculty made aware of student's learning disability (at student's request); computers; study strategies classes offered by learning disabilities program; volunteer notetaking assistance – scribes

Entrance Requirements: Diagnostic testing at Santa Monica College

Special Facilities for: Visual, hearing and physical impairments

College Life: The Learning Disabilities Program is designed to promote independence and self advocacy.

Scholarships: See page 446.

SANTA ROSA JUNIOR COLLEGE

1501 MENDOCINO AVENUE
SANTA ROSA, CALIFORNIA 95401-4395
(707) 527-4278
E-MAIL: bnichols@santarosa.edu **WEB SITE: www.santarosa.edu**

Name of Special Program: Disability Resources Department

Administrative Assistant: Brenda Nichols (707) 524-1567

General Information: Two-Year Community College; Enrollment: 38,000; **Tuition:** Residents – $26 per unit, Non-Residents – $203 per unit; **Room and Board:** No college housing available. Beautiful campus situated in suburban environ 55 miles north of San Francisco. Close to the ocean and rivers. **Academic and Vocational Programs:** Semester system, liberal arts, occupational, vocational, business and medical certificates and AA and AS degrees. Programs for transfer to a four-year colleges are available.

Special Program: Enrollment in Special Program: 400; Cost: None. In the

summer, support services are available for students taking mainstream classes: tutoring, test-taking facilitation, note-taking assistance, academic advising for students with learning disabilities
Staff: Learning disabilities specialists; process tutors; special classes
Program Features: Oral and extended time testing; individual and small group tutoring sessions; basic study skills; developmental program; note-taking assistance – scribes; tape recorders; limited course load (first year) recommended; taped texts; faculty made aware of student's learning disability; adapted computer technology; High-Tech Center for Disabled; vocational support program
Entrance Requirements: Documentation of learning disability; testing: WAIS, Woodcock-Johnson psychoeducational battery
Special Facilities for: Visual, hearing and physical impairments

SIERRA COLLEGE
5000 ROCKLIN ROAD
ROCKLIN, CALIFORNIA 95677
(916) 781-0553; FAX: (916) 789-2967
WEB SITE: www.sierracollege.edu

Name of Special Program: Learning Opportunities Center
Director: Michelle Devol
General Information: Two-Year Community College; Enrollment: 16,000; **Tuition:** Residents – $26 per unit, Non-Residents – $186 per unit, International Students – $192 per unit; **Room and Board:** College housing available. A 327-acre rural campus in a suburban area, 15 miles east of Sacramento (State Capitol) and an hour and a half to San Francisco. The college is near Lake Tahoe and ski areas in the gold country. **Majors:** Accounting, agricultural technologies, agronomy/soil/crop/animal sciences, art/fine arts, automotive technologies, biology/biological sciences, business administration/commerce/management, carpentry, chemistry, communication, computer/information sciences, construction technologies, corrections/ criminal justice, drafting and design, education, electrical/electronics technologies, engineering, equestrian studies, fashion merchandising, fire science, food services, forestry, geology, economics, horticulture, industrial arts, interior design, journalism, law enforcement/police sciences, legal secretary, liberal arts/general studies, manufacturing, marketing/retailing/merchandising, medical secretary, metallurgical/mining technology, nursing, photography, real estate, surveying, teacher aid, welding
Special Program: Enrollment in Special Program: 360; Cost: None. *Summer Program:* Sierra College offers test proctoring, liaison for incoming students and extended time for college assessment test.

Staff: Learning disabilities specialists; instructional assistants
Program Features: Oral and extended time testing; individual and small group tutoring sessions; taped texts; tape recorders; note-taking assistance – scribes; basic study skills; faculty made aware of student's learning disability; auditing and visual training classes
Entrance Requirements: Documentation of learning disability; learning disabilities specialist report; diagnostic testing at Sierra College; testing: WAIS, IEP
Special Facilities for: Physical impairments
College Life: Sierra College has the reputation of having one of the finest learning disability programs in the state. Students find the atmosphere extremely supportive.
Scholarships: See page 446.

SKYLINE COLLEGE
3300 COLLEGE DRIVE
SAN BRUNO, CALIFORNIA 94066-1698
(650) 738-4280, (650) 738-4329 TTD; FAX: (650) 738-4228
WEB SITE: www.skylinecollege.net

Name of Special Program: Developmental Skills Program
Coordinator: Linda Van Sciver
General Information: Two-Year Community College; Enrollment: 9,000; **Tuition:** Residents – $26 per unit, Non-Residents – $169 per unit; **Room and Board:** No college housing available. A suburban campus 10 minutes from downtown San Francisco, 10 minutes from the California coast and beaches. Also features a European semester exchange. **Majors:** Allied health, biology, business/management, communications, computer/information sciences, diagnostic/treatment services, education, environmental design, fine arts, home economics, letters/literature, marketing distribution, mathematics, multi/interdisciplinary studies, music, parks and recreation, physical sciences, psychology, science technologies, social sciences, visual/performing arts
Special Program: Enrollment in Special Program: 130; Cost: None. *Summer Program:* Single assessment/eligibility course offered, limited to eight to ten students; 1:1 assessment
Staff: Learning disabilities specialists; content tutors (faculty members); special counselors
Program Features: Extended time testing; taped texts; tape recorders; note-taking assistance – scribes; limited course load (first year); basic study skills; individual and small group tutoring sessions; developmental program; faculty made aware of student's learning disability (at student's request)

Entrance Requirements: Documentation of learning disability; learning disabilities specialist report; testing: WAIS, Woodcock-Johnson-R, WRAT, Ravens Matrices
Special Facilities for: Visual, hearing and physical impairments

SOLANO COMMUNITY COLLEGE
4000 SUISUN VALLEY ROAD
FAIRFIELD, CALIFORNIA 94534-4017
(707) 864-7000 X234
WEB SITE: www.solano.cc.ca.us

Name of Special Program: Disabled Student Programs and Services (DSP&S), Learning Disabilities Center
Director: Ella Tolliver, Ph.D.
General Information: Two-Year Community College; Enrollment: 12,000; **Tuition**: Residents – $26 per unit, Non-Residents – $186 per unit; **Room and Board:** No college housing available. A 192-acre suburban campus with easy access to Sacramento and San Francisco, 11 miles from Vallejo. **Majors:** Agribusiness / agricultural production, agricultural sciences, biology, business / management, business / office, chemistry, civil technologies, communications and technologies, computer / information sciences, education, engineering and technologies, environmental design, ethnic studies, fine arts, health sciences, home economics, industrial production, languages, letters / literature, marketing / distribution, mathematics, mechanical / electromechanical technologies, mechanics / repairers, multi / interdisciplinary studies, music, physics, precision production, protective services, psychology, public affairs, social sciences, visual / performing arts, vocational home economics
Special Program: Enrollment in Special Program: 100, Cost: None
Staff: Learning disabilities specialists; peer tutors; special counselors
Program Features: Oral and extended time testing; small group tutoring sessions; limited course load (as needed); note-taking assistance – scribes; tape recorders; taped texts; faculty made aware of student's learning disability; strategies instruction
Entrance Requirements: Documentation of learning disability; learning disabilities specialist report; diagnostic testing at Solano Community College; California Community College Eligibility Assessment; testing: WAIS, Woodcock-Johnson-R, SEC, psychological report
Special Facilities for: Visual, hearing and physical impairments

SOUTHWESTERN COLLEGE
900 OTAY LAKES ROAD
CHULA VISTA, CALIFORNIA 92010
(619) 421-6700 X5396
WEB SITE: www.swc.cc.ca.us

Name of Special Program: Disability Support Services
Director: Dr. Malia Flood
General Information: Two-Year Community College; Enrollment: 19,000; **Tuition:** Residents – $26 per unit, Non-Residents – $150 per unit; **Room and Board:** No college housing available. A 158-acre suburban campus with easy access to San Diego. **Academic and Vocational Programs:** Semester system, liberal arts, occupational, vocational, business and medical certificates and AA and AS degrees. Programs for transfer to a four-year colleges are available.
Special Program: Enrollment in Special Program: 100; Cost: None
Staff: Learning disabilities specialists; peer tutors; special counselors
Program Features: Oral and extended time testing; individual and small group tutoring sessions; basic study skills; note-taking assistance – scribes; tape recorders; taped texts; faculty made aware of student's learning disability (at student's request); program to improve comprehension—text comprehension and composition—called grammar mapping (with Apple computer component)
Entrance Requirements: Documentation of learning disability; learning disabilities specialist report; handwritten essay; diagnostic testing at Southwestern College; California Community College Eligibility Assessment; testing: WAIS, SEC, psychological report, Woodcock-Johnson psychoeducational battery
Special Facilities for: Visual, hearing and physical impairments

TAFT COLLEGE
29 EMMONS PARK DRIVE
TAFT, CALIFORNIA 93268
(661) 763-7700; FAX: (661) 763-7705
WEB SITE: www.taftcollege.edu

Name of Special Program: Learning Assistance Program
Director: Jeff Ross
General Information: Two-Year Community College; Enrollment 3,160; **Tuition:** Residents – $26 per unit, Non-Residents – $151 per unit; **Room and Board:** $1,574 per semester. A 15-acre rural campus in a small town, 40 miles from Bakersfield. Founded in 1922. **Majors:** Biology, business / management, business / office, chemistry, communications, com-

puter/information sciences, education, engineering and technologies, fine arts, geological sciences, health sciences, industrial production, letters/literature, library/archival sciences, mathematics, mechanical/electromechanical technologies, mechanics/repairers, multi/interdisciplinary studies, parks and recreation, physics, precision production, protective services, psychology, social sciences, visual/performing arts
Special Program: Enrollment in Special Program: 80; Cost: None.
Staff: Learning disabilities specialists; content tutors (faculty members)
Program Features: Oral and extended time testing; taped texts; note-taking assistance – scribes; basic study skills (non-credit); developmental program; tape recorders; individual and small group tutoring sessions; registration assistance; faculty made aware of student's learning disability
Entrance Requirements: Diagnostic testing at Taft College
Special Facilities for: Visual, hearing and physical impairments

VENTURA COLLEGE
4667 TELEGRAPH ROAD
VENTURA, CALIFORNIA 93003
(805) 654-6300
WEB SITE: www.venturacollege.edu

Name of Special Program: Learning Disability Program
Director: Dr. Lyn MacConnaire
General Information: Two-Year Community College; Enrollment: 15,000; **Tuition:** Residents – $26 per unit, Non-Residents – $155 per unit; **Room and Board:** No college housing available. A 112-acre suburban campus 60 miles north of Los Angeles. Founded in 1925. **Majors:** Agribusiness/agricultural production, agricultural sciences, allied health, architecture, biology, botany, business/management, business/office, chemistry, civil technologies, communications and technologies, computer/information sciences, construction trades, crafts/design, diagnostic/treatment sciences, education, engineering and technologies, environmental control technologies and design, ethnic studies, fine arts, geological sciences, health sciences, home economics, industrial production, languages, law, letters/literature, marketing, distribution, mathematics, mechanical/electromechanical technologies, mechanics/repairers, multi/interdisciplinary studies, music, parks and recreation, philosophy, physical sciences, physics, precision production, protective services, psychology, public affairs, renewable natural resources, social sciences, visual/performing arts, vocational home economics, zoology
Special Program: Enrollment in Special Program: 400; Cost: None
Staff: Learning disabilities specialists; content tutors (faculty members); peer tutors; special counselors

Program Features: Oral and extended time testing; individual and small group tutoring sessions; limited course load (first year); basic study skills; note-taking assistance – scribes; tape recorders; taped texts; developmental program; faculty made aware of student's learning disability
Entrance Requirements: Documentation of learning disability; learning disabilities specialist report; diagnostic testing at Ventura College; testing: WAIS, Woodcock-Johnson – both sections
Special Facilities for: Visual, hearing and physical impairments
Scholarships: See page 446.

WEST HILLS COMMUNITY COLLEGE
300 CHERRY LANE
COALINGA, CALIFORNIA 93210
(559) 934-2333
E-MAIL: JoyceSmyers@westhillscollege.com
WEB SITE: www.westhillscollege.com/coalinga

Name of Special Program: Disabled Student Programs and Services (DSPS)
Director: Joyce Smyers
General Information: Two-Year Community College; Enrollment: 4,290; **Tuition:** Residents – $26 per unit, Non-Residents – $151 per unit; **Room and Board:** $2,201–2,530.60 per semester. A rural campus in a small town, 60 miles from Fresno. The city of Coalinga is relatively small with 10,000 population. West Hills Community College is a major source of employment in the community. The community is very supportive of the students, staff and faculty. **Majors:** Agribusiness/agricultural production, agricultural sciences, biology, business/management, business/office, chemistry, communications, computer/information sciences, crafts/design, education, engineering and technologies, geological sciences, health sciences, industrial production, marketing/distribution, mathematics, mechanical/electromechanical technologies, mechanics/repairs, multi/interdisciplinary studies, music, physical sciences, physics, precision production, protective services, psychology, science technologies, social sciences
Special Program: Enrollment in Special Program: 71; Cost: None
Staff: Learning disabilities specialist; peer tutors; special counselors; content tutors (faculty members)
Program Features: Oral and extended time testing; note-taking assistance – scribes; taped texts; tape recorders; individual tutoring sessions; academic advising for students with learning disabilities; basic study skills; faculty made aware of student's learning disability
Entrance Requirements: Documentation of learning disability; learning

disabilities specialist report; diagnostic testing at West Hills Community College; California Community College Eligibility Assessment; testing: WAIS, Woodcock-Johnson psychoeducational battery, IEP, psychological report
Special Facilities for: Visually, hearing and physical impairments
College Life: Small campus with individual attention and monitoring of progress/needs
Scholarships: See page 446.

WEST LOS ANGELES COLLEGE
9000 OVERLAND AVENUE
CULVER CITY, CALIFORNIA 90230-3500
(310) 287-4450; FAX: (310) 287-4417
E-MAIL: israelf@wlac.edu **WEB SITE: www.wlac.edu**

Name of Special Program: Disability Support Program and Services (DSPS)
Director: Adrienne Foster; *Learning Specialist:* Fran Israel
General Information: Two-Year Community College; Enrollment: 8,000; **Tuition:** Residents – $26 per unit, Non-Residents – $159 per unit; **Room and Board:** No college housing available. A 69-acre urban campus in a large town, 10 miles from Los Angeles. Founded in 1968. **Majors:** Biology, business/management, business/office, chemistry, civil technologies, communications, computer/information sciences, education, fine arts, geological sciences, health sciences, languages, letters/literature, marketing/distribution, mathematics, mechanical/electromechanical technologies, multi/interdisciplinary studies, music, philosophy, physics, precision production, protective services, psychology, social sciences, vocational home economics
Special Program: Enrollment in Special Program: 100; Cost: None
Staff: Learning disabilities specialists; special counselor; peer tutors
Program Features: Oral and extended time testing; individual and small group tutoring sessions; limited course load (first year); note-taking assistance – scribes; tape recorders; taped texts; basic study skills; academic advising for students with learning disabilities; faculty made aware of student's learning disability (at student's request)
Entrance Requirements: Documentation of learning disability; diagnostic testing at West Los Angeles College; California Community College Eligibility Assessment
Special Facilities for: Visual, hearing and physical impairments

WEST VALLEY COLLEGE
14000 FRUITVALE AVENUE
SARATOGA, CALIFORNIA 95070
(408) 741-2422
E-MAIL: len_schreibstein@westvalley.edu
WEB SITE: www.westvalley.edu

Name of Special Program: Disability and Educational Support Program (DESP)
Director: Len Schreibstein
General Information: Two-Year Community College; Enrollment: 11,000; **Tuition:** Residents – $26 per unit, Non-Residents – $157 per unit plus resident fees; **Room and Board:** No college housing available. An urban campus located at the base of the Santa Cruz Mountains, 10 miles from San Jose. **Majors:** Allied health, architecture, biology, business / management, business / office, chemistry, civil technologies, communications, computer / information systems, crafts / design, education, engineering and technologies, environmental design, fine arts, health sciences, home economics, industrial production, languages, law, letters / literature, marketing / distribution, mathematics, multi / interdisciplinary studies, parks and recreation, philosophy, physics, precision production, protective services, psychology, social sciences, visual / performing arts, vocational home economics
Special Program: Enrollment in Special Program: 200; Cost: None
Staff: Learning disabilities specialists; peer tutors; special counselors
Program Features: Oral and extended time testing, individual and small group tutoring sessions; basic study skills; note-taking assistance – scribes; tape recorders; taped texts; limited course load (first year); faculty made aware of student's learning disability
Entrance Requirements: Learning disabilities specialist report; diagnostic testing at West Valley Community College; testing: WAIS, Woodcock-Johnson psychoeducational battery, SEC, psychological report
Special Facilities for: Visual, hearing and physical impairments

COMMUNITY COLLEGE OF AURORA

16000 EAST CENTRE TECH PARKWAY, SUITE S-202E
AURORA, COLORADO 80011-9036
(303) 361-7395 V/TDD; FAX: (303) 340-7543
E-MAIL: reniece.jones@ccaurora.edu
WEB SITE: www.ccaurora.edu

Name of Special Program: Accessibility Services Office
Coordinator: Reniece Jones
General Information: Two-Year Community College; Enrollment: 5,000; **Tuition:** Residents – $176.50 per credit hour, Non-Residents – $368.90 per credit hour; **Room and Board:** $2,900 with a weekly meal plan. The Community College of Aurora is a two-year state college located in Aurora, a suburb of Denver and is located about 30 miles east of the Rocky Mountains. The goals of Community College of Aurora are to provide the first two years of college and university education for students who wish to transfer to a baccalaureate degree-granting institution; vocational and technical education for students who are seeking job preparation, career mobility, and/or job retraining; education that strengthens the academic background of the students and prepares them to pursue their educational and career goals. **Degrees:** AA, AS, AGS, and AAS. The AA and AS degrees are designed to prepare students for advanced standing (junior level) in colleges and universities granting baccalaureate degrees. The AGS degree is available for students who want to complete a broad program of courses without the constraints of specialization. This degree is not intended for transfer, but some courses in the degree may be transferable. The AAS degree prepares students for entry-level employment in a given occupation or for upgrading/stabilizing employment. These programs are not intended for transfer, but some courses within the degree may be transferable. AAS degrees are offered in accounting, banking and financial services, computer information systems, criminal justice, early childhood education and management, management, marketing and paralegal. Community College of Aurora also offers certificates in those areas mentioned above.
Special Program: Enrollment in Special Program: 100; Cost: None
Staff: Learning disabilities specialists; content tutors (faculty members); special counselors; sign language; oral interpreter
Program Features: Oral and extended time testing; individual and small group tutoring sessions; limited course load (first year); note-taking assistance – scribes; tape recorders; taped texts; basic study skills; academic advising for students with learning disabilities; faculty made aware of student's learning disability; word processing with assistive technology class is a year-round, three-credit course

Entrance Requirements: Documentation of learning disability; learning disabilities specialist report; SAT/ACT untimed scores accepted; assessment for placement if ACT/SAT is not available; diagnostic testing at Community College of Aurora for all students; medical evaluation; testing: WAIS, IEP, psychological report
College Life: Aurora is a small college with an average of 20 people in a class, thus providing much one-on-one contact with the instructors.

COMMUNITY COLLEGE OF DENVER
P.O. BOX 173363, CAMPUS BOX 204
DENVER, COLORADO 80217-3363
(303) 556-8455; FAX: (303) 556-4563
E-MAIL: sharon.walton-hunt@ccd.edu **WEB SITE: www.ccd.edu**

Name of Special Program: Special Learning Support Program
Director: Sharon Walton-Hunt
General Information: Two-Year Community College; Enrollment: 5,000; **Tuition:** Residents – $1,833 per 12 credit hours, Non-Residents – $4,141.80 per 12 credit hours; **Room and Board:** No college housing but available apartments are nearby. An urban campus with an impressive landscape surrounding the college. It is within walking distance of downtown Denver and Larimer Square. **Degrees:** AA, AS and AGS with a university parallel. Transfer Programs in nursing, accounting, computer information systems, dental hygiene, drafting for industry. AAS and certificate programs are also offered.
Special Program: Enrollment in Special Program: 200; Cost: None
Summer Program: A Freshman Experience Class is offered for students with learning disabilities.
Staff: Learning disabilities specialists; peer tutors; content tutors (faculty members); special counselors
Program Features: Oral and extended time testing; individual and small group tutoring sessions; basic study skills; note-taking assistance – scribes; tape recorders; taped texts; developmental program; limited course load (first year); academic advising for students with learning disabilities; faculty made aware of student's learning disability
Entrance Requirements: Documentation of learning disability; diagnostic testing at Community College of Denver
Special Facilities for: Visual, hearing and physical impairments

PIKES PEAK COMMUNITY COLLEGE
5675 SOUTH ACADEMY BLVD.
COLORADO SPRINGS, COLORADO 80906-5498
(719) 540-7128; FAX: (719) 540-7523
WEB SITE: www.ppcc.edu

Name of Special Program: Office of Accommodative Services and Instructional Support (OASIS)
Director: Michael Nusen
General Information: Two-Year Community College; Enrollment: 5,800; **Tuition:** Residents – $62.90 per credit hour, Non-Residents – $313.75 per credit hour; **Room and Board:** No college housing available. An urban college, 60 miles south of Denver in the foothills of the Rocky Mountains and Pikes Peak. **Majors:** Subjects are offered for transfer to four-year colleges and a variety of vocational fields.
Special Program: Enrollment in Special Program: 60; Cost: Ranges from none to the cost of one hour tuition
Staff: Learning disabilities specialists; peer tutors
Program Features: Oral and extended time testing; individual and small group tutoring sessions; basic study skills; note-taking assistance – scribes; tape recorders; taped texts; developmental program; limited course load (first year); academic advising for students with learning disabilities; faculty made aware of student's learning disability
Entrance Requirements: No requirements for admission, open door policy
Special Facilities for: Visual, hearing and physical impairments

CONNECTICUT

HOUSATONIC COMMUNITY TECHNICAL COLLEGE
900 LAFAYETTE BLVD.
BRIDGEPORT, CONNECTICUT 06604-4704
(203) 332-5018; FAX: (203) 332-5123
E-MAIL: llangella@hcc.commnet.edu
WEB SITE: www.hctc.commnet.edu

Name of Special Program: Disabilities Support Services, a program of the Academic Support Center
Director of Academic Support Center: Marianne Tecun (203) 332-5139; *Disabilities Support Coordinator:* Lynne Langella
General Information: Two-Year Community College; Enrollment: 4,272; **Tuition:** Residents – $1,176 per semester; Non-Residents – $3,528 per semester; **Room and Board:** No college housing available. A four-acre urban campus in a small city between Boston and New York, featuring one

of the best and largest art collections of any community college in the U.S.A. **Majors:** Business/management, business/office, communications, computer/information sciences, education, engineering, fine arts, medical laboratory technologies, multi/interdisciplinary studies, protective services, public affairs, rehabilitation services, vocational home economics, drug and alcohol rehabilitation counselor, human services
Special Program: Enrollment in Special Program: 300; Cost: None
Staff: Learning disabilities specialists; peer tutors; content tutors (faculty members); special counselors
Program Features: Oral and extended time testing; individual and small group tutoring sessions; limited course load (first and second years); note-taking assistance – scribes; tape recorders; taped texts; basic study skills; developmental program; academic advising for students with learning disabilities; faculty made aware of student's learning disability; evaluation of learning styles and study skills
Entrance Requirements: Documentation of disability
Special Facilities for: Visual, hearing, and physical impairments
College Life: A new campus featuring excellent accessibility for physically challenged students and the oldest and most comprehensive program in the community technical college system in Connecticut. Housatonic Community Technical College prides itself on creating a supportive environment where students and staff work closely, and know each other on a first name basis. The college is fortunate to have a faculty that fully supports the needs of students with learning disabilities. A strong collaborative effort is a part of the Housatonic Technical College program.

FLORIDA

BREVARD COMMUNITY COLLEGE

1519 CLEARLAKE ROAD
COCOA, FLORIDA 32922
(321) 433-5598; FAX: (321) 433-5679
E-MAIL: FertelL@brevardcc.edu **WEB SITE: www.brevardcc.edu**

Name of Special Program: Office for Students with Disabilities
Director: Dr. Lyndi Fertel
General Information: Two-Year Community College; Enrollment 8,000; **Tuition:** Residents – $56.50 per academic credit, $46.47 per vocational credit; Non-Residents – $210.25 per academic credit, $180.30 per vocational credit; **Room and Board:** No college housing available. Suburban 100-acre campus in a large town, 50 miles from Orlando. Brevard Community College has four integrated campuses – in Cocoa, Melbourne, Palm Bay and Titusville – that serve over 25,000 students. On the Cocoa campus

special features include a planetarium and solar observatory. **Degrees:** Associate in Arts, Associate in Applied Sciences, Applied Technical Diploma, College Credit Certificate, Postsecondary Adult Vocational Certificate

Special Program: Enrollment in Special Program: 285; 700 registered last year; Cost: None

Staff: Learning disabilities specialists, content tutors (faculty members)

Program Features: Oral and extended time testing; individual and small group tutoring sessions; limited course load (first year); note-taking assistance – scribes; tape recorders; taped texts; academic advising for students with learning disabilities; faculty made aware of student's learning disability (at student's request); developmental program; extended time testing in a quiet room; administration of placement tests

Entrance Requirements: Documentation of learning disability; learning disabilities specialist report; SAT / ACT untimed scores accepted; diagnostic testing at Brevard Community College (not required for entrance); testing: WAIS, psychological report

Special Facilities for: Visual, hearing and physical impairments

College Life: Caring faculty and staff of the Office for Students with Disabilities, wonderful Florida weather, nearby ocean and many public beaches, Orlando attractions only an hour away, and learning disabilities specialists on staff add to the college experience at Brevard.

Scholarships: See page 447.

BROWARD COMMUNITY COLLEGE

225 EAST LAS OLAS BLVD.
FORT LAUDERDALE, FLORIDA 33301
(954) 201-7655; FAX: (954) 201-7492
E-MAIL: bcranmer@broward.edu WEB SITE: www.broward.edu

Name of Special Program: Disability Services

Coordinator and Learning Disabilities Specialist: Beverly Cranmer

General Information: Two-Year Community College; Enrollment: 55,000; **Tuition:** Residents – $69.80 per credit hour, Non-Residents – $242.05 per credit hour; **Room and Board:** No college housing available. Broward Community College consists of four campuses, located in the greater Fort Lauderdale area. **Degrees:** Associate of Arts Degree Progams, Associate of Science Degree Programs, certificate programs in specialized areas and advanced technical certificates

Special Program: Enrollment in Special Program: 750; Cost: None

Staff: Disabilities specialists; peer tutors; sign language interpreters

Program Features: Oral and extended time testing; individual tutoring

sessions; note-taking assistance – scribes; tape recorders; taped texts; limited course load (first year); academic advising for students with learning disabilities; faculty made aware of student's learning disability; Kurzweil readers; word processors; FM systems; adaptive hardware and software
Entrance Requirements: Documentation of disability; SAT/ACT untimed scores accepted; testing: WAIS, Woodcock-Johnson psychoeducational battery – achievement tests, psychological report
Special Facilities for: Visual, hearing and physical impairments

CHIPOLA JUNIOR COLLEGE
3094 INDIAN CIRCLE
MARIANNA, FLORIDA 32446-2053
(850) 718-2417; FAX: (850) 718-2255
E-MAIL: duncang@chipola.edu **WEB SITE: www.chipola.edu**

Name of Special Program: Office of Students with Disabilities
Counselor: Gayle Duncan
General Information: Two-Year Community College; Enrollment: 1,400; **Tuition:** Residents – $64 per credit hour, Non-Residents – $193 per credit hour; **Room:** Double Room – $600 per semester The college is located in the Florida Panhandle, a rural area abounding in forests, rivers and lakes. Situated in Marianna near the banks of the Chipola River, the campus uses only about 40 of its 105 acres. The remainder is in its natural state, covered with pines, cedars and hardwoods. **Majors:** Courses offered include year-round academic and vocational subjects.
Special Program: Enrollment in Special Program: 71; Cost: None
Staff: Learning disabilities specialists; peer tutors
Program Features: Oral and extended time testing; individual tutoring sessions; note-taking assistance – scribes; tape recorders; taped texts; academic advising for students with learning disabilities; faculty made aware of student's learning disability
Entrance Requirements: Documentation of learning disability; SAT/ACT untimed scores accepted; student must meet criteria for acceptance to community college; testing: psychological report
Special Facilities for: Physical impairments
College Life: Chipola Junior College offers a caring staff with many services including motorized carts for physically impaired students. Instructors are understanding and willing to work with every student when possible. The college has a very diverse population of students and offers many possibilities for student interaction.

MIAMI-DADE COMMUNITY COLLEGE - NORTH CAMPUS
11380 NORTHWEST 27th AVENUE
MIAMI, FLORIDA 33167-3495
(305) 237-1272; FAX: (305) 237-1831 **WEB SITE: www.mdc.edu**
Director: Paul Edwards (305) 237-1146; pedwards@mdc.edu

INTERAMERICAN CAMPUS
627 SOUTHWEST 27th AVENUE
MIAMI, FLORIDA 33135
(305) 237-6360; FAX: (305) 237-6085
and
KENDALL CAMPUS
11011 SOUTHWEST 104th STREET
MIAMI, FLORIDA 33176-3393
(305) 237-2767
Coordinator: Mercy Mata (305) 237-0809, mmata@mdc.edu
Learning Disabilities Specialists: Michelle McGrew-Claret (305) 237-0856, mmcgrewc@mdc.edu; Jan Sabella (305) 237-0658, jsabella@mdc.edu

Name of Special Program: ACCESS Services Department
General Information: Two-Year Community College; Enrollment: 48,943; **Tuition:** Residents – $64.05 per credit hour, Non-Residents – $219.15 per credit hour; **Room and Board:** No college housing available. A multi-campus college, located in a large city. **Majors:** Agribusiness/agricultural production, allied health, architecture, area studies, biology, business/management, business/office, chemistry, civil technologies, communications and technologies, computer/information sciences, crafts/design, diagnostic/treatment services, education, engineering and technologies, environmental design, fine arts, geological sciences, health sciences, home economics, industrial production, law, letters/literature, marketing/distribution, mathematics, mechanical/electromechanical technologies, mechanics/repairers, medical laboratory technologies, multi/interdisciplinary studies, music, parks and recreation, philosophy, physical sciences, physics, precision production, protective services, psychology, public affairs, rehabilitation services, religion, renewable natural resources, social sciences, visual/performing arts, vocational home economics
Special Program: Enrollment in Special Program: 300; Cost: None; Tutoring cost: None
Staff: Learning disabilities specialists; content tutors (faculty members); special counselors
Program Features: Oral and extended time testing; taped texts; tape recorders; basic study skills; note-taking assistance – scribes; remedial/developmental program; individual and small group tutoring sessions; academic advising for students with learning disabilities; faculty made

aware of student's learning disability through student's accommodation forms; integrated use of computers in tutorial center

Entrance Requirements: Documentation of learning disability; SAT/ACT untimed scores accepted; all documentation is helpful. A minimum of documentation is required for initial acceptance.

Special Facilities for: Visual, hearing and physical impairments

College Life: Miami Dade Community College provides an innovative approach that integrates students with learning disabilities into mainstream classes while offering support and tutoring through ACCESS Services Department. Long experience and an emphasis on computer-aided learning make Miami Dade Community College a great place to learn.

Scholarships: Kendall Campus, see page 447.

MIAMI-DADE COMMUNITY COLLEGE - WOLFSON CAMPUS

300 NORTHEAST SECOND AVENUE
MIAMI, FLORIDA 33132-2297
(305) 237-3371 (Dr. Ken Marquard, kmarquar@mdc.edu);
FAX: (305) 237-3645
(305) 237-3994 (Dr. Bruce Smitley, bsmitley@mdc.edu)
WEB SITE: www.mdc.edu

Name of Special Program: ACCESS Services Department

Director: Dr. Ken Marquard

Assistant Director and Learning Disabilities Specialist: Dr. Bruce Smitley

General Information: Two-Year Community College; Enrollment: 24,000; **Tuition:** Residents – $54 per credit hour, Non-Residents – $199.90 per credit hour; **Room and Board:** No college housing available. The Wolfson Campus is located in downtown Miami near the Port of Miami and the American Airlines Arena. Miami-Dade Community College – Wolfson is an urban inner city institution, 62.4% Hispanic, 21.2% African-American, 14.5% non-Hispanic, 1.3% other. It is near many cultural and recreational areas. **Majors:** Agribusiness, agricultural production, allied health, architecture, area studies, biology, business/management, business/office, chemistry, civil technologies, communications and technologies, computer/information sciences, crafts/design, diagnostic/treatment services, education, engineering and technologies, environmental design, fine arts, geological sciences, health sciences, home economics, industrial production, law, letters/literature, marketing/distribution, mathematics, mechanical/electromechanical technologies, mechanics/repairers, medical laboratory technologies, multi/interdisciplinary studies, music, parks and recreation, philosophy, physical sciences, physics, precision produc-

tion, protective services, psychology, public affairs, rehabilitation services, religion, renewable natural resources, social sciences, visual/performing arts, vocational home economics. Job cooperative programs and internships available.
Special Program: Accommodations for students with learning disabilities: 130; Cost: None.
Staff: Learning disabilities specialists; peer tutors; special counselors; content tutors (faculty members); vocational educational specialist; lab manager; adaptive technology specialist
Program Features: Oral and extended time testing; tape recorders; taped texts; note-taking assistance – scribes; developmental program; individual and small group tutoring sessions; basic study skills; faculty made aware of student's learning disability (at student's request); Kurzweil reader; Franklin Master spellers; SAT/ACT testing provided with accommodations; visual tech; computer laboratory; academic software; specialized programs including Word Scholar and Open Book Unbound. Additional program for vocational students with learning disabilities: Professional Skills Program which integrates basic reading, writing and math skills with vocational strategies and adaptive technologies.
Entrance Requirements: Documentation of learning disability; learning disabilities specialist report; SAT/ACT extended time scores accepted; medical documentation required
Special Facilities for: Visual, hearing and physical impairments

GEORGIA

GEORGIA PERIMETER COLLEGE – CLARKSTON CAMPUS

555 NORTH INDIAN CREEK DRIVE
CLARKSTON, GEORGIA 30021-2396
(678) 891-3385
WEB SITE: www.gpc.edu
and
DECATUR CAMPUS
3205 PANTHERSVILLE ROAD
DECATUR, GA 30034-3897
(678) 891-2441
and
ROCKDALE/NEWTON CAMPUS
1115 WEST AVENUE
CONYERS, GA 30012-9448
E-MAIL: bmartin@gpc.edu or mclark@gpc.edu

Director: Bonnie Martin, *CDS Coordinator:* Dr. Mavis Clarke

ALPHARETTA CENTER AT GSU
3705 BROOKSIDE PARKWAY
ALPHARETTA, GA 30022
and
DUNWOODY CAMPUS
2101 WOMACK ROAD
DUNWOODY, GA 30338-4497
E-MAIL: manders3@gpc.edu
Coordinator: Michael Anderson, (770) 274-5235, manders3@gpc.edu

Name of Special Program: Center for Disability Services
General Information: Two-Year Community College; Enrollment: 11,900; **Tuition:** Residents – $771 per semester, Non-Residents – $3,083 per semester; **Room and Board:** No college housing available. Georgia Perimeter College -Clarkston Campus is near the Atlanta metro area with easy access to Atlanta. **Degrees:** Associate of Arts, Associate of Science, Career Programs, Associate of Applied Science and Dual Programs
Special Program: Enrollment in Special Program: 150–175; Cost: None
Staff: Learning disabilities specialists; professional tutors; special counselors; tutoring lab
Program Features: Oral and extended time testing; taped texts; note-taking assistance – scribes; tape recorders; individual and small group tutoring sessions; limited course load; basic study skills; developmental program; faculty made aware of student's learning disability; orientation; academic advisement; separate test rooms; scanners; voice output and voice-activated computers
Entrance Requirements: Documentation of learning disability; SAT/ACT untimed scores accepted; diagnostic testing at Georgia Perimeter College; medical evaluation if there is a medical condition requiring accommodations; testing: WAIS-R, WISC-R, WISC-III, Stanford-Binet if needed for $300
Special Facilities for: Visual, hearing and physical impairments, also psychological disabilities, head injuries and other medical disabilities

REINHARDT COLLEGE
7300 REINHARDT COLLEGE CIRCLE
WALESKA, GEORGIA 30183-2981
(770) 720-5567
E-MAIL: srr@reinhardt.edu **WEB SITE: www.reinhardt.edu**

Name of Special Program: Academic Support Office
Director: Sylvia Robertson
General Information: Two-Year/Four-Year Private College; Enrollment:

1,000; **Tuition:** $13,950; **Room and Board:** $5,800. Located in a small town in the rolling foothills of northwestern Cherokee County in Waleska, Georgia, 45 miles north of Atlanta. Affiliated with the United Methodist Church. **Degree Programs:** Associate's degree in arts, education, fine arts, Bachelor's degree in business administration, communication, liberal studies, fine arts, biology, psychology, history, sociology, English, religion.
Special Program: Enrollment in Special Program: 60; Cost: $972 per course tutored per semester.
Staff: Learning disabilities specialists; content tutors (faculty members)
Program Features: Oral and extended time testing; taped texts; note-taking assistance – scribes; tape recorders; individual and small group tutoring sessions; limited course load (first year); basic study skills; developmental program; faculty made aware of student's learning disability
Entrance Requirements: Documentation of learning disability; SAT or ACT untimed scores accepted; medical evaluation (as requested); handwritten essay; testing: WAIS, psychological report,
Special Facilities for: Visual, hearing and physical impairments
Scholarships: See page 447.

ILLINOIS

COLLEGE OF LAKE COUNTY

19351 WEST WASHINGTON STREET
GRAYSLAKE, ILLINOIS 60030
(847) 543-2474; FAX: (847) 543-3474
E-MAIL: bremedi@clcillinois.edu **WEB SITE: www.clcillinois.edu**

Name of Special Program: Office for Students with Disabilities
Director: Beth Remedi
General Information: Two-Year Community College; Enrollment: 15,000; **Tuition:** Residents – $71 per credit hour, Out-of-District Residents – $196 per credit hour, Out-of-State Residents – $267 per credit hour; **Room and Board:** No college housing available. The College of Lake County is located approximately 60 miles north of Chicago. **Degrees:** Associate in Arts, Associate in Science, Associate in Engineering Science, 50 career programs
Special Program: Enrollment in Special Program: 170; Cost: None
Staff: Learning disabilities specialist; content tutors (faculty members)
Program Features: Oral and extended time testing; note-taking assistance – scribes; individual and small group tutoring sessions; basic study skills; taped texts; tape recorders; faculty made aware of student's learning disability
Entrance Requirements: Documentation of learning disability; testing: psychological report
Special Facilities for: Visual, hearing and physical impairments

College Life: The College of Lake County provides personalized attention to students requiring individualized delivery of services.

ELGIN COMMUNITY COLLEGE
1700 SPARTAN DRIVE
ELGIN, ILLINOIS 60123
(847) 214-7220
E-MAIL: arhoades@elgin.edu **WEB SITE: www.elgin.edu**

Name of Special Program: Disability Services
Director: Annabelle Rhoades
General Information: Two-Year Community College; Enrollment: 6,000; **Tuition:** Residents – $84 per credit hour, Out-of-District Residents – $276.93 per credit hour, Out-of-State Residents – $349.61; **Room and Board:** No college housing available. A 119-acre campus in a suburban area with easy access to Chicago. **Degrees:** Transfer associate's degrees, terminal associate's degrees, diplomas and certificates
Special Program: Enrollment in Special Program: 85; Cost: None
Staff: Learning disabilities specialist; content tutors
Program Features: Oral and extended time testing; note-taking assistance – scribes; individual tutoring sessions; limited course load; study skills; developmental program; academic advising for students with learning disabilities; faculty made aware of student's learning disability (at student's request); books-on-tape
Entrance Requirements: Documentation of learning disability
Special Facilities for: Visual, hearing and physical impairments
College Life: A small and personal college.
Scholarships: See page 448.

HARPER COLLEGE
1200 WEST ALGONQUIN ROAD
PALATINE, ILLINOIS 60067
(847) 925-6266; FAX: (847) 925-6267
E-MAIL: pherrera@harpercollege.edu
WEB SITE: www.harpercollege.edu

Name of Special Program: Access and Disabilities Office/PASS (Program for Achieving Student Success)
Learning Disabilities Services Coordinator: Pascuala Herrera
General Information: Two-Year State College, Enrollment: 26,000; **Tuition:** Residents – $81 per credit hour, Illinois Out-of-District Residents – $288 per credit hour, Non-Residents and International Students – $362 per cred-

it hour; **Room and Board:** Nearby apartments range from $600 to $900 a month. A 200-acre suburban campus 25 miles from Chicago. **Majors:** Allied health, biology, business/management/office, chemistry, communications/technologies, computer/information sciences, diagnostic/treatment services, education, engineering/technologies, environmental design, fine arts, health sciences, home economics, industrial production, law, letters/literature, marketing/distribution, mathematics, mechanical/electromechanical technologies, mechanics/repairers, multi/interdisciplinary, music, parks and recreation, physical sciences, physics, protective services, psychology, social sciences, visual/performing arts
Special Program: Enrollment in Special Program: 60–80; Cost: $450 for one hour, $600 for two hours. *Summer Program:* ORN 101 is a one-credit two-day seminar offered for incoming freshmen.
Staff: Learning disabilities specialists; professional tutors; learning disabilities advocate and counselors
Program Features: Testing accommodations; tape recorders; taped texts; basic study skills; note-taking assistance – scribes; developmental classes; individualized tutoring sessions; reduced course load; progress monitoring
Entrance Requirements: Documentation of learning disability; handwritten essay; ACT untimed score accepted; diagnostic testing at Harper College ($300 fee); intake interview for new students; testing: SEC, psychological report
Special Facilities for: Visual, deaf/hard of hearing and physical impairments
College Life: Successful academic support program with individualized assistance. Good overall support within Disability Services with experienced, professional staff.
Scholarships: See page 448.

ILLINOIS VALLEY COMMUNITY COLLEGE

815 NORTH ORLANDO SMITH AVENUE
OGLESBY, ILLINOIS 61348-9692
(815) 224-2720; FAX: (815) 224-3033
E-MAIL: tina_hardy@ivcc.edu **WEB SITE: www.ivcc.edu**

Name of Special Program: Special Populations
Director: Tina Hardy
General Information: Two-Year Community College, Enrollment: 4,500; **Tuition:** Residents – $63.25 per credit hour, Non-Residents – $244.71 per credit hour; **Room and Board**: No college housing available. Illinois Valley Community College is on a 410-acre campus, located in a rural area 100 miles southwest of Chicago. **Degrees:** Associate in Arts and Sciences, and Certificates of Vocations and Achievements

Special Program: Enrollment in Special Program: 90; Cost: None
Staff: Learning disabilities specialists; peer tutors; special counselors
Program Features: Oral and extended time testing; individual and small group tutoring sessions; academic advising for students with learning disabilities; note-taking assistance – scribes; tape recorders; taped texts; basic study skills; developmental program; faculty made aware of student's learning disability (at student's request)
Entrance Requirements: Documentation of learning disability; learning disabilities specialist report; diagnostic testing at Illinois Valley Community College; testing: WAIS, IEP, psychological report
Special Facilities: Limited facilities available for visual, hearing and some physical impairments
College Life: Illinois Valley Community College has a caring faculty and excellent support services.

McHENRY COUNTY COLLEGE
8900 U.S. HIGHWAY 14
CRYSTAL LAKE, ILLINOIS 60012
(815) 455-8676; FAX: (815) 455-3766
E-MAIL: balbright@mchenry.edu **WEB SITE: www.mchenry.edu**

Name of Special Program: Special Needs Program
Coordinator: Beverly Albright
General Information: Two-Year Community College; Enrollment: 11,700; **Tuition:** Residents – $68 per credit, Out-of-District Residents – $267.93 per credit, Out-of-State and International Students – $312.54 per credit; **Room and Board:** No college housing available. A 109-acre suburban campus, located 40 miles northwest of Chicago in McHenry County. **Majors:** Full transfer program with Associate of Arts degree, Associate of Science degree, Associate of Fine Arts degree, and Associate of Engineering Studies degree. A wide range of occupational degrees and certificates is also offered.
Special Program: Enrollment in Special Program: 300; Cost: None
Staff: Learning disabilities specialists; content tutors (faculty members); peer tutors; special counselors
Program Features: Oral and extended time testing; individual and small group tutoring sessions; note-taking assistance – scribes; basic study skills; tape recorders; taped texts; developmental program; academic advising for students with learning disabilities; faculty made aware of student's learning disability
Entrance Requirements: Documentation of learning disability; learning disabilities specialist report

Special Facilities for: Visual, hearing and physical impairments
College Life: Caring from a well-qualified faculty and staff and lots of personal attention.
Scholarships: See page 449.

MORAINE VALLEY COMMUNITY COLLEGE
10900 SOUTH 88th AVENUE
PALOS HILLS, ILLINOIS 60465-0937
(708) 974-5711; FAX: (708) 974-8330
E-MAIL: sievers@morainevalley.edu
WEB SITE: www.morainevalley.edu

Name of Special Program: Center for Disability Services
Director: Debbie Sievers
General Information: Two-Year Community College, Enrollment: 20,000; **Tuition:** Residents – $1,608 for 24 credit hours, Out-of-District Residents – $5,000, Out-of-State Residents – $6,000; **Room and Board:** No college housing available. A 202-acre suburban campus in a large town, seven miles southwest of Chicago. **Majors:** Allied health, business/management, business/office, civil technologies, computer/information sciences, diagnostic/treatment services, engineering technologies, health sciences, industrial production, marketing/distribution, mechanical/repairers, medical laboratory technologies, multi/interdisciplinary studies, parks and recreation, precision production, protective services; rehabilitation services, vocational home economics
Special Program: Enrollment in Special Program: 250; Cost: $100 for LDSS, Sect I testing for in-house students, $200 for non-students
Staff: Learning disabilities specialists; special counselor
Program Features: Oral and extended time testing; individual and small group tutoring sessions; basic study skills; note-taking assistance – scribes; tape recorders; taped texts; faculty made aware of student's learning disability
Entrance Requirements: Documentation of learning disability; learning disabilities specialist report; handwritten essay; SAT/ACT untimed scores accepted; diagnostic testing at Moraine Valley Community College; testing: WAIS, IEP, psychological report
Special Facilities for: Visual, hearing and physical impairments
College Life: Small class sizes, excellent instructors, special accommodations, wide selection of career, certificate and transfer programs
Scholarships: See page 449.

PARKLAND COLLEGE
2400 WEST BRADLEY AVE.
CHAMPAIGN, ILLINOIS 61821-1899
(217) 351-2588, (217) 353-2251 TTY; FAX: (217) 351-2581
E-MAIL: nrowley@parkland.edu WEB SITE: www.parkland.edu

Name of Special Program: Learning Resource Services Center
Coordinator: Marilyn Ryan; *Disability Accommodations Specialist:* Nancy Rowley; *Learning Disabilities Specialist:* Evelyn Brown
General Information: Two-Year Community College; Enrollment: 10,000; **Tuition**: Residents – $72 per credit hour, Illinois Out-of-District Residents – $203 per credit hour, Out-of-State and International Students – $298 per credit hour; **Room and Board:** Privately operated dormitory available and housing referral service. Parkland College District 505 serves a combination of rural and urban areas located in Champaign, Illinois. The Champaign-Urbana population is about 140,000 including students of the University of Illinois. Parkland College is located on a 233-acre suburban campus and houses the William M. Staeckel Planetarium and a new Child Development Center in addition to other notable programs. **Degrees:** Two-year associate degrees and one-year certificate and transfer programs are offered in a variety of majors. Medical occupations, veterinary technology and equine management are some of the strongest areas of interest.
Staff: Learning disabilities specialists; peer tutors; testing assistants
Program Features: Oral and extended time testing; individual and small group tutoring sessions; limited course load (first year); note-taking assistance; basic study skills; tape recorders; taped texts; faculty made aware of student's learning disability; one-on-one strategy sessions; assistive technology lab including Kurzweil reader, Arkenstone software and scanner, Dragon Dictate, Jaws. Additional computer access is available. One section of Psychology 109 course is designed for students with learning disabilities. Individual strategy sessions designed around individual needs.
Entrance Requirements: Must be admitted to the college; documentation of learning disability; ACT untimed scores accepted or assessment test
Special Facilities for: Visual, hearing and physical impairments
Scholarships: See page 450.

WAUBONSEE COMMUNITY COLLEGE
ROUTE 47 AT WAUBONSEE DRIVE
SUGAR GROVE, ILLINOIS 60554-9799
(630) 466-7900 X2564; FAX/TTY: (630) 466-4649
E-MAIL: ihansen@waubonsee.edu
WEB SITE: www.waubonsee.edu

Name of Special Program: Access Center for Students with Disabilities
Manager: Iris Hansen
General Information: Two-Year Community College; Enrollment: 4,500; **Tuition:** Residents – $67 per credit hour, Illinois Out-of-District Residents – $208.81 per credit hour, Out-of-State Residents – $235.56 per credit hour; **Room and Board:** No college housing available. **Majors:** Liberal arts, interpreter training, nursing, pre-engineering, respiratory therapy, auto body, heating-ventilation-air conditioning, fire science, hazardous waste treatment, therapeutic massage
Special Program: Enrollment in Special Program: 285; Cost: None. The percentage of students with learning disabilities receiving a degree in two years is 15%.
Staff: Learning disabilities specialists; content tutors (faculty members); special counselor; peer tutors.
Program Features: Oral and extended time testing; tape recorders; taped texts; basic study skills; developmental program; note-taking assistance – scribes; individual and small group tutoring sessions; limited course load (first year); academic advising for students with learning disabilities; faculty made aware of student's learning disability; advocacy and leadership training
Entrance Requirements: Documentation of learning disability; handwritten essay; testing: WAIS, psychological report (both are optional)
Special Facilities for: Visual, hearing and physical impairments

INDIANA

IVY TECH STATE COLLEGE/A PARTNER IN THE COMMUNITY COLLEGE OF INDIANA
3501 FIRST AVENUE
EVANSVILLE, INDIANA 47710-3398
(812) 429-2865; FAX: (812) 429-9834
E-MAIL: pehlen@ivytech.edu **WEB SITE: www.ivytech.edu**

Name of Special Program: ACCESS
Director: Peggy Ehlen
General Information: Two-Year State Community College; Enrollment:

4,500; **Tuition:** Residents – $87.75 per credit hour, Non-Residents – $178.50 per credit hour; **Room and Board:** No college housing available. Ivy Tech State College in the Evansville region is located on a 15-acre urban campus, approximately 10 miles from the Ohio River. **Programs of Study:** Accounting, automotive, business administration, computer information systems, design technology, electronics technology, English/communications, general studies, industrial technology, interior design, manufacturing technology, math/physical science, medical assistant, nursing, office administration, practical nursing, psychology/social sciences, surgical technology, visual communications, criminal justice, early childhood education, health and human services, environmental design, graphic design, biotechnology, paramedic science (Liberal Arts degrees through Vincennes University)
Special Program: Special tutoring is provided on first-come, first-serve basis; Enrollment in Special Program: 25; Cost: None
Staff: Learning disabilities specialist
Program Features: Oral and extended time testing; academic advising for students with learning disabilities; note-taking assistance – scribes; tape recorders; taped texts; basic study skills; developmental program; faculty made aware of student's learning disability; scanner; Open Book; Naturally Speaking; Jaws
Entrance Requirements: Current documentation of learning disability; high school diploma or GED

IVY TECH STATE COLLEGE/COLLEGE OF INDIANAPOLIS STATE
50 WEST FALL CREEK PARKWAY NORTH DRIVE
INDIANAPOLIS, INDIANA 46208-5752
(317) 921-4908 V/TDD; FAX: (317) 921-4753
E-MAIL: sdunn@ivytech.edu
WEB SITE: www.ivytech.edu/indianapolis

Name of Special Program: Disability Support Services
Director: Sharon Dunn
General Information: Two-Year State Community College; Enrollment: 10,159; **Tuition:** Residents – $87.75 per credit, Non-Residents – $178.50 per credit hour; **Room and Board:** No college housing available. A 10-acre urban campus in a large city. **Programs of Study:** Business, Health and Human Services, Applied Science and Technology **Degrees:** Associate and Applied Science degrees; technical certificates and transfer programs; Liberal Arts degree through Vincennes University/Community College of Indianapolis Partnership
Special Program: Enrollment in Special Program: 300; Cost: None

Staff: Learning disabilities specialist; content tutors (faculty members); special counselors
Program Features: Oral and extended time testing; tape recorders; development program; faculty made aware of student's learning disability; note-taking assistance – scribes; basic study skills
Entrance Requirements: Learning disabilities specialist report
Special Facilities for: Visual, hearing and physical impairments
College Life: Ivy Tech/Indianapolis offers a full range of support services and accommodations to assist students in regular classrooms. As a two-year open enrollment college, students are able to enter the work force rapidly or transfer to complete a four-year degree through a partnership with other state schools.

VINCENNES UNIVERSITY
1002 NORTH FIRST STREET
VINCENNES, INDIANA 47591
(812) 888-4214; FAX: (812) 888-5531
E-MAIL: jkavanaugh@vinu.edu or slaue@vinu.edu
WEB SITE: www.vinu.edu

Name of Special Program: Student Transition into Educational Program (STEP)
Co-Directors: Jane Kavanaugh and Susan Laue
General Information: Two-Year Public Community College; Enrollment: 4,900; **Tuition:** Residents – $113.82 per credit hour, Non-Residents – $284.13 per credit hour; **Room and Board:** $3,220–3,393 per semester. A rural campus on 100 acres, 125 miles southwest of Indianapolis on Highway 41. Founded in 1801 by President William Henry Harrison, Vincennes University is a comprehensive community college that features a full-service student residential environment. **Programs of Study:** Business, health, physical education and recreation, humanities, science and mathematics, social science, health occupations, public service, technologies, occupational and academic transfer programs and majors with over 170 associate programs leading to entry to a four-year university or to the workforce
Special Program: Enrollment in Special Program: 120, limited to 60 in fall semester; Cost: $385 per semester. *Summer Program:* BRIDGE – specifically designed for incoming students during the last summer session – an all inclusive academic and social program. Contact: Hope Clausman, (812) 888-4149, summerbridge@vinu.edu or hclausman@vinu.edu
Staff: Learning disabilities specialists; content tutors (faculty members); peer tutors

Program Features: Oral and extended time testing; individual and small group tutoring sessions; limited course load (first year); academic advising for students with learning disabilities; tape recorders; taped texts (Recording for the Blind & Dyslexic); basic study skills; development program; Spelling Aces; specialized classes for STEP students
Entrance Requirements: Documentation of learning disability; learning disabilities specialist report; diagnostic testing at Vincennes University; teacher recommendation; testing: WAIS, psychological report
Special Facilities for: Visual, hearing and physical impairments
College Life: A community college with a residential campus, which includes a variety of sports, clubs, sororities and fraternities.

IOWA

DES MOINES AREA COMMUNITY COLLEGE

2006 SOUTH ANKENY BLVD.
ANKENY, IOWA 50021
(515) 964-6469
E-MAIL: skmeredith@dmacc.edu **WEB SITE: www.dmacc.edu**

Name of Special Program: STRIVE (Selected Training Received in Vocational Education), a vocational/technical training program for students requiring resource assistance
Coordinator: Sharon Meredith
General Information: Two-Year Community College; Enrollment: 21,000; **Tuition:** Residents – $98 per credit hour, Non-Residents – $196 per credit hour; **Room and Board:** Campus apartments privately owned. A suburban campus located on a 304-acre site, six miles north of Des Moines within the city limits of Ankeny. The campus is easily accessible from both Interstate 35 and 80. **Majors:** Accounting and bookkeeping, agribusiness, architectural millwork, auto collision repair technology, auto mechanics technology, building maintenance, building trades, CAP-Chrysler, criminal justice, culinary arts, data entry (spring only), diesel technology, early child development, fashion/design, graphic design, graphic technologies, greenhouse production, heating, air-conditioning, refrigeration technology, hospitality business, information processing support, landscape design, office assistant, office specialist, retailing, sales and management, tool and diemaking, turf maintenance, welding
Special Program: Enrollment in Special Program: 100; Cost: None. The percentage of students with learning disabilities receiving a degree in two years is 20%.
Staff: Learning disabilities specialists; content tutors (faculty members)
Program Features: Oral and extended time testing; individual and small

group tutoring sessions; note-taking assistance – scribes; taped texts; tape recorders; basic study skills; developmental program; faculty made aware of student's learning disability
Entrance Requirements: Documentation of learning disability; learning disabilities specialist report; IEP, including vocational training goals and objectives; diagnostic testing at Des Moines Area Community College
Special Facilities for: Visual, hearing and physical impairments
College Life: STRIVE staff has excellent working relationships with Des Moines Area Community College faculty. Low turnover rate in staff who have an understanding of the program and class requirements.

INDIAN HILLS COMMUNITY COLLEGE
525 GRANDVIEW
OTTUMWA, IOWA 52501
1-800-726-2585 X5218
E-MAIL: mstewart@indianhills.edu
WEB SITE: www.indianhills.edu

Name of Special Program: Transition Program
Dean of Academic Services: Mary Stewart
General Information: Two-Year Community College; Enrollment: 2,915; **Tuition:** Residents – $99 per credit hour, Non-Residents – $149 per credit hour; **Room and Board:** $2,325–2,445, depending on accommodations. Indian Hills Community College is located on a 400-acre campus in northeastern Ottumwa, a small city of about 25,000 residents. **Programs**: *Business Technologies:* computer programmer/analyst, computer programming/management, administrative secretarial and bookkeeping. *Health Occupations:* nursing, child development, health information technology, physical therapist, assistant radiologic technology and practical nursing. *Advanced Technologies:* agricultural power technology, automotive technology, automotive collision technology, aviation maintenance technology, aviation pilot training, computer systems/networks technology, diesel power technology, drafting technology, electronic/telecommunications technology, laser/electro-optics technology, machine technology, robotics/automation technology, automotive repair, appliance servicing, building trades and electronics/computer occupations. *Service Occupations:* criminal justice, food service, and turf and greenhouse management
Special Program: Enrollment in Special Program: 30; Cost: $1,950–2,925 Tuition, $450 Fees
Staff: Learning disabilities specialists; content tutors (faculty members); peer tutors
Program Features: Oral and extended time testing; individual tutoring sessions; limited course load (first year); note-taking assistance – scribes;

basic study skills; developmental program; faculty made aware of student's learning disability; separate curriculum available
Entrance Requirements: On-campus visit; personal interview

IOWA CENTRAL COMMUNITY COLLEGE
330 AVENUE M
FORT DODGE, IOWA 50501
(515) 576-0099 X2254
E-MAIL: lundeen@iowacentral.com or lundberg@iowacentral.com
WEB SITE: www.iowacentral.com

Name of Special Program: Student Success Center – Special Needs Office
Coordinator: Shelley Lundeen; *Coordinator of Special Needs:* Heather Lundberg (515) 576-0099 X2245
General Information: Two-Year Community College; Enrollment: 3,198; **Tuition:** Residents – $93 per credit hour, Non-Residents – $139.50 per credit hour; **Room and Board:** Coed dormitories are available. Apartments for the physically disabled are also available. Iowa Central Community College is located in a community of 28,000. There are two semesters, three summer sessions, winter interim session, varsity athletics, international studies program, performing arts. **Degrees**: Associate of Arts, Associate of Science, Associate of General Studies, Associate of Applied Science
Special Program: Enrollment in Special Program: 34
Staff: Learning disabilities specialists; content tutors (faculty members); peer tutors; special counselors
Program Features: Oral and extended time testing; individual tutoring sessions; limited course load (first year); academic advising for students with learning disabilities; note-taking assistance – scribes; taped texts; tape recorders; basic study skills; developmental program; faculty made aware of student's learning disability
Entrance Requirements: Documentation of learning disability: learning disabilities specialist report; diagnostic testing at Iowa Central Community College

SOUTHEASTERN COMMUNITY COLLEGE: NORTH CAMPUS
1015 SOUTH GEAR AVENUE
WEST BURLINGTON, IOWA 52655-0180
(319) 752-2731 X5098; FAX: (319) 752-4957
E-MAIL: aorchard@scciowa.edu; WEB SITE: www.scciowa.edu

Name of Special Program: Secondary Transitional Education Program (STEP)
Coordinator: Ann Orchard
General Information: Two-Year Community College; Enrollment: 2,537; **Tuition:** Residents – $97 per semester hour, Non-Residents – $109 per semester hour; Room and Board: $9,024 per semester. A 160-acre suburban campus in a large town, 200 miles from Chicago, Illinois. **Majors:** Agribusiness/agricultural production, allied health, business/management, business/office, civil technologies, computer/information sciences, engineering and technologies, environmental control technologies, health sciences, mechanical/electromechanical technologies, mechanics/repairers, multi/interdisciplinary studies, precision production, protective services, gunsmithing
Special Program: Enrollment in Special Program: 45; Cost: None
Staff: Learning disabilities specialists; content tutors (faculty members)
Program Features: Oral and extended time testing; individual and small group tutoring sessions; limited course load (first year); basic study skills; note-taking assistance – scribes; tape recorders; taped texts; developmental program; faculty made aware of student's learning disability
Entrance Requirements: Documentation of learning disability; learning disabilities specialist report; testing: SEC; limited to Iowa residents who are currently receiving Special Education Services in AEA 16 (Area Education Association – (319) 753-6561). All students take ASSEP Test for entrance into college.
Special Facilities for: Physical impairments

WALDORF COLLEGE
106 SOUTH 6th STREET
FOREST CITY, IOWA 50436
800-292-1903; FAX: (641) 585-8194
E-MAIL: murraym@waldorf.edu WEB SITE: www.waldorf.edu

Name of Special Program: Learning Disabilities Program (LDP)
Director of the Academic Achievement Center: Michelle Murray
General Information: Two/Three-Year Private College; Enrollment: 650; **Tuition, Room and Board:** $21,790 per year. A 25-acre rural campus in a small town, two and one-half hours from Minneapolis and Des Moines.

Waldorf College is affiliated with the Evangelical Lutheran Church in America. **Degrees:** AA degree program which prepares for most four-year liberal arts/professional degrees, BA degree program in communications (print media, journalism and electronic media), business (management or finance and banking), humanities and elementary education
Special Program: Enrollment in Special Program: 28; Limited to 20 freshmen; Cost: $400 for freshmen per semester, $300 for sophomores per semester. *Summer Program:* Orientation prior to school year focuses on learning and study styles/strategies, time management, transition from high school, getting to know the college setting, and developing a support system
Staff: Learning disabilities specialists; peer tutors; special counselors
Program Features: Oral and extended time testing; individual and small group tutoring sessions; limited course load (first year); academic advising for students with learning disabilities; basic study skills; note-taking assistance – scribes; tape recorders; taped texts; developmental program; faculty made aware of student's learning disability
Entrance Requirements: Documentation of learning disability; SAT/ACT untimed scores accepted; testing: WAIS or WISC, IEP, psychological report
College Life: Waldorf is a small Lutheran college. This makes the students accepting of differences in others. Faculty are very willing to give extra time in their offices to work with students individually.
Scholarships: See page 450.

MARYLAND

COLLEGE OF SOUTHERN MARYLAND

8730 MITCHELL ROAD, P.O. BOX 910
LA PLATA, MARYLAND 20646-0910
(301) 934-7611; FAX: (301) 934-7699
E-MAIL: patsc@csmd.edu, glennisd@csmd.edu
WEB SITE: www.csmd.edu

Name of Special Program: Student Success Center
Director: Pat Schroeder; *Academic Support Services/ADA Coordinator,* Glennis Daniels-Bacchus (301) 934-2251 X7614
General Information: Two-Year Community College; Enrollment: $5,000–6,000; **Tuition:** Charles, St. Mary's and Calvert County Residents – $94 per credit hour, Other Maryland Residents – $160 per credit hour, Out-of-State Residents – $201 per credit hour; **Room and Board:** No college housing available. A 175-acre suburban campus, La Plata is within 30-50 minutes from Washington, D.C., near Chesapeake Bay and the Potomac River. Other campuses are in Leonardtown, Prince Frederick and Waldorf, Maryland. **Degrees:** Associate in Applied Science (AAS), Associate in Arts

(AA), Certificate Programs
Special Program: Enrollment in Special Program: 75; Cost: None
Staff: Learning disabilities specialists; content tutors (faculty members); special counselors
Program Features: Oral and extended time testing; individual and small group tutoring sessions; basic study skills; note-taking assistance – scribes; taped texts; tape recorders; developmental program; academic advising for all students with learning disabilities; faculty made aware of student's learning disability
Entrance Requirements: Documentation of learning disability; SAT/ACT untimed scores accepted; testing: psychological report
Special Facilities for: Visual, hearing and physical impairments

HOWARD COMMUNITY COLLEGE
LITTLE PATUXENT PARKWAY
COLUMBIA, MARYLAND 20144
(410) 772-4822
WEB SITE: www.howardcc.edu

Name of Special Program: Student Support Services
Director: Kathleen McSweeney (410) 772-4606
General Information: Two-Year Community College; Enrollment: 3,496; **Tuition:** Howard County Residents – $105 per credit hour, Maryland Residents – $188 per credit hour, Out-of-State Residents – $223 per credit hour; **Room and Board:** No college housing available. Located beside a lake on a 120-acre wooded campus with easy access to Baltimore and Washington, D.C. **Majors:** Allied health, biology, botany, business/management, business/office, chemistry, communications, computer/information sciences, crafts/design, education, engineering and technologies, fine arts, health sciences, industrial production, law, letters/literature, marketing/distribution, mechanical/electromechanical technologies, multi/interdisciplinary studies, music, physical sciences, physics, psychology, social sciences, visual/performing arts, zoology
Special Program: Enrollment in Special Program: 225; Cost: None
Staff: Learning disabilities specialists; content tutors (faculty members); special counselors
Program Features: Oral and extended time testing; individual and small group tutoring sessions; limited course load; basic study skills; note-taking assistance – scribes; taped texts; tape recorders; developmental program; faculty made aware of student's learning disability; computer lab
Entrance Requirements: Documentation of learning disability; testing: WAIS, SEC, psychological report
Special Facilities for: Visual, hearing and physical impairments

MONTGOMERY COMMUNITY COLLEGE
51 MANNAKEE STREET
ROCKVILLE, MARYLAND 20850
(301) 279-5058, (301) 294-9672 TTY; FAX: (301) 279-5097
E-MAIL: rose.sachs@montgomerycollege.edu
WEB SITE: www.montgomerycollege.edu

Name of Special Program: College Access Program in Disability Support Services Department
Department Chair, Counselor/Prescriptive Learning Specialist: Rose Sachs
General Information: Two-Year Community College; Enrollment: 20,930; **Tuition:** Montgomery County Residents – $93 per semester hour, Out-of County Residents – $191 per semester hour, Out-of-State Residents – $257 per semester hour; **Room and Board:** No college housing available. An 85-acre suburban campus in a small city, 12 miles north of Washington, DC. **Majors**: General education, arts and sciences, over 50 curricula. AA, AAS and AS degrees, as well as certificates
Special Program: Enrollment in Special Program: 50; Cost: None. The College Access Program serves students with specific language-based learning disabilities who have the potential and motivation for success in college classes, but who first require a developmental program in language skills.
Staff: Learning disabilities specialists; peer tutors; special counselors
Program Features: Oral and extended time testing; individual tutoring sessions; limited course load; study skills; note-taking assistance – scribes; tape recorders (provided by student); taped texts (Recording for the Blind & Dyslexic); developmental program; faculty made aware of student's learning disability (at student's request); computer lab; adaptive equipment. College Access Program classes include four non-credit developmental classes in English and reading and two one-credit student development courses in study habits and college orientation to academic and student services. Mandatory tutoring sessions and an individual skills laboratory support classroom instruction.
Entrance Requirements: Documentation of learning disability, educational evaluation with the prescriptive specialist, writing sample, a complete Disability Support Services intake packet, interview with a counselor for students with disabilities; teacher evaluations; diagnostic testing at Montgomery Community College; learning disability primary disability; testing: WAIS, IEP, psychological report
Special Facilities for: Visual, hearing and physical disabilities

LESLEY UNIVERSITY
29 EVERETT STREET
CAMBRIDGE, MASSACHUSETTS 02138-2790
(617) 349-8181
E-MAIL: threshld@mail.lesley.edu WEB SITE: www.lesley.edu

Name of Special Program: The Threshold Program
Director: James S. Wilbur
General Information: Private Two/Three-Year College-Based Program at Lesley University; Enrollment: 6,262; **Threshold Program Tuition:** $27,400; **Room and Board:** $10,750. An urban campus, adjacent to Harvard University in Cambridge, Massachusetts. Founded in 1982. **Majors:** Threshold is a comprehensive, non-degree campus-based program at Lesley University for highly motivated young adults with diverse learning disabilities and other special needs. Most students test in the low to average range. Business services, early childhood education, human services
Special Program: Enrollment in Special Program: 65
Staff: Learning disabilities specialists; specialists in related fields (faculty members); vocational counselors. All faculty have advanced degrees in their specialized areas of instruction.
Program Features: Orientation program, combination of course work and field placement, individualized structured curriculum, independent and consumer skills courses; programming in social and psychological development, vocational training in business services, early childhood and human services. Transition Year (3rd year) recommended – tuition, $8,150. Graduates earn six college credits upon completion of the two-year program. An additional three university credits are received upon completion of Transition Year.
Entrance Requirements: Personal interview; testing: WAIS-R III, educational achievement tests, psychological report. Financial aid available. Interested candidates must submit a FAFSA form.

MASSACHUSETTS BAY COMMUNITY COLLEGE
50 OAKLAND STREET
WELLESLEY HILLS, MASSACHUSETTS 02181-5399
(781) 239-2626
WEB SITE: www.massbay.edu

Name of Special Program: College Integration Project
Coordinator: Dr. Rita Hayward
General Information: Two-Year Community College; Enrollment: 3,388; **Tuition:** Residents – $119 per credit hour, Non-Residents – $325 per credit

hour; **Room and Board:** No college housing available. A suburban campus located on a scenic 84-acre site, one mile west of the intersection of Routes 128 and 9, approximately ten miles west of Boston. **Majors:** accounting, accounting with microcomputer applications, banking and finance, biotechnology, coding and medical record review, communications, computer maintenance, diagnostic ultrasonography, early childhood education, government procurement and contract management, interior design, liberal arts, licensed practical nursing, management/marketing, nuclear medicine, office management, paralegal, plastics technology, social work , travel and tourism, word processing. The college also offers pilot programs in allied health and technology called clusters, where students take introduction to allied health professions, writing and mathematics as a block with faculty who meet weekly; all work in all subjects geared toward allied health. Introduction to technology, writing and math has the same type of approach.

Special Program: Enrollment in Special Program: 14–20, limited to 30; Cost: None

Staff: Learning disabilities specialists; peer tutors; mentor tutors

Program Features: Oral and extended time testing; individual and small group tutoring sessions; limited course load (first year); basic study skills; developmental program; note-taking assistance – scribes; faculty made aware of student's learning disability; tape recorders; taped texts; self-advocacy groups; adaptive computer equipment

Entrance Requirements: Documentation of learning disability; learning disabilities specialist report; handwritten essay; testing: WAIS, IEP, psychological report

Special Facilities for: Visual, hearing and physical impairments

MOUNT WACHUSETT COMMUNITY COLLEGE

444 GREEN STREET
GARDNER, MASSACHUSETTS 01440
(978) 630-9316
E-MAIL: r.thibodeau@mwcc.mass.edu or j.kulig@mwcc.mass.edu
WEB SITE: www.mwcc.mass.edu

Name of Special Program: Visions Program TRIO – Student Support Services

Director: Ruth Thibodeau; *Learning Disabilities Specialist:* Joyce Kulig (978) 630-9185

General Information: Two-Year Community College; Enrollment: 2,564; **Tuition:** Massachusetts Residents – $136 per credit hour, New England Residents – $148.50 per credit hour, Non-Residents and International

Students – $341 per credit hour; **Room and Board:** No college housing available. Mount Wachusett Community College is on a 270-acre campus located in a rural area in north central Massachusetts with easy access to Boston. **Majors:** Business administration, automotive technology, art, deaf studies, child study, computer graphic design, criminal justice, executive office administration, human services, liberal arts, nursing, physical therapist assistant
Special Program: Enrollment in Special Program: 100; Cost: None
Staff: Learning disabilities specialists; peer tutors
Program Features: Oral and extended time testing; individual tutoring sessions; limited course load (first year); basic study skills; note-taking assistance – scribes; tape recorders; taped texts; developmental program; academic advising for students with learning disabilities; faculty made aware of student's learning disability
Entrance Requirements: Documentation of learning disability
Special Facilities for: Visual, hearing and physical impairments
College Life: Disability staff and counseling staff work closely together as a team to provide the best possible services for students with disabilities.
Scholarships: See page 451.

MICHIGAN

WASHTENAW COMMUNITY COLLEGE

4800 EAST HURON RIVER DRIVE, P.O. BOX D-1
ANN ARBOR, MICHIGAN 48106-1610
(734) 973-3342; FAX: (734) 477-8517
E-MAIL: debrag@wccnet.edu
WEB SITE: www.wccnet.edu

Name of Special Program: Learning Support Services
Coordinator: Debra Guerrero; *Learning Disabilities Specialist:* Debra Urquhart (734) 973-3493 debra@wccnet.edu
General Information: Two-Year Community College; Enrollment: 11,089; **Tuition:** In-District Residents – $71 per credit hour; Out-of-District Residents – $116 per credit hour, Out-of-State Residents – $153 per credit hour; **Room and Board:** No college housing available. Washtenaw Community College is located in a beautifully landscaped and wooded area near Ann Arbor's downtown area. The college offers state-of-the-art vocational programs. Students can attend three semesters per calendar year. **Degrees:** Associate in Arts, Associate in Science, Associate in Applied Science, Associate in Nursing, Associate in Business, certificates in occupational programs.
Special Program: Enrollment in Special Program: 50; Cost: None

Staff: Learning disabilities specialists; peer, professional/paraprofessional tutors; counselors; advisors
Program Features: Oral and extended time testing; individual and small group tutoring sessions; limited course load; note-taking assistance – scribes; taped texts; tape recorders; academic advising for students with learning disabilities; basic study skills; developmental courses; computer software; Kurzweil 3000 reader; Dragon Naturally Speaking
Entrance Requirements: Documentation of learning disability; learning disabilities specialist report; medical evaluation; must meet admissions criteria; testing: psychological report
College Life: Washtenaw Community College faculty work very closely with students registered in Learning Support Services. The staff in Learning Support Services foster caring and understanding of students with a learning disability so they can succeed.
Scholarships: See page 451.

MINNESOTA

COLLEGE OF ST. CATHERINE: MINNEAPOLIS
601 SOUTH 25th STREET
MINNEAPOLIS, MINNESOTA 55454
(651) 690-7777; FAX: (651) 690-7848
E-MAIL: careerinfo@admin.stkate.edu
WEB SITE: www.stkate.edu

Name of Special Program: Services for Students with Disabilities
Learning Disabilities Specialists: Kathy Whaley and Deborah Churchill
General Information: Four-Year Private College with Two-Year Healthcare Program; Enrollment: 3,682; **Tuition:** $460 per credit hour; **Room:** $1,250 single room, includes local phone per semester. A one-acre urban campus in the heart of the popular Twin Cities with wonderful cultural, athletic and outdoor opportunities. **Majors:** Chemical dependency family treatment, coding specialist, health and wellness counseling, health care interpreter, holistic therapies, medical record technician/health information specialist, medical transcription specialist, nursing/mobility option, occupational therapy assistant, phlebotomy, physical therapist assistant, radiography, respiratory therapist, sonography. Health care and human service career opportunities are offered through associate degree and certificate programs. Associate of Arts degree, Center for Contemporary Montessori Programs
Special Program: Enrollment in Special Program: 50; Cost: None
Staff: Learning disabilities specialist; peer tutors; professional tutors, reading and testing specialists; disabilities specialist – vision

Program Features: Oral and extended time testing; individual and small group tutoring sessions; extended program; note-taking assistance; taped texts; basic study skills; developmental courses; academic advisement; vision impairment program
Entrance Requirements: Documentation of disability
Special Facilities for: Visual, hearing and physical impairments

HIBBING COMMUNITY COLLEGE
1515 EAST 25th STREET
HIBBING, MINNESOTA 55746
(218) 262-6745
E-MAIL: shellyflaten@hcc.mnscu.edu WEB SITE: www.hcc.mnscu.edu

Name of Special Program: Disability Services
Director: Shelly Flaten
General Information: Two-Year Community College; Enrollment: 3,145; **Tuition:** Residents – $131.90 per credit hour, Non-Residents – $161.05 per credit hour; **Room and Board:** College housing available and housing lists provided. The College is located next to U.S. Highway 169 on the Iron Range of northeastern Minnesota, 75 miles northwest of Duluth. Hibbing occupies seven ultramodern buildings, linked together with glassed-in walkways. The Boundary Waters Canoe Area is one and one-half hours north of Hibbing. **Degrees:** Associate in Arts, Associate in Science, Associate in Applied Science. One-year occupational programs are also available in the secretarial and clerical areas, and students successfully completing these programs are awarded the one-year certificate of attendance.
Special Program: Enrollment in Special Program: 50; Cost: None. *Summer Program:* Early Start is a summer program offered to all students. It is designed especially for the inexperienced or apprehensive college student. This workshop helps students brush up on their writing and math skills and gain confidence in many other areas. Cost: None
Staff: Learning disabilities specialists; peer tutors; special counselors
Program Features: Oral and extended time testing; individual and small group tutoring sessions; registration assistance; note-taking assistance – scribes; tape recorders; taped texts; basic study skills; developmental program; faculty made aware of student's learning disability (at student's request); any reasonable accommodation
Entrance Requirements: Documentation of learning disability
Special Facilities for: Visual, hearing and physical impairments

METROPOLITAN COMMUNITY COLLEGE – LONGVIEW

500 SOUTHWEST LONGVIEW ROAD
LEE'S SUMMIT, MISSOURI 64081-2105
(816) 672-2053; FAX: (816) 672-2719
E-MAIL: maryellen.jenison@mcckc.edu WEB SITE: www.mcckc.edu

Name of Special Program: Academic Bridges to Learning Effectiveness (ABLE)
Director: Mary Ellen Jenison
General Information: Two-Year Community College; Enrollment: 8,117; **Tuition:** Residents – $78 per credit hour, Out-of-District Residents and Qualifying Johnson County, Kansas Residents – $138 per credit hour, Out-of-State Residents – $185 per credit hour, International Students – $218 per credit hour; **Room and Board:** No college housing available. The Longview campus overlooks Longview Lake in Lee's Summit and is on land donated to the Metropolitan Community Colleges of Kansas City, Missouri, by the family of R.A. Long, a pioneer lumberman. The campus's seven buildings include an exceptional recreational center and one that houses the college's nationally prominent automotive technology program. In 2001, Longview became the first community college to achieve *Time* magazine/*Princeton Review's* College-of-the-Year honors. Students earn semester hours for liberal arts, preprofessional or vocational degrees. Cooperative programs are offered with Johnson County Community College. **Transfer Degrees:** Associate in Arts, Associate in Computer Science, Associate in Engineering, Associate in Science. Associate in Applied Science degrees in graphic design, accounting, general business, management, computer science and information systems, construction management, marketing and retailing, office management, database, networking, programming, technical support, web and multimedia, biotechnology, audio engineering technology, automotive technology, collision repair technology, Ford ASSET, GM ASEP, or general automotive, mechanical or merchandising, grounds and turf management, land surveying, music technology, power plant technology, railroad operations, correctional science, forensic chemistry, chef apprenticeship, food and beverage or hotel/motel, correctional services, drug addiction services, mental health services, youth care services, mortuary science. Certificates in accounting assistant or clerk, computerized accounting, entrepreneurial studies, supervision, supply chain logistics, administrative assistant, database, networking, programming, technical support, web and multimedia, biotechnology, automotive technology, collision repair technology, mechanical or merchandising, grounds and turf management, horticulture, land surveying, power plant technology, correctional science, drug addiction services, mental health services, workers in developmental dis-

abilities, youth development worker, youth work.
Special Program: Enrollment in Special Program: 50–80, limited to 80; Cost: $35 per credit hour. *Summer Program:* Students may enroll in first-semester block of ABLE courses and / or a variety of general studies courses with support through ABLE. Cost: $35 per credit hour. Optional. The percentage of students with learning disabilities receiving degrees in two years is 9%; in four years is 15%, and in five or more years is 21%. ABLE is designed to teach students skills and knowledge they need to successfully pursue a variety of goals. The above figures count only students who have earned associate degrees through the Metropolitan Community Colleges or who have reported back to us that they have earned associate degrees.
Staff: Learning disabilities specialists; peer tutors; special counselors
Program Features: Oral and extended time testing; individual and small group tutoring sessions; basic study skills; note-taking assistance – scribes; tape recorders; taped texts; developmental program; faculty made aware of student's learning disability; support groups; specialized courses on college orientation; decision-making; assertiveness; legal rights and responsibilities; self-advocacy; academic advising for students with learning disabilities; mentoring of first-semester students
Entrance Requirements: Documentation of learning disability; learning disabilities specialist report; documentation of brain injury, if applicable; testing: WAIS, psychological and neuropsychological report
Special Facilities for: Visual, hearing and physical impairments
College Life: Longview has a history of being at the forefront in providing services to students with disabilities. The ABLE program has been recognized both statewide and nationally for the services provided to students with learning disabilities. The college faculty and staff focus on providing friendly, quality services to all students.
Scholarships: See page 452.

METROPOLITAN COMMUNITY COLLEGE – PENN VALLEY

3201 SOUTHWEST TRAFFICWAY
KANSAS CITY, MISSOURI 64111
(816) 759-4089
E-MAIL: patricia.goodwin@mcckc.edu **WEB SITE: www.mcckc.edu**

Name of Special Program: Academic Bridges to Learning Effectiveness (ABLE)
Director: Patricia Goodwin
General Information: Two-Year Community College; Enrollment: 6,100; **Tuition:** Residents – $78 per credit hour, Out-of-District and Qualifying

Johnson County, Kansas Residents – $138 per credit hour, Out-of-State Residents – $185 per credit hour, International Students – $218; **Room and Board:** No college housing available. Located near Penn Valley Park and minutes north of the Country Club Plaza, Penn Valley Community College is a huge enclosed campus that includes the Francis Child Development Institute and the Anna and Kemper Carter Center for the Visual Arts and Imaging Technology. **Majors:** Students may pursue programs in liberal arts as well as preprofessional or vocational areas. Cooperative programs are offered with Johnson County Community College and Kansas City, Kansas, Community College. Transfer Degrees: Associate in Arts, Associate in Computer Science, Associate in Engineering, Associate in Science. Associate in Applied Science degrees in graphic design, accounting, general business, management, computer science and information systems, construction management, marketing and retailing, office management, database, networking, programming, technical support, web and multimedia, biotechnology, dental assisting, occupational therapy assistant, paramedic (EMT), physical therapy assistant, professional nursing, radiologic technology, respiratory care, child growth and development, fashion design and merchandising, interior design, auto engineering technology, music technology, power plant technology, railroad operations, correctional science, juvenile services, mental health, forensic chemistry, chef apprenticeship, food and beverage or hotel/motel, correctional services, drug addiction services, mental health services, youth care services, mortuary science, paralegal technology. Certificates in digital press technician, accounting assistant or clerk, computerized accounting, entrepreneurial studies, supervision, supply chain logistics, administrative assistant, database, networking, programming, technical support, web and multimedia, biotechnology, dental assisting, health and information technology – coding specialist, medical transcription, paramedic (EMT), practical nursing, surgical technology, child growth and development, interior design, horticulture, automotive technology, collision repair technology, mechanical or merchandising, grounds and turf management, power plant technology, correctional science, drug addiction services, mental health services, workers in development disabilities, youth development worker, youth work

Special Program: Enrollment in Special Program: 25–30, limited to 45; Cost: $35 per credit hour in addition to regular tuition and fees. *Summer Program:* Students may enroll in first-semester block of ABLE courses and/or a variety of general studies courses with the support through ABLE. Up to 12 first-semester students are accepted in the summer semester. Cost: $35 per credit hour. Optional. The percentage of students with learning disabilities receiving a degree in two years is 9%, in four years is 15% and in five or more years is 21%.

Staff: Learning disabilities specialists; peer tutors; special counselors.
Program Features: Oral and extended time testing; individual and small group tutoring sessions; basic study skills; note-taking assistance – scribes; tape recorders; taped texts; developmental program; faculty made aware of student's learning disability; support groups; specialized courses on college orientation; decision-making; assertiveness; legal rights and responsibilities; self-advocacy
Entrance Requirements: Documentation of learning disability; testing: WAIS, psychological or neuropsychological report
Special Facilities for: Visual, hearing and physical impairments
College Life: Penn Valley has a district-wide reputation of providing a warm and caring environment for students with disabilities. The ABLE program is recognized throughout the Kansas City metropolitan area as an effective transition program for students with learning disabilities who wish to work toward a degree or certificate. The faculty and staff are dedicated to providing a quality education to all students.
Scholarships: See page 452.

ST. LOUIS COMMUNITY COLLEGE AT FLORISSANT VALLEY

3400 PERSHALL ROAD
FERGUSON, MISSOURI 63135-1408
(314) 513-4551, (314) 513-4552 TTY; FAX: (314) 513-4876
E-MAIL: smatthews@stlcc.edu WEB SITE: www.stlcc.edu/access

Name of Special Program: Access Office, disAbility Support Services
Director: Suelaine Matthews
General Information: Two-Year Community College; Enrollment: 7,000; **Tuition:** District Residents – $78 per credit hour, Other Missouri Residents – $103 per credit hour, Out-of-State Residents – $138 per credit hour; **Room and Board:** No college housing available. A 108-acre suburban campus in metropolitan St. Louis. **Majors:** Biology, business/management, business/office, chemistry, civil technologies, communications and technologies, computer/information sciences, education, engineering and technologies, fine arts, home economics, industrial production, literature, marketing/distribution, mathematics, mechanical/electromechanical technologies, multi/interdisciplinary studies, music, physics, psychology, social sciences, visual/performing arts, vocational home economics
Special Program: Enrollment in Special Program: 80; Cost: None
Staff: Learning disabilities specialists; peer tutors; special counselors
Program Features: Oral and extended time testing; individual and small group tutoring sessions; limited course load; academic advising for students with learning disabilities; basic study skills; note-taking assistance –

scribes; tape recorders; taped texts; developmental program; adapted computers; WYNN, Kurzweil readers; faculty made aware of student's learning disability
Entrance Requirements: Documentation of learning disability; diagnostic testing at St. Louis Community College at Florissant Valley; testing: WAIS, psychological report
Special Facilities for: Visual, hearing and physical impairments

NEW HAMPSHIRE

NEW HAMPSHIRE COMMUNITY TECHNICAL COLLEGE AT LACONIA

379 BELMONT ROAD
LACONIA, NEW HAMPSHIRE 03246
(603) 524-3207
E-MAIL: mbaldwin@nhctc.edu WEB SITE: www.laconia.nhctc.edu

Name of Special Program: Teaching and Learning Center
Director: Maureen Lamper
General Information: Two-Year Community Technical College; Enrollment: 350; **Tuition:** Residents – $164 per credit hour, Non-Residents – $376 per credit hour, New England Regional Students' Program – $246 per credit hour, Co-op tuition higher; **Room and Board:** No college housing available. A 325-acre campus located in the middle of northern New England, within a two-hour drive of Boston, and a 45-minute drive from Manchester, New Hampshire. Situated on a hill overlooking the picturesque Lakes Region and, on the horizon, the beautiful White Mountains. **Majors:** Graphic arts, business management, fire and electrical technologies, hospitality management, automotive/marine technology, accounting, computer technology, human services, arts and sciences, early childhood education, restaurant management, lodging and conference management. General Associate's degree in applied science. Certificate programs include legal and nursing assistant, office technologies, personal computer applications and hazardous materials.
Special Program: Enrollment in Special Program: 30; Cost: None. Pre-Tech Program (as applicable). Remedial courses in reading, writing, mathematics and study skills; Cost: $108 per credit
Staff: Learning disabilities specialist; content tutors (faculty members); peer tutors; counselors
Program Features: Oral and extended time testing; individual and small group tutoring sessions; basic study skills; limited course load; note-taking assistance – scribes; taped texts (extra cost); faculty made aware of student's learning disability (at student's request); student-paced learning;

some assisted technology
Entrance Requirements: Open admissions to college; documentation of learning disability; learning disabilities specialist report; ACT Asset Test administered at New Hampshire Community Technical College (available untimed); interview with admissions; teacher recommendation; medical evaluation (if applicable); high school transcript; Wechsler or other standardized intelligence test

NEW JERSEY

ATLANTIC CAPE COMMUNITY COLLEGE
5100 BLACK HORSE PIKE
MAYS LANDING, NEW JERSEY 08330
(609) 343-5090; FAX: (609) 343-4926
E-MAIL: estewart@atlantic.edu or lmcglynn@atlantic.edu
WEB SITE: www.atlantic.edu

Name of Special Program: Student Support Services
Program Coordinator: Eric Stewart; *Counselor:* Lucille McGlynn
General Information: Two-Year Community College; Enrollment: 3,675; **Tuition:** Residents – $79 per credit, Out-of-County Residents – $158 per credit, Out-of-State Residents – $316 per credit; **Room and Board:** No college housing available. A 546-acre suburban campus 20 minutes from Atlantic City with easy access to Philadelphia. **Degree Programs:** Accounting and finance, biology, business administration, chemistry, child development/care, computer information systems/programming/corrections/juvenile justice, criminal justice, culinary arts, education, general studies, history, hospitality management, humanities, legal assistant, liberal arts, literature, marine science, mathematics, nursing, occupational therapy assistant, physical therapist assistant, pre-law, psychology, respiratory therapy, science and mathematics, social work, sociology, studio art, e-travel
Special Program: Enrollment in Special Program: 150; Cost: None
Staff: Learning disabilities specialists; special counselors; peer tutors
Program Features: Oral and extended time testing; individual and small group tutoring sessions; limited course load (first year); academic advising for students with learning disabilities; note-taking assistance – scribes; tape recorders; taped texts; basic study skills; developmental program; faculty made aware of student's learning disability
Entrance Requirements: Documentation of learning disability; learning disabilities specialist report; basic skills placement exam
College Life: Coordinator is accessible, faculty is cooperative and accom-

modating, Dean of Students and Director of Counseling are strong student advocates. Also, Coordinator advocates for special students as well as emphasizes self-advocacy.

BROOKDALE COMMUNITY COLLEGE
765 NEWMAN SPRINGS ROAD
LINCROFT, NEW JERSEY 07738-1597
(732) 224-2730; FAX: (732) 530-7417
E-MAIL: efoley@brookdalecc.edu or cfreeman@brookdalecc.edu
WEB SITE: www.brookdalecc.edu

Name of Special Program: Learning Disabilities Support Program
Director: Elaine Foley (732) 224-2729; *Learning Disabilities Assistant:* Clare Freeman (732) 224-2973
General Information: Two-Year Community College; Enrollment: 12,000 **Tuition:** Monmouth County Residents – $91.75 per credit, Other New Jersey Residents – $183.50 per credit, Non-Residents – $225 per credit, Added fees per semester – $19.25 per credit for general services – maximum $288.75; **Room and Board:** No college housing available. A 221-acre small town campus, located on the site of a century-old horse breeding farm, with easy access to New York City. **Degrees:** Associate of Arts, Associate of Science and Associate in Applied Science
Special Program: Cost: Four credit courses plus $75 lab fee. *Summer Program:* "Transition to College" is a support course for students with learning disabilities to help them prepare for the transition to college. College survival skills are introduced, e.g., communication skills, college vocabulary, reading and writing, time management, setting priorities, taking responsibility for academic tasks and active studying.
Staff: Learning disabilities specialists; special counselors; reading specialists who tutor many different subjects
Program Features: Academic skills workshops; developmental program; individual tutoring; liaison with faculty, counselors, staff; faculty made aware of student's learning disability (at student's request); word processing for learning disabled course; summer orientation course: introduction to college study skills
Entrance Requirements: Teacher evaluations; references by counselors, faculty, staff, self

CAMDEN COUNTY COLLEGE
P.O. BOX 200, COLLEGE DRIVE
BLACKWOOD, NEW JERSEY 08012
(856) 227-7200 X4430; FAX: (856) 374-4975
E-MAIL: jkinzy@camdencc.edu WEB SITE: www.camdencc.edu

Name of Special Program: Program for the Academically Challenged Student (PACS)
Director: Joanne Kinzy
General Information: Two-Year Community College; Enrollment: 12,000; **Tuition:** Residents – $79 per credit hour, Non-Residents – $83 per credit hour; **Room and Board:** No college housing available. Camden County College is situated on 320 acres in a small town with easy access to Philadelphia. **Degrees:** Camden County College offers over 75 degree and certificate programs in career and transfer education.
Special Program: Enrollment in Special Program: 350; Cost: None. *Summer Program:* The PACS Program offers a freshman orientation, two-credit, five-week summer class. This class provides strategies for note taking, test taking, time management, improving memory, career exploration and more.
Staff: Learning disabilities specialists; tutor coordinator and content tutors (faculty members); peer tutors
Program Features: Extended time testing; basic study skills courses; small group tutoring sessions; limited course load; note-taking assistance – scribes; academic advising for students with learning disabilities; faculty made aware of student's learning disability (at student's request); bridge classes available
Entrance Requirements: Documentation of learning disability; learning disabilities specialist report; medical evaluation; testing: WAIS, IEP, psychological report
Special Facilities for: Visual, hearing, and physical impairments

MIDDLESEX COUNTY COLLEGE
2600 WOODBRIDGE AVENUE
EDISON, NEW JERSEY 08818
(732) 906-2507; FAX: (732) 906-7767
WEB SITE: www.middlesexcc.edu

Name of Special Program: Project Connections
Director: Mary Jane Warshaw
General Information: Two-Year Community College; Enrollment: 10,500; **Tuition:** Residents – $81.55 per credit, Non-Residents – $163.10 per credit; **Room and Board:** No college housing available. A 200-acre suburban campus in a small city, five miles from New Brunswick and 40 minutes from

New York City. The college offers more than 550 courses including cooperative work experiences, clinical involvements, and laboratory assignments that parallel classroom studies. **Degrees:** Associate of Arts, Associate of Science, Associate of Applied Science. One-year certificate programs are available through the Continuing Education Division.
Special Program: Enrollment in Special Program: 160; Cost: None. Project Connections is a comprehensive academic and counseling support service for students with learning disabilities who are enrolled in mainstream programs at Middlesex County College.
Staff: Learning disabilities specialists; special counselors; content tutors
Program Features: Study skills courses; individual and small group tutoring sessions
Entrance Requirements: Documentation of learning disability; learning disabilities specialist report; teacher evaluation; medical evaluation (if applicable); testing: WAIS, psychological report
Special Facilities for: Visual, hearing, and physical impairments

OCEAN COUNTY COLLEGE
COLLEGE DRIVE, P.O. 2001
TOMS RIVER, NEW JERSEY 08754-2001
(732) 255-0456; FAX: (732) 255-0458
E-MAIL: jfischer@ocean.edu or mreustle@ocean.edu
WEB SITE: www.ocean.edu

Name of Special Program: Project Academic Skills Support (PASS)
Director: Maureen G. Reustle, *Dean of Academic Services*
General Information: Two-Year County College; Enrollment: 9,000; **Tuition:** County Residents – $113 per semester hour, Out-of-County Residents – $145 per semester hour, Out-of-State Residents and International Students – $220 per semester hour. **Room and Board:** No college housing available. A 275-acre suburban campus in a large town, 60 miles from Philadelphia and 90 miles from New York City **Majors:** Allied health, administrative office management, banking/finance, biotechnology, business administration, business studies/accounting, computer science, criminal justice, engineering, environmental science, fire science, gerontology, histotechnician, human services technician, liberal arts, management, marketing, networking support specialist, nursing, paralegal, public relations, teaching assistant/child care, visual communications technology, web support specialist.
Special Program: Enrollment in Special Program: 350; Cost: None
Staff: Learning disabilities specialists; content tutors (faculty members); special counselors

Program Features: Oral and extended time testing; individual and small group tutoring sessions; limited course load (first year); basic study skills; note-taking assistance – scribes; tape recorders; taped texts; academic advising for students with learning disabilities; developmental program; faculty made aware of student's learning disability (at student's request); academic skill support class; individual and small group counseling; faculty training; peer mentors; transition support for high school students
Entrance Requirements: Documentation of learning disability; learning disabilities specialist report; placement test; intake interview; diagnostic testing at Ocean County College; handwritten essay; testing: WAIS, psychological report
Special Facilities for: Visual, hearing and physical impairments
Scholarships: See page 452.

NEW YORK

HUDSON VALLEY COMMUNITY COLLEGE

80 VANDENBURGH AVENUE
TROY, NEW YORK 12180
(518) 629-7154, (518) 629-7596 TDD; FAX: (518) 629-4831
E-MAIL: negropab@hvcc.edu **WEB SITE: www.hvcc.edu**

Name of Special Program: Disability Resource Center
Director: Pablo Negron; *Learning Disabilities Specialist:* Jennifer Miller (518) 629-7552
General Information: Two-Year Community College; Enrollment: 7,850; **Tuition:** Residents – $1,350 per semester, Non-Residents – $4,050 per semester. **Room and Board:** Off-campus housing only. Founded in 1953, Hudson Valley Community College is a two-year public institution located on the southern outskirts of Troy, in close proximity to Schenectady and Albany, New York State's capitol. In addition, this tri-city area offers an exciting array of cultural and recreational facilities including the Empire State Plaza, the New York State Museum, Saratoga Performing Arts Center, Saratoga Race Track, Proctor's Theater, as well as major ski resorts in the Adirondack, Catskill, and Berkshire Mountains. There are many recreational activities available including boating, camping, swimming, skating and hiking. **Degrees:** Associate degrees offered in School of Business and Public Administration, School of Engineering Technologies and Industrial Technologies, School of Health Sciences, and School of Liberal Arts and Sciences
Special Program: Enrollment in Special Program: 225; Cost: None. *Summer Program:* A three-week summer course to sharpen math, reading, writing,

and learning styles called "Smart Start" is available to incoming students at no charge.
Staff: Learning disabilities specialists; content tutors (faculty members); peer tutors; special counselors
Program Features: Oral and extended time testing; individual and small group tutoring sessions; limited course load (first year); basic study skills; note-taking assistance – scribes; tape recorders; taped texts; developmental program; academic advising for students with learning disabilities; faculty made aware of student's learning disability; Franklin language master spellcheckers; learning lab taught by the learning disabilities specialist; one-hour weekly seminar-style class designed to encourage self-advocacy and facilitate the transition to college. Assistive technology available including training on devices such as Kurzweil Omni 3000 reading systems; Dragon Naturally Speaking and Dragon Dictate.
Entrance Requirements: Recent documentation of learning disability; teacher evaluation; testing: WAIS, Woodcock Johnson-R
Special Facilities for: Visual, hearing and physical impairments
College Life: Hudson Valley Community College has always been a leader in providing accommodations for students with disabilities. A learning assistance lab where our students receive scheduled assistance with math, reading and writing is available. Also the learning disabilities specialist conducts a course seminar designed to help students make a smooth transition to the college environment. Topics discussed include: understanding what a learning disability is, accommodations available for students with learning disabilities, course expectation, and campus and community support services.
Scholarships: See page 453.

JEFFERSON COMMUNITY COLLEGE
COFFEN STREET
WATERTOWN, NEW YORK 13601
(315) 786-2288; FAX: (315) 786-2459
E-MAIL: strainham@sunyjefferson.edu
WEB SITE: www.sunyjefferson.edu

Name of Special Program: Learning Skills Center
Learning Disability Specialist: Sheree Trainham
General Information: Two-Year Community College; Enrollment: 2,500; **Tuition:** Residents – $1,464 per semester, Non-Residents – $2,184 per semester; **Room and Board:** No college housing available. Jefferson Community College is located in the city of Watertown, adjacent to Interstate Route 81. **Degrees:** AAS in accounting, individual studies, nurs-

ing, banking, office technologies, business administration, computer information systems, paralegal, science lab technician. AOS in hospitality and tourism. Certificates in accounting, office studies, computer information systems, retail merchandising, criminal justice and hospitality and tourism
Special Program: Enrollment in Special Program: 44; Cost: None
Staff: Learning disabilities specialists; special counselors; peer tutors; content tutors (faculty members)
Program Features: Oral and extended time testing; note-taking assistance – scribes; individual and small group tutoring sessions; limited course load (first year); basic study skills; tape recorders; taped texts; academic advising for students with learning disabilities; developmental program in reading, English, math; faculty made aware of student's learning disability
Entrance Requirements: Documentation of learning disability; SAT/ACT untimed scores accepted; testing: WAIS, IEP, psychological report
Special Facilities for: Visual, hearing and physical impairments
College Life: Jefferson Community College provides educational, cultural and community development opportunities through personalized, affordable, quality education and services for the community and its citizens. On campus there are six varsity teams for men: basketball, baseball, golf, soccer, lacrosse and cross country skiing; and five varsity sports for women: basketball, softball, volleyball, soccer and crosscountry skiing.

KINGSBOROUGH COMMUNITY COLLEGE – CUNY

2001 ORIENTAL BLVD. – MANHATTAN BEACH
BROOKLYN, NEW YORK 11235
(718) 368-5175
E-MAIL: acolarossi@kingsborough.edu
WEB SITE: www.kingsborough.edu

Name of Special Program: Special Services for Students with Disabilities
Director: Dr. Anthony Colarossi
General Information: Two-Year Community College; Enrollment: 15,000; **Tuition:** New York City Residents – $1,550 per semester, Non-Residents – $190 per credit; **Room and Board:** No college housing available. A 67-acre urban campus in a very large city, 10 miles from midtown Manhattan. **Degrees:** Associate in Arts, Associate in Science, Associate in Applied Science
Special Program: Enrollment in Special Program: 350; Cost: None
Staff: Learning disabilities specialists; special counselors
Program Features: Oral and extended time testing; note-taking assistance – scribes; individual and small group tutoring sessions; basic study skills;

tape recorders; taped texts; faculty consultation for students with learning disabilities; special orientation; career decision-making courses
Entrance Requirements: Documentation of learning disability
Special Facilities for: Visual, hearing and physical impairments

LA GUARDIA COMMUNITY COLLEGE – CUNY
31-10 THOMSON AVENUE
LONG ISLAND CITY, NEW YORK 11101
(718) 482-5260; FAX: (718) 482-6055
WEB SITE: www.lagcc.cuny.edu

Name of Special Program: Office for Students with Disabilities/The Learning Project
Director: Matthew S. Joffe
General Information: Two-Year Community College; Enrollment: 11,000; **Tuition:** Residents – $120 per credit, Non-Residents – $190 per credit; **Room and Board:** No college housing available. An urban campus in a very large city, close to Manhattan. **Degrees:** Associate in Arts, Associate in Science, Associate in Applied Science
Special Program: Enrollment in Special Program: 225; Cost: None
Staff: Learning disabilities specialists; special counselors; peer tutors; content tutors (faculty members)
Program Features: Oral and extended time testing; note-taking assistance – scribes; individual tutoring sessions; basic study skills; tape recorders; taped texts; academic advising for students with learning disabilities; developmental program; faculty made aware of student's learning disability
Entrance Requirements: Documentation of learning disability; learning disabilities specialist report; medical evaluation; diagnostic testing at La Guardia Community College; testing: WAIS, IEP, psychological report
Special Facilities for: Visual, hearing and physical impairments

NEW YORK CITY TECHNICAL COLLEGE – CUNY
300 JAY STREET
BROOKLYN, NEW YORK 11201-2983
(718) 260-5143; FAX: (718) 260-5198
E-MAIL: ffogelman@citytec.cuny.edu
WEB SITE: www.citytech.cuny.edu

Name of Special Program: Student Support Services
Director: Faith Fogelman
General Information: Two-Year Technical College; Enrollment: 12,000;

Tuition: Residents – $2,000 per semester, Non-Residents – $360 per credit hour; **Room and Board:** No college housing available. An urban campus in a large city. **Majors:** Allied health, business/management/office, civil technologies, communications, computer/information sciences, construction trades, crafts/design, diagnostic/treatment services, engineering technologies, environmental control technologies, home economics, hospitality management, marketing/distribution, mechanical/electromechanical technologies, mechanics repairers, medical laboratory technologies, multi/interdisciplinary studies, precision production, public affairs
Special Program: Enrollment in Special Program: 150; Cost: None
Staff: Learning disabilities specialist; peer tutors; content tutors (faculty members); special counselors
Program Features: Oral and extended time testing; basic study skills; tape recorders; individual and small group tutoring sessions; developmental program; taped texts; note-taking assistance – scribes; learning disabilities writing class; faculty made aware of student's learning disability (at student's request)
Entrance Requirements: Documentation of learning disability; learning disabilities specialist report; medical evaluation; handwritten essay; documentation collected after admission; testing: SEC, psychological report
Special Facilities for: Visual, hearing and physical impairments

ONONDAGA COMMUNITY COLLEGE

4941 ONONDAGA ROAD
SYRACUSE, NEW YORK 13215
(315) 498-2245; FAX: (315) 498-2977
E-MAIL: hazzardn@sunyocc.edu **WEB SITE: www.sunyocc.edu**

Name of Special Program: Office of Services for Students with Special Needs (OSSSN)
Director: Nancy Hazzard (315) 498-2119
General Information: Two-Year Community College; Enrollment: 8,000; **Tuition:** County Residents – $1,605, Other New York State Residents – $3,886.50, Non-Residents – $5,491.50; **Room and Board:** No college housing available. A rural campus of 181 acres on Onondaga Hill, four miles from Syracuse. **Majors**: Accounting, automotive technology, machine trades, architectural technology, banking, business administration, computer science and technology, credit union operations, criminal justice, data processing, drafting, early child care, electrical technology, engineering science, fire protection technology, food service administration, general studies, graphic arts and advertising technology, hotel technology, humanities, human services, insurance, interior design, labor studies,

machine operator, mathematics and science, mechanical technology, music, nursing, office technology, administrative assistant, photography, electronic media, recreation leadership, respiratory care, secretarial science, surgical technology, physical therapy, professional cooking assistant, medical records, word processing
Special Program: Enrollment in Special Program: 350; Cost: None. *Summer Program:* A one-credit course is offered during the summer in study strategies for students with learning disabilities.
Staff: Learning disabilities specialists; content tutors (faculty members); peer tutors; counselors
Program Features: Oral and extended time testing; individual tutoring sessions; limited course load (first year); note-taking assistance – scribes; tape recorders; taped texts; basic study skills; developmental program; faculty made aware of student's learning disability (at student's request)
Entrance Requirements: Documentation of learning disability; testing: WAIS, psychological report
Special Facilities for: Visual, hearing and physical impairments

TROCAIRE COLLEGE
360 CHOATE AVENUE
BUFFALO, NEW YORK 14220
(716) 826-1200 X1321; FAX: (716) 828-6107
E-MAIL: truaxn@trocaire.edu **WEB SITE: www.trocaire.edu**

Name of Special Program: Students with Special Needs
Director: Sister Mary Norine Truax
General Information: Two-Year Private College; Enrollment: 1,000; **Tuition:** $4,925 per semester; **Room and Board:** No college housing available. **Programs:** Business, hotel management, nursing (RN, LPN), surgical technology, radiology, liberal arts
Special Program: Enrollment in Special Program: 12; Cost: None
Staff: Learning disabilities specialist
Program Features: Oral and extended time testing; individual and small group tutoring sessions; limited course load (first year); note-taking assistance – scribes; academic advising for students with learning disabilities; tape recorders; developmental program; faculty made aware of student's learning disability
Entrance Requirements: Documentation of learning disability; testing: IEP
College Life: Classes are small. Students with special needs meet once a week with the coordinator.

NORTH CAROLINA

ASHEVILLE-BUNCOMBE TECHNICAL COMMUNITY COLLEGE

340 VICTORIA ROAD
ASHEVILLE, NORTH CAROLINA 28801
(828) 254-1921 X141; FAX: (828) 281-9704
E-MAIL: Aclingenpeel@abtech.edu
WEB SITE: www.abtech.edu

Name of Special Program: Disability Services Office
Coordinator: Annie Clingenpeel
General Information: Two-Year State Community College; Enrollment: 12,000; **Tuition:** Residents – $639, Non-Residents – $3,512; **Room and Board:** No college housing available. Nestled between the Blue Ridge and Great Smokey Mountains, the home of the Biltmore Estate, Asheville is an excellent place to live. AB Tech offers a semester calendar, liberal arts, occupational studies. **Programs:** Allied health and public service, arts and sciences, business and hospitality education, continuing education, engineering and applied technology, information system security, web technologies, computer information technology, digital media
Special Program: Enrollment in Special Program: 130; Cost: None
Staff: Learning disabilities specialist; peer tutors
Program Features: Oral and extended time testing; small group tutoring sessions; limited course load (first year); note-taking assistance – scribes; academic advising for students with learning disabilities; basic study skills; tape recorders; taped texts; developmental program; faculty made aware of student's learning disability (at student's request); Jaws
Entrance Requirements: Documentation of learning disability; learning disabilities specialist report; testing: WAIS, psychological report
Facilities for: Visual, hearing and physical impairments
College Life: AB Tech offers offers small classes, has a friendly environment and is committed to student success.

CENTRAL PIEDMONT COMMUNITY COLLEGE

P.O. BOX 35009
CHARLOTTE, NORTH CAROLINA 28235-5009
(704) 330-6556; FAX: (704) 330-6230
E-MAIL: patricia_adams@cpcc.edu **WEB SITE: www.cpcc.edu**

Name of Special Program: Disability Services
Counselor: Patricia Adams
General Information: Two-Year State Community College; Enrollment: 70,000; **Tuition:** Residents – $39.50 per credit hour with a $632 maximum, Non-Residents – $219.50 per credit hour with a $3,512 maximum; **Room**

and Board: No college housing available. A 37-acre urban campus located in a large city. **Programs:** Associate degrees in arts, fine arts, science and applied science; technical certificate programs designed to prepare students for immediate employment; job training programs to further a career or launch a new one; and specialized training in police and fire science fields

Special Program: Enrollment in Special Program: 130; Cost: None

Staff: Learning disabilities counselor; lab facilitator

Program Features: Oral and extended time testing; individual and small group tutoring sessions; limited course load (first year); note-taking assistance – scribes; academic advising for students with learning disabilities; basic study skills; tape recorders; taped texts; developmental program; faculty made aware of student's learning disability; student support group

Entrance Requirements: Documentation of learning disability; psychological report

Support Services for: Visual, hearing and physical impairments

SURRY COMMUNITY COLLEGE
630 SOUTH MAIN STREET
DOBSON, NORTH CAROLINA 27017
(336) 386-8121; FAX: (336) 386-3690
E-MAIL: brackenl@surry.edu **WEB SITE: www.surry.edu**

Name of Special Program: Special Population

Director: Laura Bracken

General Information: Two-Year State Community College; Enrollment: 3,500; **Tuition:** Residents – $39.50 per credit hour, Non-Residents – $219.50 per credit hour; **Room and Board:** No college housing available. College offers small student/professor ratios in a rural quiet setting with classes offered on a semester basis. **Programs:** Associate in Arts degree in art education, business education marketing, business administration, criminal justice, English, English education, history, physical education, social work, nursing, elementary, middle and special education, political science. Associate in Science degree in biology, biology education, chemistry, chemistry education, computer science, math education. Associate in Applied Sciences in viticulture and enology technology

Special Program: Enrollment in Special Program: 60; Cost: None

Staff: Learning disabilities counselor; content tutors (faculty members); peer tutors

Program Features: Oral and extended time testing; individual and small group tutoring sessions; note-taking assistance – scribes; academic advising

for students with learning disabilities; basic study skills; tape recorders; taped texts; faculty made aware of student's learning disability (at student's request); assistive technology
Entrance Requirements: Documentation of learning disability; medical evaluation; testing: WAIS, IEP, psychological report
Special Facilities for: Visual, hearing and physical impairments
College Life: Friendly staff, small classes, academic advising and confidentiality

WILKES COMMUNITY COLLEGE
P.O. BOX 120, 1328 SOUTH COLLEGIATE DRIVE
WILKESBORO, NORTH CAROLINA 28697-0120
(336) 838-6560; FAX: (336) 838-6277
E-MAIL: nancy.sizemore@wilkescc.edu
WEB SITE: www.wilkescc.edu

Name of Special Program: Student Support Services
Director: Kim Faw (Direct correspondence to Nancy Sizemore, Disability Services.)
General Information: Two-Year State Community College; Enrollment: 2,200; **Tuition:** Residents – $39.50 per credit hour, Non-Residents – $219.50 per credit hour; **Room and Board:** No college housing available. A 140-acre rural campus in the foothills of the Blue Ridge Mountains, within minutes of the Blue Ridge Parkway and national parks. **Degrees:** Associate degrees in general education, computer sciences, fine arts, dance and music, viticulture, accounting, architectural, automotive systems, broadcasting, building construction, business administration, criminal justice, culinary, early childhood, electronics engineering, horticulture, hotel and restaurant, human services, industrial maintenance, information systems, medical assisting, medium heavy duty vehicles, nursing, office systems, speech-language pathology. Diploma and certificates in dental and medical assisting, business and public services technologies, human services technology, industrial and engineering technology.
Special Program: Enrollment in Special Program: 70; Cost: None
Staff: Learning disabilities specialists; content tutors; peer tutors; special counselors
Program Features: Oral and extended time testing; individual and small group tutoring sessions; limited course load (first year); note-taking assistance – scribes; academic advising for students with learning disabilities; tape recorders; taped texts; basic study skills; developmental program; faculty made aware of student's learning disability; students may attend part-time

Entrance Requirements: Documentation of learning disability; learning disabilities specialist report; diagnostic testing at Wilkes Community College; testing: WAIS-III, IEP, psychological report; achievement test; visual motor test
Special Facilities for: Visual, hearing and physical impairments
College Life: Comprehensive services are offered to accommodate students with learning disabilities.
Scholarships: See page 454.

NORTH DAKOTA

MINOT STATE UNIVERSITY: BOTTINEAU
105 SIMRALL BLVD.
BOTTINEAU, NORTH DAKOTA 58318-1198
1-800-542-6866, (701) 228-5479; FAX: (701) 228-5614
E-MAIL: Jan.Nahinurk@misu.nodak.edu
WEB SITE: www.misu-b.nodak.edu

Name of Special Program: Student Learning Center
Director and Learning Disabilities Specialist: Jan Nahinurk
General Information: Two-Year State University; Enrollment: 551; **Tuition:** Residents and Canadian Provinces – $2,830, Non-Residents – $4,245, MN – $3,856; SD, MT – $3,535; **Room:** $1,290; **Board:** $1,992. Minot State University: Bottineau is on a 35-acre campus located in northcentral North Dakota about 13 miles from the Canadian border and 80 miles from Minot. It is in close proximity to the International Peace Garden, J. Clark Salyer National Refuge, Denbigh Experimental Forest, the Turtle Mountains. The offices of the North Dakota Forest Service provide a natural setting to support unique training programs. **Majors:** Agriculture, art, biology, business administration/education, chemistry, education, English, health professions, history, home economics, journalism, mathematics, music, parks and recreation, pre-law, pre-pharmacy, pre-veterinary medicine, social science, urban forestry, wildlife management. Vocational technologies: horticulture, landscaping, nursery practice, flowershop and greenhouse management, marketing and management, office education, wildlife and fisheries, parks and recreation, urban forestry, information processing, administrative assistant, computerized office management, legal secretary, medical assistant, medical secretary, accounting, water technology, network engineering
Special Program: Enrollment in Special Program: 20; Cost: None
Staff: Learning disabilities specialist; content tutors (faculty members); peer tutors
Program Features: Extended time testing; individual and small group

tutoring sessions; note-taking assistance; basic study skills class; developmental classes; faculty made aware of student's learning disability; career awareness and job search classes
Entrance Requirements: Documentation of learning disability; ACT untimed scores accepted; testing: WAIS, IEP, psychological report

OHIO

CENTRAL OHIO TECHNICAL COLLEGE
1179 UNIVERSITY DRIVE
NEWARK, OHIO 43055
(740) 366-9246
WEB SITE: www.cotc.edu/studentlife/ODSabout.asp

Name of Special Program: Learning Assistance Center/Office for Disability Services
Learning Disabilities Specialist: Dr. Peter Prewett
General Information: Two-Year Technical College, Enrollment: 1,350; **Tuition:** Residents – $1,152 for 12-15 credit hours, Non-Residents – $2,052 for 12-15 credit hours; **Room and Board:** No college housing available. A 155-acre suburban campus in a large town, 30 miles from Columbus. College offers two-year technical/vocational degree programs. **Majors:** Accounting, business management, secretarial science, computer programming, nursing, radiographic, medical sonography, physical therapist assistant, baby childhood development, criminal justice, electronics, electromechanical, mechanical and drafting design technologies
Special Program: Enrollment in Special Program: 30; Cost: None
Staff: Learning disabilities specialists; peer tutors; special counselors
Program Features: Oral and extended time testing; taped texts; tape recorders; note-taking assistance - scribes; basic study skills; developmental program; individual and small group tutoring sessions; limited course load (first year); faculty made aware of student's learning disability (at student's request)
Entrance Requirements: Documentation of learning disability; learning disabilities specialist report; diagnostic testing at Central Ohio Technical College; handwritten essay; testing: WAIS, SEC, psychological report
Special Facilities for: Visual, hearing and physical impairments

CUYAHOGA COMMUNITY COLLEGE – EASTERN CAMPUS
4250 RICHMOND ROAD
HIGHLAND HILLS VILLAGE, OHIO 44122-6195
(216) 987-2034; FAX: (216) 987-2423
E-MAIL: maryann.sender@tri-c.edu
WEB SITE: www.tri-c.edu

Name of Special Program: ACCESS/DSS/Vocational Education Program
Program Manager: Mary Sender
General Information: Two-Year Community College; Enrollment: 12,000; **Tuition:** County Residents – $80.54 per credit hour, Out-of-County Ohio Residents – $106.48 per credit hour, Out-of-State Residents – $218.04 per credit hour; **Room and Board:** No college housing available. Cuyahoga Community College is made up of three campuses located in or near the city of Cleveland. **Degrees:** Associate degrees in Arts, Science, Applied Business, Applied Science, Technical Studies. One-year certificates and post-degree professional certificates
Special Program: Enrollment in Special Program: 300; Cost: None. *Summer Program:* The summer program includes introduction to college life, time management skills, strategies for becoming a more independent student and study skills.
Staff: Learning disabilities specialists; peer tutors; content tutors (faculty members); special counselors
Program Features: Oral and extended time testing; individual and small group tutoring sessions; limited course load (first year); academic advising for students with learning disabilities; basic study skills; note-taking assistance – scribes; tape recorders; taped texts through RFB; developmental program; faculty made aware of student's learning disability (at student's request); adaptive equipment
Entrance Requirements: Documentation of learning disability; diagnostic testing at Cuyahoga Community College; testing: WAIS, IEP, psychological report
Special Facilities for: Visual, hearing and physical impairments
College Life: Cuyahoga Community College offers students with learning disabilities a secure environment where their academic needs can be met. Close contact with a learning disabilities advisor and personal contact with instructors are encouraged as well as easy access to adaptive equipment to assist students in their areas of weakness.
Scholarships: See page 454.

**OHIO STATE UNIVERSITY
AGRICULTURAL TECHNICAL INSTITUTE
1328 DOVER ROAD
WOOSTER, OHIO 44691
(330) 264-3911 X1253; FAX: (330) 262-7634
E-MAIL: miller.2920@osu.edu WEB SITE: www.ati.osu.edu**

Name of Special Program: Office for Disability Services / Office of Student Affairs
Coordinator: Sean Miller
General Information: Two-Year State College; Enrollment: 740; **Tuition, Room and Board:** Ohio Residents – $12,033 for three quarters, Non-Residents – $23,256 for three quarters. A 136-acre rural campus in a large town, 30 minutes from Akron. **Degrees:** Agribusiness / agricultural production / sciences, environmental design, renewable natural resources, science technologies, vocational home economics
Special Program: Enrollment in Special Program: 75; Cost: None
Staff: Learning disabilities specialists; peer tutors; content tutors (faculty members)
Program Features: Oral and extended time testing; individual and small group tutoring sessions; limited course load (first year); academic advising for students with learning disabilities; tape recorders; note-taking assistance – scribes; basic study skills; taped texts; developmental program; faculty made aware of student's learning disability; assistive technology
Entrance Requirements: Documentation of learning disability; ACT untimed scores accepted; placement tests; testing: WAIS, IEP, psychological report
Special Facilities for: Visual, hearing and physical impairments
College Life: Small classes, specialized services, many services to support all students

**OHIO STATE UNIVERSITY AT LIMA
4240 CAMPUS DRIVE
LIMA, OHIO 45804
(419) 995-8453; FAX: (419) 995-8483
E-MAIL: meyer.193@osu.edu WEB SITE: www.lima.ohio-state.edu**

Name of Special Program: Office for Disability Services
Coordinator: Karen Meyer
General Information: Two-Year Branch Campus of Regional Four-Year University; Enrollment: 1,178; **Tuition:** Residents – $5,310, Non-Residents – $16,533. A 565-acre suburban campus in a small town, midway between Columbus and Toledo. **Majors:** Begin coursework at Lima in any of the

Ohio State University's 170 bachelor's degree programs offered at the Columbus campus. **Bachelor's Degrees:** elementary education, biology, history, psychology, English, general business, family financial management
Special Program: Enrollment in Special Program: 25; Cost: None. The percentage of students with learning disabilities receiving degrees in four years is 75% and in five or more years is 25%.
Staff: Learning disabilities specialist
Program Features: Oral and extended time testing; note-taking assistance - scribes; basic study skills; tape recorders, taped texts, developmental program; academic advising for students with learning disabilities: faculty made aware of student's learning disability
Entrance Requirements: Documentation of learning disability; learning disabilities specialist report; handwritten essay; ACT untimed scores accepted; medical evaluation; testing: psychological report
Special Facilities for: Visual, hearing and physical impairments

OHIO STATE UNIVERSITY AT MARION

1465 MOUNT VERNON AVENUE
MARION, OHIO 43302-5695
(740) 725-6247
E-MAIL: hazelett.2@osu.edu WEB SITE: www.marion.ohio-state.edu

Name of Special Program: Learning Disabilities Services
Coordinator: Margaret C. Hazelett
General Information: Two-Year Branch Campus of Regional Four-Year State University; Enrollment: 1,277; **Tuition:** Ohio Residents – $5,310, Non-Residents – $16,533; **Room and Board:** No college housing available. A regional campus which serves a seven-county area, situated 45 miles north of the main university campus in Columbus. **Majors:** Begin coursework at Marion in any of the Ohio State University's 170 bachelor's degree programs offered at the Columbus campus. **Bachelor's Degrees:** business, education, English history, psychology, and nursing
Special Program: Enrollment in Special Program: 8; Cost: None
Staff: Learning disabilities specialist; peer tutors; staff tutors
Program Features: Oral and extended time testing; taped texts; note-taking assistance – scribes; basic study skills; developmental program; tape recorders; individual and small group tutoring sessions; limited course load (first year); academic advising for students with learning disabilities; faculty made aware of student's learning disability
Entrance Requirements: Documentation of learning disability; learning disabilities specialist report; SAT/ACT untimed scores accepted; handwritten essay; diagnostic testing at Ohio State University at Marion; test-

ing: WAIS, IEP, psychological report
Special Facilities for: Visual, hearing and physical impairments
College Life: Campus is small, attractive, and well situated. The faculty, student body and staff members are very sensitive to the needs of the student with learning disabilities. There is a great deal of support provided to students with learning disabilities, as well as a positive campus environment.

OHIO STATE UNIVERSITY AT NEWARK
1179 UNIVERSITY DRIVE
NEWARK, OHIO 43055
(740) 366-9441
E-MAIL: czang@cotc.edu **WEB SITE: www.newark.osu.edu**

Name of Special Program: Learning Assistance Center / Disability Services
Director: Connie Zang
General Information: Two-Year Branch Campus of Regional Four-Year State University; Enrollment: 1,867; **Tuition:** Ohio Residents – $5,310, Non-Residents – $16,533; **Room and Board:** No college housing available. A 150-acre suburban campus in a large town, 28 miles east of the main university campus in Columbus. **Majors:** Agriculture, allied medical professions, architecture, art, arts and sciences, business, dental hygiene, dentistry, education, engineering, human ecology, law, medicine, music, natural resources, nursing, optometry, pharmacy, social work, veterinary medicine
Special Program: Enrollment in Special Program: 28; Cost: None
Staff: Learning disabilities specialists; peer tutors; special counselors
Program Features: Oral and extended time testing; taped texts; note-taking assistance – scribes; basic study skills; developmental program; tape recorders; individual and small group tutoring sessions; limited course load (first year); faculty made aware of student's learning disability (at student's request)
Entrance Requirements: Documentation of learning disability; learning disabilities specialist report; handwritten essay; diagnostic testing at Ohio State University at Newark; testing: WAIS, SEC, psychological report
Special Facilities for: Visual, hearing and physical impairments

BLUE MOUNTAIN COMMUNITY COLLEGE

2411 NORTHWEST CARDEN AVENUE
PENDLETON, OREGON 97801
(541) 278-5807; FAX: (541) 278-5888
E-MAIL: aspiegel@bluecc.edu **WEB SITE: www.bluecc.edu**

Name of Special Program: Services for Students with Disabilities
Director: Amy Spiegel
General Information: Two-Year Community College; Enrollment: 1,250; **Tuition:** Residents – $60.20 per credit hour, Non-Residents – $120.40 per credit hour; **Room and Board:** No college housing available. A 170-acre rural campus, located in the dry, open spaces of Eastern Oregon. Pendleton is known for its World-Class Pendleton Round-Up each September and for the Pendleton Woolen Mills. **Majors:** Liberal Arts: agriculture, anthropology, art, biology, business administration, business education, chemistry, computer science, criminal justice, economic education, English, foreign languages, general studies, geography, geology, health, history, math, music, nursing, physical education, physics, political science, psychology, sociology, speech and theatre. Professional Technical: accounting, agriculture, dental assistant, civil engineering, drafting, electronic engineering, general business, human services, marketing, and nursing, Distance Education: web-based BMCC online, video courses, auto courses, satellite
Special Program: Enrollment in Special Program: 100; Cost: None. The percentage of students with learning disabilities receiving a degree in two years is 5% and in four years is 60%.
Staff: Learning disabilities specialist; peer tutors; learning diagnostician; Special Services providers.
Program Features: Oral and extended time testing; taped texts; tape recorders; note-taking assistance – scribes; basic study skills; developmental program; individual and small group tutoring sessions; limited course load (first year); academic advising for students with learning disabilities; faculty made aware of student's learning disability; transition planning
Entrance Requirements: Documentation of learning disability; diagnostic testing at Blue Mountain Community College; testing: WAIS, WJR, psychological report
Special Facilities for: Visual, hearing and physical impairments
College Life: The college is small enough to offer personalized attention and at the same time nurture the independence and self-advocacy of the students with learning disabilities.

LINN-BENTON COMMUNITY COLLEGE
6500 PACIFIC BLVD., SOUTHWEST
ALBANY, OREGON 97321
(541) 917-4683; TTY (541) 917- 4703; FAX: (541) 917-4703
E-MAIL: adero.allison@linnbenton.edu
WEB SITE: www.linnbenton.edu

Name of Special Program: Office of Disability Services (ODS)
Coordinator: "Adero" C.E. Allison, Ph.D.
General Information: Two-Year Community College; Enrollment 3,651; **Tuition:** Residents – $62 per credit hour, Non-Residents – $163 per credit hour, International Students – $175 per credit hour; **Room and Board:** No college housing available. A rural campus of 104 acres, centrally located in the Willamette Valley, two miles south of Albany and 11 miles east of Corvallis. **Degrees:** Associate of Applied Science, Associate of Arts, Associate of General Studies, Associate of Science, Associate of General Studies – Technology Option. Certificates are offered in a number of professional technical programs.
Special Program: Enrollment in Special Program: 199; Cost: None
Staff: Learning disabilities specialists; peer tutors; content tutors (faculty members); special counselors
Program Features: Oral and extended time testing; taped texts; tape recorders; note-taking assistance – scribes; basic study skills; individual tutoring and small group sessions; faculty made aware of student's learning disability; test accommodations; assistive technology
Entrance Requirements: Documentation of disability; testing: WAIS, psychological report
Special Facilities for: Visual, hearing and physical impairments
College Life: A very supportive staff and faculty.

MOUNT HOOD COMMUNITY COLLEGE
26000 SOUTHEAST STARK STREET
GRESHAM, OREGON 97030
(503) 491-6923; FAX: (503) 491-7549
E-MAIL: dsoweb@mhcc.edu **WEB SITE: www.mhcc.edu**

Name of Special Program: Disability Services
Coordinator: Liz Johnson
General Information: Two-Year Community College; Enrollment; 8,100; **Tuition:** Residents – $1001 per semester, Non-Residents – $213 per credit hour; **Room and Board:** No college housing available. Washington, California, Idaho and Nevada residents may attend Mount Hood Community College and pay in-state tuition. Mount Hood Community

College is located 12 miles east of Portland, at the west end of the Columbia River Gorge. **Degrees:** Associate of Applied Science, Associate of Arts, Associate of General Studies. Certificates are offered in a number of professional technical programs.
Special Program: Enrollment in Special Program: 150; Cost: None
Staff: Learning disabilities specialists; peer tutors; special counselors
Program Features: Oral and extended time testing; taped texts; tape recorders; note-taking assistance – scribes; basic study skills; developmental program; individual and small group tutoring sessions; limited course load (first year); academic advising for students with learning disabilities; faculty made aware of student's learning disability; adapted computer lab
Entrance Requirements: Documentation of disability; testing: psychological report
Special Facilities for: Visual, hearing and physical impairments
College Life: Through accommodations which are tailored to individual needs, Mount Hood Community College assures students with learning disabilities an equal opportunity to succeed at the college level without compromising their right to privacy or their personal dignity.
Scholarships: See page 455.

PENNSYLVANIA

COMMUNITY COLLEGE OF ALLEGHENY COUNTY SOUTH CAMPUS

1750 CLAIRTON ROAD, ROUTE 885
WEST MIFFLIN, PENNSYLVANIA 15122
(412) 469-6215; FAX: (412) 469-6371
E-MAIL: emason@ccac.edu **WEB SITE: www.ccac.edu**

Name of Special Program: Supportive Services
Director: Esther M. Mason
General Information: Two-Year Community College; Enrollment: 10,690; **Tuition:** Residents – $80 per credit, Out-of-County Residents – $160, Out-of-State Residents – $240; **Room and Board:** No college housing available. The campus is located on a 200-acre site near Century III Mall. The six-story modern educational facility contains lecture halls, classrooms, a learning assistance center, a community library, an adult center, a theater, offices and a student dining area. A solar-heated greenhouse is adjacent to the campus complex. **Majors:** Allied health, biology, business/management/office, chemistry, civil technologies, communications, computer/information sciences, construction trades, crafts/design, diagnostic/treatment services, education, engineering and technologies, fine arts, health sciences, home economics, industrial production, languages, law, market-

ing/distribution, mathematics, mechanical/electromechanical technologies, mechanics/repairers, medical laboratory technologies, multi/interdisciplinary studies, parks and recreation, physics, precision production, psychology, protective services, public affairs, rehabilitation services, science technologies, social sciences, transportation, visual/performing arts, vocational home economics
Special Program: Enrollment in Special Program: 150; Cost: None
Staff: Learning disabilities specialist; content tutors (faculty members); special counselors
Program Features: Oral and extended time testing; individual and small group tutoring sessions; limited course load (first year); note-taking assistance – scribes; tape recorders; taped texts; basic study skills; developmental program; academic counseling; faculty made aware of student's learning disability; personal/career counseling; learning disability support group
Entrance Requirements: Documentation of learning disability; learning disabilities specialist report; diagnostic testing at Community College of Allegheny County – South Campus; teacher evaluation
Special Facilities for: Visual, hearing and physical impairments

NORTHAMPTON COMMUNITY COLLEGE

3835 GREEN POND ROAD
BETHLEHEM, PENNSYLVANIA 18020
(610) 861-5342; FAX: (610) 861-5075
E-MAIL: LDemshock@northampton.edu
WEB SITE: www.northampton.edu

Name of Special Program: Disability Services
Coordinator: Laraine Demshock
General Information: Two-Year Community College; Enrollment: 7,500; **Tuition:** Residents – $159 per credit, Out-of-County Residents – $207 per credit, Out-of-State Residents – $307 per credit; **Room and Board:** $1,410 per semester, apartment: $1,516 per semester; food plans vary from $580 to $1,020 per semester. A 165-acre suburban campus in a small city, 60 miles north of Philadelphia. The Monroe campus is located at Old Mill Road, P.O. Box 530, Tannersville, PA 18372, (570) 620-9221. **Majors:** Accounting, communication design, architectural technology, banking, biological science, business administration and management, computer-aided design, chemistry, chemical technology, computer data processing/information systems and science, criminal justice, dental hygiene, education, electronics technology, emergency services technology, engineering, funeral service, general studies, hotel/restaurant management, interior design, liberal arts,

library technical assistant, math/physical science, office administration, radio/TV, radiologic technology, real estate, small business management and travel tourism, automotive tech, criminal justice, culinary arts, early childhood education, fine arts, manufacturing engineering tech, nursing, social work, sports management, veterinary tech, special education
Special Program: Enrollment in Special Program: 270; Cost: None
Staff: Learning disabilities specialists; peer tutors; special counselors; content tutors (faculty members)
Program Features: Oral and extended time testing; taped texts; tape recorders; developmental program; individual and small group tutoring sessions; limited course load; basic study skills; faculty made aware of student's learning disability; adaptive computer lab
Entrance Requirements: Documentation of learning disability; learning disabilities specialist report; testing: WAIS, psychological report (testing must be current, within three years of application)
Special Facilities for: Visual, hearing and physical impairments

READING AREA COMMUNITY COLLEGE
P.O. BOX 1706, 10 SOUTH SECOND STREET
READING, PENNSYLVANIA 19603
(610) 372-4721 X5060; FAX: (610) 607-6257
E-MAIL: mmitchell@racc.edu **WEB SITE: www.racc.edu**

Name of Special Program: Center for Counseling and Academic Development
Director: Maria Mitchell
General Information: Two-Year Community College; Enrollment: 5,000; **Tuition:** County Residents – $67 per credit hour, Other Pennsylvania Residents – $134 per credit hour, Non-Residents – $201 per credit hour; **Room and Board:** No college housing available. An urban setting approximately 55 miles west of Philadelphia. Term schedule for Fall, Winter and Spring is 10 weeks. Summer Term is 2–5 week modules. Internships and co-ops available in specific curriculums. Open Admission – may apply any term for enrollment. **Majors:** Accounting and accounting transfer; administrative assistant, basic secretarial skills, biological sciences transfer, business administration, business ed transfer, business management, computer information systems/information technology, culinary arts, early childhood education transfer, education technology, electrical engineering technology, electronics engineering technology, heating, ventilation and air conditioning, human resources, human services worker, industrial maintenance, legal secretary, liberal arts transfer, machine tool technology, medical lab technology, medical secretary, RN, LPN, pre-law

transfer, professional pilot, respiratory care, special ed para-educator, travel and tourism, communications transfer

Special Program: Enrollment in Special Program: 90; Cost: None. *Summer Program:* One-credit course in "College Success Strategies" (required of all incoming students). Basic courses in reading, writing, math and study skills are offered. The percentage of students with learning disabilities receiving a degree in two years is 5%, in four years is 40% and in five or more years is 60%.

Staff: Learning disabilities specialists; content tutors (faculty members); peer tutors; special counselors

Program Features: Oral and extended time testing; individual and small group tutoring sessions; basic study skills; note-taking assistance – scribes; tape recorders; taped texts; developmental program; academic advising for students with learning disabilities; faculty made aware of student's learning disability; test scanners; voice-activated software

Entrance Requirements: Documentation of learning disability; psychological report

Special Facilities for: Visual, hearing and physical impairments

College Life: Small class sizes enable students to receive focused instruction. Strong tutorial services and one-to-one tutoring are available.

RHODE ISLAND

COMMUNITY COLLEGE OF RHODE ISLAND: KNIGHT CAMPUS

400 EAST AVENUE
WARWICK, RHODE ISLAND 02886-1807
(401) 825-2164
E-MAIL: amcmahon@ccri.edu **WEB SITE: www.ccri.edu**
Disability Services Advisor: Alda McMahon

FLANAGAN CAMPUS

1762 LOUISQUISSET PIKE
LINCOLN, RHODE ISLAND 02865-4585
(401) 333-7329
E-MAIL: seramian@ccri.edu
Disability Services Advisor: Susan Eramian

LISTON CAMPUS

1 HILTON STREET
PROVIDENCE, RHODE ISLAND 02905-2304
(401) 455-6064
E-MAIL: solausen@ccri.edu
Disability Services Advisor: Shelly Olausen

Rhode Island (continued) – Two-Year Programs

Name of Special Program: Access to Opportunity
General Information: Two-Year Community College; Enrollment: 15,000; **Tuition:** Residents – $1,127 per semester, Non-Residents – $3,314 per semester; **Room and Board:** No college housing available. Community College of Rhode Island offers classes at three major campuses and nine satellite locations throughout Rhode Island. The campus housing special programs is located nine miles from Providence. **Majors:** Associate level degrees in allied health, business administration, chemistry, computer studies and information processing, criminal justice/legal studies, dental health, engineering, fine arts, human services, industrial technology, nursing, office administration and general studies/liberal arts. Several one-year certificate programs are also offered.
Special Program: Enrollment in Special Program: 75; Cost: None
Staff: Disabilities specialists; content tutors; special counselors
Program Features: Individual tutoring sessions; academic advising; career exploration; job readiness; transfer advising
Entrance Requirements: Documentation of disability; other documentation as appropriate; math, reading and English placement testing results
Special Facilities for: Visual, hearing and physical impairments
College Life: Community College of Rhode Island is an open enrollment public institution with a full array of support services and academic accommodations available to qualified students with documented disabilities. Courses are offered during evening and weekend hours at locations throughout the state.
Scholarships: See page 456.

TEXAS

ALVIN COMMUNITY COLLEGE

3110 MUSTANG ROAD
ALVIN, TEXAS 77511
(281) 756-3531; FAX: (281) 756-3843
E-MAIL: ecross.@alvincollege.edu
WEB SITE: www.alvincollege.edu

Name of Special Program: Disability Services Office
Director: Eileen Cross
General Information: Two-Year Community College; Enrollment: 2,438; **Tuition:** Residents – $500 per 12 credit hours, Non-Residents – $1,458 per 12 credit hours; **Room and Board:** No college housing available. A 113-acre small town campus with easy access to Houston. **Majors:** Accounting, art/fine arts, biology, business administration/management, child care/child and family studies, communication, computer program-

ming / technologies, corrections, court reporting, drafting and design, electrical and electronics technologies, law enforcement / police sciences, legal secretarial studies, liberal arts / general studies, math, medical secretarial studies, mental health / rehabilitation counseling, music, nursing, paralegal studies, physical education, physical sciences, radio and television, respiratory therapy, secretarial studies / office management, theater arts / drama, voice

Special Program: Enrollment in Special Program: 60; Cost: None

Staff: Learning disabilities specialists

Program Features: Oral and extended time testing; taped texts; tape recorders; note-taking assistance – scribes; basic study skills; developmental program; academic advising for students with learning disabilities; faculty made aware of student's learning disability (at student's request); learning style exploration; interest inventories; SODA (student organization)

Entrance Requirements: Documentation of learning disability; learning disabilities specialist report; entrance test can be local / state

Special Facilities for: Visual, hearing and physical impairments

EL PASO COMMUNITY COLLEGE: VALLE VERDE CAMPUS
919 HUNTER
EL PASO, TEXAS 79915
(915) 831-2426; FAX: (915) 831-2244
E-MAIL: janl@epcc.edu **WEB SITE: www.epcc.edu**
Director: Jan Lockhart

MISSION DEL PASO CAMPUS
10700 GATEWAY EAST
EL PASO, TEXAS 79927
(915) 831-7024; FAX: (915) 831-6062
E-MAIL: juans@epcc.edu
Campus Representative: Juan Segovia

TRANSMOUNTAIN CAMPUS
9570 GATEWAY BLVD. NORTH
EL PASO, TEXAS 79924
(915) 831-5808; FAX: (915) 831-5179
E-MAIL: charlesy@nmail.epcc.edu
Campus Representative: Charles Yakubovsky

NORTHWEST CAMPUS
6701 SOUTH DESERT ROAD
EL PASO, TEXAS 79932
(915) 831-8815; FAX: (915) 831-8861

E-MAIL: gerryp@nmail.epcc.edu
Campus Representative: Gerry Perez

RIO GRANDE CAMPUS
100 WEST RIO GRANDE AVENUE
EL PASO, TEXAS 79902
(915) 831-4198; FAX: (915) 831-4170
E-MAIL: maryc@nmail.epcc.edu
Campus Representative: Mary Chavez

Name of Special Program: Center for Students with Disabilities
General Information: Two-Year Community College; Enrollment: 13,409; **Tuition:** Residents – $666 for 12 credit hours, Non-Residents – $903 for 12 credit hours; **Room and Board:** No college housing available. Urban campuses in a large city, three miles from Juarez, Mexico. Founded in 1969. **Majors:** Agribusiness/agricultural, allied health, architecture, biology, business management/office, chemistry, civil/communications technologies, computer/information sciences, construction trades, crafts/ design, diagnostic treatment, education, engineering/environmental control technologies/design, fine arts, geological sciences, health sciences, industrial production, languages, letters/literature, marketing/distribution, mechanical/electromechanical, mechanics/repairers, medical laboratory technologies, multi/interdisciplinary studies, music, parks and recreation, precision production, protective services, psychology, social sciences, transportation, visual/performing arts, vocational home economics
Special Program: Enrollment in Special Program: 479; Cost: None
Staff: Learning disabilities specialists; special counselors; content tutors
Program Features: Oral and extended time testing; taped texts; note-taking assistance – scribes; basic study skills; developmental program; individual and small group tutoring sessions; faculty made aware of student's learning disability (at student's request); academic advising for students with learning disabilities; reader service; adaptive equipment; instruction in using recorders, NCR paper and assistive listening devices providing note-taking guidance in conjunction with class
Entrance Requirements: Documentation of learning disability; diagnostic testing at El Paso Community College if needed and requested by student
Special Facilities for: Visual, hearing and physical impairments
College Life: New students are requested to attend a "Learning to Learn" series along with new student orientation.

SAN ANTONIO COLLEGE
1300 SAN PEDRO AVENUE
SAN ANTONIO, TEXAS 78212
(210) 733-2347; FAX: (210) 733-2242
E-MAIL: mgomez@accd.edu **WEB SITE: www.accd.edu/sac**

Name of Special Program: disABILITY Support Services
Coordinator/Counselor: Maria T. Gomez
General Information: Two-Year Community College; Enrollment: 21,000; **Tuition:** Residents – $659 for 12 credit hours, Non-Residents – $2,171 for 12 credit hours; **Room and Board**: No college housing available. Founded in 1925. A 45-acre urban campus in the downtown area of San Antonio. **Majors:** Agribusiness / agricultural production, allied health, architecture, business / management, business / office, chemistry, communications technologies, computer / information sciences, construction trades, education, engineering and technologies, geological sciences, health sciences, letters / literature, library / archival sciences, mathematics, medical laboratory technologies, multi / interdisciplinary studies, parks and recreation, physical sciences, physics, precision production, protective services, psychology, public affairs, social sciences, visual / performing arts, vocational education
Special Program: Enrollment in Special Program: 300; Cost: None
Staff: Learning disabilities specialists; peer tutors; special counselors; content tutors (faculty members)
Program Features: Oral and extended time testing; individual and small group tutoring sessions; limited course load (first year); academic advising for students with learning disabilities; basic study skills; note-taking assistance – scribes; taped texts; developmental program; faculty made aware of student's learning disability (at student's request); student development (SPEV) for students with learning disabilities (academic and personal success)
Entrance Requirements: Documentation of learning disability; medical report; high school transcript or GED scores, testing: Woodcock-Johnson psychoeducational battery, psychological report
Special Facilities for: Visual, hearing and physical impairments
College Life: "One stop shopping" method of enrollment. All aspects of admissions, residency, placement testing, course advisement / scheduling, FAX service in one unit.

VERMONT

LANDMARK COLLEGE
(COLLEGE FOR STUDENTS WITH LEARNING DISABILITIES)
RIVER ROAD, R.R. I, BOX 1000
PUTNEY, VERMONT 05346
(802) 387-6711; FAX: (802) 387-6860
E-MAIL: admissions@landmark.edu
WEB SITE: www.landmark.edu

Dean of Admissions: Dale M. Herold
Landmark College is an associate degree-granting institution that is exclusively for students with dyslexia, ADHD/ADD or language-based learning disabilities. Its goal is to prepare students to enter or return to other colleges or universities.
Admission to Landmark College is based on a diagnosis of dyslexia, ADHD/ADD or other specific learning disability, average to superior intelligence, and high motivation to undertake the program. Once the application is received and reviewed, the qualified candidate may be invited to the campus for a testing session and a personal interview, following which the admissions decision will be made.
The degree program offers traditional liberal arts classes which meet for four and one-half hours per week, not the customary three. This additional time allows instructors both to convey the material, either through lecture or discussion sessions, and to provide the study skills needed to fully assimilate the material.
Because so many students with learning disabilities have inadequate language skills, Landmark College offers non-credit skills courses that build students' skills of composition, reading, spelling, study skills, mathematics, comprehension and word processing.
General Information: Two-Year Private College; Enrollment: 410 (All have dyslexia, ADHD/ADD or other learning disabilities.) **Tuition:** $36,000; **Room and Board:** $7,500. Landmark College is on a rural 125-acre wooded campus, two and one-quarter hours from Boston and three and one-half hours from New York City. Major ski areas are within one hour's ride.
Degrees: Associate of Arts in general studies; business studies.
Summer Program: Three-week intensive program focusing on skills development, reading and reading comprehension, effective writing or composition skills, organizational and study skills. Students take writing, study skills and either math or speech communications. All summer classes meet for an hour and fifteen minutes a day (non-credit). Cost: $3,600
Staff: Learning disabilities specialists; special counselors; faculty members, advisors
Program Features: Learning strategies; basic study skills; developmental program; college skills program; faculty made aware of student's learning

disability; non-credit skills development in summer session; language skills remediation
Entrance Requirements: Documentation of learning disability or ADHD; learning disabilities specialist report; SAT scores accepted; teacher evaluation/recommendations; handwritten essay; personal on-campus interview; average to superior intelligence; high motivation; testing: WAIS-R, psychological report
Special Facilities for: Physical impairments
Scholarships: See page 457.

VIRGINIA

NEW RIVER COMMUNITY COLLEGE

P.O. BOX 1127
DUBLIN, VIRGINIA 27084
(540) 674-3600 X4358; FAX: (540) 674-3649
E-MAIL: nrdixoj@nr.edu **WEB SITE: www.nr.edu**

Name of Special Program: Learning Enrichment and Achievement Program (LEAP)
Director: Jeananne Dixon
General Information: Two-Year Community College; Enrollment: 4,000; **Tuition:** Residents – $72.50 per credit hour, Non-Residents – $235.35 per credit hour; **Room and Board:** No college housing available. A 100-acre rural campus located in Dublin, Virginia. **Programs:** Occupational/technical education, university parallel/college transfer education, general education, continuing education, special training programs, developmental courses, special regional and community services
Special Program: Enrollment in Special Program: 130; Cost: None. *Summer Prep Program:* One-week introduction to college and academic strategies. Cost: $35
Staff: Learning disabilities specialists; content tutors; peer tutors; special counselors
Program Features: Oral and extended time testing; individual and small group tutoring sessions; limited course load (first year); basic study skills; note-taking assistance – scribes; tape recorders; taped texts; developmental classes; faculty made aware of student's learning disability
Entrance Requirements: Documentation of learning disability; testing: WAIS, IEP, psychological report
Special Facilities for: Visual, hearing and physical impairments

CHIPPEWA VALLEY TECHNICAL COLLEGE

BUSINESS EDUCATION CENTER
620 WEST CLAIREMONT AVENUE
EAU CLAIRE, WISCONSIN 54701-6162
800-547-2882 X6234, (715) 833-6234
800-833-6509 TTY, (715) 852-1344 TTY; FAX: (715) 833-6470
E-MAIL: vdeford@cvtc.edu or schambers@cvtc.edu
WEB SITE: www.cvtc.edu

Name of Special Program: Disability Services
Administrator: Sherry Chambers; *Disability Services Assistant:* Vivian De Ford
General Information: Two-Year State Vocational and Technical College; Enrollment 6,000; **Tuition:** Residents – $87 per credit hour, Non-Residents – $536.30 per credit hour; **Room and Board:** No college housing available. Founded in 1912. An urban campus in a small city, 90 miles east of Minneapolis-St Paul, Minnesota. Noted for its outdoor sports such as fishing, hunting, skiing and hiking. **Majors:** Agribusiness/agricultural production, agricultural sciences, allied health, architecture, business/management, business/ office, child care, civil technologies, computer/information sciences, construction trades, diagnostic/treatment services, engineering technologies, environmental control technologies, health sciences, industrial production, law, marketing/distribution, mechanical/electromechanical technologies, mechanics/repairers, medical laboratory technologies, precision production, protective services
Special Program: Enrollment in Special Program: 173; Cost: None. The Serve Lab is open twelve (12) hours a week during summer school. It is available to students with a documented disability.
Staff: Learning disability specialists; peer tutors
Program Features: Oral and extended time testing; taped texts; basic study skills; limited course load (first year); individual and small group tutoring sessions; note-taking assistance – scribes; faculty made aware of student's disability; developmental program; tape recorders; FM systems, interpreters, adaptive equipment, assistive technology instruction, others as needed/requested
Entrance Requirements: Documentation of disability; COMPASS (accommodation form found on web site)
Special Facilities for: Visual, hearing and physical impairments

GATEWAY TECHNICAL COLLEGE: KENOSHA CAMPUS
3520 30th AVENUE
KENOSHA, WISCONSIN 53144-1690
(262) 564-2366; (262) 564-2206 TTY
E-MAIL: gieseb@gtc.edu and sullivanj@gtc.edu
WEB SITE: www.gtc.edu

RACINE CAMPUS
1001 SOUTH MAIN STREET
RACINE, WISCONSIN 53403-7379
(262) 619-6200; (262) 619-6206 TTY

ELKHORN CAMPUS
400 COUNTY ROAD H
ELKHORN, WISCONSIN 53121
(262) 741-8476

Name of Special Program: Special Needs Support
Transition Counselor: Barbara Giese *for students under 21 years of age*
Special Needs Counselor: Jack Sullivan *for students over 21 years of age*
General Information: Two-Year Technical College; Enrollment: 26,451 (three campuses); **Tuition:** Residents – $80.50 per credit, Non-Residents – $510.30 per credit; **Room and Board:** No college housing available. Founded in 1911. An urban campus in a small city, 40 miles south of Milwaukee, with easy access to Chicago. **Majors:** Agribusiness/agricultural production, business/management, business/office, civil technologies, communications/engineering technologies, environmental design, health sciences, industrial production, mechanical/electromechanical technologies, protective services, transportation, vocational home economics
Special Program: Enrollment in Special Program: 524 plus 678 seen for diagnostic intake each year; Cost: None
Staff: Special needs counselors; content tutors (faculty members); peer tutors; transition specialist
Program Features: Oral and extended time testing; taped texts; tape recorders; note-taking assistance – scribes; basic study skills (non-credit); academic prep program; individual and small group tutoring sessions; limited course load; meetings with instructors and students to discuss modifications; meetings with learning skills specialist to develop employment plan
Entrance Requirements: Documentation of learning disability or learning disabilities specialist report; placement test
Accessibility for: Visual, hearing and physical impairments; emotional disability, attention deficit disorder, all ADA disabilities
College Life: Long-standing support system with special needs instructors acting as liaisons

MILWAUKEE AREA TECHNICAL COLLEGE
700 WEST STATE STREET
MILWAUKEE, WISCONSIN 53233-1443
(414) 297-6581; (414) 297-6986 TDD; FAX: (414) 297-8142
E-MAIL: spainc@matc.edu. WEB SITE: www.matc.edu

Name of Special Program: Disability Services
Manager: Carolyn Spain
General Information: Two-Year Community College; Enrollment: 44,000; **Tuition:** Associate Degree and Diploma – $1,437.05 for 15 credits, Four-Year College Transfer – $1,900.55 for 15 credits; **Room and Board:** No college housing available. A 10-acre urban campus in a very large city with easy access to Chicago and Minneapolis. **Majors:** Agribusiness/agricultural production/sciences, allied health, business/management/office, chemistry, civil technologies, communications and technologies, computer/information sciences, crafts/design, diagnostic/treatment services, education, engineering technologies, environmental control technologies, health sciences, home economics, industrial production, marketing/distribution, mechanical/electromechanical technologies, mechanics/repairers, medical laboratory technologies, physical sciences, precision production, protective services, public affairs, rehabilitation services, visual/performing arts, vocational home economics
Special Program: Enrollment: 400; Cost: None
Staff: Learning disabilities specialists; peer tutors; content tutors (faculty members); staff advisors
Program Features: Oral and extended time testing; individual and small group tutoring sessions; limited course load (first year); note-taking assistance – scribes; tape recorders; taped texts; basic study skills; academic advising for students with learning disabilities; faculty made aware of student's learning disability; adaptive equipment; special learning center for students with disabilities with state-of-the-art computer equipment, software programs and assistive listening technology
Entrance Requirements: Documentation of learning disability; learning disabilities specialist report; admissions testing at Milwaukee Area Technical College
Special Facilities for: Visual, hearing and physical impairments

NORTHEAST WISCONSIN TECHNICAL COLLEGE
P.O. BOX 19042, 2740 WEST MASON STREET
GREEN BAY, WISCONSIN 54307-9042
(920) 498-5447; FAX: (920) 498-5618
WEB SITE: www.nwtc.edu

Name of Special Program: Special Needs Service Program
Dean: Bridget Goldman
General Information: Two-Year State College; Enrollment: 5,117; **Tuition:** Residents – $96.40 per credit hour, Non-Residents – $545.70 per credit hour; **Room and Board:** No college housing available. Founded in 1913. A suburban campus in a small city, 129 miles from Milwaukee. **Majors:** Agriculture, business and marketing, business and industry, health occupations, protective services, and trade and industry
Special Program: Enrollment in Special Program: 250; Cost: None
Staff: Learning disabilities specialists; content tutors (staff members); peer tutors; special counselors
Program Features: Oral and extended time testing; individual and small group tutoring sessions; limited course load (first year); note-taking assistance – scribes; tape recorders; taped texts; basic study skills; developmental program; faculty made aware of student's learning disability
Entrance Requirements: Documentation of learning disability; learning disabilities specialist report (recommended); diagnostic testing at Northeast Wisconsin Technical College (recommended)
Special Facilities for: Visual, hearing and physical impairments

WAUKESHA COUNTY TECHNICAL COLLEGE
800 MAIN STREET
PEWAUKEE, WISCONSIN 53072-4698
(262) 691-5210
E-MAIL: djilbert@wctc.edu
WEB SITE: www.wctc.edu

Name of Special Program: The Learning Place
Coordinator of Special Services: Deborah Jilbert
General Information: Two-Year Vocational Technical College; Enrollment: 9,096; **Tuition:** Residents – $87 per credit, Non-Residents – $536.30 per credit; **Room and Board:** No college housing available. A suburban campus in a large town, 25 miles from Milwaukee. Part of the Wisconsin Technical Colleges System. **Majors:** Allied health, business management, office management, communications, diagnostic treatment services, engineering technologies, health sciences, industrial production, marketing and distribution, mechanical technologies, electromechanical technolo-

gies, mechanics / repairers, precision production, protective services, vocational home economics
Special Program: Enrollment in Special Program: 30, Limited to 12–15 per program; Cost: Varies. *Summer Program:* A one-day transition class with limited enrollment. The program prepares the students with learning disabilities for the fall semester.
Staff: Learning disabilities specialists; peer tutors; content tutors (faculty members)
Program Features: Oral and extended time testing; individual and small group tutoring sessions; limited course load (first year); basic study skills; note-taking assistance – scribes; tape recorders and taped texts for visually impaired; academic advising for students with learning disabilities; faculty made aware of student's learning disability
Entrance Requirements: Documentation of learning disability; learning disabilities specialist report; ASSET (Admission Test – accommodations provided with approved documentation); vocational evaluation; medical evaluation; psychological testing
Special Facilities for: Visual, hearing and physical impairments
College Life: The amount of supportive services available for students enrolled in our program makes our college attractive to students with disabilities. Not only do we have extensive academic support services, we also have some specialized services for students with disabilities who need more structured programs.

Four-Year and Two-Year Colleges with Expanded Services for Students with Learning Disabilities

The following four-year and two-year colleges offer students an extensive array of services to help them achieve their academic goals.

ARIZONA

NORTHERN ARIZONA UNIVERSITY

BOX 5633
FLAGSTAFF, ARIZONA 86011-6045
(928) 523-8773; FAX: (928) 523-8747
E-MAIL: chad.loberge@nau.edu **WEB SITE: www.nau.edu**

Name of Support Services: Disability Support Services
Director: Chad Loberger
General Information: Four-Year State University; Enrollment: 15,750; **Tuition:** Residents – $4,223, Non-Residents – $12,853; **Room and Board:** $5,960. Northern Arizona University is located on a 730-acre campus in Flagstaff, Arizona, and is close to many outdoor attractions among them the Snow Bowl and the Grand Canyon. **Degrees:** BA, BS, BFA, BMus, BMus Ed, BSN, and astronomy, education, forestry and hotel/restaurant management programs
Support Services: Enrollment: 70; Cost: None
Staff: Learning disabilities specialists
Special Features: Extended time testing, individual and small group tutoring sessions; limited course load (first year); academic advising for students with learning disabilities; note-taking assistance – scribes; taped texts; tape recorders; basic study skills; support group; assistive technology lab
Entrance Requirements: Documentation of learning disability; aptitude and achievement testing; psychological report
Special Facilities for: Visual, hearing and physical impairments
College Life: Disability Support Services offers very personalized services to students with disabilities. Our support combined with strong academic programs makes the institution highly attractive.

ARKANSAS

HARDING UNIVERSITY

BOX 12233, 900 E. CENTER
SEARCY, ARKANSAS 72149-0001
(501) 279-4028; FAX: (501) 279-4217
E-MAIL: tmcleod@harding.edu **WEB SITE: www.harding.edu**

Name of Support Services: Student Support Services
Director: Jim Johnston; *Disabilities Specialist:* Teresa McLeod
General Information: Four-Year Private University; Enrollment: 4,400; **Tuition:** Residents – $306 per credit hour; **Room and Board:** $4,650 per year plus meal plan. Harding University is in the foothills of the Ozarks

and 45 minutes from Little Rock, Arkansas. **Degrees:** education, nursing, liberal arts, business, Bible, computer science
Support Services: Enrollment: 275; Cost: None
Staff: Learning disabilities specialists; peer tutors; special counselors
Special Features: Oral and extended time testing, individual and small group tutoring sessions; note-taking assistance – scribes; taped texts; tape recorders; basic study skills; advanced developmental program; faculty made aware of student's learning disability
Entrance Requirements: Documentation of learning disability; SAT/ACT untimed scores accepted; testing: WAIS, IEP, psychological report
Special Facilities for: Visual, hearing and physical impairments; accommodations are made on a case-by-case basis of accepted students.

CALIFORNIA

CALIFORNIA STATE POLYTECHNIC UNIVERSITY: POMONA
3801 WEST TEMPLE AVENUE
POMONA, CALIFORNIA 91768
(909) 869-7659 V/TDD; FAX: (909) 869-3271
E-MAIL: clschmitt@csupomona.edu
WEB SITE: www.csupomona.edu

Name of Support Services: Disability Resource Center (DRC)
Director: Dr. Catherine Schmitt-Whitaker
General Information: Four-Year State University; Enrollment: 18,700; **Annual Tuition:** Residents – $3,414, Non-Residents – $3,414 plus $226 per unit; **Room and Board:** $7,506. California State Polytechnic University: Pomona spans approximately 1,400 acres about 40 minutes from downtown areas of Los Angeles, Orange County and San Bernardino. The climate is semi-arid, with clear and dry summers and mild winters. **Degrees:** Cal Poly Pomona has seven colleges offering a multitude of Bachelor's degrees in each: Agriculture, Restaurant and Hotel Management, Science, Business, Engineering, Environmental Design and Letters, Arts and Social Science. Each college offers hands-on opportunities before graduation so students may learn applications in addition to theories.
Support Services: Enrollment: 259; Cost: None
Staff: Learning disabilities specialists; special counselors
Special Features: Oral and extended time testing, individual tutoring sessions; note-taking assistance – scribes; taped texts; tape recorders; academic advising for students with learning disabilities; faculty made aware of student's learning disability; assistive technology lab, enhanced services program offered to limited number of students (Arches)
Entrance Requirements: Documentation of learning disability; learning

disabilities specialist report; SAT/ACT untimed scores accepted; testing: psychological report
Special Facilities for: Visual, hearing and physical impairments
College Life: Through a U.S. Department of Education TRIO grant, a new department has been created to provide students with learning disabilities enhanced advising services, tutoring and individual support.
Scholarships: See page 425.

CALIFORNIA STATE UNIVERSITY: BAKERSFIELD
9001 STOCKDALE HIGHWAY
BAKERSFIELD, CALIFORNIA 93311-1099
(661) 664-3360, (661) 654-6288; FAX: (661) 664-2171
E-MAIL: ssd@csub.edu **WEB SITE: www.csub.edu**

Name of Support Services: Services for Students with Disabilities
Director: Janice Clausen
General Information: Four-Year State University; Enrollment: 8,000; **Tuition:** Residents – $1,106 per quarter, Non-Residents – $1,106 per quarter plus $226 per unit; **Room and Board:** $3,500–5,800. The 375-acre campus is located in a metropolitan city in the southern San Joaquin Valley just two hours from Los Angeles and five hours from the Bay area. Beach areas, national parks and other recreational spots are only miles away. The climate is semi-arid, with clear and dry summers and mild winters. **Majors:** Art, biology, business administration, chemistry, child adolescent and family studies, communication, computer science, criminal justice, economics, English, environmental resource management, geology, history, liberal studies, mathematics, music, natural sciences, nursing, philosophy, physical education and kinesiology, physics, political science, psychology, public administration, religious studies, sociology, Spanish, theatre arts
Support Services: Enrollment: 180; Cost: None
Staff: Learning disabilities specialist
Special Features: Oral and extended time testing; taped texts; tape recorders; note-taking assistance – scribes
Entrance Requirements: Documentation of learning disability; SAT/ACT untimed scores accepted; testing: WAIS, diagnostic testing at college
Special Facilities for: Visual, hearing and physical impairments
College Life: The goal of the Services for Students with Disabilities Office is to see that equal opportunities are provided for any students with disabilities. The Office helps mainstream students into the college environment at their optimum level by taking advantage of services and support provided by various campus departments. An important part of college life is found in campus programs and activities not just the classroom.

CALIFORNIA STATE UNIVERSITY: FULLERTON
P.O. BOX 6830, 800 NORTH STATE COLLEGE BLVD.
FULLERTON, CALIFORNIA 92834-6830
(714) 278-3117; FAX: (714) 278-2408
E-MAIL: pmiller@fullerton.edu **WEB SITE: www.fullerton.edu**

Name of Support Services: Office of Disabled Student Services
Director: Paul K. Miller
General Information: Four-Year State University; Enrollment: 30,000; **Tuition and Room:** Residents – $1,260 per semester; Non-Residents – $1,260 plus $339 per unit per semester; **Room and Board:** $6,545. California State University at Fullerton consists of a 225-acre campus in a suburban area, 30 miles east of Los Angeles. **Degrees:** Biological science, business, communications and the arts, computer and physical science, education, engineering and environmental design, health professions, and social sciences
Support Services: Enrollment: 450; Cost: None
Staff: Learning disabilities specialists
Special Features: Oral and extended time testing; note-taking assistance – scribes; taped texts; tape recorders; basic study skills; academic advising for students with learning disabilities
Entrance Requirements: Documentation of learning disability; SAT/ACT untimed scores accepted; testing: WAIS, psychological report
Special Facilities for: Visual, hearing and physical impairments

UNIVERSITY OF CALIFORNIA: RIVERSIDE
900 UNIVERSITY AVENUE
RIVERSIDE, CALIFORNIA 92521-0214
(951) 827-4538 V/TTY; FAX: (951) 827-4218
E-MAIL: marcia.schiffer@ucr.edu
WEB SITE: www.ucr.edu

Name of Support Services: Services for Students with Disabilities (Student Special Services Department)
Director: Marcia Theise Schiffer
General Information: Four-Year State University; Enrollment: 17,000; **Tuition:** Residents – $5,768; **Room and Board:** $9,350. The University of California: Riverside is on a suburban 1200-acre campus, 50 miles east of Los Angeles near mountains, desert and beaches. **Majors:** Agriculture, biological sciences, business, communication and the arts, computer and physical science, engineering and environmental design, health professions, social science
Support Services: Enrollment: 50; Cost: None

Staff: Learning disabilities specialists
Special Features: Oral and extended time testing; individual and small group tutoring sessions; note-taking assistance – scribes; taped texts; tape recorders; basic study skills; Kurzweil reader; word processors
Entrance Requirements: Documentation of learning disability; learning disabilities specialist report; SAT untimed scores accepted; testing: WAIS, psychological report; diagnostic testing at the University of California: Riverside
Special Facilities for: Visual, hearing and physical impairments

UNIVERSITY OF SOUTHERN CALIFORNIA
UNIVERSITY PARK
LOS ANGELES, CALIFORNIA 90089-5012
(213) 740-0776; FAX: (213) 740-8216
E-MAIL: ability@usc.edu **WEB SITE: www.usc.edu**

Name of Support Services: Disability Services and Programs
Director: Edward Roth, Ph.D.
General Information: Four-Year State University; Enrollment: 23,000; **Tuition:** $33,892; **Room and Board:** $10,144. The University Park campus is located three miles south of downtown Los Angeles on 155 acres. **Majors:** Communications, architecture, cinema-television, letters, arts and sciences, gerontology, pre-dentistry, engineering, fine arts, health professions, pre-law, business, accounting, pre-medicine, music, pharmacy, policy, planning and development, education, social work, theatre
Support Services: Enrollment: 350; Cost: None. The percentage of students with learning disabilities who receive a degree in five or more years is 78%.
Staff: Learning disabilities specialists; peer tutors; special counselors
Special Features: Extended time testing; individual and small group tutoring sessions; limited course load (optional); academic advising for students with learning disabilities; note-taking assistance – scribes; taped texts; learning enrichment workshops; tutoring; learning assistance
Entrance Requirements: Documentation of learning disability; learning disabilities specialist report; SAT/ACT untimed scores accepted
Special Facilities for: Visual, hearing and physical impairments

CONNECTICUT

FAIRFIELD UNIVERSITY
1073 NORTH BENSON ROAD
FAIRFIELD, CONNECTICUT 06824-5195
(203) 254-4000 X2445; FAX: (203) 254-4014
E-MAIL: wloneil@mail.fairfield.edu WEB SITE: www.fairfield.edu

Name of Support Services: Student Support Services
Director: Reverend W. Laurence O'Neil, S.J.
Assistant Director: David Ryan Soderlund
General Information: Four-Year State University; Enrollment: 5,053; **Tuition:** $27,450; **Room and Board:** $9,270. Fairfield is a Jesuit University located in Fairfield, Connecticut, on a 200-acre campus that features beautifully wooded hills and spacious lawns. The University is situated in a suburban community of 55,000, one hour from New York City and five minutes from Long Island Sound. **Majors:** Accounting, American studies, biology, chemistry, communication, computer science, economics, engineering, English, finance, history, information systems, international studies, management, marketing, mathematics, modern languages and literatures, neuroscience, nursing, philosophy, physics, politics, psychology, religious studies, sociology and anthropology, visual and performing arts
Support Services: Enrollment: 90; Cost: None
Staff: Learning disabilities specialists; peer tutors
Special Features: Oral and extended time testing; individual and small group tutoring sessions; limited course load (first year); academic advising for students with learning disabilities; note-taking assistance – scribes; tape recorders; basic study skills; faculty made aware of student's learning disability
Entrance Requirements: Documentation of learning disability; learning disabilities specialist report; SAT/ACT untimed scores accepted
Special Facilities for: Visual, hearing and physical impairments
College Life: One-on-one contact with professors, access to first-rate facilities and technology, and a wide array of co-curricula activities including Division I athletics and exciting programming at Regina A. Quick Center for the Arts give students many ways to develop new interests and expertise.

HAWAII

BRIGHAM YOUNG UNIVERSITY: HAWAII

55-220 KULANAI STREET
LAIE, HAWAII 96762
(808) 293-3211; FAX: (808) 293-3525
E-MAIL: buckinghamp@byuh.edu **WEB SITE: www.byuh.edu**

Name of Support Services: Special Needs Program
Director: Paul Buckingham
General Information: Four-Year Private University; Enrollment: 2,400; **Tuition:** $4,988; **Room and Board**: $6,000 per semester. Brigham Young University: Hawaii is 32 miles from Honolulu. **Degrees:** Bachelor of Arts, Bachelor of Fine Arts, Bachelor of Science, Bachelor of Social Work
Support Services: Enrollment: 12; Cost: None. The percentage of students with learning disabilities receiving a degree in four years is 80%.
Staff: Learning disabilities specialists; peer tutors; special counselor
Special Features: Extended time testing; individual and small group tutoring sessions; limited course load (first year); academic advising for students with learning disabilities; note-taking assistance – scribes; taped texts; tape recorders; basic study skills; faculty made aware of student's learning disability
Entrance Requirements: Documentation of learning disability; medical evaluation
Special Facilities for: Visual, hearing and physical impairments
College Life: Brigham Young University: Hawaii is a unique campus. Not only are the natural surroundings beautiful, but there is a cultural diversity amongst the students and faculty that is sensational. In this modest-sized student body, students are given the opportunity to receive a quality education and get to know and understand people from around the world.

ILLINOIS

NORTHERN ILLINOIS UNIVERSITY

947 NORTH 12th STREET
DE KALB, ILLINOIS 60115
(815) 753-1303; FAX: (815) 753-9599
E-MAIL: nancyk@niu.edu **WEB SITE: www.niu.edu**

Name of Support Services: Center for Access-Ability Resources (CAAR)
Director: Nancy Kasinski
General Information: Four-Year State University; Enrollment: 20,825; **Annual Tuition:** Residents – $4,420; **Room and Board**: $4,416. The DeKalb campus of Northern Illinois University consists of 514 acres. The campus is 65 miles from downtown Chicago and 45 miles southeast of Rockford.

Degrees: Many degrees are available within the Colleges of Liberal Arts, Sciences, Education, Visual and Performing Arts, Business, Health and Human Sciences, and Engineering.
Support Services: Enrollment: 188; Cost: None
Staff: Learning disabilities specialists; peer tutors
Special Features: Testing accommodations; basic study skills; coaching; note-taking assistance – scribes; taped texts; tape recorders; faculty made aware of student's learning disability
Entrance Requirements: Documentation of learning disability; ACT untimed scores accepted; teacher evaluation; handwritten essay; testing: WAIS, IEP, psychological report
Special Facilities for: Visual, hearing and physical impairments

SOUTHERN ILLINOIS UNIVERSITY
CAMPUS BOX 1611
EDWARDSVILLE, ILLINOIS 62026
(618) 650-3726; FAX: (618) 650-5691
E-MAIL: jfloyd@siue.edu **WEB SITE: www.siue.edu**

Name of Support Services: Disability Support Services
Director: Jane A. Floyd-Hendey
General Information: Four-Year State University; Enrollment: 13,295; **Tuition:** Residents – $4,183; Non-Residents – $7,543; **Room and Board**: $5,364. The campus of Southern Illinois University consists of 2,300 acres in a small town near St. Louis, Missouri. **Degrees:** BA, BS, BFA, BSE, BLS
Support Services: Enrollment: 120; Cost: None
Staff: Learning disabilities specialists; peer tutors
Special Features: Oral and untimed testing; individual and small group tutoring sessions; limited class load (first year), academic advising; note-taking assistance – scribes; taped texts; tape recorders; basic study skills; developmental programs; faculty made aware of student's learning disability; Kurzweil reader; word processors; personal and career counseling; learning disability support group
Entrance Requirements: Documentation of learning disability; ACT untimed scores accepted; testing: WAIS, IEP, psychological report
Special Facilities for: Visual, hearing and physical impairments

WESTERN ILLINOIS UNIVERSITY
1 UNIVERSITY CIRCLE
MACOMB, ILLINOIS 61455
(309) 298-2512; FAX: (309) 298-2361
E-MAIL: disability@wiu.edu
WEB SITE: www.student.services.wiu.edu/dss/

Name of Support Services: Disability Support Services
Director: Tara Miller
General Information: Four-Year State University; Enrollment: 13,000; **Tuition:** Residents – $2,610, Non-Residents – $5,220; **Room and Board**: $5,366 double occupancy. The Western Illinois University campus consists of more than 1,000 acres and is located 40 miles east of the Mississippi River. The University operates the Alice I. Kibbe Life Sciences Station on the Mississippi River, the Frank J. Horn Field Campus and the University Farm which provides nearby facilities for students enrolled in agriculture, biology, and recreation park and tourism administration courses. **Degrees:** BA, BB, BS, BFA, BSE, BLS
Support Services: Cost: None
Staff: Learning disabilities specialists; peer tutors
Special Features: Oral and untimed testing, limited class load (first year); note-taking assistance – scribes; taped texts; tape recorders; basic study skills; faculty made aware of student's learning disability.
Entrance Requirements: Documentation of learning disability; SAT/ACT untimed scores accepted
Special Facilities for: Visual, hearing and physical impairments

INDIANA

UNIVERSITY OF SAINT FRANCIS
2701 SPRING STREET
FORT WAYNE, INDIANA 46808
(260) 434-7677; FAX: (260) 434-7444
E-MAIL: mkruyer@sf.edu **WEB SITE: www.sf.edu**

Name of Support Services: Student Learning Center
Director: Michelle Kruyer
General Information: Four-Year Private University; Enrollment: 1,755. **Tuition:** $16,750; **Room and Board:** $5,610 double occupancy. The campus of the University of Saint Frances is located near downtown Fort Wayne in an urban setting. The university is a Catholic, coeducational institution of higher education in the liberal arts tradition. **Degrees:** Bachelor degrees in liberal arts and sciences, accounting and business administration, elemen-

tary and secondary and special education, nursing and social work. Pre-professional programs include law, dentistry, medicine and science.
Support Services: Enrollment: 40; Cost: None
Staff: Learning disabilities specialist; peer tutors
Special Features: Oral and untimed testing, limited course load (first year); individual and small group tutoring sessions; tape recorders, faculty made aware of student's learning disability; Kurzweil readers, word processors; Word Q and Dragon Naturally Speaking voice recognition software
Entrance Requirements: Documentation of learning disability; SAT/ACT untimed scores accepted; medical evaluation (if needed); requirements are dependent upon type of disability; testing: IEP, psychological report
College Life: Small class sizes, and small campus. The Student Learning Center offers a place where students with learning disabilities receive assistance with course work.

IOWA

UNIVERSITY OF IOWA

3100 BURGE
IOWA CITY, IOWA 52242-1214
(319) 335-1462; FAX: (319) 335-3973
E-MAIL: daushen-ju@uiowa.edu **WEB SITE: www.uiowa.edu**

Name of Support Services: Student Disability Services
Director: Dau-shen Ju, Ph.D.
General Information: Four-Year State University; Enrollment: 29,430; **Tuition:** Residents – $5,935, Non-Residents – $18,159; **Room:** $6,912. The 110-acre campus is in a small town 110 miles east of Des Moines and 220 miles west of Chicago. **Majors:** Biological science, business, communications and the arts, computer and physical science, education, engineering and environmental design, health professions, social science
Support Services: Enrollment: 450; Cost: None
Staff: Learning disabilities specialists; peer tutors
Special Features: Extended time testing; limited course load (first year); academic advising for students with learning disabilities; note-taking assistance – scribes; taped texts; Kurzweil readers
Entrance Requirements: Documentation of learning disability; testing: WAIS, psychological report
Special Facilities for: Visual, hearing and physical impairments
College Life: The University of Iowa has a central office serving all students with disabilities on campus (Student Disability Services). Students are assigned to specific advisors on the basis of disability, primarily. The University provides academic accommodations, if warranted, in all classes.

KANSAS

KANSAS STATE UNIVERSITY
202 HOLTON HALL
MANHATTAN, KANSAS 66506-1311
(785) 532-6441; FAX: (785) 532-6457
E-MAIL: dss@ksu.edu **WEB SITE: www.ksu.edu/dss**

Name of Support Services: Disabled Student Services
Director: Gretchen Holden
General Information: Four-Year State University; Enrollment: 22,000; **Tuition:** Residents – $4,256, Non-Residents – $12,964; **Room and Board:** $6,006. Kansas State University is located in a suburban area on a 668-acre campus, 125 miles west of Kansas City. **Degrees:** Biological science, business, communications and the arts, computer and physical science, education, engineering and environmental design, social science
Support Services: Enrollment: 266; Cost: None
Staff: Learning disabilities specialists; peer tutors
Special Features: Oral and extended time testing; small group tutoring sessions; limited course load; academic advising for students with learning disabilities; note-taking assistance – scribes; taped texts; basic study skills; faculty made aware of student's learning disability; Dragon Naturally Speaking voice recognition software; Kurzweil readers
Entrance Requirements: Documentation of learning disability; ACT untimed scores accepted; testing: WAIS, IEP, psychological report
Special Facilities for: Visual, hearing and physical impairments
Scholarships: See page 428.

MAINE

UNIVERSITY OF NEW ENGLAND
911 HILLS BEACH ROAD
BIDDEFORD, MAINE 04005-9599
(985) 448-4214; FAX: (985) 448-4423
E-MAIL: schurch@une.edu **WEB SITE: www.une.edu**

Name of Support Services: Individual Learning Program (ILP)
Coordinator: Susan M. Church
General Information: Four-Year Private University; Enrollment: 2,660; **Tuition:** $21,540; **Room and Board:** $8,730. A suburban university on the southern coast of Maine. The nearest big city is Portland. **Majors:** University of New England is comprised of the College of Arts and Sciences offering the BA, BS and AA degrees. Directed study, junior year abroad, pre-med, advisory committee personal major, certificate programs, academic minors, cooperative education. BA, BS, in humanities,

life science, management, occupational therapy, physical therapy, social/behavioral sciences, and nursing (ADN and BSN)
Support Services: Enrollment: 25 (limited to 25); Cost: Level I – $2,300 to Level III – $4,500 per year
Staff: Learning disabilities specialists
Special Features: Oral and extended time testing; individual tutoring sessions; limited course load (first year); academic advising for students with learning disabilities; basic study skills; developmental program; faculty made aware of student's learning disability (at student's request); support group; mentoring program of upper level ILP; students mentoring ILP freshmen; weekly sessions with learning specialist.
Entrance Requirements: Documentation of learning disability; teacher evaluation; learning disabilities specialist report; testing: WAIS-R, psychological report
College Life: Small classes and small college overall with the ILP well-integrated into the academic community. It gives extensive support where and when students have need.

MASSACHUSETTS

ANNA MARIA COLLEGE
50 SUNSET LANE
PAXTON, MASSACHUSETTS 01612
(508) 849-3372, X313; FAX: (508) 849-3362
WEB SITE: www.annamaria.edu

Name of Support Services: Learning Center
General Information: Four-Year Private College; Enrollment: 919; **Tuition:** $18,545; **Room and Board:** $7,415. Anna Marie College is on a 180-acre campus in the suburbs eight miles northwest of Worcester. It is a private college affiliated with the Roman Catholic Church and includes a learning resource center, an art gallery and an audiovisual center. **Degrees:** BA, BS, BBA, BFA, BM and BSN
Support Services: Enrollment: 22; Cost: None
Staff: Learning disabilities specialists
Special Features: Oral and extended time testing; individual tutoring sessions; limited course load; academic advising for students with learning disabilities; note-taking assistance – scribes; taped texts; tape recorders; basic study skills; faculty made aware of student's learning disability; word processors; personal and career counseling
Entrance Requirements: Documentation of learning disability; SAT/ACT untimed scores accepted; testing: WAIS, psychological report
Special Facilities for: Visual, hearing and physical impairments

UNIVERSITY OF MASSACHUSETTS: LOWELL
1 UNIVERSITY AVENUE, SOUTHWICK HALL, NORTH CAMPUS
LOWELL, MASSACHUSETTS 01854
(978) 934-4574; FAX: (978) 934-3042
E-MAIL: chandrika-sharma@uml.edu
WEB SITE: www.uml.edu/student-services/disability

Name of Support Services: Office of Disability Services
Director: Chandrika Sharma, Ed.D.
General Information: Four-Year State University; Enrollment: 8,600; **Tuition:** Residents – $8,166, Non-Residents – $19,066; **Room and Board:** $6,311. University of Massachusetts: Lowell is an urban campus, 26 miles north of Boston near beaches and ski areas. **Degrees:** Health professions, engineering, arts and sciences, fine arts, management and education (graduate only)
Support Services: Enrollment: 5% of accepted students; Cost: None
Staff: Learning disabilities specialists; peer tutors; content tutors (faculty members); special counselors
Special Features: Oral and extended time testing; small group tutoring sessions; limited course load; academic advising for students with learning disabilities; note-taking assistance – scribes; taped texts; tape recorders; basic study skills; faculty made aware of student's learning disability (at student's request)
Entrance Requirements: Documentation of learning disability; learning disabilities specialist report; SAT/ACT untimed scores accepted; medical evaluation (if needed); handwritten essay; testing: WAIS, psychological report
Special Facilities for: Visual, hearing and physical impairments
College Life: University of Massachusetts: Lowell provides quality service from caring individuals. We emphasize self-advocacy and tailor our services to reflect the world beyond college. There is an extremely warm and friendly environment without hand-holding.

WESTERN NEW ENGLAND COLLEGE
1215 WILBRAHAM ROAD
SPRINGFIELD, MASSACHUSETTS 01119-2684
(413) 782-1257; FAX: (413) 782-1746
E-MAIL: balpert@wnec.edu **WEB SITE: www.wnec.edu**

Name of Support Services: Student Disability Services (SDS)
Director: Dr. Bonni Alpert
General Information: Four-Year Private College; Enrollment: 4,500; **Tuition:** $24,626; **Room and Board:** $9,526. Western New England College

is on a 131-acre campus in suburban Springfield, described as the "Crossroads of New England," just 90 miles west of Boston. **Degrees:** Biological science, business, communication and the arts, computer and physical science, engineering and environment design, health professions, social science
Support Services: Enrollment: 150; Cost: None
Staff: Learning disabilities specialists; peer tutors; content tutors (faculty members); special counselors
Special Features: Oral and extended time testing; individual tutoring sessions; limited course load (first year); academic advising for students with learning disabilities; note-taking assistance – scribes; taped texts; tape recorders; basic study skills; faculty made aware of student's learning disability; assistive technological devices
Entrance Requirements: Documentation of learning disability; learning disabilities specialist report; SAT/ACT untimed scores accepted; medical evaluation; testing: WAIS, IEP, psychological report
College Life: WNEC is a community that values diversity and therfore is continually designing innovative programs and learning formats in order to support the learning needs of all students. The faculty and the disability support staff are always available to help students navigate both the academic and social environments of their college experience.
Special Facilities for: Visual, hearing and physical impairments

MICHIGAN

AQUINAS COLLEGE
1607 ROBINSON ROAD, SOUTHEAST
GRAND RAPIDS, MICHIGAN 49506-1799
(616) 632-2166; FAX: (616) 732-4431
E-MAIL: sweenjac@aquinas.edu **WEB SITE: www.aquinas.edu**

Name of Support Services: Academic Achievement Center
Coordinator: Jackie Sweeney
General Information: Four-Year Private College; Enrollment: 2,500; **Tuition:** $17,926; **Room and Board:** $5,824. Aquinas College is a Catholic institution on a 107-acre campus in an urban setting, six miles east of downtown Grand Rapids, Michigan, and about 45 minutes from Lake Michigan. **Degrees:** Professional accountancy, business administration, athletic training, biology, chemistry, economics, education, English, environmental science, history, humanities, mathematics, modern languages, music education, liturgical music, nursing, political science, psychology, sociology, sports management, sustainable business, theology
Support Services: Enrollment: 60; Cost: None

Staff: Learning disabilities specialists; peer tutors; content tutors (faculty members); special counselors
Special Features: Oral and extended time testing; individual and small group tutoring sessions; limited course load (first year); academic advising for students with learning disabilities; note-taking assistance – scribes; taped texts; basic study skills; developmental program for reading; faculty made aware of student's learning disability
Entrance Requirements: Documentation of learning disability; SAT/ACT untimed scores accepted; medical evaluation; testing: WAIS, IEP, psychological report
Special Facilities for: Visual, hearing and physical impairments
College Life: The Academic Achievement Center provides services at no additional cost on an individual need basis so as to fulfill the Aquinas goal of enabling all students to reach their full academic potential. A counselor helps with academic advising, goal setting, and career counseling with the students to improve their skills.
Scholarships: See page 431.

MINNESOTA

THE COLLEGE OF SAINT CATHERINE

2004 RANDOLPH AVENUE
ST. PAUL, MINNESOTA 55105-2514
(651) 690-6563, 1-800-656-KATE; FAX: (651) 690-6718
E-MAIL: bjmandel@stkate.edu **WEB SITE: www.stkate.edu**

Name of Support Services: Resources for Disabilities
Coordinator: Barbara Mandel
General Information: Four-Year Private College; Enrollment: 5,500; **Tuition:** $22,464; **Room Rate:** $6,120. The College of Saint Catherine is a woman's college, five miles from downtown St. Paul on a 119-acre wooded campus. The college is part of a consortium with four other private colleges. **Degrees:** Sciences, business administration, communications, arts, computer science, education, nursing and other health professions
Support Services: Enrollment: 80; Cost: None
Staff: Learning disabilities specialists; peer tutors; content tutors (faculty members); special counselors
Special Features: Oral and extended time testing; individual tutoring sessions; limited course load (first year); academic advising for students with learning disabilities; note-taking assistance – scribes; taped texts; basic study skills; faculty made aware of student's learning disability (at student's request); test-taking with computer
Entrance Requirements: Documentation of learning disability; learning

disabilities report; SAT/ACT untimed scores accepted; medical evaluation, diagnostic testing at The College of Saint Catherine; testing: WAIS, IEP, psychological report
Special Facilities for: Visual, hearing and physical impairments

MISSOURI

WEBSTER UNIVERSITY
470 EAST LOCKWOOD
ST. LOUIS, MISSOURI 63017
(314) 968-7495; FAX: (314) 968-7116
E-MAIL: mcleespa@webster.edu
WEB SITE: www.webster.edu

Name of Support Services: Services for Students with Disabilities
Director: Patricia McLeese, Ph.D.
General Information: Four-Year Private University; Enrollment: 4,200; **Tuition:** $12,880; **Room and Board:** $5,800. Webster University is 12 miles southwest of St. Louis on a 47-acre campus in a suburban area. **Degrees:** Biological science, business, communication and the arts, computer and physical science, engineering and environment design, health professions, social science
Support Services: Enrollment: 40; Cost: None
Staff: Learning disabilities specialists; peer tutors
Special Features: Oral and extended time testing; individual and small group tutoring sessions; note-taking assistance – scribes; taped texts; basic study skills; faculty made aware of student's learning disability; Kurzweil readers; computers; personal and career counseling
Entrance Requirements: Documentation of learning disability; ACT untimed scores accepted; testing: WAIS, psychological report
Special Facilities for: Visual, hearing and physical impairments

NEBRASKA

MIDLAND LUTHERAN COLLEGE
900 NORTH CLARKSON STREET
FREMONT, NEBRASKA 68025
(402) 941-6257; FAX: (402) 727-6223
E-MAIL: kramme@mlc.edu **WEB SITE: www.mlc.edu**

Name of Support Services: Academic Support Services
Director: Lisa Kramme

General Information: Four-Year Private University; Enrollment: 960; **Tuition:** $19,510; **Room and Board:** $4,950. Midland Lutheran College is located in Fremont, Nebraska, a community of 24,000, approximately 30 miles northwest of Omaha and 50 miles north of Lincoln. International travel and study abroad programs are available. **Degrees:** Associate of Arts: administrative assistant, business administration, community service, education, mathematics/computer science, paralegal studies, parish secretary, parish work, respiratory therapy, travel/tourism. Baccalaureate Degrees: Art, biology, business administration, chemistry, communication, economics, education, English, environmental science composite, history, human services composite, journalism and mass communication, math/computer science, music, natural science composite, nursing, physical education, physical science composite, psychology, religion/philosophy, social science composite, sociology, speech/theatre, youth, family ministry
Support Services: Cost: None
Staff: Disability services coordinator; peer tutors; test proctor
Special Features: Oral and extended time testing; individual and small group tutoring sessions; note-taking assistance – scribes; taped texts; tape recorders; basic study skills; faculty made aware of student's learning disablility
Entrance Requirements: Documentation of learning disability; ACT untimed scores accepted; testing: psychological report
Special Facilities for: Visual, hearing and physical impairments
College Life: With an average class size of 18 and a faculty-to-student ratio of 1:15, students have the opportunity to get to know their professors and faculty know their students. Midland Lutheran College is a caring community that values faith, learning, quality, respect and stewardship.

NEW HAMPSHIRE

NEW ENGLAND COLLEGE

THE PATHWAYS CENTER
24 BRIDGE STREET
HENNIKER, NEW HAMPSHIRE 03242-0793
(603) 428-2218; FAX: (603) 428-7230
E-MAIL: lcook@nec.edu **WEB SITE: www.nec.edu**

Name of Support Services: The Pathways Center
Coordinator: Lucy Cook
General Information: Four-Year Private University; Enrollment: 885; **Tuition:** $24,136; **Room and Board:** $8,456. Rural campus 18 miles from Concord; founded in 1946. **Majors:** Biology, business/management, com-

munications, computer/information sciences, education, engineering, fine arts, letters/literature, life sciences, marketing/distribution, mathematics, multi/interdisciplinary studies, parks and recreation, philosophy, physical sciences, psychology, public affairs, social sciences, visual/performing arts
Support Services: Services are provided on an as-needed basis.
Staff: Learning disabilities specialists; professional tutors
Special Features: Oral and extended time testing; individual and small group tutoring sessions; limited course load (first year); tape recorders
Entrance Requirements: Documentation of learning disability; ACT untimed scores accepted; testing: WAIS, psychological report

UNIVERSITY OF NEW HAMPSHIRE
4 GARRISON AVENUE
DURHAM, NEW HAMPSHIRE 03824
(603) 862-2607 V/TTY; FAX: (603) 862-4043
E-MAIL: maxine.little@unh.edu
WEB SITE: www.unh.edu/disabilityservices

Name of Support Services: Disability Service for Students
Director: Maxine Little
General Information: Four-Year State University; Enrollment: 10,800; **Tuition:** Residents – $9,778, Non-Residents – $21,498; **Room and Board:** $7,032. The University is located in the quaint town of Durham, 30 miles from the ocean and one hour from the White Mountains and Boston, Massachusetts. It is an undergraduate-oriented institution on a semester system with numerous opportunities for international studies abroad and research. **Degrees:** 100 majors and 2,000 courses are offered at the baccalaureate level through the Colleges of Liberal Arts, Engineering and Physical Sciences, Life Sciences and Agriculture, the School of Health and Human Services, the Whittemore School of Business and Economics, the Thompson School of Applied Science and University of New Hampshire Manchester.
Support Services: Enrollment: 235; Cost: None
Staff: Learning disabilities specialist; special counselors
Special Features: Oral and extended time testing; limited course load (first year); taped texts; note-taking assistance – scribes; tape recorders, faculty made aware of student's learning disability (at student's request); computers for essay exams; use of calculator; priority seating, assistive technology
Entrance Requirements: Documentation of learning disability; disabilities specialist report; medical evaluation; testing: WAIS, psychological report; achievement testing
Special Facilities for: Visual, hearing and physical impairments

College Life: Comprehensive support services in an environment which encourages self-advocacy and independence.
Scholarships: See page 433.

NEW JERSEY

RIDER UNIVERSITY

2083 LAWRENCEVILLE ROAD
LAWRENCEVILLE, NEW JERSEY 08648-3099
(609) 896-5000 X7365; FAX: (609) 895-5507
E-MAIL: blandford@rider.edu **WEB SITE: www.rider.edu**

Name of Support Services: Learning Disability Services/Education Enhancement Program
Director: Dr. Barbara Blandford
General Information: Four-Year Private University; Enrollment: 4,390; **Tuition:** $22,000; **Room and Board:** $8,000. Rider University is located on a 555-acre campus in the suburban community of Lawrenceville, New Jersey, midway between Princeton and Trenton. It is approximately 55 miles northeast of Philadelphia and 65 miles southwest of New York City. **Academic Units:** College of Business Administration; College of Liberal Arts, Education and Sciences; College of Continuing Studies and Westminister Choir College located in Princeton, New Jersey.
Support Services: Enrollment: 100; Cost: None
Staff: Learning disabilities specialists; peer tutors; special counselors
Special Features: Oral and extended time testing; individual and small group tutoring sessions; limited course load (first year); academic advising for students with learning disabilities; note-taking assistance – scribes; tape recorders; taped texts; basic study skills; developmental program; faculty made aware of student's learning disability
Entrance Requirements: Documentation of learning disability; SAT untimed scores accepted; testing: WAIS, psychological report
Special Facilities for: Visual, hearing and physical impairments
College Life: The Education Enhancement Program assists all students, including those with learning disabilities, in becoming more independent and efficient learners and in meeting the university's academic standards and attaining their personal educational goals. All students with learning disabilities are completely mainstreamed into the college environment.

NEW YORK

CITY UNIVERSITY OF NEW YORK (CUNY)

HUNTER COLLEGE

695 PARK AVENUE-HE 1124
NEW YORK, NEW YORK 10021
(212) 772-4857, (212) 650-3230 TTY; FAX: (212) 650-3449
E-MAIL: sudi.shayesteh@hunter.cuny.edu
WEB SITE: www.hunter.cuny.edu

Name of Support Services: Office of Access and Accomodations
Director: Sudi Shayesteh
General Information: Four-Year City College; Enrollment: 20,000; **Tuition:** $4,000; **Room and Board:** $5,200. The college is in an urban area in New York City and includes a learning resource center, art gallery, radio station, geography/geology laboratory and the academic computing services laboratory. **Degrees:** BA, BS, BFA, BMusic and BS education, Liberal Arts. Pre-Professionals, Internships and Exchange Programs
Support Services: Enrollment: 300; Cost: None
Staff: Learning disabilities specialists; peer tutors
Special Features: Oral and extended time testing; individual and small group tutoring sessions; academic advising for students with learning disabilities; note-taking assistance – scribes; tape recorders; faculty made aware of student's learning disability; basic study skills; developmental program; Kurzweil readers; personal and career counseling; learning disability support group; Reading Edge; computer training and assistance; multi-sensory learning disability seminars; Omni 2000 (reading computer program)
Entrance Requirements: Documentation of learning disability; SAT/ACT untimed scores accepted; diagnostic testing at Hunter College
Special Facilities for: Visual, hearing and physical impairments
College Life: A strong and effective Office for Students with Disabilities. Direct and explicit multi-sensory training.

SAINT BONAVENTURE UNIVERSITY

ST. BONAVENTURE, NEW YORK 14778-2135
(716) 375-2066; FAX: (716) 375-2072
E-MAIL: nmatthew@sbu.edu **WEB SITE: www.sbu.edu**

Name of Support Services: Disability Support Services (DSS)
Coordinator: Nancy A. Matthews
General Information: Four-Year Private University; Enrollment: 3,200; **Tuition:** $22,515; **Room and Board:** $7,706. Saint Bonaventure University is a Catholic institution in the Franciscan tradition. The 500-acre campus is

in a rural area 70 miles southeast of Buffalo and offers a golf course, spacious lawns, various indoor and outdoor recreational facilities. ***Degrees:*** Bachelor of Arts, Science, Science in Education, and Business Administration. **Majors:** Classical languages, English, French, history, philosophy, political science, psychology, social science, environment science, sociology, Spanish, visual arts, biology, chemistry, biochemistry, computer science, mathematics, medical technology, physics, accounting, finance, management sciences, marketing, elementary, education, secondary education, physical education, journalism and mass communication.
Support Services: Enrollment: 130; Cost: None
Staff: Learning disabilities specialists; peer tutors
Special Features: Oral and extended time testing; individual and small group tutoring sessions; limited course load (first year); academic advising for students with learning disabilities; note-taking assistance – scribes; taped texts; tape recorders; faculty made aware of student's learning disability; peer mentors
Entrance Requirements: Documentation of learning disability; SAT / ACT untimed scores accepted; handwritten essay; testing: WAIS, IEP, psychological report
Special Facilities for: Visual, hearing and physical impairments
College Life: In addition to providing necessary accommodations to students with disabilities, St. Bonaventure University also employs a teaching and learning center which provides and promotes both creative and dynamic instruction as well as utilities, and teaches dedicated, critical and active learning. The center affords peer tutoring in almost every subject. Students have the opportunity to meet with the coordinator of DSS on a regular weekly basis.

STATE UNIVERSITY OF NEW YORK (SUNY)

SUNY - ALBANY UNIVERSITY

1400 WASHINGTON AVENUE, CC 130/137
ALBANY, NEW YORK 12222
(518) 442-5490; FAX: (518) 442-5589
E-MAIL: cmalloch@uamail.albany.edu
WEB SITE: www.albany.edu/studentlife/ld

Name of Support Services: Learning Disabled Student Services
Learning Disability Specialist: Carolyn Malloch
General Information: Four-Year State University; Enrollment: 17,000; **Tuition:** Residents – $4,350, Non-Residents – $10,610; **Room and Board:** $8,604. Albany University is located in the capitol city of New York State. **Degrees:** Biological science, business, communication and the arts, com-

puter and physical science, engineering and environment design, health professions, social science
Support Services: Enrollment: 180; Cost: None
Staff: Learning disabilities specialists. The percentage of students with learning disabilities who receive a degree in five or more years is 67%.
Program Features: Extended time testing; limited course load (first year 12 credits); academic advising for students with learning disabilities; note-taking assistance – scribes; tape recorders; taped texts; faculty made aware of student's learning disability (at student's request); basic study skills; Kurzweil readers; individual appointments; adapt tech in main Library
Entrance Requirements: Documentation of learning disability; SAT / ACT untimed scores accepted; testing: WAIS, IEP, psychological report
Special Facilities for: Visual, hearing and physical impairments
Scholarships: See page 435.

SUNY - BINGHAMTON UNIVERSITY
BOX 6000
BINGHAMTON, NEW YORK 13902-6000
(607) 777-2686; FAX: (607) 777-6893
E-MAIL: bjfairba@binghamton.edu
WEB SITE: www.binghamton.edu

Name of Support Services: Services for Students with Disabilities
Director: B. Jean Fairbairn
General Information: Four-Year State University; Enrollment: 12,000; **Tuition:** Residents – $4,350, Non-Residents – $10,610; **Room and Board:** $7,450. Binghamton University is located in a suburban area on a 606-acre campus, one mile west of Binghamton. **Degrees:** The University consists of five schools each with a variety of majors: Harper College (Liberal Arts and Sciences), School of Management, School of Engineering, School of Nursing, and the School of Education and Human Development
Support Services: Enrollment: 100; Cost: None
Staff: Learning disabilities specialists; special counselors
Special Features: Oral and extended time testing; individual tutoring sessions; limited course load (first year); academic advising for students with learning disabilities; note-taking assistance – scribes; tape recorders; taped texts; faculty made aware of student's learning disability (at student's request); talking computer; personal and career counseling; peer advisors; adaptive computer lab; consultation and advocacy for reasonable accommodations; computer-based reader; closed circuit TV giant magnifier; portable assistive listening devices
Entrance Requirements: Documentation of learning disability; SAT / ACT

untimed scores accepted; testing: WAIS, psychological report
Special Facilities for: Visual, hearing and physical impairments
College Life: A wide range of support services for high achieving students with physical, learning or other disabilities.

SUNY – STONY BROOK UNIVERSITY
DISABILITIES SUPPORT SERVICES
133 HUMANITIES BUILDING
STONY BROOK, NEW YORK 11794-5328
(631) 632-6748; FAX: (631) 632-6747
E-MAIL: dmolloy@notes.cc.stonybrook.edu
WEB SITE: www.stonybrook.edu

Name of Support Services: Center for Disabilities Support Services
Director: Joanna Harris; *Learning Disability Specialist:* Donna Molloy
General Information: Four-Year State University; Enrollment: 18,771; **Tuition:** Residents – $4,350, Non-Residents – $10,610; **Room and Board:** $8,450. A suburban setting about 60 miles east of Manhattan on the wooded North Shore of Long Island. Full-time and part-time internships and exchange programs with schools in Germany, Ireland, Italy, France and Poland. A diverse student body with a large number of foreign students. **Degrees:** The College of Arts and Sciences offers degree programs in fine arts and humanities, biological and physical sciences, mathematics and social and behavioral sciences. Special interdisciplinary majors and programs leading to provisional certification in secondary education also are available. The College of Engineering and Applied Sciences, which works closely with industry, offers three accredited major programs in engineering, with strong emphasis on individual design and research projects. The W. Averell Harriman School for Management and Policy trains students as analysts, planners, and managers for the public, non-profit and private sectors with a major and a minor in business management. Health Sciences Center includes five professional schools and a teaching hospital. Undergraduate degrees offered in allied health professions, nursing and social welfare.
Support Services: Enrollment: 140; Cost: None
Staff: Learning disabilities specialists; peer tutors; special counselors
Special Features: Preregistration advisement; determination of appropriate accommodations; extended time testing; assistance in acquiring note takers – scribes; tutors; readers; short-term equipment loan (i.e., tape recorder); learning strategies and time management advisement; assistance with scheduling/registration; and general advisement; staff act as liaison with faculty and community agencies

Entrance Requirements: Documentation of learning disability; SAT untimed scores accepted
Special Facilities for: Visual, hearing and physical impairments

SYRACUSE UNIVERSITY
804 UNIVERSITY AVENUE, SUITE 309
SYRACUSE, NEW YORK 13244-1120
(315) 443-1128; FAX: (315) 443-1312
E-MAIL: odssched@syr.edu or shsimon@syr.edu
WEB SITE: www.syracuse.edu

Name of Support Services: Office of Disability Services
Director: Stephen Simon
General Information: Four-Year Private University; Enrollment: 15,000; **Tuition:** $25,720; **Room and Board:** $9,960. A four-year private co-ed university on a 200-acre campus located in a large city. **Degrees:** BA, BFA, BMus
Support Services: Enrollment: 200; Cost: None. The percentage of students with learning disabilities who receive a degree in four years is 90%, in five years 10%.
Staff: Learning disabilities specialists; special counselors
Special Features: Oral and extended time testing; individual and small group tutoring sessions; academic advising for students with learning disabilities; note-taking assistance – scribes; taped texts; tape recorders; basic study skills
Entrance Requirements: Documentation of learning disability; SAT untimed scores accepted; diagnostic testing at Syracuse University

NORTH CAROLINA

BELMONT ABBEY COLLEGE
100 BELMONT–MT. HOLLY ROAD
BELMONT, NORTH CAROLINA 28012-1802
(704) 825-6820; FAX: (704) 825-6670
E-MAIL: betsysechler@bac.edu
WEB SITE: www.belmontabbeycollege.edu

Name of Support Services: Learning Disability Support Services
Director: Dr. Elizabeth S. Sechler
General Information: Four-Year Private College; Enrollment: 940; **Tuition:** $15,358; **Room and Board:** $7,960. Belmont Abbey College is a coeducational non-profit liberal arts college, affiliated with the Roman Catholic

Church. The 650-acre campus is in a suburban area, 10 miles southwest of Charlotte. **Majors:** Accounting, biology, business management, chemistry, computer studies, economics, elementary, middle and secondary education, education and non-licensure, English, fine arts, history, medical technology, philosophy, political science, pre-law, psychology, recreational studies, therapeutic recreation, sociology, theology
Support Services: Enrollment: 50; Cost: None
Staff: Academic counseling staff
Special Features: Oral and extended time testing; limited course load (first year); basic study skills; academic advising for students with learning disabilities; faculty made aware of student's learning disability (at student's request)
Entrance Requirements: Documentation of learning disability; testing: WAIS, psychological report
Special Facilities for: Visual, hearing and physical impairments
College Life: Belmont Abbey College has a favorable ratio of faculty to students and is a small campus community.

NORTH CAROLINA STATE UNIVERSITY
BOX 7509, STUDENT HEALTH CENTER
RALEIGH, NORTH CAROLINA 27695-7509
(919) 515-7653; FAX: (919) 513-2840
E-MAIL: cheryl_branker@ncsu.edu **WEB SITE: www.ncsu.edu**

Name of Support Services: Disability Services for Students
Director: Dr. Cheryl Branker, Associate Vice Provost
General Information: Four-Year State University; Enrollment: 29,637; **Tuition:** Residents – $2,391.50, Non-Residents – $8,490.50; **Room and Board:** $3,248. North Carolina is a land grant institution that was established in 1887. The 1,640-acre campus is in an urban area in Raleigh. **Degrees:** Baccalaureate degrees are offered in the nine colleges on the university campus: Agriculture and Life Science, Engineering, Education and Psychology, Forest Resources, Humanities and Social Sciences, Management, Physical and Mathematics Science, Design
Support Services: Enrollment: 220; Cost: None
Staff: Learning disabilities specialists; peer tutors
Special Features: Oral and extended time testing; limited course load (first year); note-taking assistance – scribes; taped texts; tape recorders; adaptive equipment as well as information about the campus and the resources available to the students. Students meet regularly on an individual basis with coordinators in the Disability Services office.
Entrance Requirements: Documentation of learning disability within past

three years; testing: WAIS, psychological report
Special Facilities for: Visual, hearing and physical impairments

OHIO

CLEVELAND INSTITUTE OF ART

11141 EAST BLVD.
CLEVELAND, OHIO 44106-1700
(216) 421-7400; FAX: (216) 754-2557
E-MAIL: jmilenski@gate.cia.edu **WEB SITE: www.cia.edu**

Name of Support Services: Tutoring Program
Associate Director of Academic Services: Jill Milenski
General Information: Five-Year State Institute; Enrollment: 600; **Tuition:** $13,508.50; **Room and Board:** $4,568. Cleveland Institute of Art is in the urban University Circle area and is home to museums, hospitals, Cox Western Reserve University, Cleveland Institute of Music and Cultural Center of Cleveland. **Degrees:** Cleveland Institute of Art is a five-year art college offering a BFA in ceramics, enameling, glass, jewelry and metals, fiber, sculpture, painting, photo, drawing/printmaking, industrial design, interior design, illustration, graphic design, medical illustration, technology and integrated media (TIME). MFA in medical illustration and TIME
Support Services: Enrollment: 36; Cost: None. The percentage of students with learning disabilities who receive a degree in five or more years is approximately 75%.
Staff: Learning disabilities specialists; peer tutors
Special Features: Oral and extended time testing; limited course load (first year); academic advising for students with learning disabilities; note-taking assistance – scribes; taped texts; tape recorders; basic study skills; faculty made aware of student's learning disability; computer with "Talking Dictionary" Thesaurus; computer-based writing center; website; workshops
Entrance Requirements: Documentation of learning disability

OHIO STATE UNIVERSITY: MANSFIELD
OFFICE FOR DISABILITY SERVICES
CONARD LEARNING CENTER
1680 UNIVERSITY DRIVE
MANSFIELD, OHIO 44906
(419) 755-4304; FAX: (419) 755-4016
E-MAIL: mclane.15@osu.edu
WEB SITE: www.mansfield.ohio-state.edu

Name of Support Services: Office for Disability Services
Learning Disabilities Specialist: Michelle McLane
General Information: Four-Year State University; Enrollment: 1,215; **Tuition:** Residents – $8,667, Non-Residents – $17,559; **Room and Board:** $6,792. Campus apartments are available; cost varies. Ohio State University: Mansfield is in a rural setting halfway between Cleveland, and Columbus, Ohio. The 600-acre campus is in a suburban area two miles from Mansfield. **Degrees:** Bachelor's degrees in business, early and middle childhood education, English, history and psychology can be completed on the Mansfield campus. Most of the required coursework in criminology and sociology can be completed on the Mansfield campus. Other degree programs offered through Ohio State University may be started on the Mansfield campus.
Support Services: Enrollment: 35; Cost: None
Staff: Learning disabilities specialists; peer tutors; content tutors (faculty members)
Special Features: Oral and extended time testing; individual tutoring sessions; limited course load (first year); academic advising for students with learning disabilities; note-taking assistance – scribes; taped texts; basic study skills; developmental program; faculty made aware of student's learning disability; adaptive computers; Dragon Dictate; Omnipage 9.0 (scanning)
Entrance Requirements: Documentation of learning disability; ACT untimed score accepted; testing: WAIS, IEP, psychological report
Special Facilities for: Visual, hearing and physical impairments
College Life: Ohio State University: Mansfield is a small campus. Students have a variety of technologies available to support their disability.

UNIVERSITY OF TOLEDO
OFFICE OF ACCESSIBILITY
1400 SNYDER MEMORIAL MAIL STOP 110
TOLEDO, OHIO 43606-3390
(419) 530-4981; FAX: (419) 530-6137
E-MAIL: lyost@utnet.utoledo.edu **WEB SITE: www.utoledo.edu**

Name of Support Services: Office of Accessibility
Interim Director: Lisa Yost
General Information: Four-Year State University; Enrollment: 19,480; **Tuition:** Residents – $7,054, Non-Residents – $15,865; **Room and Board:** $4,156 per semester. The university is located on a 400-acre campus in a large city. **Degrees:** AA, AS, BA, BS
Support Services: Enrollment: 400; Cost: None
Staff: Learning disabilities specialists; special counselors
Special Features: Oral and extended time testing; individual and small group tutoring sessions; note-taking assistance – scribes; taped texts; tape recorders; faculty made aware of students' learning disability; disability developmental program; priority registration
Entrance Requirements: Documentation of learning disability; testing: WAIS, psychological report
Special Facilities for: Visual, hearing and physical impairments
Scholarships: See page 437.

OREGON

SOUTHERN OREGON UNIVERSITY
1250 SISKIYOU BLVD.
ASHLAND, OREGON 97520
(541) 552-6213; FAX: (541) 552-8462
E-MAIL: lowriet@sou.edu **WEB SITE: www.sou.edu**

Name of Support Services: Disability Services for Student (DSS)
Director: Theresa Lowrie
General Information: Four-Year State University; Enrollment: 4,500; **Tuition:** Residents – $2,480; Non-Residents – $10,702. The 175-acre campus is in a small town 10 miles southeast of Medford. **Degrees:** BA, BS, BFA, and Associate degrees
Support Services: Enrollment: 75; Cost: None
Staff: Learning disabilities specialist
Special Features: Oral and extended time testing; note-taking assistance – scribes; academic advising for students with learning disabilities; taped texts; basic study skills; faculty made aware of student's learning

disability; personal and career counseling; computers
Entrance Requirements: Documentation of learning disability; learning disabilities specialist's report (within three years); testing: WAIS, psychological report

UNIVERSITY OF OREGON
5278 UNIVERSITY OF OREGON
EUGENE, OREGON 97403-5278
(541) 346-1155; FAX: (541) 346-6013
E-MAIL: disabsrv@darkwing.uoregon.edu
WEB SITE: www.uoregon.edu

Name of Support Services: Disability Services (DS); Student Support Services (SSS)
Director: Steve Pickett
General Information: Four-Year State University; Enrollment: 21,000; **Tuition:** Residents – $4,875, Non-Residents – $16,416; **Room and Board:** $6,570. The University of Oregon is located in Eugene, the third largest city in the state. The 280-acre campus is an arboretum of more than 500 species and more than 3,000 specimens of trees. Campus buildings date from 1876 when Deady Hall opened, to 1999 when the William W. Knight Law Center was completed. The Museum of Natural History is located at 15th Avenue and Columbia Street. Across campus is the Museum of Art, which is noted for its collections of Oriental and Northwest Art. **Degrees:** Students select their courses from departments and programs in the College of Arts and Sciences and from six professional schools and colleges. The University has full accreditation from the Southwest Association of School and Colleges. Teaching, research, and a spirit of sharing are characteristics of the campus learning community.
Support Services: DS Enrollment: 478; Cost: None; *SSS* Enrollment: 340; Cost: None
Staff: Learning disabilities specialists; special counselors
Special Features: Disability Services – Oral and extended time testing; note-taking assistance – scribes; taped texts; limited course load (first year); academic advising for students with learning disabilities; faculty made aware of student's learning disability; adaptive technology lab. *Student Support Services* – Individual and small group tutoring sessions; basic study skills; special classes and workshops
Entrance Requirements: Disability Services – Documentation of learning disability; SAT/ACT untimed scores accepted; teacher evaluation; hand-written essay. *Student Support Services* – must be registered with Disability Services
Special Facilities for: Visual, hearing and physical impairments

KUTZTOWN UNIVERSITY OF PENNSYLVANIA
15200 KUTZTOWN ROAD
KUTZTOWN, PENNSYLVANIA 19530
(610) 683-4108; FAX (610) 683-1520
E-MAIL: richter@kutztown.edu **WEB SITE: www.kutztown.edu**

Name of Support Services: Disability Services
Director: Patricia J. Richter
General Information: Four-Year, State University; Enrollment: 8,500; **Tuition, Room and Board:** Residents – $6,177.80 per semester, Non-Residents – $9,889.30 per semester. Picturesque 328-acre campus in a Pennsylvania Dutch community midway between Allentown and Reading. Highways, buses and airports provide easy access to New York and Philadelphia. **Majors:** Counseling and psychological service, criminal justice/social work, dance, economics, elementary education, English, fine arts, foreign languages, geography, health, history, liberal science, music, nursing, philosophy, physical sciences, political science, psychology, secondary education, special education, speech, theatre, telecommunications
Support Services: Enrollment: 300; Cost: None
Staff: Learning disabilities specialist; content tutors (faculty members); special counselors; peer tutors
Special Features: Oral and extended time testing; individual and/or small group tutoring sessions; academic advising for students with learning disabilities, note-taking assistance – scribes; taped texts; tape recorders; basic study skills; faculty made aware of student's learning disability
Entrance Requirements: Documentation of learning disability; SAT/ACT untimed scores accepted; handwritten essay; testing: WAIS, psychological report
Special Facilities for: Visual, hearing and physical impairments

UNIVERSITY OF PITTSBURGH AT BRADFORD
300 CAMPUS DRIVE
BRADFORD, PENNSYLVANIA 16701
(814) 362-7674; FAX: (814) 362-7684
E-MAIL: boyce@exchange.upb.pitt.edu
WEB SITE: www.upb.pitt.edu

Name of Support Services: Disability Resource Services (DRS)
Director: Dr. Gillian Boyce
General Information: Four-Year State University; Enrollment: 1,105; **Tuition:** Residents – $9,888, Non-Residents – $19,776; **Room and Board:** $6,720. The University is in a rural area two hours from Buffalo, New York.

Skiing and outdoor recreation facilities are 20-30 minutes away. **Degrees:** Bachelor and Associate degrees plus professional preparations and credential programs in elementary and secondary education. Semester-at-Sea is a unique opportunity.
Support Services: Enrollment: 10; Cost: None
Staff: Learning disabilities specialist; peer tutors
Special Features: Oral and extended time testing; individual and / or small group tutoring sessions; limited course load (first year); note-taking assistance – scribes; taped texts; tape recorders; basic study skills; faculty made aware of student's learning disability; personal and career counseling
Entrance Requirements: Documentation of learning disability; self-disclosure / documentation
Special Facilities for: Visual, hearing and physical impairments
College Life: Small classes and high ratio of faculty to students makes for success.

WIDENER UNIVERSITY
ONE UNIVERSITY PLACE
CHESTER, PENNSYLVANIA 19013-5792
(610) 499-1266; FAX: (610) 499-1192
E-MAIL: rebecca.a.corsey@widener.edu
WEB SITE: www.widener.edu

Name of Special Program: Enable
Director: Rebecca Corsey McKeogh, Ph.D.
General Information: Four-Year Private University; Enrollment: 2,400; **Tuition:** $21,400; **Room and Board:** $7,700. Widener University is 15 minutes south of Philadelphia. The campus has active sports, theatre, Greek life, and focused interest clubs. **Degrees:** Pre-law, pre-med, arts and sciences, management, nursing, hotel and restaurant management, engineering and teacher certification programs.
Special Program: Enrollment in Special Program: 189; Cost: None
Staff: Learning disabilities specialists; peer tutors; content tutors (faculty members); special counselors (available through other academic support programs)
Program Features: Oral and extended time testing; individual and small group tutoring sessions; limited course load (first year); academic advising for students with learning disabilities; note-taking assistance – scribes; taped texts; faculty made aware of student's learning disability (at student's request); basic study skills; developmental program.
Entrance Requirements: Documentation of learning disability
Special Facilities for: Visual, hearing and physical impairments

College Life: Widener provides personalized academic planning, skills building and emotional support so that students internalize the process and function successfully more and more independently.

RHODE ISLAND

JOHNSON AND WALES UNIVERSITY
8 ABBOTT PARK PLACE
PROVIDENCE, RHODE ISLAND 02903
800-343-2565, (401) 598-4689; FAX: (401) 598-4657
E-MAIL: mberstein@jwu.edu
WEB SITE: www.jwu.edu/prov/stu_succ.htm

Name of Special Program: Center for Academic Support/Special Needs
Director: Meryl Berstein
General Information: Four-Year Private University; Enrollment: 10,000; **Tuition:** $19,875; **Room and Board:** $7,299–9300. The downtown location of the university offers many business, cultural, educational and recreational facilities, such as the Providence Performing Arts Center, Providence Public Library, Trinity Square Repertory Company, Providence Civic Center, Rhode Island State House, Rhode Island School of Design and Brown University. The university offers opportunities to pursue practical careers in business, food service, hospitality or technology. The calendar is a trimester type offering internships and cooperative plans. There are also campuses in Florida, Colorado, North Carolina, South Carolina and Virginia. **Majors:** Accounting, advertising/public relations, teacher education, business administration, computers/business applications, court reporting, direct response retailing, entrepreneurship, equine studies, fashion merchandising, finance and investment, international business, health care administrator, management, marketing, paralegal studies, retailing, sales management, secretarial studies, technical business management, culinary arts, baking and pastry arts, food and beverage management, hotel-restaurant management, restaurant/leisure management, restaurant institutional management, travel-tourism management, applied computer science, computerized drafting, electronic technology
Staff: Learning disabilities specialists; content tutors (faculty members); peer tutors; special counselors
Program Features: Extended time testing; individual and small group tutoring sessions; reduced course load; tape recorders; taped texts; note-taking assistance – scribes; basic study skills; faculty made aware of student's learning disability; preferential scheduling
Special Facilities for: Visual, hearing and physical impairments

TENNESSEE

UNIVERSITY OF TENNESSEE: KNOXVILLE

2227 DUNFORD HALL
915 VOUNTEER BLVD.
KNOXVILLE, TENNESSEE 37996-4020
(865) 974-6087; FAX: (865) 974-9552
E-MAIL: ods@utk.edu or esinger1@utk.edu
WEB SITE: www.utk.edu

Name of Support Services: Office of Disability Services
Director: Emily Singer
General Information: Four-Year Private College: Enrollment: 25,000; **Annual Tuition**: Residents – $5,140; Non-Residents – $16,210; **Room and Board:** $1,200–5,000 per semester. The University of Tennessee: Knoxville is located in East Tennessee about one hour's drive from the Great Smoky Mountains. The University was the state's first public university and is a comprehensive land-grant research institution currently ranked among the nation's top 50 public universities. **Degrees:** Bachelor, Master and Doctoral degrees through the Colleges of Arts and Sciences, Agricultural Sciences and Natural Resources, Architecture and Design, Business Administration, Communication and Information, Engineering, Nursing, Social Work, Education, Health and Human Sciences
Support Services: Enrollment: 1,000; Cost: None
Staff: Learning disabilities specialists
Special features: Oral and extended time testing; limited course load; note-taking assistance – scribes; taped texts; tape recorders; faculty made aware of student's learning disability (at student's request); assistive technology, Kurzweil reader
Entrance Requirements: Documentation of learning disability; testing: WAIS, IEP
Special Facilities for: Visual, hearing and physical impairments
College Life: For those students who want a large university, we have a dedicated support staff and a strong commitment from the university to work with our students.

TEXAS

SOUTHERN METHODIST UNIVERSITY

SMU BOX 355
DALLAS, TEXAS 75275-0355
(214) 768-4557; FAX: (214) 768-1255
E-MAIL: rmarin@mail.smu.edu **WEB SITE: www.smu.edu**

Name of Support Services: Services for Students with Disabilities
Coordinator: Rebecca Marin
General Information: Four-Year Private University; Enrollment: 9,500; **Tuition:** $12,700; **Room and Board:** $7,045. Southern Methodist University is a non-sectarian private institution affiliated with the United Methodist Church. It is situated five miles north of downtown Dallas on a 164-acre campus. **Degrees**: The College of Humanities and Science, School of the Arts, School of Business and School of Engineering and Applied Science offer bachelor's degrees.
Support Services: Enrollment: 164; Cost: None
Staff: Learning disabilities specialist; peer tutors; content tutors (faculty members)
Special Features: Individual tutoring sessions; note-taking assistance – scribes; tape recorders; basic study skills; faculty made aware of student's learning disability; Kurzweil readers; personal and career counseling; testing in separate room
Entrance Requirements: Documentation of learning disability in keeping with the "Guidelines for Documenting a Learning Disability" issued by the Association on Higher Education and Disability (AHEAD)
College Life: Southern Methodist University is attractive to students with learning disabilities because of the small size of its campus, its good faculty/student ratio, and the generally small size of its classes.

UNIVERSITY OF HOUSTON

307 STUDENT SERVICE CENTER
48 CALHOUN ROAD
HOUSTON, TEXAS 77204-3022
(713) 743-2255; FAX: (713) 743-5396
E-MAIL: camoruso@uh.edu **WEB SITE: www.uh.edu**

Name of Support Services: Center for Students with disABILITIES
Director: Cheryl Amoruso
General Information: Four-Year State University; Enrollment: 32,000; **Tuition:** Residents – $12,480; **Room and Board:** $10,630. University of Houston is situated on a 540-acre campus in an urban area three miles from the Houston business district. **Degrees**: Degrees are offered through

the following colleges: Architecture, Business Administration, Education, Engineering, Hotel and Restaurant Management, Humanities and Fine Arts, Communications, Natural Sciences and Mathematics, Optometry, Social Sciences, Technology, Law Center, Pharmacy, Graduate School of Social Work

Support Services: Enrollment: 900; Cost: None

Staff: Learning disabilities specialist; peer tutors

Special Features: Oral and extended time testing; individual tutoring sessions; limited course load (if needed); academic advising for students with learning disabilities; note-taking assistance – scribes; taped texts; tape recorders (may be used but not provided); basic study skills; faculty made aware of student's learning disability; accessible computer hardware and software

Entrance Requirements: Documentation of learning disability; SAT/ACT untimed scores accepted; diagnostic testing at University of Houston; testing: WAIS, Woodcock-Johnson-R

Special Facilities for: Visual and hearing impairments

College Life: Our staff is experienced and dedicated to students with disabilities of all types. We feel that we go the extra mile for our students. We teach our students to focus on their strengths and to be good self-advocates.

Scholarships: See page 438.

UNIVERSITY OF NORTH TEXAS
UNION – SUITE 322, P.O. BOX 310770
DENTON, TEXAS 76203-0770
(940) 565-4323; FAX: (940) 369-7969
E-MAIL: ronv@unt.edu **WEB SITE: www.unt.edu/oda**

Name of Support Services: Office of Disability Accommodation (ODA)

Director: Ron Venable

General Information: Four-Year State University; Enrollment: 25,000; **Annual Tuition:** Residents – $2,096, Non-Residents – $6,513; **Room and Board:** $4,417. University of North Texas is located within the Dallas/Fort Worth area on 412 acres in the city of Denton. The University has access to many cultural, educational and employment opportunities. **Degrees**: The University is known for specialization in music, visual arts, pre-law, premedicine, fashion design, teacher education and hotel restaurant management, also fine programs in business and community service.

Support Services: Enrollment: 500+; Cost: None

Staff: Learning disabilities specialist; peer tutors

Special Features: Oral and extended time testing; individual tutoring sessions; limited course load (first year); note-taking assistance – scribes;

taped texts; tape recorders; basic study skills; developmental program; faculty made aware of student's learning disability; TASP/Discovery
Entrance Requirements: Documentation of learning disability; learning disabilities specialist report; SAT/ACT untimed scores accepted; testing: WAIS, psychological report; diagnostic testing at University of North Texas; reports must be current and within three years
Special Facilities for: Visual, hearing and physical impairments
College Life: Services are individualized within a mainstreamed environment.

UTAH

UTAH STATE UNIVERSITY

0101 OLD MAIN HALL
LOGAN, UTAH 84322-0101
800-259-2966, (435) 797-0740, (435) 797-2444 TTY; FAX: (435) 797-0130
E-MAIL: diane.baum@usu.edu WEB SITE: www.usu.edu

Name of Support Services: Disability Resource Center (DRC)
Director: Diane Craig Baum
General Information: Four-Year State University; Enrollment: 15,766; **Annual Tuition:** Residents – $3,614, Non-Residents – $10,616; **Room and Board:** $3,560. The University is located on 332 acres 96 miles north of Salt Lake City. **Degrees:** BA, BS, BBA
Support Services: Enrollment: 250; Cost: None
Staff: Learning disabilities specialists; peer tutors
Special Features: Oral and extended time testing; note-taking assistance – scribes; taped texts; tape recorders; basic study skills; academic advising for students with learning disabilities; Kurzweil readers; personal and career counseling
Entrance Requirements: Documentation of learning disability; learning disabilities specialist report; SAT/ACT untimed scores accepted: testing: psychological report, medical evaluation; diagnostic testing at Utah State University
Special Facilities for: Visual, hearing and physical impairments
Scholarships: See page 439.

VERMONT

SAINT MICHAEL'S COLLEGE
ONE WINOOSKI PARK
COLCHESTER, VERMONT 05439
(802) 654-2818; FAX: (802) 654-2591
WEB SITE: www.smcvt.edu

Name of Support Services: Support Services
Contact Person: Antonia Messuri
General Information: Four-Year Private College; Enrollment: 1,900; **Tuition:** $28,280, **Room and Board:** $6,990. **Degrees:** Bachelor of Arts degrees
Support Services: Enrollment: 140; Cost: None
Staff: Learning disabilities specialists; peer tutors; content tutors (faculty members); special counselors. The percentage of students with learning disabilities who receive a degree in four years is 76%.
Special Features: Oral and extended time testing; individual and small group tutoring sessions; limited course load (first year); academic advising for students with learning disabilities; note-taking assistance – scribes; taped texts; tape recorders; basic study skills; faculty made aware of student's learning disability (at student's request); computers; Kurzweil readers; personal and career counseling; learning disability support group
Entrance Requirements: Documentation of learning disability; learning disabilities specialist report; testing: WAIS
Special Facilities for: Visual, hearing and physical impairments

WASHINGTON

WASHINGTON STATE UNIVERSITY
ADMIN. ANNEX 205
PULLMAN, WASHINGTON 99164
(509) 335-1566 V/TTY; FAX: (509) 335-8511
E-MAIL: schaeff@wsu.edu **WEB SITE: www.wsu.edu**

Name of Support Services: Disability Resource Center
Coordinator: Susan Schaeffer, Ph.D.
General Information: Four-Year State University; Enrollment: 20,000; **Tuition:** Residents – $5,888, Non-Residents – $15,628; **Room and Board:** $5,598. Washington State University is situated 70 miles from Spokane. **Degrees:** Bachelor of Arts
Support Services: Enrollment: 600; Cost: None. The percentage of students with learning disabilities who receive a degree in four years is 67%, in five or more years is 78%.

Staff: Learning disabilities specialists
Special Features: Oral and extended time testing; individual and small group tutoring sessions; limited course load (first year); academic advising for students with learning disabilities; note-taking assistance – scribes; taped texts; tape recorders; basic study skills; faculty made aware of student's learning disability; computers; Kurzweil readers; personal and career counseling
Entrance Requirements: Documentation of learning disability; SAT/ACT untimed scores accepted; diagnostic testing at college; medical evaluation; testing: WAIS, IEP, psychological report
Special Facilities for: Visual and hearing impairments

WEST VIRGINIA

SALEM INTERNATIONAL UNIVERSITY

223 WEST MAIN STREET, P.O. BOX 500
SALEM, WEST VIRGINIA 26426-0500
(304) 782-5633; FAX: (304) 782-5592
E-MAIL: lmarsh@salemiu.edu **WEB SITE: www.salemiu.edu**

Name of Support Services: Academic and Personal Counseling Services Center
Director: Lisa Marsh
General Information: Four-Year Private University; Enrollment: 560; **Tuition:** $10,000; **Room and Board:** $4,790. The Salem campus is located in a small town near Pittsburgh, Pennsylvania, and Charleston, West Virginia. The University operates on a modular schedule where students take one course per month, 3 to 5 hours a day. **Majors:** Applied computer information sciences, aviation, biology, business administration, criminal justice, education, equine career and pre-veterinary studies, Japanese studies, liberal studies
Support Services: Cost: None
Staff: Learning disabilities specialists; peer tutors
Special Features: Oral and extended time testing; individual and small group tutoring sessions; academic advising for students with learning disabilities; note-taking assistance – scribes; taped texts; tape recorders; basic study skills; faculty made aware of student's learning disability (at student's request); support services with additional programs available for qualified students
Entrance Requirements: Documentation of learning disability; SAT/ACT untimed scores accepted
College Life: Many students find the modular schedule system very help-

ful because they only have two courses every eight weeks which equals one term or semester. Students with learning disabilities often see this as an advantage even though the coursework is intensive.

WISCONSIN

ALVERNO COLLEGE
3400 SOUTH 43rd STREET
MILWAUKEE, WISCONSIN 53234-3922
(414) 382-6026; FAX: (414) 382-6354
E-MAIL: colleen.barnett@alverno.edu
WEB SITE: www.alverno.edu

Name of Support Services: Office for Student Accessibility
Coordinator: Colleen Barnett
General Information: Four-Year Private College; Enrollment: 2,160; **Tuition:** $15,984; **Room and Board:** $5,954. Alverno College is a women's college affiliated with the Roman Catholic Church. It is situated on a 52-acre campus in an urban area, near Lake Michigan on Milwaukee's southside. **Majors:** Studio art, art education/therapy, biology, broadfield science, social studies, business and management, chemistry, community leadership and development, elementary/middle education, English, history, international business, mathematics, music/education/therapy, nursing, philosophy, professional communications, psychology, religious studies, social science
Support Services: Enrollment: 48; Cost: None
Staff: Learning disabilities specialist; peer tutors
Special Features: Oral and extended time testing; individual and small group tutoring sessions; limited course load (first year); note-taking assistance – scribes; taped texts; tape recorders; basic study skills; developmental program; faculty made aware of student's learning disability; Kurzweil readers; voice recognition software
Entrance Requirements: Documentation of learning disability; ACT untimed scores accepted; testing: WAIS, IEP, psychological report
Special Facilities for: Visual, hearing and physical impairments

CALIFORNIA

PASADENA CITY COLLEGE

1570 EAST COLORADO BLVD.
PASADENA, CALIFORNIA 91106-2003
(626) 585-7127; FAX: (626) 585-7566
E-MAIL: elweller@pasadena.edu WEB SITE: www.pasadena.edu

Name of Support Services: Disabled Student Programs and Services (DSPS)
Director: Kent T. Yamauchi; *Learning Disabilities Specialist:* Emy Lu Weller
General Information: Two-Year Community College; Enrollment: 2,300; **Tuition:** Residents – $26 per unit, Non-Residents – $151 per unit; **Room and Board**: No college housing available. The College is located in an urban area, sponsoring 16-week semesters in spring and fall, a 6- to 10-week session in the summer and a 6-week winter intersession. **Degrees:** Associate of Arts, Associate of Science, AA certificates
Support Services: Enrollment: 450; Cost: None. *Summer Program:* Provides registration assistance for fall; develops student educational contract which specifies services and accommodations.
Staff: Learning disabilities specialist; peer tutors; special counselors
Special Features: Oral and extended time testing, small group tutoring sessions; limited course load (first year); taped texts; tape recorders; basic study skills; academic advising for students with learning disabilities; basic study skills; faculty made aware of student's learning disability; Kurzweil readers; personal and career counseling; High Tech Computer Lab
Entrance Requirements: Documentation of learning disability; California Community College Eligibility Assessment
Special Facilities for: Visual, hearing and physical impairments
College Life: Beautiful campus with many vocational options as well as transfer curriculum. Very stable, expert DSPS staff.
Scholarships: See page 445.

SADDLEBACK COLLEGE

28000 MARGUERITE PARKWAY
MISSION VIEJO, CALIFORNIA 92692
(949) 582-4885; FAX: (949) 347-1526
E-MAIL: randerson@saddleback.edu or dcrary@saddleback.edu
WEB SITE: www.saddleback.edu

Name of Support Services: Special Services (Disabled Student Programs and Services)

Director: Randy Anderson; *Learning Disability Specialist:* Diane Crary
General Information: Two-Year Community College; Enrollment: 23,000; **Tuition:** Residents – $26 per unit, Out-of-State Residents – $177 per unit; **Room and Board**: No college housing available. **Degrees:** Associate of Arts, Associate of Science, AA Certificates
Support Services: Enrollment: 450; Cost: None. *Summer Program:* College Link for high school seniors is designed primarily for students with disabilities: College Success, Self Advocacy, and Computer Access Lab. Enrollment is through the Special Services Office.
Staff: Learning disabilities specialists; special counselors
Special Features: Oral and extended time testing, note-taking assistance – scribes; tape texts (E text); basic study skills; academic advising for students with learning disabilities; developmental program (special classes); faculty made aware of student's learning disability (at student's request); alternate media; adapted computer lab
Entrance Requirements: Documentation of learning disability; diagnostic testing at Saddleback College
College Life: Very caring, progressive staff, excellent facilities, including a High Tech Center for student with disabilities

FLORIDA

SEMINOLE COMMUNITY COLLEGE

100 WELDON BLVD.
SANFORD, FLORIDA 32773
(407) 708-2110; FAX: (407) 328-2484
E-MAIL: paishond@scc-fl.edu **WEB SITE: www.scc-fl.edu**

Name of Support Services: Disability Support Services
Director: Dottie Paishon
General Information: Two-Year Community College: Enrollment: 32,000; **Tuition:** Residents – $69.36 per credit hour, Non-Residents – $248.30 per credit hour; **Room and Board:** No college housing available. Seminole Community College provides learning opportunities at two campuses, an instructional center, business, high schools and outreach centers throughout Seminole County. The Seminole Community College campus at Sanford, Lake Mary resides on 200 acres of beautiful rolling countryside. The college is 15 miles north of Orlando, bordered by Sanford on the North and Lake Mary on the West. **Degrees:** AA, AS, specialized career certificates, continuing professional education, customized workplace training, adult education, and community, leisure and youth programs
Support Services: Enrollment: 425; Cost: None
Staff: Learning disabilities specialists; peer tutors

Special Features: Oral and extended time testing, individual and small group tutoring sessions, limited course load (first year), academic advising for students with learning disabilities, note-taking assistance – scribes, taped texts, tape recorders, developmental program
Entrance Requirements: Documentation of learning disability; SAT/ACT untimed scores accepted; diagnostic testing at Seminole Community College; testing: WAIS, psychological report
Special Facilities for: Visual, hearing and physical impairments

ILLINOIS

JOHN WOOD COMMUNITY COLLEGE

1301 SOUTH 48th STREET
QUINCY, ILLINOIS 62305
(217) 641-4352; (217) 224-4309 TDD
E-MAIL: akers@jwcc.edu **WEB SITE: www.jwcc.edu**

Name of Support Services: Support Services Center – Disability Services
Coordinator: Rose-Marie Akers
General Information: Two-Year Community College; Enrollment: 1,478; **Tuition:** Residents – $89 per credit hour, Non-Residents – $189 per credit hour; **Room and Board:** No college housing available. A suburban campus 140 miles northwest of St. Louis, Missouri. **Degrees:** AA, AS, AAS, certificates in agriculture, electronics technology, business, early childhood education, CAD emergency services, nursing, office technology, physical therapy assistant, truck driver training, liberal arts
Support Services: Enrollment: 75; Cost: None
Staff: Learning disabilities specialist; content tutors; peer tutors; special counselors; case coordinators
Special Features: Oral testing and extended time; individual and small group tutoring sessions; limited course load; academic advising for students with learning disabilities; note-taking assistance – scribes; taped texts; tape recorders, basic study skills; developmental program; instruction to improve self-esteem; career exploration and job development; self-advocacy training
Entrance Requirements: Documentation of learning disability; psychological report
Special Facilities for: Visual, hearing and physical impairments
Scholarships: See page 448.

KISHWAUKEE COLLEGE
21193 MALTA ROAD
MALTA, ILLINOIS 60150-9699
(815) 825-2086; FAX: (815) 825-2072
E-MAIL: fenske@kishwaukeecollege.edu
WEB SITE: www.kishwaukeecollege.edu

Name of Support Services: Special Needs
Coordinator: Karen Fenske
General Information: Two-Year Community College; Enrollment: 2,576; **Tuition:** District Residents – $65 per credit hour, Out-of-District Residents – $233.24 per credit hour, Out-of-State Residents – $261.69 per credit hour; **Room and Board:** No college housing available. Kishwaukee College is located on a 120-acre rural campus with easy access to Chicago. **Degrees**: Kishwaukee College offers five transfer degrees, 62 occupational degrees and certificates as well as customized occupational retraining, Adult Basic Education and community-based interest courses. The college works with four area community colleges and several major universities through co-op agreements and telecommunication technology.
Support Services: Enrollment: 60; Cost: None
Staff: Learning disabilities specialists; content tutors (faculty members); peer tutors; special counselors
Special Features: Oral and extended time; individual and small group tutoring sessions; limited course load (first year); academic advising for students with learning disabilities; note-taking assistance – scribes; taped texts; tape recorders, basic study skills; developmental program; faculty made aware of student's learning disability; Wynn readers
Entrance Requirements: Documentation of learning disability
Special Facilities for: Visual, hearing and physical impairments
College Life: Focusing on individual educational needs requires a recognition of the student diversity. Therefore, the college provides support services and educational services to meet individual needs. As an institution whose mission is student learning, Kishwaukee College is committed to providing education which will assist individuals in developing to their optimum capacity.

LAKE LAND COLLEGE
5001 LAKE LAND BLVD.
MATTOON, ILLINOIS 61938
(217) 234-5259; FAX: (217) 234-5390
E-MAIL: ehartke@lakeland.cc.il.us
WEB SITE: www.lakeland.cc.il.us/specialneeds

Name of Support Services: Special Needs Office
Director: Emily M. Hartke
General Information: Two-Year Community College; Enrollment: 4,710; **Tuition:** Residents – $55.50 per semester hour, Non-Residents – $141.86 per semester hour, Out-of-State Residents – $272.27 per semester hour. **Room and Board:** No college housing available. A 304-acre rural campus with easy access to Champaign. **Degrees:** AA, AS, AAS, certificates
Support Services: Enrollment: 200; Cost: None
Staff: Learning disabilities specialists; content and skills tutors; special needs counselors
Special Features: Oral and extended time; individual and small group tutoring sessions; academic advising for students with learning disabilities; note-taking assistance – scribes; taped texts; tape recorders, basic study skills; developmental program; faculty made aware of student's learning disability; assistive technology
Entrance Requirements: Documentation of learning disability; support services application
Special Facilities for: Visual, hearing and physical impairments

LINCOLN LAND COMMUNITY COLLEGE
P.O. BOX 19256, 5250 SHEPHERD ROAD
SPRINGFIELD, ILLINOIS 62794-9256
(217) 786-2828; FAX: (217) 786-2310
E-MAIL: linda.chriswell@llcc.edu **WEB SITE: www.llcc.edu**

Name of Support Services: Special Needs
Director: Linda Chriswell
General Information: Two-Year Community College; Enrollment: 14,000; **Tuition:** Residents – $62.50 per credit hour, Out-of-State Residents – $317.40 per credit hour; **Room and Board:** No college housing available. The College covers all or part of 15 counties in central Illinois and is located on the south edge of the capital city. **Degrees**: AA, AS, AFA, AES, AAS, AGE, certificates of achievement or completion
Support Services: Enrollment: 300; Cost: None
Staff: Learning disabilities specialists; content tutors (faculty members); peer tutors; special counselors

Special Features: Oral and extended time; individual and small group tutoring sessions; limited course load (first year); academic advising for students with learning disabilities; note-taking assistance – scribes; taped texts; tape recorders; basic study skills; developmental program; faculty made aware of student's learning disability; adaptive assistive technology
Entrance Requirements: Documentation of learning disability; medical evaluation; handwritten essay; testing: WAIS, IEP, psychological report
Special Facilities for: Visual, hearing and physical impairments
College Life: Team effort of all employees to afford students with learning disabilities an "equal playing field" or access and equal status in higher education.

LINCOLN TRAIL COLLEGE
11220 STATE HIGHWAY 1
ROBINSON, ILLINOIS 62454
(618) 544-8657; FAX: (618) 544-4705
E-MAIL: haskinsb@iecc.edu **WEB SITE: www.iecc.edu/ltc**

Name of Support Services: Learning Skills Center
Director: Brian D. Haskins
General Information: Two-Year Community College; **Tuition:** $1,696; **Room and Board:** No college housing available. **Degrees**: AA, AS, Certificates of Achievement
Support Services: Enrollment: 50; Cost: None
Staff: Learning disabilities specialists; content tutors (faculty members); peer tutors; special counselors
Special Features: Oral and extended time; individual tutoring sessions; limited course load (first year); academic advising for students with learning disabilities; note-taking assistance - scribes; taped texts; tape recorders; basic study skills; developmental program; computers; readers; interpreters
Entrance Requirements: Documentation of learning disability; learning disabilities specialist report; diagnostic testing at college; teacher evaluations; medical evaluations
Special Facilities for: Visual, hearing and physical impairments
College Life: Lincoln Trail College is a rural community college working on a semester-based calendar. We have a very small faculty-to-student ratio and an Independent Learning Strategy.
Scholarships: See page 449.

OLNEY CENTRAL COLLEGE
305 NORTH WEST
OLNEY, ILLINOIS 62350
(618) 395-7777; FAX: (618) 392-3293
E-MAIL: koored@iecc.edu **WEB SITE: www.iecc.edu/occ**

Name of Support Services: Learning Skills Center
Director: Donita Koore
General Information: Two-Year Community College; Enrollment: 1,617; **Annual Tuition:** Residents – $6,040; Non-Residents – $7,568; **Room and Board:** No college housing available. **Degrees**: AA, AS, AFA, AES, AAS, AGE, certificates of achievement or completion
Support Services: Enrollment: 100; Cost: None. The percentage of students with learning disabilities who receive degrees in two years is 50%, in four years 80%.
Staff: Learning disabilities specialists; peer tutors
Special Features: Oral and extended time; individual tutoring sessions; academic advising for students with learning disabilities; note-taking assistance - scribes; taped texts; tape recorders; basic study skills; developmental program; word processor; personal and career counseling; faculty made aware of student's learning disability; Payne Learning Needs Inventory; large screen monitor; colored overlays; specialized computer programs; colored coded keyboard; talking dictionary; electronic math machines
Entrance Requirements: Asset and TABE Testing
Special Facilities for: Visual, hearing and physical impairments

IOWA

SCOTT COMMUNITY COLLEGE
500 BELMONT ROAD
BETTENDORF, IOWA 52722
(563) 441-4074
E-MAIL: jdial@eicc.edu
WEB SITE: www.eicc.edu

Name of Support Services: Academic Support Services and Personal, Academic, Cultural Enrichment (PACE) Program
Learning Disabilities Specialist: Jill Dial (563) 441-4027
General Information: Two-Year Community College; Enrollment: 4,000; **Tuition:** Residents – $90 per credit hour, Non-Residents – $135 per credit hour; **Room and Board:** No college housing available. Scott Community College has two locations: one on a 181-acre urban campus in Bettendorf

and one in Davenport. The area has many parks, and the Mississippi River offers ideal recreational opportunities. **Degrees**: AA, AS, AAS, certificates of achievement and completion in vocational and technical areas.
Support Services: Enrollment: 15; Cost: None
Staff: Learning disabilities specialists; special counselors
Special Features: Extended time testing; individual and small group tutoring sessions; limited course load (first year); academic advising for students with learning disabilities; taped texts; basic study skills; developmental program; assistive devices for vision impairments and reading disabilities
Entrance Requirements: Documentation of learning disability
Special Facilities for: Visual and physical impairments

KANSAS

LABETTE COMMUNITY COLLEGE

200 SOUTH 14th STREET
PARSONS, KANSAS 67357
(620) 421-6700 X1147; FAX: (620) 421-8284
E-MAIL: gwenm@labette.edu **WEB SITE: www.labette.edu**

Name of Support Services: Student Success Center
Interim Director: Gwen Morgan
General Information: Two-Year Community College; Enrollment: 1,500; **Tuition:** Kansas Residents – $67 per credit hour, Residents of Arkansas, Missouri, Oklahoma – $88 per credit hour, Non-Residents – $121 per credit hour; **Room and Board:** No college housing available. Labette Community College is located on a four-acre campus in a small town. Students come from other counties, states and countries to take advantage of the rural community and quality education that is available at Labette Community College. **Degree Programs**: Accounting, commercial art, fine art, biology, business administration, business education, business and industrial supervision, cooperative industrial training, economics, education, English, fire science, history, journalism, mathematics, music, nursing, office technology, physical education, physics, political science, psychology/sociology, radiography, respiratory care, special ed, paraprofessional training, speech and theatre, technology and tech prep, pharmaceutical tech
Support Services: Enrollment: 20; Cost: None
Staff: Learning disabilities specialists; content tutors (faculty members)
Program Features: Oral and extended time testing; individual and small group tutoring sessions; taped texts; tape recorders; note-taking assistance – scribes; basic study skills; developmental program; faculty made aware of student's learning disability

Entrance Requirements: Documentation of learning disability; SAT/ACT untimed scores accepted; medical evaluation; diagnostic testing at Labette Community College; testing: WAIS, psychological report
Special Facilities for: Visual, hearing and physical impairments

MARYLAND

THE COMMUNITY COLLEGE OF BALTIMORE COUNTY: ESSEX CAMPUS

7201 ROSSVILLE BLVD.
BALTIMORE, MARYLAND 21237-3899
(410) 780-6741, (410) 238-4601 TTY; FAX: (410) 780-6849
E-MAIL: bhunsinger@ccbcmd.edu WEB SITE: www.ccbcmd.edu

Name of Support Services: Office of Special Services
Director: Beth Hunsinger
General Information: Two-Year Community College; Enrollment: 11,200; **Tuition:** County Residents – $87 per credit hour, Non-Residents – $226 per credit hour; **Room and Board:** No college housing available. The Community College of Baltimore County is in a suburban/urban location outside Baltimore City limits. The Essex campus is one of the three campuses in the system. The other two are Catonsville and Dundalk. **Degrees:** AA, AAS, certificates
Support Services: Enrollment: 150; Cost: None
Staff: Learning disabilities specialist
Special Features: Extended time testing; individual and small group tutoring sessions; limited course load; academic advising for students with learning disabilities; note-taking assistance – scribes; taped texts; tape recorders, basic study skills; developmental program; faculty made aware of student's learning disability; adaptive technology; Dragon Dictate Jaws; Kurzweil 3000
Entrance Requirements: Documentation of learning disability; SAT/ACT untimed scores accepted
Special Facilities for: Visual, hearing and physical impairments as well as ADHD psychological disabilities
Scholarships: See page 450.

MASSACHUSETTS

BERKSHIRE COMMUNITY COLLEGE
1350 WEST STREET
PITTSFIELD, MASSACHUSETTS 01201-5786
(413) 499-4660 X1605, (413) 499-3328 TDD; FAX: (413) 499-4576
E-MAIL: pfarron@berkshirecc.edu
WEB SITE: www.berkshirecc.edu

Name of Support Services: disAbled Student Services
Coordinator: Pamela A. Farron
General Information: Two-Year Community College; Enrollment: 2,400; **Tuition:** Massachusetts Residents – $120 per credit, New England and New York Residents – $133 per credit, Non-Residents and International Students – $354 per credit; **Room and Board:** No college housing available. A traditional community college on a 180-acre site nestled in the Berkshires – a summertime cultural destination. The college is approximately one hour from Springfield, Massachusetts, and Albany, New York. **Degrees:** There are 46 associate degrees and certificate programs, plus Life Long Learning – non-credit workshops.
Support Services: Enrollment: 250; Cost: None
Staff: Learning disabilities specialist; peer tutors; special counselors
Special Features: Oral and extended time; individual and small group tutoring sessions; limited course load (first year); academic advising for students with learning disabilities; note-taking assistance – scribes; taped texts; tape recorders; basic study skills; developmental program; faculty made aware of student's learning disability; adaptive computer center
Entrance Requirements: Documentation of learning disability; testing: WAIS, IEP, psychological report
Special Facilities for: Visual, hearing and physical impairments

CAPE COD COMMUNITY COLLEGE
2240 IVANOUGH ROAD
WEST BARNSTABLE, MASSACHUSETTS 02668-1599
(508) 362-2131 X4337; FAX: (508) 362-3988
E-MAIL: jchasson@capecod.edu
WEB SITE: www.capecod.edu

Name of Support Services: O'Neill Center for Disability Services
Director: Joyce Chasson; *Learning Disability Specialist:* Dr. Richard Sommers X4317
General Information: Two-Year Community College; Enrollment: 2,258; Tuition: Residents – $122 per credit hour; Non-Residents – $328 per credit hour; **Degrees:** AA, AS, AAS, certificate programs
Support Services: Cost: None

Staff: Learning disabilities specialists; content tutors (faculty members)
Special Features: Oral and extended time; individual and small group tutoring sessions; limited course load (first year); academic advising for students with learning disabilities; note-taking assistance - scribes; taped texts; tape recorders, basic study skills workshops; developmental program; faculty made aware of student's learning disability; Kurzweil readers; word processors; personal and career counseling; adaptive computer lab
Entrance Requirements: Documentation of learning disability
Special Facilities for: Visual, hearing and physical impairments

MIDDLESEX COMMUNITY COLLEGE
591 SPRINGS ROAD
BEDFORD, MASSACHUSETTS 01730
(781) 280-3641; FAX: (781) 275-7126
E-MAIL: Disability Support Services: woodss@middlesex.mass.edu or
Transition Program: sauliche@middlesex.mass.edu
WEB SITE: www.middlesex.mass.edu

Name of Support Services: Disability Support Services (DSS)
Director: Susan Woods
General Information: Two-Year Community College; Enrollment: 8,000; **Tuition:** Residents – $120 per credit, New England Residents – $132 per credit, Non-Residents and International Students – $326 per credit; **Room and Board:** No college housing available. Middlesex Community College has two campuses – Bedford and Lowell. The Bedford campus has over 200 acres with 11 buildings close to Routes 128 and 3. The Lowell campus is located in the heart of downtown at 33 Kearney Square. **Degrees:** AA in arts, business administration, applied science, general studies, science, certificates of achievements
Support Services: Enrollment: 400; Cost: None
Staff: Learning disabilities specialists; 1:1 tutoring
Special Features: Oral and extended time; individual and small group tutoring sessions; limited course load (first year); academic advising for students with learning disabilities; note-taking assistance – scribes; taped texts; tape recorders, basic study skills; developmental classes; faculty made aware of student's learning disability; assistive tech lab/TRIO Program for Student Achievement
Entrance Requirements: Documentation of learning disability

Name of Support Services: The Transition Program
Transition Program Internship Coordinator: Evelyn Saulich (781) 280-3636
E-mail: sauliche@middlesexmass.edu
Special Features: The Transition Program, designed expressly for students

with significant learning disabilities, is also part of the Disability Support Services office. This two-year certificate program teaches consumer and business skills, independent living, and personal and social development. The cornerstone of the program is an internship each semester in local business settings. It is a particularly successful educational experience for students who would have difficulty meeting the academic/cognitive demands of standard college course work.
Special Facilities for: Visual, hearing and physical impairments

MICHIGAN

NORTHWESTERN MICHIGAN COLLEGE
1701 EAST FRONT STREET
TRAVERSE CITY, MICHIGAN 49686
(231) 995-1139; FAX: (231) 995-1253
E-MAIL: deverett@nmc.edu **WEB SITE: www.nmc.edu**

Name of Support Services: Office of Support Services
Learning Disabilities Specialist: Denyse Everett
General Information: Two-Year Community College; Enrollment: 4,000; **Tuition:** Grand Traverse County Residents – $71.15 per contact hour, Michigan Residents – $127.10 per contact hour, Out-of-State Residents and International Students – $158.60 per contact hour; **Room and Board:** $6,800. Northwestern Michigan College is located in scenic northern Michigan on a spacious 80-acre campus under the pines. A comprehensive community college with an "Open Door" policy for admissions. **Degrees:** AAS, ASA (transfer options), ADN (nursing), certificate of achievement. Northwestern Michigan has a unique partnership with the senior universities throughout Michigan. Students can complete a four-year degree without leaving Northwestern through the University Center.
Support Services: Cost: None
Staff: Learning disabilities specialists; tutorial specialist; interpreter/advisor
Special Features: Oral and extended time; small group tutoring sessions; limited course load (first year); academic advising for students with learning disabilities; note-taking assistance – scribes; taped texts; tape recorders; basic study skills; developmental classes; faculty made aware of student's learning disability (at student's request); computers; personal and career counseling
Entrance Requirements: Documentation of learning disability
Special Facilities for: Visual, hearing and physical impairments

NEW YORK

BROOME COMMUNITY COLLEGE
P.O. BOX 1017
BINGHAMTON, NEW YORK 13902
(607) 778-5234 V/TDD; FAX: (607) 778-5562
E-MAIL: pomeroy_b@sunybroome.edu
WEB SITE: www.sunybroome.edu

Name of Support Services: Student Support Services
Director: Bruce Pomeroy
General Information: Two-Year Community College (State University of New York); Enrollment: 4,962; **Tuition:** Residents – $1,407 per semester, Non-Residents – $2,814 per semester; **Room and Board:** No college housing available. **Degrees:** AA, AAS, AS, transfer programs, certificates
Support Services: Enrollment: 100–125; Cost: None
Staff: Learning disabilities specialists; content tutors (faculty members); peer tutors; special counselors
Special Features: Oral and extended time; individual and small group tutoring sessions; limited course load (first year); academic advising for students with learning disabilities; note-taking assistance – scribes; taped texts; tape recorders, basic study skills; developmental program; faculty made aware of student's learning disability; KPR 1000/3000; Dragon Dictate; Seiko Reading Pens
Entrance Requirements: Documentation of learning disability
Special Facilities for: Visual, hearing and physical impairments
College Life: We go beyond the "letter of the law" in service provisions and meet the "spirit" of the law.
Scholarships: See page 453.

FINGER LAKES COMMUNITY COLLEGE
4355 LAKESHORE DRIVE
CANANDAIGUA, NEW YORK 14424-8395
(585) 394-3500 X7390; FAX: (585) 394-5005
WEB SITE: www.flcc.edu

Name of Support Services: Services for Students with Learning Disabilities
Coordinator: Amy Nichols
General Information: Two-Year Community College (State University of New York); Enrollment: 3,229; **Tuition:** Residents – $1,450; Non-Residents – $2,900; **Room and Board:** No college housing available. A 300-acre campus in a suburban area in the Finger Lakes area of New York State. **Degrees:** AA, AAS, AS, transfer programs, certificates
Support Services: Enrollment: 180; Cost: None

Staff: Learning disabilities specialists; content tutors (faculty members); peer tutors
Special Features: Oral and extended time; individual and small group tutoring sessions; limited course load (first year); academic advising for students with learning disabilities; note-taking assistance – scribes; taped texts; tape recorders, basic study skills; developmental program; faculty made aware of student's learning disability; personal and career counseling; learning disability support group
Entrance Requirements: Documentation of learning disability; testing: WAIS-R, IEP, psychological report
Special Facilities for: Visual (limited equipment), hearing and physical impairments

HERKIMER COUNTY COMMUNITY COLLEGE
100 RESERVOIR ROAD
HERKIMER, NEW YORK 13350
(315) 866-0300 X8331; FAX: (315) 866-6957
WEB SITE: www.herkimer.edu

Name of Support Services: Office of Special Services – Student Learning Center
Special Needs Coordinator: Leslie Cornish
General Information: Two-Year Community College (State University of New York); Enrollment: 2,635; **Tuition:** Residents – $2,700, Non-Residents – $4,400, International – $5,200; **Room and Board:** $5,100. Herkimer County Community College is located in Central New York in the foothills of the Adirondacks in a rural setting. HCCC holds AJCAA national titles in lacrosse, field hockey, men's soccer, and men's basketball. **Majors:** Business administration, business, fashion/buying/merchandising, business health services, management, technology, criminal justice, forensic investigations, early childhood education, human services, liberal arts and sciences, athletic training, general studies, physical education, paralegal, occupational therapy assistant, physical therapy assistant, radio-television broadcasting, travel and tourism, Walt Disney emphasis.
Support Services: Enrollment: 200; Cost: None
Staff: Learning disabilities specialists; content tutors (faculty members); peer tutors
Special Features: Oral and extended time; individual and small group tutoring sessions; limited course load (first year); academic advising for students with learning disabilities; note-taking assistance – scribes; taped texts; tape recorders, basic study skills; developmental program; faculty made aware of student's learning disability; personal and career counseling; learning disability support group

Entrance Requirements: Documentation of learning disability; testing: WAIS, IEP, psychological report
College Life: There is a lot of support on the campus for students with disabilities. HCCC has a very active College Learning Center and Office of Special Services. The Learning Center has professional and peer tutors. There is a tutor for almost every course on campus. Counseling Center is available for personal concerns, careers and transfers.

PAUL SMITH'S COLLEGE
ROUTES 86 & 30, P.O. BOX 265
PAUL SMITHS, NEW YORK 12970
(518) 327-6414; FAX: (518) 327-6369
E-MAIL: mccartr@paulsmiths.edu
WEB SITE: www.paulsmiths.edu

Name of Support Services: Center for Accommodations Services
Learning Specialist: Roxanne McCarty
General Information: Two-Year Private College; Enrollment: 850; **Tuition:** $16,910; **Room and Board:** $7,420. Paul Smith's College is a private college situated on 14,200 acres in a rural area. **Majors:** American studies, business administration, culinary arts, ecology, environmental services, forest harvesting, hospitality, hotel and restaurant, liberal arts, technical writing, travel and tourism
Support Services: Enrollment: 80; Cost: None. *Summer Program:* Three-day orientation program; Cost: $60. Parents are included.
Staff: Learning disabilities specialists; peer tutors; special counselors
Special Features: Oral and extended time; limited course load (first year); note-taking assistance – scribes; tape recorders; faculty made aware of student's learning disability; Kurzweil personal reader
Entrance Requirements: SAT untimed scores accepted; handwritten essay
College Life: The forestry club, Adirondack experiences, radio station, winter carnival and winter weekends add to college life.

ROCKLAND COMMUNITY COLLEGE
145 COLLEGE ROAD
SUFFERN, NEW YORK 10901
(845) 574-4316; FAX: (845) 574-4462
E-MAIL: mzemek@sunyrockland.edu
WEB SITE: www.sunyrockland.edu

Name of Support Services: Office of Disability Services
Learning Disability Specialist: Marge Zemek

General Information: Two-Year Community College (State University of New York); Enrollment: 5,000; **Tuition**: Residents – $1,400 per semester, Non-Residents – $2,800 per semester; **Room and Board:** No college housing available. Rockland Community College is on 150-acre suburban campus with easy access to New York City. **Degrees:** Associate of Arts, Associate of Science, Certificates of Achievement and Completion
Support Services: Enrollment: 400; Cost: None. *Summer Program:* "Keys For Success" – a one-credit program open only for incoming freshmen with learning disabilities. Instruction in study skills, organizational skills, time management, test-taking strategies, note taking, summarizing, coping skills, campus orientation. Cost: $105 plus fees
Staff: Learning disabilities specialists
Special Features: Extended time testing, limited course load; note-taking assistance; taped texts; tape recorders; basic study skills; academic advising for students with learning disabilities; developmental program; faculty made aware of student's individually designed accommodations
Entrance Requirements: Documentation of learning disability; testing: WAIS, IEP, psychological report
Special Facilities for: Visual, hearing and physical impairments
Scholarships: See page 453.

STATE UNIVERSITY OF NEW YORK, COLLEGE OF TECHNOLOGY
ALFRED STATE COLLEGE
10 UPPER COLLEGE DRIVE
ALFRED, NEW YORK 14802
(607) 587-4506; FAX: (607) 587-3210
E-MAIL: meachahm@alfredstate.edu WEB SITE: www.alfredstate.edu

Name of Support Services: Office of Student Disability Services
Coordinator: Heather Meachem
General Information: Two- and Four-Year State College; Enrollment: 3,400; **Tuition**: Residents – $4,350, Non-Residents (Associate Degree) – $7,210; **Room and Board:** $6,700. Alfred State College is 15 miles north of the Pennsylvania border, 75 miles south of Rochester and 90 miles southeast of Buffalo. **Degrees:** Associate in Applied Science, Associate in Arts, and Associate in Science, Associate in Occupational Studies, Bachelor of Business Administration, Bachelor of Technology, Bachelor of Science, certificates of achievement and completion
Support Services: Enrollment: 200; Cost: None
Staff: Learning disabilities specialists; peer tutors
Special Features: Oral and extended time testing, individual and small group tutoring sessions; limited course load (first year); note-taking assis-

tance – scribes; taped texts; tape recorders; basic study skills; academic advising for students with learning disabilities; faculty made aware of student's learning disability; personal and career counseling; Jaws for Windows; WYNN; Reading for the Blind & Dyslexic membership
Entrance Requirements: Documentation of learning disability; testing: WAIS, psychological report
Special Facilities for: Visual, hearing and physical impairments
College Life: Supportive faculty and disability staff are eager to assist students to meet their goal of academic success.

SUFFOLK COUNTY COMMUNITY COLLEGE
AMMERMAN CAMPUS
533 COLLEGE ROAD
SELDEN, NEW YORK 11784-2899
(631) 451-4045, FAX: (631) 451-4473
E-MAIL: boycem@sunysuffolk.edu
WEB SITE: www.sunysuffolk.edu

GRANT CAMPUS
CROOKED HILL ROAD, BRENTWOOD, NEW YORK 11717
(631) 851-6250; FAX: (631) 851-6330
E-MAIL: reinauj@sunysuffolk.edu

EASTERN CAMPUS
121 SPEONK-RIVERHEAD ROAD, RIVERHEAD, NEW YORK 11901
(631) 548-3524, FAX: (631) 548-3613
E-MAIL: greenm@sunysuffolk.edu

Name of Support Services: Office of Special Services
Assistant Directors: Marlene Boyce – Ammerman Campus; Judith Taxler Reinauer – Grant Campus; Michele Green – Eastern Campus
General Information: Two-Year Community College (State University of New York); Enrollment: 22,450; **Tuition**: Residents – $1,495 per semester, Non-Residents – $2,990 per semester; **Room and Board:** No college housing available. Three campuses in small towns on Long Island with easy access to New York City. **Degrees:** Associate of Arts, Associate of Science, Associate in Applied Science, Certificates of Achievement and Completion
Support Services: Enrollment: 350 Ammerman Campus; 150 Grant Campus; 125 Eastern Campus. Cost: None
Staff: Learning disabilities specialists; content tutors (faculty members)
Special Features: Oral and extended time testing, individual and small group tutoring sessions; limited course load (first year); note-taking assistance – scribes; taped texts; tape recorders; basic study skills; academic

advising for students with learning disabilities; developmental program; faculty made aware of student's learning disability; Kurzweil readers; computers, special math courses at development level; math and writing learning center
Entrance Requirements: Documentation of learning disability; learning disabilities specialist report; testing: psychological report
Special Facilities for: Visual, hearing and physical impairments
Scholarships: See page 454.

SULLIVAN COUNTY COMMUNITY COLLEGE
112 COLLEGE ROAD
LOCH SHELDRAKE, NEW YORK 12759
800-577-5243, (845) 434-5750 X4229; FAX: (845) 434-4806
E-MAIL: hlaurent@sullivan.suny.edu
WEB SITE: www.sullivan.suny.edu

Name of Support Services: Department of Learning and Student Development Services
Counselor: Helene Laurenti
General Information: Two-Year Community College (State University of New York); Enrollment: 2,000; **Tuition:** Residents – $3,200, Non-Residents – $6,400; **Room and Board:** $6,050. Sullivan County Community College is nestled in the world-renowned Catskill Mountain Range, approximately 100 miles from New York City, and offers a wide variety of educational opportunities. **Degrees:** AA, AS, AAS, AOS. Strong liberal arts core, contemporary career-oriented programs, transfer programs, and continuing education
Support Services: Cost: None
Staff: Learning disabilities specialists; content tutors (professionals); peer tutors
Special Features: Oral and extended time testing, individual and small group tutoring sessions; note-taking assistance – scribes; taped texts; tape recorders; basic study skills; academic advising for students with learning disabilities; developmental program; faculty made aware of student's learning disability (at student's request); personal and career counseling; computer lab; open enrollment
Entrance Requirements: Documentation of learning disability; testing: WAIS, IEP, psychological report
Special Facilities for: Visual, hearing and physical impairments
College Life: Sullivan County Community College offers students with learning disabilities individual attention, screening and a wide variety of supportive services, all at no cost to the student.

OHIO

UNIVERSITY OF RIO GRANDE/COMMUNITY COLLEGE

218 NORTH COLLEGE AVENUE
RIO GRANDE, OHIO 45674
(740) 245-7339; FAX: (740) 245-7446
E-MAIL: mkimmel@rio.edu **WEB SITE: www.rio.edu**

Name of Support Services: Accessibility Services
Director: Marshall Kimmel
General Information: Two-Year State Community College; Enrollment: 2,600; **Tuition**: Residents – $96 per credit hour, Non-Residents – $115 per credit hour; **Room and Board:** $6,042. The University/Community College is in a rural setting in southeastern Ohio. **Degrees:** Associate degrees are offered through the Colleges of Professional Studies and Liberal Arts & Sciences and the Schools of Business, Technology, Fine Arts, Education, Nursing, Sciences, Social Sciences, and Humanities
Support Services: Enrollment: 78; Cost: None
Staff: Learning disabilities specialist; peer tutors
Special Features: Oral and extended time testing, individual and small group tutoring sessions; limited course load; note-taking assistance - scribes; taped texts; tape recorders; basic study skills; academic advising for students with learning disabilities; developmental program; faculty made aware of student's learning disability
Entrance Requirements: Documentation of learning disability
Special Facilities for: Visual, hearing and physical impairments
College Life: The University works through the peer and faculty tutors/mentors on a one-to-one basis with a goal of meaningful employment for each student.

PENNSYLVANIA

COMMUNITY COLLEGE OF ALLEGHENY COUNTY: ALLEGHENY CAMPUS

808 RIDGE AVENUE
PITTSBURGH, PENNSYLVANIA 15212
(412) 237-4613, (412) 237-4552 TTY; FAX: (412) 237-2721
E-MAIL: mgleser@ccac.edu **WEB SITE: www.ccac.edu**

Name of Support Services: Disability Services Supportive Services
Director: Mary Beth Doyle (412) 237-4614
LD Coordinator: Marilyn Gleser, Learning Disabilities Learning Community
General Information: Two-Year Community College; Enrollment: 16,000; **Tuition:** County Residents – $80 per credit, Other Pennsylvania Residents – $94-160 per credit, Non-Residents – $240 per credit; **Room and Board:**

No college housing available. Community College of Allegheny County: Allegheny Campus is on a large urban campus, 242 acres near three rivers by the Pirates Ball Field and Steelers Football Stadium. **Majors**: Academic programs leading to AA in Arts, AA in Sciences, AS in Applied Science and certificates

Support Services: Enrollment: 250; Cost: None

Staff: Learning disabilities specialists; peer tutors; special counselors; *Summer Program* – Learning Disabilities Summer Pre-College Program (only at Allegheny Campus): A four-week pre-college program emphasizing study skills, reading, English and math and transition from high school to college.

Special Features: Oral and extended time testing, individual and small group tutoring sessions; limited course load (first year); note-taking assistance – scribes; taped texts; tape recorders; basic study skills; academic advising for students with learning disabilities; developmental program; faculty made aware of student's learning disability (at student's request); personal and career counseling; Block Learning Community; pre-college program

Entrance Requirements: Documentation of learning disability

Special Facilities for: Visual, hearing and physical impairments

College Life: First two levels of developmental classes are blocked for students with learning disabilities. Facilitated study groups, tutoring opportunities and availability of one-on-one counseling support all contribute to college success for students with learning disabilities.

COMMUNITY COLLEGE OF ALLEGHENY COUNTY: BOYCE CAMPUS

595 BEATTY ROAD
MONROEVILLE, PENNSYLVANIA 15146
(724) 325-6620, (724) 325-6733 TTY; FAX: (724) 325-6797
E-MAIL: pflorentine@ccac.edu **WEB SITE: www.ccac.edu**

Name of Support Services: Disability Services Support Services

Director: Patricia Florentine

General Information: Two-Year Community College; Enrollment: 2,620; **Tuition:** County Residents – $80 per credit, Other Pennsylvania Residents – $94-160 per credit, Non-Residents – $240 per credit. **Room and Board:** No college housing available. Community College of Allegheny County: Boyce Campus is in a suburban setting, east of Pittsburgh. The major access is from Route 22, Route 48 and Pennsylvania Turnpike, Exit 6. **Majors**: Hospitality management, business, teacher's education, computer/information science, engineering, computer-aided drafting, criminal justice,

communication, journalism, fitness sports and lifetime recreation, pre-athletic training, banking, occupational therapy assistant, physical therapy assistant, radiologic technologist, diagnostic medical sonographics (ultrasonics), surgical technologist, and many others.
Support Services: Enrollment: 225; Cost: None. The percentage of students with learning disabilities who receive a degree in two years is 15%, in 3 years 45% and in four years 40%.
Staff: Learning disabilities specialists; technical specialist.
Special Features: Oral and extended time testing, individual and small group tutoring sessions; note-taking assistance – scribes; taped texts; tape recorders; basic study skills; academic advising for students with learning disabilities; developmental program; faculty made aware of student's learning disability (at student's request); learning styles assessment and strategies
Entrance Requirements: Documentation of learning disability; placement tests in English, reading and math
Special Facilities for: Visual, hearing and physical impairments
College Life: The College builds self-esteem for students with learning disabilities as well as helps to develop academic skills and assistance with study skills and time management.

COMMUNITY COLLEGE OF ALLEGHENY COUNTY: NORTH CAMPUS

8701 PERRY HIGHWAY
PITTSBURGH, PENNSYLVANIA 15237
(412) 369-3686, (412) 369-4110 TTY; FAX: (412) 369-3635
E-MAIL: kwhite@ccac.edu **WEB SITE: www.ccac.edu**

Name of Support Services: Disability Services Support Services
Director: Kathleen White
General Information: Two-Year Community College; Enrollment: 4,000; **Tuition:** County Residents – $80 per credit, Other Pennsylvania Residents – $94-160 per credit, Out-of-State Residents – $240 per credit; **Room and Board:** No college housing available. Community College of Allegheny County: North Campus is in a suburban setting, near Pittsburgh. **Degrees**: Associate degree categories: university parallel, technologies, applied services and trades, business careers, applied arts, health-related, math and sciences, building trade technologies, engineering and sciences, social services
Support Services: Enrollment: 450; Cost: None
Staff: Learning disabilities specialists
Special Features: Oral and extended time testing, individual and small group tutoring sessions; limited course load (first year); note-taking assistance – scribes; tape texts; tape recorders; basic study skills; academic

advising for students with learning disabilities; developmental program; faculty made aware of student's learning disability (at student's request)
Entrance Requirements: Documentation of learning disability
Special Facilities for: Visual, hearing and physical impairments
College Life: Services for students with learning disabilities are tailored to the individual's needs.

TEXAS

AMARILLO COLLEGE

2200 SOUTH WASHINGTON, P.O. BOX 447
AMARILLO, TEXAS 79178-0001
(806) 371-5436; (806) 345-5570
E-MAIL: rossnagel-bj@actx.edu **WEB SITE: www.actx.edu**

Name of Support Services: disAbility Services
Coordinator: Brenda Rossnagel
General Information: Two-Year Community College; Enrollment: 7,500; **Tuition:** District Residents – $738.75 per semester, Other Texas Residents – $978.75 per semester, Non-Residents – $1,488.75 per semester; **Room and Board:** $5,200 per year. Amarillo College is on a 58-acre suburban campus near Palo Duro Canyon, a national park. **Degrees**: Transfer associate, terminal associate and certificate programs
Support Services: Enrollment: 150 - 200; Cost: None
Staff: Learning disabilities specialists; content tutors (faculty members); peer tutors
Special Features: Oral and extended time testing, individual and small group tutoring sessions; limited course load (first year); note-taking assistance – scribes; taped texts; tape recorders; basic study skills; academic advising for students with learning disabilities; developmental program; faculty made aware of student's learning disability
Entrance Requirements: Documentation of learning disability; testing: WAIS, IEP, psychological report
Special Facilities for: Visual, hearing and physical impairments

CENTRAL TEXAS COLLEGE
CENTRAL CAMPUS
P.O. BOX 1800
KILLEEN, TEXAS 76540-1800
(254) 526-1863; FAX: (254) 526-1700
E-MAIL: denise.pergl@ctcd.edu
WEB SITE: www.ctcd.edu

Name of Support Services: Learning Disability Support Services
Coordinators: Denise Pergl
General Information: Two-Year Community College; Enrollment: 10,061; **Tuition:** Residents – $512, Non-Residents – $2,080; **Room and Board:** $2,990. Central Texas College is on a 500-acre suburban campus with easy access to Austin. **Degrees:** Associate in Arts, Associate in Science, Associate in Applied Science, Associate in General Studies, and Certificate programs
Support Services: Enrollment: 100; Cost: None
Staff: Learning disability counselor/coordinator
Special Features: Extended time testing, individual tutoring sessions; taped texts/exams; tape recorders; basic study skills; academic advising for students with learning disabilities; faculty made aware of student's learning disability; equipment check-out includes language masters, laptop computers, overlays
Entrance Requirements: Documentation of learning disability within last three years
Special Facilities for: Visual, hearing and physical impairments

DEL MAR COLLEGE
101 BALDWIN
CORPUS CHRISTI, TEXAS 78404
(361) 698-1298; FAX: (361) 698-1092
E-MAIL: kcarrol@delmar.edu **WEB SITE: www.delmar.edu**

Name of Support Services: Special Services
Director: Jo Ann Luckie; *Intervention Specialist:* Kay Carrol
General Information: Two-Year Community College; Enrollment: 12,000; **Tuition:** District Residents – $925 per semester, Out-of-District Residents – $2,425, Out-of-State Residents and International Students – $2,980; **Room and Board:** No college housing available. Del Mar College is on a 159-acre campus within 200 miles of San Antonio, Austin, Houston and Mexico. Corpus Christi is a city of 250,000 on Corpus Christi Bay and the Gulf of Mexico. Shipping, farming, cattle ranching and oil are important to the area. **Degrees:** AA, AS, AAS and certificates
Support Services: Enrollment: 700; Cost: None

Staff: Disabilities specialists; peer tutors; special counselors
Special Features: Oral and extended time testing, individual tutoring sessions; limited course load (first year); note-taking assistance – scribes; taped texts; basic study skills; academic advising for students with learning disabilities; developmental program; faculty made aware of student's learning disability; computers; learning disability support group; Kurzweil readers; diagnostician; adaptive equipment; learning labs
Eligibility Requirements: Documentation of learning disability; learning disabilities specialist report; SAT/ACT untimed scores accepted; medical evaluation; diagnostic testing at Del Mar College; handwritten essay; testing: WAIS, IEP, psychological report
Special Facilities for: Visual, hearing and physical impairments
Scholarships: See page 456.

EL CENTRO COMMUNITY COLLEGE
801 MAIN STREET
DALLAS, TEXAS 75202-3604
(214) 860-2073; FAX: (214) 860-2233
E-MAIL: mjw5320@dcccd.edu
WEB SITE: www.elcentrocollege.edu

Name of Support Services: Disability Services
Assistant Coordinator: Michelle Watson
General Information: Two-Year Community College; Enrollment: 11,500; **Tuition:** County Residents – $36 per credit hour, Other Texas Residents – $66 per credit hour, Out-of-State Residents – $106 per credit hour; **Room and Board:** No college housing available. El Centro Community College is one of seven colleges in the Dallas County Community College system. El Centro is an urban campus located in downtown Dallas. **Degrees:** AA, AS, AAS, technical occupational programs and certificates
Support Services: Enrollment: 69; Cost: None
Staff: Learning disabilities specialists; peer tutors; special counselors
Special Features: Oral and extended time testing, individual and small group tutoring sessions; limited course load (first year); note-taking assistance – scribes; taped texts; tape recorders; basic study skills; academic advising for students with learning disabilities; developmental program; faculty made aware of student's learning disability; computers; Kurzweil readers; personal and career counseling
Entrance Requirements: Documentation of learning disability
Special Facilities for: Visual, hearing and physical impairments
College Life: El Centro offers outstanding services and the college is easily accessible to students with physical disabilities.

NORTH HARRIS COLLEGE
2700 W.W. THORNE DRIVE
HOUSTON, TEXAS 77073
(281) 618-5481; FAX: (281) 618-7107
E-MAIL: tgarza@nhmccd.edu **WEB SITE: www.nhmccd.edu**

Name of Support Services: Disability Services Office
Coordinator: Teresa Garza (281) 618-5680
General Information: Two-Year Community College; Enrollment: 10,070; North Harris College is one of five colleges in the North Harris Montgomery Community College District and is located on a 185-acre, suburban campus in Houston. **Tuition:** District Residents – $672 for 15 credit hours, Other Texas Residents – $1,272 for 15 credit hours, Out-of-State Residents – $1,497 for 15 credit hours; **Room and Board:** Some off-campus housing. **Degrees:** AA, AS, AAS and certificates
Support Services: Enrollment: 250; Cost: None
Staff: Learning disabilities specialists; peer tutors; special counselors
Special Features: Oral and extended time testing, individual and small group tutoring sessions; limited course load (first year); note-taking assistance – scribes; taped texts; tape recorders; basic study skills; academic advising for students with learning disabilities; developmental program; word processors; optical scanner / reader, diagnostic services
Entrance Requirements: Documentation of learning disability; diagnostic testing at North Harris College
Special Facilities for: Visual, hearing and physical impairments
Scholarships: See page 457.

VIRGINIA

TIDEWATER COMMUNITY COLLEGE - NORFOLK CAMPUS
300 GRANBY STREET
NORFOLK, VIRGINIA 23510-1909
(757) 822-1213, 822-1226, 822-1248 TDD; FAX: (757) 822-1214
E-MAIL: jrashada@tcc.edu
WEB SITE: www.tcc.edu

CHESAPEAKE CAMPUS
1428 CEDAR ROAD
CHESAPEAKE, VA 23320
(757) 822-5125

PORTSMOUTH CAMPUS
7000 COLLEGE DRIVE
PORTSMOUTH, VA 23703
(757) 822-2200

VIRGINIA BEACH CAMPUS
1700 COLLEGE CRESCENT
VIRGINIA BEACH, VA 23456
(757) 822-7211

Name of Support Services: Learning Disabilities Services
Student Services Disabilities Counselor: Janice H. Rashada (all four campuses)
General Information: Two-Year Community College; Enrollment: 33,000; **Tuition:** Residents – $81.00 per credit hour, Non-Residents – $246.05 per credit hour; **Room and Board:** No college housing available. Tidewater Community College, founded in 1968, has grown from a single location to four campuses with an Advanced Technology Center and a Visual Arts Center in Portsmouth. TCC also offers classes at local military bases and local area schools. **Degrees:** Associate in Arts in fine / liberal arts; Associate in Science in business, engineering general studies, science, computer science, social sciences; Associate in Applied Science in agricultural, arts and design technology, business, engineering / industrial, health, public service; diploma, certificates and career studies
Support Services: Enrollment: 450; Cost: None
Staff: Learning disabilities specialists; content tutors (faculty members); peer tutors; special counselors; deaf specialist
Special Features: Oral and extended time testing, individual and small group tutoring sessions; limited course load (first year); note-taking assistance – scribes; taped texts; tape recorders; basic study skills; academic advising for students with learning disabilities; developmental program; learning disability support group; faculty made aware of student's learning disability; Arkenstone Reader; Dragon Dictate; Phonic Ear; four-track recorders; Language Masters; Portable equipment checkout; comprehensive testing
Entrance Requirements: Documentation of learning disability; learning disabilities specialist report; medical evaluation; open admissions; testing: WAIS, psychological report
Special Facilities for: Visual, hearing and physical impairments
Scholarships: See page 458.

WASHINGTON

WALLA WALLA COMMUNITY COLLEGE
500 TAUSICK WAY
WALLA WALLA, WASHINGTON 99362-9267
(509) 527-4262; FAX: (509) 527-4480
E-MAIL: claudia.angus@wwcc.edu
WEB SITE: www.wwcc.edu

Name of Support Services: Services for Students with Disabilities
Disabilities Coordinator: Claudia Angus
General Information: Two-Year Community College; Enrollment: 13,000; **Tuition:** Residents – $1,767, Non-Residents – $2,679; **Room and Board:** No college housing available. Walla Walla Community College is located on 125 acres in a small rural town. **Majors:** Liberal arts and studies, business administration, nursing, agriculture, health and related services, computer education, engineering and applied sciences, vocational and home economics
Staff: Learning disabilities specialist; peer tutors; special counselors
Special Features: Oral and extended time testing, individual and small group tutoring sessions; limited course load (first year); note-taking assistance – scribes; taped texts; tape recorders; basic study skills; academic advising for students with learning disabilities; developmental program; faculty made aware of student's learning disability; other features as indicated by documentation
Entrance Requirements: Documentation of learning disability; medical evaluation for ADD / ADHD; testing: WAIS, psychological report
Special Facilities for: Visual, hearing and physical impairments

WISCONSIN

LAKESHORE TECHNICAL COLLEGE
1290 NORTH AVENUE
CLEVELAND, WISCONSIN 53015-1414
(888) GO-TO-LTC (468-6582); FAX: (888) 468-6211
E-MAIL: rivi.hatt@gotoltc.edu WEB SITE: www.gotoltc.edu

Name of Support Services: Learning Support Services
ADA/Learning Support Services Specialist: Rivi Hatt
General Information: Two-Year Community College; Enrollment: 2,270; **Tuition:** Residents – $87 per credit hour, Non-Residents – $536.30 per credit hour; **Room and Board:** No college housing available. Lakeshore Technical College is located in the village of Cleveland, Wisconsin, halfway between the cities of Manitowoc and Sheboygan near Lake Michigan in east-central Wisconsin. The campus is easily reached by following I-43 (Exit 137), 50 miles north of Milwaukee and 50 miles south of

Green Bay. **Programs:** Certificates, technical diplomas, associate degrees, as well as apprentice, trade extension and preparation courses
Support Services: Enrollment: 60; Cost: None
Staff: Learning disabilities specialist; peer tutors; special counselors
Special Features: Oral and extended time testing, individual and small group tutoring sessions; limited course load (first year); note-taking assistance – scribes; taped texts; tape recorders; basic study skills; academic advising for students with learning disabilities; developmental program; faculty made aware of student's learning disability; Kurzweil 3000 and other assistive technology
Entrance Requirements: Documentation of learning disability; SAT/ACT untimed scores accepted; testing: IEP, psychological report
Special Facilities for: Visual, hearing and physical impairments
College Life: Lakeshore Technical College was awarded a national recognition for serving students having disabilities. There is a flexible admissions policies for persons having disabilities.

Colleges Providing Services for Students with Learning Disabilities

COLLEGES PROVIDING SERVICES FOR STUDENTS WITH LEARNING DISABILITIES

The following Colleges provide services for students with Learning Disabilities but do not have specific full-time programs. The type of college – whether a two- or four-year – appears in parentheses next to the college name.

Abbreviation Key for Services

OET: Oral and Extended Time Testing	**BSS:** Basic Study Skills
ITS: Individual Tutoring Sessions	**DP:** Developmental Program
SGTS: Small Group Tutoring Sessions	**FALD:** Faculty Made Aware of Student's Learning Disability
LCL: Limited Course Load	**KR:** Kurzweil Readers
AA: Academic Advising for LD Students	**DD:** Dragon Dictate
NTA: Note-Taking Assistance	**WP:** Word Processors
TR: Tape Recorders	**PCC:** Personal and Career Counseling
TT: Taped Texts	**LDSG:** LD Support Group

ALABAMA

Jacksonville State University *(4 -yr)*
Disability Support Services (DSS)
700 Pelham Road, North
Jacksonville, Alabama 36265-1602
256-782-5093 V/TDD;
Fax: 256-782-5025
E-mail: dmiller@jsucc.jsu.edu
Web Site: www.jsu.edu
Director: Daniel Miller
Disability Specialist LD/ADHD: Adam Green
Services: OET, ITS, SGTS, LCL, AA, NTA, TR, BSS, FALD, KR, WP, PCC, LDSG, Individualized Postsecondary Program
Scholarships: See page 423.

Troy State University *(4-year)*
Adaptive Needs Program
215 Trojan Center
Troy, Alabama 36082
334-670-3219; Fax: 334-670-3810
E-mail: dsellers@.troy.edu
Web Site: www.troy.edu
Director: Deborah G. Sellers
Services: OET, ITS, SGTS, LCL, NTA, TR, TT, BSS, AA, DP, PCC, FALD, Registration assistance, Check-out of Adaptive Equipment

Univ. of South Alabama *(4-year)*
Disabled Student Services
307 University Blvd.
Mobile, Alabama 36688-0002
251-460-7212; Fax: 251-460-6157
E-mail: aagnew@usouthal.edu
Web Site: www.southalabama.edu
Director: Andrea C. Agnew
Services: OET, LCL, AA, NTA, TR, TT, BSS, DP, FALD, PCC, WP, Arkenstone Reader

ARKANSAS

East Arkansas Community College *(2-year)*
Office of Disability & Health Services
1700 Newcastle Road
Forrest City, Arkansas 72335
870-633-4480 x304; Fax: 870-633-7222
E-mail: mtinsley@eacc.edu
Web Site: www.eacc.edu
Contact Person: Melvin Tinsley
Services: OET, ITS, NTA, TR, DP, FALD, PCC, SGTS

CALIFORNIA

Califomia State University: Fresno *(4-year)*
Services for Students with Disabilities
Henry Hadden Library 1049
5200 North Barton, MSML 125
Fresno, California 93740-8014
559-278-2811, 559-278-3084 TDD; Fax: 559-278-4214
E-mail: caroles@csufresno.edu
Web Site: www.csufresno.edu
Director: Carole Snee
Services: OET, NTA, TR, TT, BSS, AA, FALD, KR, WP, PCC, LDSG, Computer Lab

California State University: East Bay *(4-year)*
Student Disability Resource Ctr.
25800 Carlos Bee Blvd.
Hayward, California 94542-3057
510-885-3868; Fax: 510-885-4775
Web Site: www.csueastbay.edu
Director: Pennijean Savage
Services: OET, ITS, SGTS, NTA, TR, TT, BSS, FALD, PCC

Fullerton College *(2-year)*
Disability Support Services
321 East Chapman Avenue
Fullerton, California 92832
714-992-7270; 714-871-9192 TDD
E-mail: lcampbell@fullcoll.edu
Web Site: www.fullcoll.edu
Coordinator: Lisa Campbell
Services: OET, ITS, NTA, TR, TT, BSS, DP, AA, FALD, KR, WP
Scholarships: See page 443.

Holy Names University *(4-year)*
Academic Affairs/Student Support Services
3500 Mountain Blvd.
Oakland, California 94619
510-436-1321; Fax: 510-436-1199
Services: OET, ITS, SGTS, LCL, AA, NTA, TT, BSS, FALD, PCC, LDSG

Humboldt State Univ. *(4-year)*
Student Disability Resource Center (SDRC)
1 Harpst Street
Arcata, California 95521-8299
707-826-4678; Fax: 707-826-5397
E-mail: sdrc@humboldt.edu
Web Site: www.sdrc.humboldt.edu
Services: OET, ITS, NTA, TR, TT, AA, FALD (at student's request)

Merced College *(2-year)*
Disabled Student Services
3600 M Street
Merced, California 95348
209-384-6155; 209-384-6311 TDD
Director: Richard Marashlian
Services: OET, NTA, TR, TT, FALD

Reedley College *(2-year)*
Disabled Student Services
995 North Reed Avenue
Reedley, California 93654
559-638-0332
Web Site: www.reedleycollege.edu
Director: Janice Emerzian
Services: OET, ITS, LCL, NTA, TR, TT, BSS, FALD, KR, WP, PCC, LDSG

San Diego State University/ Imperial Valley Campus *(2-yr)*
Disabled Student Services
720 Heber Avenue
Calexico, California 92231
760-768-5509
Web Site: www.ivcampus.sdsu.edu
Services: OET, ITS, SGTS, LCL, AA, NTA, TR, TT, BSS, FALD

Sonoma State University *(4-year)*
Disabled Student Services
1801 East Cotati Avenue
Salizar Hall 1049
Rohnect Park, California 94928-3808

707-664-2677, 707-664-2958 TDD;
Fax: 707-664-3330
E-mail: sasweb@sonoma.edu
Web Site: www.sonoma.edu
Director: Michael Daine Ph.D.
Services: ET, AA, NTA, TT, BSS, Promote Self-Advocacy

Univ. of California: Irvine *(4-yr)*
100 Disability Services Center
Irvine, California 92697-5250
949-824-7494, 949-824-6272 TDD;
Fax: 949-824-3083
E-mail: dsc@uci.edu
Web Site: www.disability.uci.edu
Director: Jan Serrantino
Services: OET, ITS, LCL, NTA, TR, TT, AA, BSS, FALD (at student's request), Adaptive Technology Lab, PCC

COLORADO

Colorado Northwestern Community College *(2-year)*
Student Support Special Services
500 Kennedy Drive
Rangely, Colorado 81648-3598
800-562-1105 X285, 970-675-3285
E-mail: lee.stanley@cncc.edu
Web Site: www.cncc.edu
Director: Lee Stanley
Services: OET, ITS, SGTS, NTA, TR, TT, BSS, DP, AA, FALD (at student's request), Voice Synthesizer, Arkenstone Reader, PCC,

Colorado State Univ. *(4-year)*
Resources for Disabled Students
100 General Services (RDS)
Fort Collins, Colorado 80523
970-491-6385 V/TDD;
Fax: 970-491-3457
E-mail: rkreston@laman.colostate.edu
Web Site: www.colostate.edu/depts/RDS
Director: Rosemary Kreston
Services: ET, ITS, LCL, AA, NTA, TT, TR, BSS, FALD (at student's request), Assistive Technology

Front Range Community College *(2-year)*
Special Services
3645 West 112th Avenue
Westminster, Colorado 80031
303-404-5302, 303-404-5577 TTY;
Fax: 303-438-9524
E-mail:
JoAnna.Bennett@frontrange.edu
Web Site: www.frontrange.edu
Director: JoAnna Bennett
Services: OET, ITS, SGTS, LCL, NTA, TR, TT, BSS, DP, FALD, Assistive Computer Technology

Metropolitan State College *(4-yr)*
Disability Services
P.O. Box PAR-177
Denver, Colorado 80217-3363
303-556-8387, 303-556-8484 TTY;
FAX: 303-556-2074
Web Site: www.mscd.edu
Director: Lisa McGill
Services: OET, ITS, SGTS, LCL, NTA, TR, TT, BSS, DP, FALD, WP, PCC, LDSG, Computer Lab

Northeastern Junior College *(2-yr)*
Comprehensive Learning Center
100 College Drive
Sterling, Colorado 80751
970-521-6679; Fax: 970-522-4945
Web Site: www.njc.edu
Director: Donelle Hogarth
Services: OET, ITS, SGTS, LCL, NTA, TR, TT, BSS, DP, FALD, WP, PCC

Univ. of Colorado: Denver *(4-yr)*
Office of Disability Resources and Services
Box 1118 AR-177

Denver, Colorado 80217-3363
303-556-3450, 303-556-4766 TDD;
FAX: 303-556-2074
E-mail: lisa.mcgill@cudenver.edu
Web Site: www.cudenver.edu
Director: Lisa McGill
Services: OET, ITS, SGTS, LCL, NTA, TR, TT, BSS, DP, FALD, WP, PCC, LDSG, Computer Lab

CONNECTICUT

Eastern Connecticut State University *(4-year)*
Office of Disability Services
80 Windham Street
Willimantic, Connecticut 06226
203-456-2231
Web Site: www.easternct.edu
Services: OET, ITS, SGTS, LCL, NTA, TR, BSS, FALD, Assistive Tech

Northwestern Connecticut Community-Technical College *(2-year)*
Services for Students with Disabilities
Park Place East
Winsted, Connecticut 06098
203-738-6307 V/TTY;
Fax: 203-379-4465
E-mail:
rdennerlein@nwcc.commnet.edu
Web Site: www.nwctc.commnet.edu
Director: Roseann Dennerlein
Services: OET, AA, TT, TR, AA, WP, ITS, NTA, FALD (at student's request), KR

Norwalk Community Technical College *(2-year)*
Services for Students with Disabilities
188 Richards Avenue
Norwalk, Connecticut 06854
203-875-7192
Web Site: www.nctc.commnet.edu
ADA Coordinator: Lori Orvetti
Services: Accommodations are based on documentation.

University of New Haven *(4-yr)*
Disability Services and Resources
300 Boston Post Road
West Haven, Connecticut 06516
203-932-7331 V/TDD
Web Site: www.newhaven.edu
Services: OET, ITS, SGTS, LCL, AA, NTA, TR, TT, BSS, DP, FALD, PCC, WP, Adaptive Technology

DISTRICT OF COLUMBIA

Catholic University of America *(4-year)*
Disability Support Services
207 Pryzbyla Center
620 Michigan Avenue NE
Washington, D.C. 20064
202-319-5211; Fax: 202-319-5126
E-mail:
cua-disabilityservices@cua.edu
Web Site: www.cua.edu
Director: Emily K. Singer
Services: OET, ITS, SGTS, LCL, AA, NTA, TT, TR, BSS, FALD, Assistive Technology, Early Registration

George Washington Univ. *(4-year)*
Disability Support Services
800 21st Street NW
Marvin Center, Suite 242
Washington, D.C. 20052
202-994-8250 V/TDD
Fax: 202-994-7610
E-mail: dss@gwu.edu
Web Site: www.gwu.edu
Director: Christy Willis
Services: OET, ITS, SGTS, LCL, AA, NTA, FALD, TR, TT, KR, WP, DP, PCC, LDSG, Computer Lab
Scholarships: See page 426.

Howard University *(4-year)*
Special Student Services
Howard Center Suite 725
2225 Georgia Avenue, NW
Washington, D.C. 20059
202-238-2420
E-mail: bwilliams@howard.edu
Web Site: www.howard.edu
Dean/Special Student Services: Barbara Williams
Services: OET, ITS, TT, NTA, BSS, FALD, KR, PCC

FLORIDA

Baptist College of Florida *(4-year)*
Disability Services
5400 College Drive
Graceville, Florida 32440
850-263-3261
E-mail: mail@baptistcollege.edu
Web Site: www.baptistcollege.edu
Director/Sr VP: Dr. R.C. Hammack
Services: OET, ITS, NTA, TR, FALD

Edison Community College *(2-yr)*
Student Support Services
8099 College Parkway SW
Fort Myers, Florida 33919
239-489-9427
Web Site: www.edison.edu
Services: OET, ITS, AA, NTA, TT, DP, BSS, DP, FALD, WP, KR

Flagler College *(4-year)*
Disability Services
74 King Street, PO Box 1027
St. Augustine, Florida 32085
904-829-6481; 904-829-0094
Web Site: www.flagler.edu
Services: OET, AA, NTA, TT, TR, BSS, FALD

Florida Community College at Jacksonville *(2-year)*
Disabled Student Services
101 West State Street Room A1093
Jacksonville, Florida 32202
904-633-8488 V/TDD
Web Site: www.fccj.org
Services: OET, ITS, SGTS, LCL, NTA, TR, TT, BSS, DP, FALD,

Gulf Coast Community College *(2-year)*
Disability Support Services
5230 West Highway 98
Panama City, Florida 32401
904-872-3834
E-mail: lvandalen@gulfcoast.edu
Web Site: www.gulfcoast.edu
Director: Linda Van Dalen
Services: OET, ITS, SGTS, LCL, AA, NTA, TR, TT, BSS, FALD, WP, PCC, LDSC, KR

Indian River Community College *(2-year)*
Student Disability Services (SDS)
3209 Virginia Avenue
Fort Pierce, Florida 34981-5596
772-462-7782; Fax: 772-462-4699
E-mail: rbrant@ircc.edu or tvalencia@ircc.edu
Web Site: www.ircc.edu
Director: Terry Valencia
Counselor: Rhoda Brant
Services: OET, SGTS, LCL, AA, NTA, TR, TT, BSS, DP, FALD, KR, WP, PCC, Computer Lab

Palm Beach Atlantic College *(4-yr)*
Disabilities Services
901 South Flagler Drive Box 24708
West Palm Beach, Florida 33401
561-803-2100; 800-238-3998
Web Site: www.pba.edu
Director: Dr. Emery D. Twoey
Services: OET, AA, BSS, FALD

Pensacola Junior College *(2-year)*
Disability Support Services

PNS Bldg. 6
1000 College Blvd.
Pensacola, Florida 32504-8998
850-484-1637 V/TDD/TTY
E-mail: jnickles@pjc.edu
Web Site: www.pjc.edu
Director: Dr. James Nickles
Services: OET, ITS, SGTS, LCL, AA, NTA, TR, TT, BSS, DP, FALD, KR, WP, PCC, adaptive equipment

St. Johns River Community College *(2-year)*
Disabled Student Services
5001 St. Johns Avenue
Palatka, Florida 32177-3897
386-312-4035; Fax: 386-312-4029
E-mail: kristiannsweet@sjrcc.edu
Web Site: sjrcc.edu
Director: Shirley Kennedy, Ph.D.
Services: OET, NTA, TR, BSS, DP, FALD

Tallahassee Comm. College *(2-yr)*
Disability Support Services
444 Appleyard Drive
Tallahassee, Florida 32304
850-201-8430
E-mail: dss@tcc.fl.edu
Web Site: www.tcc.fl.edu
Coordinator: Margaret L. Hardee
Services: OET, ITS, AA, NTA, TT, TR, Adaptive Computer Lab

University of Central Florida *(4-yr)*
Student Disability Services
Student Resource Center Room 132
Orlando, Florida 32816
407-823-2371; 407-823-2116 TDD
E-mail: sds@mail.ucf.edu
Web Site: www.sds.ucf.edu
Director: Dr. Philip N. Kalfin
Services: OET, SGTS, LCL, NTA, TR, TT, BSS, FALD (at student's request), KR, WP, PCC

University of Miami *(4-year)*
Accessibility Resources
Whitten University Center
1306 Stanford Drive
Coral Gables, Florida 33124-6990
305-284-2374; Fax: 305-284-1999
Web Site: www.miami.edu
Director: Mayra L. Diaz
Services: OET, ITS, SGTS, LCL, NTA, TR, TT, BSS, FALD (at student's request), Accommodations as supported in the psychoeducational evaluation

GEORGIA

Emory University *(4-year)*
Office of Disability Services
110 Administration Building
Atlanta, Georgia 30322
404-727-6016; Fax: 404-727-1126
E-mail: jpsmile@emory.edu
Web Site: www.emory.edu
Coordinator: Jessalyn P. Smiley
Services: OET, ITS, SGTS, LCL, AA, NTA, TR, TT, BSS, FALD, LDSG, WP, PCC

Georgia Southern College *(4-yr)*
Counseling & Career Development Center
Statesboro, Georgia 30460
912-681-5541; Fax: 912-681-0834
Web Site: www.georgiasouthern.edu
Director: Dr. David Matthews
Coordinator: Wayne Akins
Services: OET, ITS, SGTS, LCL, NTA, TR, TT, BSS, DP, FALD, KR, WP, PCC

HAWAII

Hawaii Community College *(2-yr)*
Ha'awi Kokua Program
200 West Kawili Street
Bldg. 388 Room 104

Hilo, Hawaii 96720-4091
808-933-0702 V/TTY
E-mail: kkane @hawcc.hawaii.edu
Web Site: www.hawcc.hawaii.edu
Counselor: Karen Kane
Services: OET, ITS, SGTS, AA, NTA, TT, TR, BSS, FALD, PCC, KR, WP, LCL for dorming requirements
Scholarships: See page 448.

Kaua`i Community College *(2-yr)*
Student Services Office
3-1901 Kaumuali`i Highway
Lihu`e, Hawaii 96766-9591
808-245-8314; Fax: 808-245-8297
Web Site: www.kauaicc.hawaii.edu
Services: OET, ITS, SGTS, LCL, AA, TR, TT, BSS, DP, FALD, PCC

University of Hawaii at Hilo *(4-yr)*
University Disabilitye Services
200 West Kawili Street
Hilo, Hawaii 96720-4091
808-933-0816, 808-933-3334 TTY
E-mail: shirachi@hawaii.edu
Web Site: www.uhh.hawaii.edu
Director: Susan Shirachi
Services: OET, ITS, SGTS, AA, NTA, TT, TR, BSS, FALD, Assistive Technology

IDAHO

Lewis-Clark State College *(4-year)*
Disability Services
500 Eighth Avenue
Lewiston, Idaho 83501
208-792-2313
E-mail: dmundel@lcsc.edu
Web Site: www.lcsc.edu
Coordinator: Debi Mundell
Services: OET, ITS, SGTS, LCL, AA, NTA, TR, TT, BSS, DP, FALD, WP, PCC

ILLINOIS

Black Hawk College *(2-year)*
Student Accommodations Office
6600 34th Avenue
Moline, Illinois 61265-5899
309-796-5949; Fax: 309-792-5901
E-mail: lourasha@bhc.edu
Web Site: www.bhc.edu
Services: OET, ITS, SGTS, LCL, AA, NTA, TR, TT, BSS, DP, FALD (at student's request), PCC, KR

City Colleges of Chicago *(2-year)*
Daley College
Karen Lee 773-838-2578
Kennedy-King College
Derrick Smith 773-602-5278
Malcolm X. College
Jamin Israel 312-850-7342
Olive-Harvey College
Rae Gully 773-291-6345
Truman College
Linda Ford 773-907-4725
Harold Washington College
Deborah Miles 312-553-6096
Wright College
Teri Prokes 773-481-8015
Inquiries should be addressed to the individual Special Needs Coordinators (see above) or the Information Center below:
City Colleges of Chicago
Information Center/Special Needs
226 West Jackson Street
Chicago, Illinois 60606-6997
312-553-2500; FAX: 312-553-3328
Web Site: www.ccc.edu
Services: OET, LCL, NTA, TT, DP, FALD, WP, PCC, AA

Danville Area Community College *(2-year)*
Student Support Services
2000 E. Main Street
Room 113 Cannon Hall

Martin Luther King Memorial Way
Danville, Illinois 61832-5199
217-443-8747; Fax: 217-443-8898
E-mail: pmcconn@dacc.edu
Web Site: www.dacc.edu
Coordinator: Penny J. McConnell
Services: OET, ITS, SGTS, AA, NTA, TR, TT, BSS, DP, PCC, FALD (at student's request)

Governors State University *(2 yr)*
Disability Support Services
1 University Parkway
University Park, Illinois 60466
708-534-4508
E-mail: r-sweeney@govst.edu
Web Site: www.govst. edu
Coordinator: Robin Sweeney
Services: OET, AA, NTA, TT, TR, Specialized computer software

Illinois Central College *(2-year)*
Access Services
One College Drive
East Peoria, Illinois 61635-0001
309-694-5749; 309-694-5721 TTY;
Fax: 309-694-5450
E-mail: tingles@icc.edu
Web Site: www.icc.edu
Director: Terri Ingles
Services: OET, NTA, TR, TT, AA, FALD

Richland Community College *(2-yr)*
Learning Accommodation Services
One College Park
Decatur, Illinois 62521
217-875-7200 x362
E-mail: matkins@richland.edu
Web Site: www.richland.edu
Director: Mary Atkins
Services: OET, ITS, SGTS, LCL, NTA, TT, TR, BSS, DP, FALD, WP, LDSG

St. Xavier University *(4-year)*
Learning Center & Disability Services
3700 West 103rd Street
Chicago, Illinois 60655
773-298-3308; 773-298-3956
E-mail: zientara@sxu.edu
Web Site: www.sxu.edu
Director: Sue Zientara
Services: OET, ITS, SGTS, NTA, TT, BSS, DP, FALD (at student's request), PCC, Priority Registration

Shawnee Community College *(2-yr)*
Special Needs Services
8364 College Road
Ullin, Illinois 62992
618-634-2242; 618-634-3228
E-mail: annieh@shawneecc.edu
Web Site: www.shawneecc.edu
Counselor: Annie P. Hubbard
Services: OET, ITS, SGTS, LCL, AA, NTA, TT, TR, BSS, DP, FALD

Truman College *(2-year)*
Special Needs Office
1145 West Wilson Avenue
Chicago, Illinois 60640
773-907-4725
E-mail: lford@ccc.edu.edu
Web Site: www.trumancollege.cc.edu
Director: Linda Ford
Services: OET, ITS, SGTS, LCL, AA, NTA, TT, TR, BSS, FALD

INDIANA

Indiana Institute of Technology *(4-year)*
Student Support Services
1600 East Washington Blvd.
Fort Wayne, Indiana 46803
800-937-2448
E-mail: mcscudder@indianatech.edu
Web Site: www.indianatech.edu

Director: Mary C. Scudder
Services: OET, ITS, SGTS, LCL, TR, BSS, WP, PCC

Indiana University *(4-year)*
Disability Services for Students
601 East Kirkwood Hall, #327
Bloomington, Indiana 47405-2801
812-855-3508; Fax: 812-855-7650
E-mail: ferguson@indiana.edu
Web Site: www.indiana.edu/~iubdss
Coordinator: Jody Ferguson
Services: OET, AA, LCL, TR, NTA TT, BSS, FALD, WP, KR, PCC
Scholarships: See page 427.

Indiana University: Southeast *(4-yr)*
Disability Services
UC South Room 006
4201 Grant Line Road
New Albany, Indiana 47150-6405
812-941-2243; Fax: 812-941-2542
E-mail: wallach@ius.edu
Web Site: www.ius.edu
Director: Hannah Wallace
Services: OET, ITS, SGTS, LCL, AA, NTA, TR, BSS, KR, WP, FALD

Ivy Tech Community College Northeast *(2-year)*
Disability Support Services
3800 North Anthony Blvd.
Fort Wayne, Indiana 46805
260-480-4197
E-mail: ketter@ivytech.edu
Web Site: www.ivytech.edu/fortwayne
Contact: Kristi Etter
Services: OET, ITS, SGTS, LCL, AA, NTA, TR, BSS, FALD, KR, WP

Ivy Tech Community College Southern Indiana *(2-year)*
Disability and Support Services
8204 Highway 311
Sellersburg, Indiana 47172-1897
812-246-3301 X4197
E-mail: dshaw@ivytech.edu
Web Site: www.ivytech.edu/sellersburg
Counselor: Denise Shaw
Services: OET, ITS, SGTS, LCL, AA, NTA, TT, TR, BSS, FALD

Manchester College *(4-year)*
Services for Students with Disabilities
604 College Avenue
North Manchester, Indiana 46962
260-982-5076
E-mail: dshowe@manchester.edu
Web Site: www.manchester, edu
Director: Denise S. Howe
Services: OET, ITS, SGTS, LCL, NTA, BBS, PPC, Disabilities Support Group, Computer Network Available

Valparaiso University *(4-year)*
Disability Support Services
Miller Hall 126
651 South College Avenue
Valparaiso, Indiana 46383-6493
219-464-5456
Web Site: www.valpo.edu
Director: Sherry DeMik
Services: OET, ITS, LCL, AA, NTA, TT, TR, BSS, FALD, Evaluation after student has been admitted to the university

IOWA

Coe College *(4-year)*
Academic Achievement Program
1220 First Avenue, NE
Cedar Rapids, Iowa 52402
319-399-8547
Director: Lois Kabela-Coates
E-mail: lkabela@coe.edu
Web Site: www.coe.edu
Services: OET, ITS, SGTS, LCL, AA, NTA, TT, BSS, FALD, WP, PCC

Muscatine Community College *(2-year)*
Academic Achievement Program
152 Colorado Street
Muscatine, Iowa 52761
(563) 288-6013
Coordinator: Kathy A. Trosen
E-mail: ktrosen@eicc.edu
Web Site: www.eicc.edu
Services: OET, ITS, LCL, NTA, TR, TT, BSS, DP, FALD

North Iowa Area Community College *(2-year)*
Special Needs
500 College Drive, AB104
Mason City, Iowa 50401-7299
641-422-4105
Web Site: www.niacc.edu
Services: OET, ITS, SGTS, AA, TR, TT, NTA, BSS, DP, FALD, WP, PCC, LDSG

Southwestern Community College *(2-year)*
Special Needs Program
1501 West Townline Street
Creston, Iowa 50801
641-782-7081 x458, 1-800-247-4023; Fax: 641-782-3312
E-mail: pantini@swcciowa.edu
Web Site: www.swcciowa.edu/disabilities
Coordinator: Deb Pantini
Services: OET, ITS, SGTS, LCL, BSS, DP, FALD

KANSAS

Barclay College *(4-year)*
Office of Student Disability Services
607 North Kingman
Haviland, Kansas 67059
620-862-5252
E-mail: admissions@barclaycollege.edu
Web Site: www.barclaycollege.edu
Services: OET, ITS, FALD

Fort Scott Community College *(2-yr)*
Student Support Services
2108 South Horton
Fort Scott, Kansas 66701
316-223-2700; Fax: 316-223-6530
E-mail: damonf@ftscott.edu
Web Site: www.ftscott.edu
Coordinator: Lynne Wheeler
Services: OET, ITS, SGTS, NTA, TR, TT, BSS, DP, FALD (at student's request)

Hutchinson Community College *(2-year)*
Student Support Services
Parker Student Union
1300 North Plum
Hutchinson, Kansas 67501
800-289-3501 x3564; 620-665-3564
E-mail: eldera@hutchcc.edu
Web Site: www.hutchcc.edu
Director: Jeanette Cecil
Services: OET, TT, NTA, FALD

Kansas City Kansas Community College *(2-year)*
Disability Resource Center
7250 State Avenue
Kansas City, Kansas 66112
913-288-7670 V/TDD
E-mail: vwebb@kckcc.edu
Web Site: www.kckcc.edu
Faculty Director: Valerie Webb
Services: OET, TR, TT, LCL, NTA, BSS, ITS, SGTS, DP, FALD, Assistive Technology

Wichita State University *(4-year)*
Disability Services
1845 North Fairmount
Wichita, Kansas 67260-0132
316-978-3309 V/TDD; Fax: 316-978-3114

Web Site: www.witchita.edu
Director: Grady Landrum
Services: OET, NTA, TR, TT, BSS, FALD (at student's request), WP, PCC, Individual Study Sessions, KR

KENTUCKY

Morehead State University *(4-year)*
Disability Services
223 Allie Young Hall
Morehead, Kentucky 40351
606-783-5188; Fax: 606-783-5083
E-mail: e.day@moreheadstate.edu
Web Site: www.morehead.edu
Coordinator: Evangeline Day
Services: OET, ITS, SGTS, TT, BSS, DP, FALD (at student's request), TR (provided by student), Kurzweil 3000

Murray State University *(4-year)*
Services for Students with Learning Disabilities
P.O. Box 9
Murray, Kentucky 42071-0009
270-762-2018; Fax: 270-762-4339
E-mail:
cindy.clemson@murraystate.edu
Web Site:
www.murraystate.edu/secsv/ssld
Coordinator: Cindy Clemson
Services: OET, ITS, SGTS, TR, TT, BSS, DP, FALD
Scholarships: See page 429.

Northern Kentucky Univ. *(4-year)*
Office of Disability Services
Nunn Drive
Highland Heights, Kentucky 41099
859-572-5180
E-mail: roths@nku.edu
Web Site: www.nku.edu
Director: Sue Roth
Services: OET, ITS, SGTS, LCL, AA, NTA, TT, TR, BSS, DP, FALD

University of Louisville: Belknap Campus *(4-year)*
Disability Resource Center
120 Robbins Hall
Louisville, Kentucky 40292
502-852-6938; Fax: 502-852-0924
E-mail:
clpatu01@qwise.louisville.edu
Web Site: www.louisville.edu
Director: Cathy Patus
Services: OET, ITS, AA, NTA, TR, TT, BSS, DP, FALD (at student's request), KR, WP, PCC, LDSG

Western Kentucky Univ. *(4-year)*
Student Disability Services
1906 College Heights Blvd., #21052
Bowling Green, Kentucky 42101-3576
270-745-5004; 207-745-3030 TDD
Fax: 270-745-6289
Web Site: www.wku.edu
Director: David Coffey
Services: OET, AA, NTA, TT, TR, FALD, WP, PCC

LOUISIANA

Louisiana State University at Alexandria *(2-year with limited 4-year program)*
Services for Students with Disabilities (SSD)
8100 Highway 71 South
Alexandria, Louisiana 71302
318-473-6545; Fax: 318-473-6580
E-mail: studentservices@lsua.edu
Web Site: www.lsua.edu
Director: Dr. Dee Slavant
Services: LCL, AA, TR, BSS, DP, FALD

University of Louisiana at Lafayette *(4-year)*
Services for Students with Disabilities
104 University Circle, P.O. Box 44010
Lafayette, Louisiana 70504-4010
337-482-5252; Fax: 337-482-1340
E-mail: ssd@louisiana.edu
Web Sites: www.louisiana.edu
www.disability.louisiana.edu
Coordinator: Dr. Carol Landry
Services: OET, ITS, SGTS, AA, LCL, NTA, TT, TR, BSS, FALD, PCC, Adaptive Computer Lab

University of Louisiana at Monroe *(4-year)*
Counseling Center - Students with Special Needs
700 University Drive
Monroe, Louisiana 71209-1135
318-342-5220
E-mail: kfoster@ulm.edu
Director: Karen Foster
Web Site: www.ulm.edu
Services: OET, ITS, AA, NTA, TT, BSS, DP, FALD, WP, PCC

MARYLAND

Catonsville Community College *(2-year)*
Disability Support Services
800 South Rolling Road
Baltimore, Maryland 21228
410-455-6946, 410-455-4163 TTY
E-mail: jhodge@ccbcmd.edu
Web Site: www.ccbcmd.edu
Coordinator: Jill Hodge
Services: OET, ITS, SGTS, LCL, NTA, TR, TT, BSS, FALD, KR, WP, PCC, Computer Lab

Chesapeake College *(2-year)*
Disability Services for Students
P.O. Box 8
Wye Mills, Maryland 21679
410-822-5400 X250,
410-827-9164 TDD
Web Site: www.chesapeake.edu
Services: OET, ITS, SGTS, LCL, NTA, TR, TT, BSS, DP, FALD, WP, PCC

Hagerstown Community College *(2-yr)*
Student Support Services
11400 Robinwood Drive
Hagerstown, Maryland 21742
301-790-2800 x551; Fax: 301-739-0737
Coordinator/Testing and Tutoring: Dawn Schoenenberger
Services: OET, ITS, SGTS, LCL, AA, NTA, TR, TT, FALD, WP, KR, Assistive Technology, Scanners, Bookwise/Reading Edge

Harford Community College *(2-year)*
Disability Support Services
401 Thomas Run Road
Bel Air, Maryland 21015-1698
410-836-4402, 410-836-4199 TTY;
Fax: 410-836-4200
E-mail: bnaughto@harford.edu
Web Site: www.harford.edu
Director: Brandy Naughton
Services: OET, ITS, SGTS, LCL, AA, NTA, TR, TT, BSS, DP, FALD (at student's request), KR, WP, PCC

Johns Hopkins University *(4-year)*
Disability Services
3400 North Charles Street
Baltimore, Maryland 21218
410-516-8949; Fax: 410-516-5300
E-mail: phayeslip@jhu.edu
Web Site: www.jhu.edu

Associate Director: Peggy Hayeslip
Services: OET, ITS, SGTS, LCL, AA, NTA, TR, BSS, FALD, KR, WP, PCC, Computer Technology

Loyola College in Maryland *(4-yr)*
Center for Academic Services and Support
4501 North Charles Street
Baltimore, Maryland 21210
410-617-2663; Fax: 410-617-2034
E-mail: labrown@loyola.edu
Web Site: www.loyola.edu
Assistant Director: Leslie Brown
Services: OET, ITS, SGTS, LCL, AA, NTA, TR, TT, BSS, FALD, PCC, Computers, LDSG, Adaptive Equipment, Kurzweil 3000, Dragon Dictate

Towson State University *(4-year)*
Disability Support Services
7720 York Road
Towson, Maryland 21252
410-704-2638; 410-704-4423 TTD; Fax: 410-704-4247
E-mail: swillemin@towson.edu
Web Site: www.towson.edu
Director: Susan Willemin
Services: OET, ITS, SGTS, LCL, AA, NTA, TR, TT, BSS, FALD, KR, WP, PCC

MASSACHUSETTS

Bentley College *(4-year)*
Counseling & Student Development
175 Forest Street
Waltham, Massachusetts 02452-4705
781-891-2274; Fax; 781-891-2474
E-mail: rdanchise@bentley.edu
Web Site: www.bentley.edu
Director: Roger Danchise, Ph.D.
Services: OET, ITS, LCL, AA, NTA, TT, TR, BSS, FALD, LDSG, KR, WP

Boston College *(4-year)*
Disability Services
140 Commonwealth Avenue
Chestnut Hill, Massachusetts 02467
617-552-8055; Fax: 617-552-6075
Assistant Director: Kathleen Duggan
E-mail: dugganka@bc.edu
Web Site: www.bc.edu
Services: OET, ITS, SGTS, LCL, NTA, AA, TT, TR, FALD, KR, WP

Brandeis University *(4-year)*
Disabilities and Support Services
415 South Street
Waltham, Massachusetts 02454
781-736-3470
E-mail: brodgers@brandeis.edu
Web Site: www.brandeis.edu
Coordinator: Beth Rodgers-Kay
Services: ET, TR, TT, BSS, AA

Bristol Community College *(2-yr)*
Office of Disability Services
777 Elsbree Street
Fall River, Massachusetts 02720-7395
508-678-2811 x2955; Fax: 508-730-3297
Web Site: www.bristol.mass.edu
Director: Jan Baptist
Services: OET, ITS, SGTS, LCL, AA, NTA, TR, TT, BSS, DP, FALD, WP, PCC, Adaptive Computing
Scholarships: See page 450.

Clark University *(4-year)*
Disability Services/Academic Advising Center
950 Main Street
Worcester, Massachusetts 01610
508-793-7468; Fax: 508-421-3700
E-mail: jdaigneault@clarku.edu
Web Site: www.clarku.edu
Coordinator: Jane Daigneault
Services: OET, ITS, SGTS, LCL, AA, TT, BSS, FALD

Eastern Nazarene College *(4-year)*
Center for Academic Services
23 East Elm Avenue
Quincy, Massachusetts 02170
617-745-3836
E-mail: cas@enc.edu
Web Site: www.enc.edu
Services: OET, ITS, SGTS, AA, BSS, DP, FALD (at student's request), Computer Lab

Harvard College *(4-year)*
Accessible Education Office
20 Garden Street
Cambridge, Massachusetts 02138
617-496-8707; 617-496-3720 TTY
E-mail: aeo@fas.harvard.edu
Web Site: www.college.harvard.edu
Director: Louise H. Russell
Services: OET, ITS, NTA, TR, TT, BSS, FALD, Volunteer Readers

Smith College *(4-year)*
Office of Disability Services
College Hall, Room 9
Northampton, Massachusetts 01063
413-585-2071; 2072 TTY/TDD;
Fax: 413-585-4498
E-mail: lrausche@smith.edu
Web Site: www.smith.edu/ods
Director: Laura Rauscher
Services: OET, ITS, SGTS, LCL, NTA, TR, TT, FALD (at student's request)

University of Massachusetts: Boston *(4-year)*
Ross Center for Disability Services
100 Morrissey Blvd.
Boston, Massachusetts 02125-3393
617-287-7430; Fax: 617-287-5525
E-mail: marshall.milner@umb.edu
Web Site: www.umb.edu
Acting Director: Marshall Milner
Services: OET, ITS, AA, NTA, BSS, Adaptive Computer Lab, Preferred Registration

University of Massachusetts: Dartmouth *(4-year)*
Disabled Student Services
285 Old Westport Road
North Dartmouth, Massachusetts 02747-2300
508-999-8711; Fax: 508-999-8719
E-mail: cjohnson@umassd.edu
Director: Carole J. Johnson
Services: OET, ITS, AA, NTA, TR, TT, FALD, LDSG, Special Workshops

Wheaton College *(4-year)*
Disability Services
25 East Main Street
Norton, Massachusetts 02766
508-286-8215, 508-286-5682 TTY;
Fax: 508-286-5621
E-mail: mbledsoe@wheatonma.edu
Web Site: www. wheatoncollege.edu
Assistant Dean: Martha Bledsoe
Services: OET, LCL, AA, NTA, TT, TR, BBS, FALD
Scholarships: See page 431.

MICHIGAN

Adrian College *(4-year)*
Access Services for Students with a Disability
110 South Madison Street
Adrian, Michigan 49221-2575
517-265-5161 x4413;
Fax: 517-264-3181
E-mail: jmccloskey@adrian.edu
Web Site: www.adrian.edu
Director: Jane McCloskey
Services: OET, ITS, SGTS, LCL, AA, NTA, TR, TT, BSS, DP, FALD

Ferris State University *(4-year)*
Disabilities Services
820 Campus Drive, Starr 317
Big Rapids, Michigan 49307-2251
231-591-3772 V/TDD;
Fax: 231-591-3686

E-mail: merwine@ferris.edu
Web Site: www.ferris.edu
Director: Eunice Merwin
Services: OET, ITS, SGTS, AA, NTA, TT, TR, BS, DP, FALD, Arkenstone Reader

Glen Oaks Community College *(2-year)*
Disability Support Services
62249 Shimmel Road
Centreville, Michigan 49032-9719
269-467-9945; Fax: 269-467-9068
E-mail: lraven@glenoaks.edu
Web Site: www.glenoaks.edu
Counselor: Lyle Raven
Services: OET, ITS, SGTS, LCL, AA, NTA, TT, TR, BSS, DP, FALD

Grand Rapids Community College *(2-year)*
Disability Support Services
143 Bostwick Avenue NE
Grand Rapids, Michigan 49503
616-234-4140; Fax: 616-234-4965
Coordinator: Anne Sherman
Services: OET, ITS, LCL, AA, NTA, TT, BSS, Academic Advising

Hope College *(4-year)*
Academic Support Center
Van Zoeren Room 269
41 Graves Place
Holland, Michigan 49423
616-395-7830; Fax: 616-395-77617
E-mail: jheisler@hope.edu
Web Site: www.hope.edu
Director: Jacqueline Heisler
Services: ET, ITS, SGTS, LCL, AA, NTA, TR, BSS, FALD (at student's request), KR, WP, LDSG, Computer Lab

Jackson Community College *(2-yr)*
Center for Student Success
2111 Emmons Road
Jackson, Michigan 49201
517-796-8415
E-mail: bethany.rogers@jccmi.edu
Web Site: www.jccmi.edu
Coordinator: Bethany Rogers
Services: OET, ITS, SGTS, AA, NTA, TT, TR, BSS workshops, FALD

Kalamazoo Valley Community College *(2-year)*
Special Services
6767 West O Avenue
Kalamazoo, Michigan 49003
269-488-4397, 269-488-4358 TTY
Web Site: www.kvcc.edu
Special Services Advisor: Lois Baldwin X5384
Services: OET, ITS, SGTS, LCL, AA, NTA, TR, TT, BSS, DP, FALD, KR, WP, PCC, Assistance with Organization, Time Management Skills

Kellogg Community College *(2-yr)*
Support Services
450 North Avenue
Battle Creek, Michigan 49017
269-965-4150
E-mail: supportservices@kellogg.edu
Web Site: www.kellogg.edu
Services: OET, ITS, SGTS, LCL, NTA, TR, TT, BSS, DP, FALD, PCC, KR, WP

Lake Michigan College *(2-year)*
Special Populations
2755 East Napier Avenue
Benton Harbor, Michigan 49022
269-927-8100
E-mail: moely@lakemichigancollege.edu
Web Site: www.lakemichigancollege.edu

Coordinator: Eloise L. Moely x5191
Services: OET, ITS, SGTS, LCL, NTA, TR, TT, BSS, DP, FALD, PCC, KR, WP

Madonna University *(4-year)*
Offices of Disability Resources
36600 Schoolcraft Road
Livonia, Michigan 48150-1173
734-432-5641 V/TTY
E-mail: mmeldrum@madonna.edu
Web Site: www.madonna.edu
Director: Michael W. Meldrum
Services: OET, ITS, SGTS, AA, NTA, TR, BSS, FALD, PCC, WP

Michigan Technological University *(4-year)*
Services for Students with Disabilities
1400 Townsend Drive
Houghton, Michigan 49931-1295
906-487-2212; Fax: 906-487-3060
E-mail: gbmelton@mtu.edu
Web Site: www.mtu.edu
Coordinator: Dr. Gloria B. Melton
Services: OET, ITS SGTS, LCL, AA, NTA, TR, TT, BSS, FALD, Special Enlargement Monitor, CCTV

Mid-Michigan Community College *(2-year)*
Disability Services
1375 South Clare Avenue
Harrison, Michigan 48625-9247
989-386-6636
Web Site: www.midmich.edu
Coordinator: Susan Cobb
5805 East Pickard Street
Mount Pleasant, Michigan 48858
989-773-6622
ASC Specialist: Ann Kedrowski
Services: OET, ITS SGTS, LCL, AA, NTA, TR, TT, BSS, DP, FALD

Mott Community College *(2-year)*
DisAbility Services for Students
1401 East Court Street
Flint, Michigan 48503
810-762-0399 V/TTY
E-mail: sbutka@mcc.edu
Web Site: www.mcc.edu
Director: Delores Deen
Services: OET, ITS, SGTS, NTA, TR, TT, DP, FALD, KR, WP, PCC

Oakland Community College *(2-yr)*
Programs for Academic Support Services (PASS)
2900 Featherstone Road
Auburn Hills, Michigan 48326
248-232-4080; 248-232-4081 TDD
Web Site: www.oaklandcc.edu
Services: OET, LCL, ITS, SGTS, NTA, TR, TT, BSS, DP, FALD

Oakland University *(4-year)*
Disability Support Services
2200 North Squirrel Road
Rochester, Michigan 48309-4401
248-370-3266
E-mail: lgsisson@oakland.edu; dss@oakland.edu
Web Site: www4.oakland.edu
Director: Linda G. Sisson
Services: OET, ITS, SGTS, LCL, AA, NTA, TR, TT, BSS, FALD (at student's request), DP, scanned/E-text

Saginaw Valley State University *(4-year)*
Disability Services
7400 Bay Road
University Center, Michigan 48710
989-964-7000; Fax: 989-964-7258
E-mail: disability-services@svsu.edu
Web Site: www.svsu.edu/disabilityservices
Services: OET, ITS, SGTS, LCL, AA, NTA, TR, TT, BSS, FALD, WP, PCC,

Computerized Tutorials Screen Readers, Adaptive Technology

St. Clair County Community College *(2-year)*
Academic Achievement Center
323 Erie, P.O. Box 5015
Port Huron, Michigan 48061-5015
810-989-5555; Fax: 810-989-5579
E-mail: npecorilli@sc4.edu
Web Site: www.sc4.edu
Counselor: Nancy Pecorilli
Services: OET, ITS, SGTS, LCL, AA, NTA, TR, TT, BSS, FALD, KR

Southwestern Michigan College *(2-year)*
Special Populations Program
58900 Cherry Grove Road
Dowagiac, Michigan 49047
269-687-4801; 800-456-8675; Fax: 269-782-1331
E-mail: ssullivan@swmich.edu
Web Site: www.swmich.edu
Coordinator: Susan Sullivan
Services: OET, ITS, SGTS, LCL, AA, NTA, TT, TR, BSS, DP, FALD, WP, PCC, LDSG (in the form of a special study skills class).
Scholarships: See page 451.

MINNESOTA

Concordia University *(4-year)*
Disability Services
275 North Syndicate Street
St. Paul, Minnesota 55104-5494
651-641-8272 V/TTY
E-mail: schrieber@csp.edu
Web Site: www.csp.edu/disability
Director: David Schreiber
Services: OET, ITS, SGTS, LCL, AA, NTA, TR, TT, BSS, DP, FALD

Crown College *(4-year)*
Academic Success and Study Lab
8700 College View Drive
St. Bonifacius, Minnesota 55375-9001
952-446-4216; Fax: 952-446-4149
E-mail: carlbluml@crown.edu
Web Site: www.crown.edu
Director: Lori Carlblum
Services: OET, ITS, SGTS, LCL, AA, NTA, TT, TR, BSS, FALD

Minnesota State University, Moorhead *(4-year)*
Disability Services
1104 7th Avenue South
Moorhead, Minnesota 56563
218-477-5859; Fax: 218-477-2430
E-mail: toutges@mnstate.edu
Web Site: www.mnstate.edu
Coordinator: Greg Toutges
Services: OET, NTA, TT, FALD

Ridgewater College *(2-year)*
Disability Services
2 Century Avenue
Hutchinson, Minnesota 55350
800-722-1151
Web Site: www.ridgewater.mnscu.edu
Director: Tammy Becker
Services: OET, ITS, SGTS, LCL, NTA, AA, TR, TT, BSS, DP, FALD, WP, PCC, LDSG

Rochester Community and Technical College *(2-year)*
Disability Services
851 30th Avenue SE
Rochester, Minnesota 55904
507-280-2968
E-mail: travis.kromminga@roch.edu
Web Site: www.roch.edu
Director: Travis Kromminga
Services: OET, ITS, AA, NTA, TR, TT, BSS, FALD, KR, WP, Adaptive Computer Lab

St. Cloud State University *(4-year)*
Student Disability Services
216 Atwood Center
720 Fourth Avenue, South
St. Cloud, Minnesota 56301-4498
320-308-4080
E-mail: sds@stcloudstate.edu
Web Site: www.stcloudstate.edu/sds
Director: Owen Zimpel
Services: OET, NTA, TT, FALD

MISSISSIPPI

University of Mississippi *(4-year)*
Student Disability Services
234 Martindale Center, PO Box 1848
University, Mississippi 38677
662-915-7128; Fax: 662-915-5972
E-mail: sds@olemiss.edu
Web Site: www.olemiss.edu
Director: Ardessa Minor
Services: OET, ITS, SGTS, LCL, AA, NTA, TR, TT, BSS, FALD

MISSOURI

Fontbonne University *(4-year)*
The Kinkel Center for Academic Resources
6800 Wydown Blvd.
St. Louis, Missouri 63105
314-719-3627; Fax: 314-719-3614
Director: Jane Snyder, Ed.D.
E-mail: jsnyder@fontbonne.edu
Web Site: www.fontbonne.edu
Services: OET, ITS, SGTS, NTA, TR, BSS, DP, FALD KR, WP, PCC

Metropolitan Community College Maple Woods *(2-year)*
Access Services
2601 NE Barry Road
Kansas City, Missouri 64156
816-437-3095; Fax: 816-437-3049
E-mail: janet.weaver@mcckc.edu
Web Site: www.mcckc.edu
Outreach Counselor: Janet Weaver
Services: OET, ITS, SGTS, NTA, TR, TT, BSS, DP, WP, PCC, FALD

Mineral Area College *(2-year)*
Disability Support Services
5270 Flat River Road
Park Hills, Missouri 63601
573-518-2152; Fax: 573-518-2354
E-mail: lleftridge@mineralarea.edu
Web Site: www.mineralarea.edu
Director: Lisa Leftridge
Services: OET, ITS, SGTS, LCL, AA, NTA, TR, TT, BSS, DP, PCC, FALD, Assistive Technology

University of Missouri: Kansas City *(4-year)*
Services for Students with Disabilities
5100 Rockhill
Kansas City, Missouri 64110
816-235-5696; Fax: 816-235-6363
E-mail: disability@umkc.edu
Web Site: www.umkc.edu
Coordinator: Scott Laurent
Services: OET, NTA, TT, TR, FALD, WP, BSS, KR, PCC, LCL

Washington University in St. Louis *(4-year)*
Disability Resources
One Brookings Drive, Box 1136
St. Louis, Missouri 63130
314-935-4062
E-mail: kmosley@wustl.edu
Web Site: www.wustl.edu
Coordinator: Kaslina Love Mosley
Services: OET, NTA, TT, TR, FALD, BSS, KR, WP, PCC

MONTANA

Montana State University: Billings *(4-year)*
Disability Support Services
1500 University Drive
Billings, Montana 59101-0298
406-657-2283 V/TTY;
Fax: 406-657-1658
E-mail: tcarey@msubillings.edu
Web Site: www.msubillings.edu/dss
Director: Trudy Carey
Services: OET, ITS, SGTS, LCL, AA, NTA, TT, TR, BSS, PCC, FALD (at student's request), KR, Arkenstone, Open Book
Scholarships: See page 432.

Montana State University: Great Falls College of Technology *(2-year)*
Disability Services
2100 16th Avenue South
Great Falls, MT 59405
(406) 771-4311; Fax: (406) 771-4342
E-mail: jdavis@msugf.edu
Web Site: www.msugf.edu
Director: Jill Davis
Services: OET, ITS, SGTS, NTA, TR, BSS, DP, AA, FALD (at student's request), Voice Recognition Software, Screen/Test Readers, Word Prediction Software

Montana State University: Northern *(4-year)*
Disability Services
Cowan Hall 213C
Havre, Montana 59501
406-265-4117
E-mail: wjlanier@msun.edu
Web Site: www.msun.edu
Coordinator: William Lanier
Services: OET, ITS, SGTS, AA, NTA, TR, TT, BSS, WP, PCC

NEBRASKA

Doane College *(4-year)*
Student Support Services
1014 Boswell Avenue
Crete, Nebraska 68333-2430
800-333-6263, 402-826-8586;
Fax: 402-826-8600
E-mail: sherri.hanigan@doane.edu
Web Site: www.doane.edu
Director: Sherri Hanigan
Services: OET, ITS, SGTS, LCL, NTA, TT, TR, BSS, DP, FALD (at student's request)

University of Nebraska: Kearney *(4-year)*
Student Support Services
905 West 25th Street
Kearney, Nebraska 68849
308-865-8214; Fax: 308-865-8286
E-mail: zellerg@unk.edu
Web Site: www.unk.edu
Director: Dr. Gail Zeller
308-865-8988
Services: OET, ITS, SGTS, BSS, FALD (at student's request), KR, WP, PCC

University of Nebraska: Lincoln *(4-year)*
Services for Students with Disabilities
132 Canfield Admin. Bldg.
P.O. Box 880401
Lincoln, Nebraska 68588-0401
402-472-3787; Fax: 402-472-0080
E-mail: vcheney2@unl.edu
Web Site: www.unl.edu/ssd
Director: Veva Cheney
Services: OET, LCL, NTA, TT, WP, Priority Registration, Computers with Assistive Technology (Zoom Text, Jaws, WYNN, Inspiration, Read & Write, Dragon Naturally Speaking), Braille, Sign Language Interpreters, C Print (real time captioning) and Accessible Rooms

Western Nebraska Community College *(2-year)*
Disability Services
1601 East 27th Street
Scottsbluff, Nebraska 69361-1899
308-635-6090
E-mail: stephens@wncc.net
Web Site: www.wncc.net
Director: Norm Stephenson
Services: OET, ITS, LCL, NTA, TR, TT, BSS, DP, FALD, WP, PCC

NEW HAMPSHIRE

Hesser College *(2-year)*
Academic Support Center
3 Sundial Avenue
Manchester, NH 03103
603-668-6660
Web Site: www.hesser.edu
Director: Deborah Jameson
Services: ITS, SGTS, LCL, TR, BSS, FALD, WP, PCC, Computer Lab

NEW JERSEY

Gloucester County College *(2-year)*
Dept. of Special Needs Services
1400 Tanyard Road
Sewell, New Jersey 08080
856-415-2281; Fax: 856-468-6902
E-mail: dcook@gccnj.edu
Web Site: www.gccnj.edu
Coordinator: Dennis Cook
Services: OET, ITS, SGTS, LCL, AA, NTA, TR, TT, BSS, DP, FALD, KR, WP

NEW MEXICO

New Mexico State Univ. *(4-year)*
Services for Students with Disabilities
P.O. Box 30001, MS 4149
Las Cruces, New Mexico 88003-8001
505-646-6840; 505-646-1918 TDD; Fax: 505-646-5222
Web Site: www.nmsu.edu/~ssd
Coordinator: Michael Armendariz
Services: OET, LCL, NTA, TT, FALD, WP, Arkenstone, Brattle Accessible Computers

New Mexico Institute of Mining and Technology *(4-year)*
Counseling and Disability Services
801 LeRoy Place
Socorro, New Mexico 87801
505-835-5443
Web Site: www.nmt.edu
Director: Laurie Tacheny Borden
Services: OET, ITS, SGTS, LCL, NTA, TT, FALD, WP, One-on-One Counseling

Northern New Mexico College *(2-year)*
Special Needs Department
921 Paseo de Onate
Espanola, New Mexico 87532
505-747-2152; Fax: 505-747-2180
E-mail: kimd@nnmc.edu
Web Site: www.nnmc.edu
Director: Kim Dickman
Services: OET, ITS, SGTS, BSS, NTA, TR, DP, AA, Library Assistance, Resume Assistance

Santa Fe Community College *(2-yr)*
Special Services
6401 South Richards Ave
Santa Fe, New Mexico 87502-4187
505-428-1701
E-mail: dmatsui@sfccnm.edu
Web Site: www.sfccnm.edu
Coordinator: Dennis Matsui
Services: OET, ITS, LCL, NTA, TR, TT, BSS, DP, FALD

NEW YORK

Bryant and Stratton College: Henrietta Campus *(2-year)*
Learning Center

1225 Jefferson Road
Rochester, New York 14623
585-292-5627
E-mail: dmarcuri@bryantstratton.edu
Web Site: www.bryantstratton.edu
Counselor: Dawn M. Arcuri
Services: OET, ITS, SGTS, AA, NTA, TT, BSS, FALD (at student's request)

Cazenovia College *(2-year & 4-year)*
Student Support Services
43 Lincklaen Street, 1st Floor
Cazenovia, New York 13035
1-800-654-3210 X7308; 315-655-7308
Web Site: www.cazenovia.edu
Director: Cynthia Pratt
Services: ITS, SGTS, TR, TT, DP, FALD

City University of New York (CUNY)

City College – CUNY *(4-year)*
Student Disability Services
Convent Avenue at 138th Street
New York, New York 10031
212-650-5913; Fax: 212-650-5772
Acting Director: Laura Farres
E-mail: sds@ccny.cuny.edu
Web Site: www.ccny.cuny.edu/student_affairs/disabilities
Services: OET, ITS, SGTS, LCL, TT, TR, BSS, FALD, AA, NTA, KR, WP, PCC

College of Staten Island – CUNY *(4-year)*
Disability Services
1P-101, 2800 Victory Blvd.
Staten Island, New York 10314
718-982-2510, 718-982-2515 TTY; Fax: 718-982-2117
E-mail: nielson@mail.csi.cuny.edu
Web Site: www.csi.cuny.edu/disabilityservices
Director: Margaret Venditti
Services: OET, ITS, SGTS, LCL, AA, NTA, TR, TT, BSS, DP, FALD (at student's request), KR, WP, PCC
Summer Program: See page 408.

Queens College – CUNY *(4-year)*
Office of Special Services for Students with Disabilities
171 Kiely Hall
65-30 Kissena Blvd.
Flushing, New York 11367-1597
718-997-5870; Fax: 718-997-5895
Web Site: www.qc.edu
Director: Dr. Mirian Detres-Hickey
Services: OET, ITS, SGTS, LCL, NTA, TR, TT, BSS, DP, FALD, KR, Support Groups
Summer Program: See page 411.

Colgate University *(4-year)*
Academic Program Support
13 Oak Drive
Hamilton, New York 13346-1386
315-228-7225, 315-228-6001 TTY; Fax: 315-824-7831
E-mail: lwaldman@mail.colgate.edu
Web Site: www.colgate.edu
Director: Lynn Waldman
Services: OET, ITS, SGTS, LCL, AA, NTA, TR, TT, BSS, FALD, WP, LDSG

College of New Rochelle *(4-year)*
Learning Disabilities Student Services
29 Castle Place
New Rochelle, New York 10805
914-654-5599; Fax: 914-654-5866
E-mail: jbristol@cnr.edu
Web Site: www.cnr.edu
Director: Joan Bristol
Services: OET, ITS, AA, NTA, TT, TR, PCC, FALD

Columbia-Greene Community College *(2-year)*
Office of Special Services
4400 Route 23

Hudson, New York 12534
518-828-4181 x3437,
518-828-1399 TTY
Web Site: www.sunycgcc.edu
Director: Catherine M. Tretheway
Services: OET, ITS, SGTS, LCL, NTA, TR, TT, BSS, DP, FALD, WP, KR, PCC

Cornell University *(4-year)*
Office of Equal Opportunity
234 Day Hall
Ithaca, New York 14853-2801
607-254-4636; Fax: 607-255-5396
Web Site: www.cornell.edu
Services: OET, ITS, LCL, AA, TR, NTA, TT, FALD, KR, WP, PCC, LDSG, Mentoring Program

Dutchess Community College *(2-year)*
Disabled Student Services
53 Pendell Road
Poughkeepsie, New York 12601
914-431-8037
E-mail: perez@sunydutchess.edu
Web Site: www.sunydutchess.edu
Director: Paula Perez
Services: OET, ITS, SGTS, LCL, AA, NTA, TR, TT, BSS, DP, FALD, KR, WP, PCC, Computer Lab
Scholarship: See page 453.

D'Youville College *(4-year)*
Disability Services
320 Porter Avenue
Buffalo, New York 14201
716-829-7775
E-mail: connorsm@dyc.edu
Web Site: www.dyc.edu
Director: Sr. Mary Brendan Connors
Services: OET, ITS, SGTS, LCL, AA, NTA, BSS, DP, FALD (at student's request)

Fulton Montgomery Community College *(2-year)*
Learning Center
2805 State Route 67
Johnstown, New York 12095
518-762-5502
E-mail: ellie.fosmire@fmcc.suny.edu
Web Site: www.fmcc.suny.edu
Coordinator: Ellie Fosmire
Services: OET, ITS, SGTS, LCL, BSS, NTA, TR, TT, DP, FALD

Ithaca College *(4-year)*
Academic Support Services for Students with Disabilities
953 Danby Road
Ithaca, New York 14850
607-274-1005; Fax: 607-274-3957
E-mail: acssd@ithaca.edu
Web Site: www.ithaca.edu
Coordinator: Leslie Shettino
Services: OET, AA, NTA, TR, TT, FALD

Jamestown Community College *(2-year)*
Disability Support Services
P.O. Box 20, 525 Falconer Street
Jamestown, New York 14702-0020
716-665-5220 x2459;
Fax: 716-487-2626
E-mail: nancycallahan@mail.sunyjcc.edu
Web Site: www.sunyjcc.edu
Coordinator: Nancy Callahan
Services: OET, ITS, AA, NTA, TR, TT, BSS, DP, FALD (at student's request)

Medaille College *(4-year)*
Office of Disability Services
18 Agassiz Circle
Buffalo, New York 14214
716-880-2391
Web Site: www.medaille.edu

Services: OET, ITS, NTA, TR, BSS, DP, FALD

Nassau Community College (*2-yr*)
Center for Students with Disabilities
One Education Drive
Garden City, New York 11530-6793
516-572-7241; Fax: 516-572-9874
E-mail: schimsj@ncc.edu
Web Site: www.sunynassau.edu
Director: Janis Schimsky
Services: ET, ITS, SGTS, LCL, AA, NTA, TT, BSS, KR, WP, PCC

New York Institute of Technology (*4-year*)
Disability Services
P.O. Box 8000, Northern Blvd.
Old Westbury, New York 11568-8000
516-686-7683; Fax: 516-686-7891
E-mail: cdavid01@nyit.edu
Web Site: www.nyit.edu
Coordinator: Colleen Davidson
Services: OET, ITS, NTA, TR, FALD (at student's request), PCC, BSS, Computers.
Scholarships at Old Westbury: See page 434.

Niagara County Community College (*2-year*)
Disabled Student Services
3111 Saunders Settlement Road
Sanborn, New York 14132-9460
716-614-6280; Fax: 716-614-6700
E-mail: drilling@niagaracc.suny.edu
Web Site: www.niagaracc.suny.edu
Coordinator: Karen A. Drilling
Services: OET, ITS, SGTS, LCL, NTA, TR, BSS, DP, FALD (at student's request), WP, PCC,
Liaison with Outside Agencies

Niagara University (*4-year*)
Specialized Support Services
Seton Hall 1st Floor
Niagara University, New York 14109
716-286-8076; Fax: 716-286-8063
E-mail: ds@niagara.edu
Web Site: www.niagara.edu
Services: OET, SGTS, LCL, AA, TR, NTA, TT, BSS, FALD, KR, WP, PCC, Monitoring of Academic Progress, Access to electronic textbooks based on eligibility

Pace University (*4-year*)
Disability Services
1 Pace Plaza
New York, New York 10038
212-346-1526
E-mail: rraskin@pace.edu
Web Site: www.pace.edu
Coordinator: Dr. Richard H. Raskin
Services: OET, ITS, SGTS, AA, NTA, FALD, PCC

Rensselaer Polytechnic Inst. (*4-year*)
Disability Services for Students
110 Eighth Street
Troy, New York 12180
518-276-2746; Fax: 518-276-4839
Web Site: www.rpi.edu
Assistant Dean: Debra Hamilton
Services: OET, ITS, SGTS, LCL, AA, NTA, TR, TT, BSS, FALD

Russell Sage College (*4-year*)
Disability Services
45 Ferry Street
Troy, New York 12180
518-292-1764
E-mail: academicsupport@sage.edu
Web Site: www.sage.edu
Coordinator: M. Katherine Norman
Services: OET, SGTS, LCL, AA, NTA, TR, BSS, FALD, WP, PCC

Skidmore College *(4-year)*
Support Services
815 North Broadway
Saratoga Springs, New York 12866
518-580-8150; Fax: 518-580-5781
E-mail: cguile@skidmore.edu
Web Site: www.skidmore.edu
Coordinator: Cynthia Guile
Services: OET, ITS, LCL, AA, NTA, TR, TT, BSS, FALD

State University of New York (SUNY)

SUNY – Farmingdale State College *(2-year & 4 year)*
Support Services for Students with Disabilities
Route 110
Farmingdale, New York 11735
631-420-2411; Fax: 631-420-2163
E-mail: edelmamp@farmingdale.edu
Web Site: www.farmingdale.edu
Director: Malka Edelman
Services: OET, AA, NTA, TR, DP, FALD (at student's request)

SUNY – College at Brockport *(4-year)*
Office for Students with Disabilities
350 New Campus Drive
Brockport, New York 14420-2947
585-395-5409 V/TTY;
Fax: 585-395-5291
E-mail: osdoffic@brockport.edu
Web Site: www.brockport.edu
Services: OET, LCL, NTA, TT, TR, KR, WP, PCC, FALD, Alternate Test Location, Exams Read Aloud
Scholarships: See page 435.

SUNY – College at Cortland *(4-yr)*
Student Disability Services Office
P. O. Box 2000
Cortland, New York 13045
607-753-2066
E-mail: gomezu@cortland.edu
Web Site: www.cortland.edu
Interim Director: Ute Gomez
Services: OET, ITS, NTA, TR, TT, BSS, PCC, KR, FALD

SUNY – College at New Paltz *(4-yr)*
Disability Resource Center
75 South Manheim Blvd.
New Paltz, New York 12561-2499
845-257-3020; Fax: 845-257-3952
E-mail: drc@newpaltz.edu
Web Site: www.newpaltz.edu
Director: Portia Altman
Services: OET, ITS, SGTS, LCL, AA, NTA, TT, BBS, FALD (at student's request), WP, PCC, LDSG

SUNY – College at Plattsburgh *(4-year)*
Student Support Services
Angell College Center 110
Plattsburgh, New York 12901
518-564-2810; Fax: 518-564-2807
E-mail: michele.carpentier@plattsburgh.edu
Web Site: www.plattsburgh.edu
Director: Michele Carpentier
Services: OET, ITS, SGTS, LCL, AA, NTA, TR, TT, BSS, DP, FALD (at student's request), KR, WP, PCC, LDSG, Specialized Advisement

SUNY – College of Agriculture and Technology at Cobleskill *(4-year)*
DisAbility Support Services
Route 7
Cobleskill, New York 12043
518-255-5282; Fax: 518-255-6430
E-mail: abarnolk@cobleskill.edu
Web Site: www.cobleskill.edu
Coordinator: Lynn K. Abarno
Services: OET, ITS, SGTS, NTA, BSS, TT, DP, FALD (at student's request)

SUNY – College of Technology at Canton *(4-year)*
Accommodative Services
34 Cornell Drive, Campus Center 235
Canton, New York 13617
315-386-7392; Fax: 315-379-3877
E-mail: leev@canton.edu
Web Site: www.canton.edu
Director: Veigh Mehan Lee
Services: OET, ITS, SGTS, LCL, AA, NTA, TT, TR, BSS, DP, FALD
Scholarships: See page 436.

SUNY – College of Technology at Delhi *(2-year)*
Services for Students with Disabilities
2 Main Street
Delhi, New York 13753
607-746-4593; Fax: 607-746-4368
Web Site: www.delhi.edu
Director: Michele DeFreece
Services: OET, ITS, SGTS, NTA, BSS, DP, FALD, KR

SUNY – College of Technology at Morrisville *(2-year)*
Disability Services
038 Onondaga Hall
Morrisville, New York 13408
315-684-6349; Fax: 315-684-6116
Web Site: www.morrisville.edu
Services: OET, ITS, SGTS, LCL, AA, NTA, TR, BSS, FALD, WP, Voice Input and Output Computer System

SUNY – Institute of Technology at Utica/Rome *(4-year)*
Counseling and Special Programs
208 Campus Center
Utica, New York 13504-3050
315-792-7160; Fax: 315-792-7112
E-mail: mary.browndepass@sunyit.edu
Web Site: www.sunyit.edu
Director: Mary Brown-DePass x7805
Services: OET, ITS, SGTS, LCL, NTA, TR, TT, BSS, FALD, PCC

NORTH CAROLINA

Blue Ridge Community College *(2-year)*
Disability Services
DW Sink Jr Bldg Room 127
Flat Rock, North Carolina 28731
828-694-1813
E-mail: judys@blueridge.edu
Web Site: www.blueridge.edu
Director: Judy Stoneham
Services: OET, ITS, NTA, TR, BSS, KR, FALD

Catawba Valley Community College *(2-year)*
Program for Students with Disabilities
2550 Highway 70 SE
Hickory, North Carolina 28602
828-327-7000 x4222
E-mail: whorvath@cvcc.edu
Web Site: www.cvcc.edu
Director: Wanda Horvath
Services: OET, ITS, AA, NTA, TT, TR, BSS, DP, FALD, PCC

Pitt Community College *(2-year)*
Disability Services
P.O. Drawer 7007, Highway 11S
Greenville, North Carolina 27835-7007
252-493-7294
Web Site: www.pitt.cc.nc.us
Director: Michael L. Bridgers
Services: OET, ITS, SGTS, AA, NTA, TT, TR, BSS, DP, PCC, FALD

Sandhills Community College *(2-yr)*
Disability Services
3395 Airport Road
Pinehurst, North Carolina 28374
910-695-3707

E-mail: ashm@sandhills.edu
Web Site: www.sandhills.edu
DS Provider: Madie Ash
Services: OET, ITS, TT, TR, NTA, DP, PCC, FALD

Tri-County Community College *(2-year)*
Special Services Office
4600 East U.S. 64
Murphy, North Carolina 28906
828-835-4259
E-mail: lhowell@tricounty.edu
Web Site: www.tricountycc.edu
Special Needs Counselor: Linda Howell
Services: OET, ITS, SGTS, LCL, AA, NTA, TR, TT, BSS, DP, FALD, WP, PCC

University of North Carolina: Charlotte *(4-year)*
Disability Services
9201 University City Blvd.
Charlotte, North Carolina 28223
704-687-4355; Fax: 704-687-3226
E-mail: dissrvcs@email.uncc.edu
Web Site: www.ds.uncc.edu
Director: Jo Ann A. Fernald
Services: OET, LCL, AA, NTA, TR, TT, FALD, PCC, Converting Text to Braille
Scholarships: See page 436.

University of North Carolina: Greensboro *(4-year)*
Office of Disability Services
Suite 215 EUC, P.O. Box 26170
Greensboro, North Carolina 27402-6170
336-334-5440 V/TTY; Fax: 336-334-4412
E-mail: ods@uncg.edu
Web Site: www.uncg.edu
Director: Mary Culkin
Services: OET, NTA, TR, TT, BSS, FALD

Western Carolina University (4-yr)
Student Support Services
137 Killian Annex
Cullowhee, North Carolina 28723
(828) 227-7127; FAX: (828) 227-7078
E-mail: mellen@wcu.edu
Web Site: www.wcu.edu
Director: Carol Mellen
Services: OET, ITS, SGTS, LCL, AA, NTA,TR, TT, BSS, FALD, WP, PCC, Arkenstone readers

NORTH DAKOTA

Mayville State University *(4-year)*
Academic Support Center
330 Third Street, NE
Mayville, North Dakota 58257
701-788-4747
E-mail: kyllo@mayvillestate.edu
Web Site: www.mayvillestate.edu
Coordinator: Greta Kyllo
Services: OET, ITS, SGTS, AA, NTA, TR, TT, BSS, DP (algebra and English), PCC, FALD (at student's request), Institutional Membership in RFB&D, Personal Notebook 24-hour Computer Access, WP

University of North Dakota *(4-yr)*
Disability Support Services
P.O. Box 9040
Grand Forks, North Dakota 58202-9040
701-777-3425; Fax: 701-777-4170
E-mail: dss@und.nodack.edu
Web Site: www.und.nodak.edu
Director: Deb Glennen
Services: OET, NTA, TT,

OHIO

Bowling Green State University Firelands *(2-year)*
Disability Services
One University Drive
Huron, Ohio 44839
419-433-5560 x20748, x20614
E-mail: pnemitz@bgnet.bgsu.edu
Web Site: firelands.bgsu.edu
Coordinator: Penny Nemitz
Services: OET, ITS, SGTS, LCL, AA, NTA, TR, BSS, DP, FALD, WP, PCC

Case Western Reserve Univ. *(4-yr)*
Disability Resources
10900 Euclid Avenue
Cleveland, Ohio 44106-7062
216-368-5230; Fax: 216-368-8826
E-mail: disability@case.edu
Web Site: www.case.edu
Coordinator: Susan Sampson
Services: OET, ITS, SGTS, LCL, NTA, TT, TR, BSS, FALD (at student's request), KR, WP, PCC, Electronic Learning Center

Cleveland State University *(4-year)*
Disability Services
2121 Euclid Avenue
Cleveland, Ohio 44115
216-687-2015; Fax: 216-687-9320
E-mail: r.c.yurick@csuohio.edu
Web Site: www.csuohio.edu
Coordinator: Kate Yurick
Services: OET, ITS, SGTS, LCL, AA, NTA, TR, TT, BSS, PCC, FALD, Computer/WordProcessing Stations, Preferred Registration

Columbus State Community College *(2-year)*
Disability Services
550 East Spring Street
Columbus, Ohio 43215
614-287-2570 V/TTY;
Fax: 614-287-6054
E-mail: disability@cscc.edu
Web Site: www.cscc.edu
Director: Wayne Cocchi
Services: OET, ITS, NTA, TR, TT, BSS, DP, Education Plan Report, WP, PCC, Computer Use – Scanner, Voice Synthesis

Cuyahoga Community College: Metropolitan Campus *(2-year)*
Access/Disability Services
2900 Community College Avenue
Cleveland, Ohio 44115-3196
216-987-4344; Fax: 216-987-4941
E-mail: grace.banda@tri-c.edu
Web Site: www.tri-c.edu/access
Coordinator: Grace Banda
Services: OET, ITS, SGTS, LCL, AA NTA, TR, TT, BSS, DP, FALD, KR, WP, PCC, LDSG

Cuyahoga Community College: Western Campus *(2-year)*
Access/Disabled Student Services
11000 West Pleasant Valley Road
Parma, Ohio 44130-5199
216-987-5077; Fax: 216-987-5118
E-mail: rose.kolovrat@tri-c.edu
Web Site: www.tri-c.edu/access
Director: Rose Kolovrat
Services: OET, ITS, SGTS, LCL, NTA, AA, TR, TT, BSS, PCC, FALD (at student's request)

Edison Community College *(2-yr)*
Disability Support Services
1973 Edison Drive
Piqua, Ohio 45356
937-778-7837; Fax: 937-778-1820
E-mail: malolepszy@edisonohio.edu
Web Site: www.edisonohio.edu
Coordinator: Jill Malolepszy-Boeke
Services: OET, ITS, SGTS, AA, NTA, TT, TR, BSS, DP, FALD, PCC

Franklin University *(4-year)*
Disability Services
201 South Grant Avenue
Columbus, Ohio 43215
614-797-4700; Fax: 614-797-4799
E-mail: access@franklin.edu
Web Site: www.franklin.edu
Services: OET, ITS, SGTS, LCL, NTA, TR, TT, BSS, DP, FALD, WP, PCC, LDSG

Kent State University *(4-year)*
Student Accessibility Services
Ground Floor DeWeese Center
Kent, Ohio 44242-0001
330-672-3391; Fax: 330-672-3763
E-mail: lmcgloth@kent.edu
Web Site: www.kent.edu
Coordinator: Laura McGlothlin
Services: OET, ITS, SGTS, LCL, NTA, TT, TR, BSS, FALD, KR, WP, PCC

Ohio Wesleyan Univ. *(4-year)*
Learning Disabilities Assistance Ctr.
61 South Sandusky Street
Delaware, Ohio 43015
740-368-3280
E-*mail:* arc@owu.edu
Web Site: www.owu.edu
Director: Dr. Lydia Block x3857
Services: ET, BSS, TR, FALD
Scholarships: See page 436.

Otterbein College *(4-year)*
Academic Support Center
One Otterbein College
Westerville, Ohio 43081-2006
614-823-1618; Fax: 614-823-1983
E-mail: lmonaghan@otterbein.edu
Web Site: www.otterbein.edu
Coordinator: Leah Monaghan
Services: OET, ITS, BSS, DP, AA, NTA, FALD

Sinclair Community College *(2-year)*
Office of Disability Services
444 West Third Street
Dayton, Ohio 45402-1460
937-512-5113
E-mail: robin.moore-cooper@sinclair.edu
Web Site: www.sinclair.edu
Coordinator: Robin Moore-Cooper
Services: OET, ITS, SGTS LCL, NTA, TR, TT, BSS, DP, FALD, KR, PCC
Scholarships: See page 455.

University of Akron: Wayne College *(2-year)*
Learning Support Services
1901 Smucker Road
Orrville, Ohio 44667
330-684-8963; Fax: 330-684-8989
E-mail: juliabeyeler@uakron.edu
Web Site: www.wayne.uakron.edu
Director: Dr. Julia Beyeler
Services: OET, ITS, LCL, AA, NTA, TR, TT, BSS, DP, FALD (at student's request)

University of Cincinnati *(4-year)*
Disability Services
210 University Pavilion
Cincinnati, Ohio 45221-0213
513-556-6823; Fax: 513-556-1383
E-mail: debra.merchant@uc.edu
Web Site: www.uc.edu
Director: Debra Merchant
Services: OET, ITS, SGTS, LCL, AA, NTA, TR, TT, BSS, DP, FALD, KR and Reading Edge, Scribe for Tests, WP, PCC, Priority Registration

Wright State University (4-year)
Disability Services
3640 Colonel Glenn Highway
Dayton, Ohio 45435-0001
937-775-5680; Fax: 937-775-5844

E-mail:
disabilityservices@wright.edu
Web Site: www.wright.edu
Services: OET, SGTS, LCL, NTA, TT, TR, BSS, DP, PCC, LDSG, Specialized Orientation Classes

OKLAHOMA

East Central University *(4-year)*
Student Support Services
1100 East 14th Street
Ada, Oklahoma 74820
580-310-5300
E-mail: dwest@ecok.edu
Web Site: www.ecok.edu
Director: Dwain West
Services: OET, ITS, SGTS, LCL, NTA, TR, TT, BSS, DP, FALD, PCC, WP

Oral Roberts University *(4-year)*
Disability Services
7777 South Lewis Avenue
Tulsa, Oklahoma 74171
918-495-7018
E-mail: droberson@oru.edu
Web Site: www.oru.edu
Director: Don Roberson
Services: OET, ITS, SGTS, AA, TT, TR, NTA, BSS, FALD, KR, PCC

Rose State College *(2-year)*
Student Disabilities
6420 Southeast 15th Street
Midwest City, Oklahoma 73110
405-733-7407
Web Site: www.rose.edu
Services: OET, ITS, SGTS, AA, NTA, TT, BSS, DP, FALD (at student's request), KR, WP/with Sound Proof, PCC

Tulsa Community College *(2-year)*
disABLED Student Resource Center
909 South Boston Ave., Room 331B
Tulsa, Oklahoma 74119
918-595-7115; Fax: 918-595-8398
E-mail: lwilliam@tulsacc.edu
Web Site: www.tulsacc.edu
Counselor: Yolanda R. Williams
Services: OET, LCL, AA, NTA, TR, TT, BSS, FALD, KR, WP, DP

University of Oklahoma *(4-year)*
Office of Disability Services
620 Elm Avenue, Suite 166
Norman, Oklahoma 73019-0340
405-325-3852; 405-325-4173 TDD;
Fax: 405-325-4491
E-mail: ods@ou.edu
Web Site: www.ou.edu
Director: Suzette Dyer
Services: OET, ITS, LCL, NTA, TT, BSS, FALD, WP, KR, Adaptive Computer Lab (Speech Synthesis, Voice Recognition Software, Braille Printer, Scanner/Reader)

OREGON

Clackamas Community College *(2-year)*
Disability Resource Center (DRC)
19600 South Molalla Avenue
Oregon City, Oregon 97045
503-657-6958 x2324
E-mail: caseys@clackamas.edu
Web Site: www.clackamas.edu
Coordinator: Casey Sims
Services: OET, ITS, SGTS, LCL, AA, NTA, TT, TR, BSS, DP, KR, WP, PCC, FALD
Scholarships: See page 455.

Lane Community College *(2-year)*
Disability Services
4000 East 30th Avenue
Eugene, Oregon 97405-0640
541-463-5150; 541-463-3079 TTY;
Fax: 541-463-4739
E-mail: disabilityservices@lanecc.edu
Web Site: www.lanecc.edu

Director: Nancy Hart
Services: OET, LCL, AA, NTA,TR, TT, FALD, PCC, WP, KR, Advocacy, Personal FM Systems

Oregon State University *(4-year)*
Services for Students with Disabilities
A202 Kerr Administration Bldg.
Corvallis, Oregon 97331
541-737-4098
E-mail: ssd@oregonstate.edu
Web Site: www.oregonstate.edu
Director: Tracy Bentley Townlin
Services: NTA, TR, TT, ITS, FALD, Alternative Testing

Portland Community College *(2-yr)*
Office for Students with Disabilities (OSD)
Sylvania ST 229
Portland, Oregon 97280-0990
503-977-4341; Fax: 503-977-4882
E-mail: wpalmer@pcc.edu
Web Site: www.pcc.edu
Coordinator: Wendy Palmer
Services: OET, ITS, AA, NTA, TR, TT, BSS, DP, PCC, FALD (at student's request),

Portland State University *(4-year)*
Disability Services
P. O. Box 751 – IASC
Portland, Oregon 97207-0751
503-725-4150; FAX: 503-725-4103
E-mail: polly@pdx.edu
Web Site: www.pdx.edu
Assistant Director: Polly Livingston
Services: OET, NTA, BSS, TT, FALD

PENNSYLVANIA

Albright College *(4-year)*
Student Support Services for the Learning Disabled Student
13th & Bern Sts., P.O. Box 15234
Reading, Pennsylvania 19612 -5234
610-921-7662; Fax: 610-921-7659
E-mail: tarchie@alb.edu
Web Site: www.albright.edu
Director: Taffenia Archie
Services: OET, ITS, LCL, NTA, AA, TT, TR, FALD, PCC, LDSG

Allegheny College *(4-year)*
Student Support Services
520 North Main Street
Meadville, Pennsylvania 16335
814-332-2898
E-mail: john.mangine@allegheny.edu
Web Site: www.allegheny.edu
Director: John Mangine
Services: OET, ITS, LCL, AA, NTA, TT, TR, BSS, FALD

Bloomsburg University of PA *(4-yr)*
Student Support Services
400 East Second Street
Bloomsburg, Pennsylvania 17815
570-389-3606; FAX: 570-389-2612
E-mail: mbloskey@bloomu.edu
Web Site: www.bloomu.edu
Director: M. Theresa Bloskey
Services: OET, ITS, SGTS, AA, LCL, NTA, TR, TT, BSS, DP, PCC, FALD

California University of Pennsylvania *(4-year)*
Office for Students with Disabilities (OSD)
250 University Avenue, Box 7
California, Pennsylvania 15419
724-938-5781; Fax: 724-938-4599
E-mail: bilitski@cup.edu
Director: Cheryl Bilitski
Web Site: www.cup.edu/osd
Services: OET, SGT, NTA, BSS, TR, TT, FALD, WP, KR

Community College of Philadelphia *(2-year)*
Center on Disabilities
1700 Spring Garden Street
Philadelphia, Pennsylvania 19130
215-751-8050
Web Site: www.ccp.edu
Director: Fran DiRosa
Services: OET, ITS, SGTS, LCL, AA, NTA, TR, TT, BSS, DP, FALD, Reader Service, Assistive Technology

Drexel University (4-year)
Office of Disability Services
3141 Chestnut Street 81-210
Philadelphia, Pennsylvania 19104
215-895-1401; Fax: 215-895-1402
E-mail: disability@drexel.edu
Web Site: www.drexel.edu
Director: Michele M. Peters
Services: OET, TR, NTA, TT, PCC, Assistive Technology, KR 3000, Dragon Dictate, Voice Recognition Software, Jaws

East Stroudsburg University *(4-yr)*
Disability Services
200 Prospect Street
East Stroudsburg, Pennsylvania 18301-2999
570-422-3954 V / TTY; Fax: 570-422-3918
E-mail: emiller@po-box.esu.edu
Web Site: www3.esu.edu
Coordinator: Edith F. Miller, Ed.D.
Services: OET, ITS, SGTS, LCL, AA, NTA, TR, TT, BSS, FALD, WP, KR
Scholarships: See page 437.

Gettysburg College *(4-year)*
Academic Advising Office
Box 414 College Union Bldg. 280
Gettysburg, Pennsylvania 17325
717-337-6579; Fax: 717-337-6906
Web Site: www.gettysburg.edu
Services: OET, ITS, SGTS, LCL, AA, NTA, TT, TR, BSS, FALD

Indiana University of Pennsylvania *(4-year)*
Disability Support Services
201 Pratt Drive, Pratt Hall Rm 216
Indiana, Pennsylvania 15705
724-357-4067 V / TTY
E-mail: catherine.dugan@iup.edu
Web Site: www.iup.edu
Director: Dr. Catherine Dugan
Services: OET, LCL, AA, NTA, TR, TT, BSS, FALD, KR, WP, PCC

Lafayette College *(4-year)*
Special Needs Support Services
1 Markle Hall
Easton, Pennsylvania 18042
610-330-5080; Fax: 610-330-5711
E-mail: robbinsr@lafayette.edu
Web Site: www.lafayette.edu
Associate Dean of Studies: Ronald E. Robbins
Services: OET, ITS, NTA, BSS, FALD

Lehigh Carbon Community College *(2-year)*
Disability Support Services
4525 Education Park Drive
Schnecksville, Pennsylvania 18078
610-799-1586; Fax: 610-799-1159
E-mail: lkelly@lccc.edu
Web Site: www.lccc.edu
Learning Specialist: Linda Kelly
Services: OET, ITS, SGTS, LCL, AA, NTA, TR, TT, BSS, DP, FALD, KR, WP, PCC, LDSG

Lock Haven University of Pennsylvania *(4-year)*
Disability Services
401 North Fairview Street
Lock Haven, Pennsylvania 17745
570-893-2926

E-mail: rjunco@lhup.edu
Web Site: www.lhup.edu
Director: Dr. Reynol Junco
Services: OET, SGTS, LCL, AA, NTA, TR, TT, BSS, FALD (at student's request)

Manor Junior College *(2-year)*
The Learning Center
700 Fox Chase Road
Jenkintown, Pennsylvania 19046
215-885-2360 x267
E-mail: mlandis@manor.edu
Web Site: www.manor.edu
Director: Michael J. Landis
Services: OET, ITS, SGTS, AA, TR, BSS, DP, FALD, WP

Pennsylvania State University: Berks Campus *(4-year)*
Disability Services
153 Franco
Reading, Pennsylvania 19610
610-396-6410; Fax: 610-396-6026
Web Site: www.bk.psu.edu
Disability Specialist: Susan Anderson
Services: OET, ITS, SGTS, LCL, AA, NTA, TR, TT, BSS, DP, FALD, KR, WP, PCC, LDSG, Computer Lab
Scholarships: See page 437.

University of the Sciences in Philadelphia *(4-year)*
Disability Support Services
600 South Forty Third Street
Philadelphia, Pennsylvania 19104-4495
215-596-8950; Fax: 215-596-8792
E-mail: b.little@usip.edu
Web Site: www.usip.edu
Assistant Dean of Students: Barbara E. Little
Services: OET, ITS, SGTS, AA, NTA, TT, TR, BSS, FALD, PCC

RHODE ISLAND

Brown University *(4-year)*
Disability Support Services
26 Benevolent Street, Box P
Providence, Rhode Island 02912
401-863-9588; Fax: 401-863-1999
E-mail: dss@brown.edu or catherine_axe@brown.edu
Web Site: www.brown.edu/dss
Coordinator: Catherine J. Axe
Services: OET, LCL, AA, NTA, TT, TR, BSS, FALD, KR, WP, PCC, Self-Advocacy Workshop

Providence College *(4-year)*
Disability Support Services
549 River Avenue
Providence, Rhode Island 02918-0001
401-865-2494; Fax: 401-865-1219
E-mail: nkudarau@providence.edu
Web Site: www.providence.edu/oas
Assistant Director: Nicole Kudarauskas
Services: OET, NTA, TT, TR, BSS, Adaptive/Assistive Hardware and Software

University of Rhode Island *(4-yr)*
Disability Services for Students
330 Memorial Union
Kingston, Rhode Island 02881
401-874-2098; Fax: 401-874-5574
E-mail: rohland@uri.edu
Web Site: www.uri.edu/disability
Coordinator: Pamela A. Rohland
Services: OET, LCL, AA, NTA, TT, TR, BSS, FALD, Coaching, Strategy Sessions Groups

SOUTH CAROLINA

Trident Technical College *(2-year)*
Services for Students with Disabilities

P.O. Box 118067, 7000 Rivers Ave.
Charleston, South Carolina 29423
843-574-6131; 843-574-6351 TTY;
Fax: 843-574-6812
E-mail: jim.orgel@tridenttech.edu
Web Site: www.tridenttech.edu
Director: Pamela Middleton
Primary Counselor: James R. Orgel
Services: OET, ITS, SGTS, LCL, AA, NTA, TR, TT, BSS, DP, FALD, PCC

SOUTH DAKOTA

National American University *(2-year & 4-year)*
Development Studies
321 Kansas City Street
Rapid City, South Dakota 57701-1708
605-394-4827; Fax: 605-394-4871
E-mail: ghytrek@national.edu
Web Site: www.national.edu
Dean of Student Services: Dr. Gayle Ashworth
Services: OET, ITS, SGTS, LCL, AA, NTA, TR, BSS, DP, FALD, WP

South Dakota State Univ. *(4-year)*
Office of Disability Services
2805 Binnewies Hall 145
Brookings, South Dakota 57007
605-688-4504; 605-688-4594 TTD;
Fax: 605-688-6450
E-mail: nancy.crooks@sdstate.edu
Web Site: www.sdstate.edu
Coordinator: Nancy Hartenhoff-Crooks
Services: OET, AA, NTA, TT, TR, BSS, FALD (at student's request), PCC

TENNESSEE

Middle Tennessee State University *(4-year)*
Disabled Student Services
P.O. Box 7
Murfreesboro, Tennessee 37132
(615) 898-2783; FAX: (615) 898-4893
1-800-433-MTSU
E-mail: dssemail@mtsu.edu
Web Site: www.mtsu.edu
Director: John Harris;
Assistant Director: Janet Norman
Services: ET, ITS, AA, NTA, TR, Adaptive Computer Equipment, Early Course Registration

Vanderbilt University *(4-year)*
Opportunity Development Center
P.O. Box 351809, Station B
Nashville, Tennessee 37235
615-322-4705; Fax: 615-343-0671
Web Site: www.vanderbilt.edu/odc
Director of ODC: Patrice A. Pierce
Disability Services Specialist: Corinne Lankford
Services: OET, SGTS, NTA, TT, FALD

TEXAS

Angelina College *(2-year)*
Special Student Services
P.O. Box 1768
Lufkin, Texas 75902
936-633-5289; Fax: 936-633-5247
E-mail: kbowser@angelina.edu
Web Site: www.angelina.edu
Coordinator: Karen Bowser
Services: OET, ITS, SGTS, LCL, AA, NTA, TR, TT, BSS, DP, FALD (at student's request)
Scholarships: See page 456.

Cedar Valley College *(2-year)*
Trio Special Support Services
3030 North Dallas Avenue
Lancaster, Texas 75134
972-860-8119; Fax: 972-860-8014
Director: Grenna Rollings
Web Site: www.cedarvalleycollege.edu

Services: OET, ITS, SGTS, LCL, NTA, TR, TT, BSS, DP, FALD, Franklin Speller, CCTV, Scanner
Scholarships: See page 456.

Hill College *(2-year)*
Student Support Services
P.O. Box 619, 112 Lamar Drive
Hillsboro, Texas 76645
254-582-2555 x217; Fax: 254-582-7591
Web Site: www.hillcollege.edu
Director: Marinel Baker
Services: OET, ITS, SGTS, LCL, AA, NTA, TT, TR, BSS, DP, FALD, PCC

Lee College *(2-year)*
Counseling Center
Disability Services Office
511 South Whiting, P.O. Box 818
Baytown, Texas 77522-0818
281-425-6384; Fax: 281-425-6382
Web Site: www.lee.edu
Director: Dr. Rosemary Coffman
Services: OET, ITS, SGTS, AA, NTA, TT, TR, DP, FALD, KR, DD

North Lake College *(2-year)*
Disability Services Office
5001 North MacArthur Blvd.
Irving, Texas 75038-3899
972-273-3165; Fax: 972-273-3164
E-mail: cag7341@dcccd.edu
Web Site: www.northlakecollege.edu
Director: Carole Gray
Services: OET, LPC, AA, TT, NTA,TR, BSS, DP, FALD, WP, PCC, KR, DNS

San Jacinto College: South *(2-year)*
Special Populations
13735 Beamer Road
Houston, Texas 77089-6099
281-922-3453; Fax: 281-929-4626
E-mail: cginn@south.sjcd.cc.edu
Web Site: www.sjcd.cc.edu
Coordinator: Connie Ginn
Services: OET, ITS, SGTS, LCL, AA, NTA, TR, TT, BSS, DP, FALD, KR

Southwestern Assemblies of God University *(4-year)*
Achievement Center
1200 Sycamore
Waxahachie, Texas 75165-2397
972-937-4010; Fax: 972-923-0488
Web Site: www.sagu.edu
Coordinator: Carrie Shrank
Services: OET, ITS, SGTS, LCL, AA, NTA, TT, TR, BSS, DP, FALD

Tarrant County College: Northeast Campus *(2-year)*
Disability Support Services (DSS)
828 Harwood Road
Hurst, Texas 76054
817-515-6333
E-mail: judy.kelley@tccd.edu
Web Site: www.tccd.edu
Coordinator: Judy Kelley
Services: OET, ITS, SGTS, AA, NTA, TT, TR, BSS, DP, FALD, WP, KR, DNS

Texas A & M University *(4-year)*
Department of Student Life
Disability Services
Cain Hall Rm B118, 1224 TAMU
College Station, Texas 77843-1224
979-845-1637; Fax: 979-458-1214
E-mail: anne@studentlife.tamu.edu
Web Site: www.tamu.edu
Coordinator: Dr. Anne Reber
Services: OET, LCL, AA, NTA, TR, TT, BSS, FALD, KR, WP, LDSG, Specialized Adaptive Technology and Internet Use

Texas A & M University: Commerce *(4-year)*
Mach 111 – Special Services
P.O. Box 3011
Commerce, Texas 75429
903-886-5833; Fax: 903-468-3220
E-mail:

Frank_Perez@tamu-commerce.edu
Web Site: www.tamu-commerce.edu
Disabilities Supervisor: Frank Perez
Services: OET, ITS, SGTS, LCL, AA, NTA, TR, TT, BSS, DP, FALD

Univ. of the Incarnate Word *(4-yr)*
Student disAbility Support Services
4301 Broadway
San Antonio, Texas 78209
210-283-3938
E-mail: rapp@uiwtx.edu or soto@uiwtx.edu
Web Site: www.uiw.edu
Director: Dr. Rhonda Rapp
Academic Counselor: Ann Soto
Services: OET, LCL, AA, NTA, TR, TT, BSS, FALD

University of Texas at El Paso *(4-yr)*
Disabled Student Services
500 West University Avenue
El Paso, Texas 79968
915-747-5148; Fax: 915-747-8712
E-mail: dss@utep.edu or jsaunders@utep.edu
Web Site: www.utep.edu
Assistant Director: James B. Saunders, Jr.
Services: OET, NTA, TT, TR, KR, DNS

UTAH

Salt Lake Community College *(2-yr)*
Disability Resource Center
4600 South Redwood Road
Salt Lake City, Utah 84130
801-957-4659; 801-957-4646 TTY
Fax: 801-957-4947
E-mail: linda.bennet@slcc.edu
Web Site: www.slcc.edu
Director: Linda Bennet
Learning Disabilities Specialist: Steven P. Lewis
Services: OET, ITS, SGTS, LCL, NTA, TR, TT, BSS, DP, Learning Disabilities Minicourse taught by Learning Disabilities Specialist
Scholarships: See page 457.

Snow College *(2-year)*
Accessibility Services
710 East 100 North
Ephraim, Utah 84627
435-283-7321; Fax: 435-283-7149
E-mail: Katie.Larsen@snow.edu
Web Site: www.snow.edu
Director: Katie Jean Larsen
Services: OET, SGTS, LCL, AA, NTA, TT, TR, BSS, FALD, WP, PCC

Westminster College *(4-year)*
Disability Services Program
1840 South 1300 East
Salt Lake City, Utah 84105
801-832-2280, 801-832-2286 TTY;
Fax: 801-832-3101
E-mail: gdewitt@westminstercollege.edu
Web Site: www.westminstercollege.edu
Director: Ginny DeWitt
Services: OET, ITS, AA, NTA, LCL, TT, TR, FALD, KR, WP, Individualized Accommodations
Scholarships: See page 439.

VERMONT

Community College of Vermont *(2-year)*
Student Support Services
CCV Administrative Offices
P.O. Box 120, Wasson Hall
Waterbury, Vermont 05676
802-241-3535; Fax: 802-241-3526
E-mail: judyj@mail.ccv.edu
Web Site: www.ccv.edu
Provost: Joyce M. Judy
Services: OET, ITS, SGTS, LCL, AA, NTA, TT, TR, BSS, DP, FALD

Norwich University *(4-year)*
Learning Support Center
158 Harmon Drive
Northfield, Vermont 05663
802-485-2130; Fax: 802-485-2684
Web Site: www.norwich.edu
Director: Paula A. Gills
Services: OET, ITS, SGTS, AA, BSS, FALD, PCC, WP

VIRGINIA

Blue Ridge Community College *(2-year)*
Disability Services
P.O. Box 80, 1 College Lane
Weyers Cave, Virginia 24486
1-888-750-2722 x2298
E-mail: gibsonb@brcc.edu
Web Site: www.brcc.edu
Coordinator: Beth Gibson
Services: OET, NTA, TR, BSS, DP, FALD

College of William and Mary *(4-yr)*
Dean of Students
Disability Services
P.O. Box 8795
Williamsburg, Virginia 23187-8795
757-221-2510; 757-221-2302 TDD; Fax: 757-221-2538
E-mail: lbcoll@wm.edu
Web Site: www.wm.edu
Assistant Dean: Lisa B. Colligan
Services: OET, NTA, TR, TT, BSS, FALD, KR, WP, PCC

Dabney S. Lancaster Community College *(2-year)*
Achievement Center
1000 Dabney Drive
Clifton Forge, Virginia 24422
540-863-2860; Fax: 540-863-2915
E-mail: ldavis@dslcc.edu
Web Site: www.dl.vccs.edu
Director: Elizabeth O. Davis
Services: OET, ITS, SGTS, AA, NTA, TR, TT, BSS, DP, FALD

Eastern Mennonite Univ. *(4-year)*
Student Disability Support Services
1200 Park Road
Harrisonburg, Virginia 22802
800-368-2665 or 540-432-4254; Fax: 540-432-4444
E-mail: hedrickj@emu.edu
Web Site: www.emu.edu
Coordinator: Joyce C. Hedrick
Services: OET, ITS, SGTS, LCL, AA, NTA, TT, TR, BSS, DP (English and Mathematics), FALD, Supportive University Faculty

Emory & Henry College *(4-year)*
Liberal Arts College
Paul Adrian Powell III Resource Center/Academic Support Servs.
Wiley Hall, Room 205
P.O. Box 947, One Garnard Drive
Emory, Virginia 24327-0947
276-944-6144; Fax: 276-944-6180
E-mail: lhoneycutt@ehc.edu
Web Site: www.ehc.edu
Director: Lisa Honeycutt
Services: OET, ITS, SGTS, AA, NTA, TR, TT, BSS, FALD (at student's request), PCC, KR, WP

Ferrum College *(4-year)*
Office of Academic Disability Services
P.O. Box 1000, Route 40 West
Ferrum, Virginia 24088
540-365-4262; Fax: 540-365-4271
E-mail: nbeach@ferrum.edu
Web Site: www.ferrum.edu
Director: Nancy S. Beach
Services: OET, ITS, SGTS, AA, NTA, TR, TT, BSS, FALD (at student's request), WP, PCC, Arkenstone

Reader, Specialized Advising
Summer Program: See page 413.

Thomas Nelson Community College *(2-year)*
Disabled Student Services
P.O. Box 9407
Hampton, Virginia 23670
804-825-2833; 804-825-2853 TDD
E-mail: baileyn@tncc.edu
Web Site: www.tncc.edu
Coordinator: Nancy Bailey
Services: OET, ITS, LCL, AA, NTA, TT, TR, BSS, DP, FALD, KR, DNS, WP, PCC, Assistive Technology

University of Virginia *(4-year)*
Learning Needs and Evaluation Ctr.
Elson Health Center
400 Brandon Ave., P.O. Box 800760
Charlottesville, Virginia 22908-0760
434-243-5180; Fax: 434-243-5188
E-mail: aea3f@virginia.edu
Web Site: www.virginia.edu/studenthealth/LNEC.html
Director: Dr. Allison Anderson
Services: OET, NTA, TT, FALD (at student's request), KR, BSS, Assistive Technology

WASHINGTON

Central Washington University *(4-year)*
Disability Support Services
400 East University Way
Ellensburg, Washington 98926-7431
509-963-2171; 509-963-2143 TDD; Fax: 509-963-3235
E-mail: campbelr@cwu.edu
Web Site: www.cwu.edu
Director: Robert A. Campbell
Services: OET, LCL, NTA, TR, TT, BSS, FALD, WP, LDSG

Evergreen State College *(4-year)*
Access Services for Students with Disabilities
2700 Evergreen Pkwy., NW
Olympia, Washington 98505
360-866-6348; Fax: 360-866-6823
E-mail: pickeril@evergreen.edu
Web Site: www.evergreen.edu
Director: Linda Pickering
Services: OET, SGTS, LCL, NTA, TR, TT, BSS, FALD, Assistive Technology

Green River Comm. College *(2-yr)*
Disability Support Services
12401 SE 320th Street
Auburn, Washington 98092
253-833-9111 x2646; 253-288-3359 TDD; Fax: 253-288-3471
E-mail: ghimes@greenriver.edu
Web Site: www.greenriver.edu
Director: Gail Himes
Services: OET, ITS, LCL, AA, NTA, TT, BSS, DP, KR, FALD, Readers and/or Scribes for Exams, Assistive Technology, Adaptive Equipment, Preferred Seating, Ergonomic Furniture

Lower Columbia College *(2-year)*
Special Services Office
1600 Maple, P.O. Box 3010
Longview, Washington 98632-0310
360-442-2311; Fax: 360-442-2919
E-mail: tcorrie@lowercolumbia.edu
Web Site: www.lowercolumbia.edu
Coordinator: Twylla Corrie
Services: OET, SGTS, LCL, NTA, TR, TT, BSS, DP, FALD (at student's request), Assistive Technology, Ergonomic Furniture

Olympic College *(2-year)*
Disability Support Services/Access Services
1600 Chester Avenue

Bremerton, Washington 98337
360-475-7540; Fax: 360-475-7436
E-mail: kfusco@oc.ctc.edu
Web Site: www.oc.ctc.edu
Director: Karen Fusco
Services: OET, ITS, LCL, AA, NTA, TR, TT, BSS, DP, FALD, Adaptive Computer Lab

Seattle Central Community College *(2-year)*
Disability Support Services
1701 Broadway, RM BE 1140
Seattle, Washington 98122
206-587-4183; Fax: 206-903-3236
Web Site: www.seattlecentral.edu
Director: Al Souma
Services: OET, ITS, NTA, TR, TT, BSS, DP, FALD, LDSG

Shoreline Community College *(2-year)*
Office of Special Services for Students with Disabilities
16101 Greenwood Avenue North
Shoreline, Washington 98133
206-546-5832
E-mail: kthompson@shoreline.edu
Web Site: www.shoreline.edu
Coordinator: Kim Thompson
Services: OET, NTA, TR, TT, BSS, DP, FALD, KR

South Puget Sound Community College *(2-year)*
Disability Support Services
2011 Mottman Road SW
Olympia, Washington 98512-6292
360-596-5261; Fax: 360-596-5709
E-mail: jshowalter@spscc.ctc.edu
Web Site: www.spscc.ctc.edu
Director: Jane Showalter
Services: OET, ITS, LCL, NTA, BSS, FALD (at student's request), PCC, TT, KR, WP

Spokane Falls Community College *(2-year)*
Disability Support Services MS 3011
3410 W. Fort George Wright Drive
Spokane, Washington 99224 -5288
509-533-4166; Fax: 509-533-3547
E-mail: benw@spokanefalls.edu
Web Site: www.spokanefalls.edu
Director: Ben Webinger
Services: OET, LCL, NTA, TR, TT, BSS, DP, FALD (at student's request), KR, WP, PCC, Colored Overlays, WYNN, Assistive Technology

University of Washington *(4-year)*
Disabled Student Services
448 Schmitz Hall, Box 355839
Seattle, Washington 98195-5839
206-543-8924, 206-543-8925 TTY; Fax: 206-616-8379
E-mail: uwdss@washington.edu
Web Site: www.washington.edu
Director: Dyane Haynes
Services: OET, LCL, NTA, TT, FALD (at student's request)

Western Washington Univ. *(4-year)*
disAbility Resources for Students
516 High Street, Old Main 110
Bellingham, Washington 98225
360-650-3083; Fax: 360-650-3715
E-mail: drs@wwu.edu
Web Site: www.wwu.edu/depts/drs
Director: David Brunnemer
Services: OET, ITS, SGTS, NTA, TT, TR, BSS, FALD, KR, Adaptive Computer Training

Yakima Valley Community College *(2-year)*
Disability Support Services
16th Avenue and Nob Hill Blvd.
Yakima, Washington 98907
509-574-4960; Fax: 509-574-6860
E-mail: mcoomer@yvcc.edu
Web Site: www.yvcc.edu

Director: Marc Coomer
Services: ITS, SGTS, TT, DP, BSS, DP, FALD, LDSG, WP, Study Skills

WEST VIRGINIA

Fairmont State College *(4-year)*
Disabilities Services
1201 Locust Avenue
Fairmont, West Virginia 26554-2491
304-367-4686; Fax: 304-366-4406
E-mail: apammer@fairmontstate.edu
Web Site: www.fairmontstate.edu
Coordinator: Andrea Pammer
Services: OET, ITS, AA, NTA, TT, BSS, DP, FALD, KR, Assistive Technology

Glenville State College *(4-year)*
Academic Support Center
200 High Street
Glenville, West Virginia 26351
304-462-4118; Fax: 304-462-7495
E-mail: Daniel.Reed@glenville.edu
Web Site: www.glenville.edu
Director: Daniel A. Reed
Services: OET, ITS, NTA, TT, TR, DP, FALD, DNS

West Virginia University *(4-year)*
Office of Disability Services
G30 Mountainlair
P.O. Box 6423
Morgantown, West Virginia 26506-6423
304-293-6700 V/TTD; Fax: 304-293-3861
E-mail: access2@mail.wvu.edu
Web Site: www.wvu.edu
Director: Dr. Richard Strasburger
Services: ET, ITS, SGTS, LCL, TR, TT, FALD, KR, PCC, Priority Preregistration, Counseling

WISCONSIN

Beloit College *(4-year)*
Educational Development Program
Student Support Services
Box 137, 700 College Street
Beloit, Wisconsin 53511-5595
608-363-2500; 608-363-2620; Fax: 608-363-2718
E-mail: ewoldtn@beloit.edu
Web Site: www.beloit.edu
Director: Nick Ewoldt
Services: OET, ITS, SGTS, NTA, FALD

Edgewood College *(4-year)*
Learning Support Services
1000 Edgewood College Drive
Madison, Wisconsin 53711
608-663-2812; Fax: 608-663-3291
E-mail: LLaz@edgewood.edu or dtobin@edgewood.edu
Web Site: www.edgewood.edu
Director: Laurie Laz
Disabilities Services Coordinator: Deb Tobin
Services: OET, ITS, SGTS, NTA, TT, BSS
Summer Program: See page 414.

Fox Valley Technical College *(2-yr)*
Special Needs Center
1825 North Bluemound Drive
P.O. Box 2277
Appleton, Wisconsin 54912-2277
920-735-5679
E-mail: schwaben@fvtc.edu
Web Site: www.fvtc.edu
Coordinator: Shary Schwabenlender
Services: OET, ITS, SGTS, LCL, AA, NTA, TT, TR, BSS, DP, FALD, WP, Arkenstone Readers

Lawrence University *(4-year)*
Academic Accomodations for Students with Disabilities

118 South Lawe Street, Box 599
Appleton, Wisconsin 54912-0599
920-832-6530; Fax: 920-832-6884
E-mail:
geoffrey.c.gajewski@lawrence.edu
Web Site: www.lawrence.edu
Associate Dean of Student Academic Services: Geoff Gajewski
Services: OET, ITS, SGTS, LCL, AA, NTA, TT, TR, BSS, FALD

Marian College *(4-year)*
Academic Support Services
45 South National Avenue
Fond du Lac, Wisconsin, 54935
920-923-8951
E-mail:
lmrogers65@mariancollege.edu
Web Site: www.mariancollege.edu
Coordinator: Lisa Rogers
Services: OET, ITS, SGTS, NTA, TR, TT, FALD, BSS, WP, PCC

Univ. of Wisconsin: Madison *(4-yr)*
McBurney Disability Resource Ctr.
905 University Avenue, Suite 100K
Madison, Wisconsin 53715-1005
608-265-5467; Fax: 608-265-2998
E-mail: woodbridge@wisc.edu
Web Site: www.wisc.edu
Director: Cathleen Trueba
Accomodations Specialist
Diane Woodbridge
Services: OET, NTA, TT, FALD, Advocacy Training, Learning Skills Instruction, WP, PCC, LDSG
Scholarships: See page 440.

Wisconsin Indianhead Technical College *(2-year)*
Student Success Center Services
1900 College Drive
Rice Lake, Wisconsin 54868
715-234-7082; Fax: 715-234-5172
Web Site: www.witechcolleges.com
Director: Herb Schweitzer
Services: OET, ITS, SGTS, AA, TR, TT, FALD, PCC, Computer-Aided Training
Summer Program: See page 422.
Scholarships: See page 458.

WYOMING

Casper College *(2-year)*
Accommodative Services
125 College Drive
Casper, Wyoming 82601
307-268-2557; Fax: 307-268-2444
E-mail: bheuer@caspercollege.edu
Web Site: www.caspercollege.edu
Counselor: Brent Heuer
Services: OET, ITS, SGTS, AA, NTA, TR, TT, BSS, DP, FALD, KR, CCTV

Laramie County Community College *(2-year)*
Disability Resource Center (DRC)
1400 East College Drive
Cheyenne, Wyoming 82007
307-778-1359, 307-778-1266 TTY
Fax: 307-778-1262
E-mail: LDignan@lccc.wy.edu
Web Site: www.lccc.wy.edu
Coordinator: Lisa Dignan
Services: OET, ITS, SGTS, AA, NTA, TR, TT, BSS, FALD, KR, WP, PCC
Scholarships: See page 458.

Summer Programs and Scholarships for Students with Learning Disabilities

The following two-year and four-year colleges have summer programs and scholarships for students with learning disabilities

COLLEGES OFFERING SUMMER TRANSITION PROGRAMS

FOUR-YEAR COLLEGES

ARKANSAS

UNIVERSITY OF ARKANSAS
GARLAND AVENUE, ARKANSAS UNION 116
FAYETTEVILLE, ARKANSAS 72701
(479) 575-3104, (479) 575-3646 TDD; FAX: (479) 575-7445
E-MAIL: ada@uark.edu **WEB SITE: www.uark.edu**

Center for Students with Disabilities
Summer Program: Academic Support for Achievement. This is a college transition program for high-achieving students with disabilities. This program provides students with a headstart at the University of Arkansas. Students, parents and professionals work together to develop an Individual College Plan. The program culminates with the planning conference at which the student's College Plan is discussed and refined. The student's rights as a college student with a disability are discussed and a schedule of action for the first year at college is developed. The student is linked with tutors, counselors and other resources either on the campus or in the community. Academic Support for Achievement assists students only with the transition to college. (Individual services and accommodations are provided by the Office for Campus Access at the University of Arkansas.) Cost: varies with individual need

COLORADO

UNIVERSITY OF DENVER
LEARNING EFFECTIVENESS PROGRAM
2050 EAST EVANS AVENUE SUITE 30
DENVER, COLORADO 80208
(303) 871-2372; FAX: (303) 871-3939
E-MAIL: LEP-info@du.edu **WEB SITE: www.du.edu/lep**

Learning Effectiveness Program
Summer Program: Students enrolled in summer school may participate in the full program for $600.

CONNECTICUT

MITCHELL COLLEGE
437 PEQUOT AVENUE
NEW LONDON, CONNECTICUT 06320
(860) 701-7141; FAX: (860) 701-5090
E-MAIL: carnevalej@mitchell.edu **WEB SITE: www.mitchell.edu**

Learning Resource Center
Summer Program: Two courses may be taken for college credit; full Learning Resource Center support is available. Cost: $3,500. Optional

FLORIDA

BEACON COLLEGE
105 EAST MAIN STREET
LEESBURG, FLORIDA 34748
(352) 787-7660; FAX: (352) 787-0721
E-MAIL: admissions@beaconcollege.edu
WEB SITE: www.beaconcollege.edu

Summer Program: The summer term is a combination of a mini master program on campus and a cultural studies program abroad. The cultural studies program enables currently enrolled students the opportunity to combine academics such as art, history, music and literature with travel opportunities. The summer 2006 trip includes stops in Italy and Greece. Approximate cost: $1,600 (does not include travel arrangements)

FLORIDA A & M UNIVERSITY
667 ARDELIA COURT
TALLAHASSEE, FLORIDA 32307
(850) 599-3180; FAX: (850) 561-2513
E-MAIL: nholmes@famu.edu **WEB SITE: www.famu.edu**

Learning Development and Evaluation Center
Summer Program: The summer transition program for high school and first-time college students with a learning disability provides intense instruction in study skills, memory skills, mathematics, reading improvement and socialization. The transition program serves as a feeder for students with a learning disability who intend to pursue postsecondary education. Cost: $1,560. Mandatory

GEORGIA

BRENAU UNIVERSITY WOMEN'S COLLEGE
ONE CENTENNIAL CIRCLE
GAINESVILLE, GEORGIA 30506
(770) 534-6134; FAX: (770) 297-5883
E-MAIL: vyamilkoski@lib.brenau.edu
WEB SITE: www.brenau.edu/learning center

Brenau Learning Center
Summer Program: The Learning Center program operates each semester of the school year, including the summer, with the same services. Summer tutoring fees are $450 per tutored course. There are some summer residential (housing) scholarships available that include paid campus work positions for full-time students.

UNIVERSITY OF GEORGIA
114 CLARK HOWELL HALL
ATHENS, GEORGIA 30602
(706) 542-8719; FAX: (706) 542-8778
E-MAIL: dshimket@uga.edu **WEB SITE: www.dissvcs.uga.edu**

Disability Resource Center (DRC)
Summer Program: Students admitted under special criteria for learning disabilities are admitted as regular students to the summer quarter. The Disability Resource Center offers special activities to orient freshmen to campus and academic life.

ILLINOIS

NATIONAL LOUIS UNIVERSITY
2840 SHERIDAN ROAD
EVANSTON, ILLINOIS 60201
(847) 475-1100 X2357
E-MAIL: jpiper@nl.edu **WEB SITE: www.nl.edu**

Center for Academic Development
Summer Program: Two-week program for students with learning disabilities who are already admitted to the university and need help with study skills, tutoring and adjustment to college life in general. Cost: $50

IOWA

SAINT AMBROSE UNIVERSITY
518 WEST LOCUST STREET
DAVENPORT, IOWA 52803
(563) 333-6275 V/TTY; FAX: (563) 333-6243
E-MAIL: SaddlerRyanC@sau.edu WEB SITE: www.sau.edu

Services for Students with Disabilities
Summer Program: A four-week summer program is designed to give students with learning disabilities a headstart on developing skills for a successful college career. A three-credit course is included. Cost: $2,700

KENTUCKY

EASTERN KENTUCKY UNIVERSITY
521 LANCASTER AVENUE, TURLEY HOUSE 1
RICHMOND, KENTUCKY 40475-3136
(859) 622-1500 V/TDD; FAX: (859) 622-6395
E-MAIL: disbellu@acs.eku.edu
WEB SITE: www.eku.edu/student services

Project SUCCESS
Summer Program: Project SUCCESS conducts a Summer Transition Program. The program is geared towards high school juniors and seniors with learning disabilities who desire to transition from secondary to post-secondary education. Attendance is approximately 40 people. First 40 receive stipend, others pay fee $40.

LOUISIANA

LOUISIANA COLLEGE
1140 COLLEGE DRIVE, BOX 545
PINEVILLE, LOUISIANA 71360
(318) 487-7629; FAX: (318) 487-7285
E-MAIL: matthews@lacollege.edu WEB SITE: www.lacollege.edu

Program to Assist Student Success (PASS)
Summer Program: The summer session consists of two five-week sessions. Many types of assistance for students with identified disabilities are available. Cost: $60 per semester hour

MAINE

UNITY COLLEGE
QUAKER HILL ROAD, RR 78, P.O. BOX 1
UNITY, MAINE 04988-9502
(207) 948-3131 X263; FAX: (207) 948-5626
E-MAIL: jhoran@unity.edu **WEB SITE: www.unity.edu**

Learning Resource Center
Summer Program: The Summer Institute of Unity College is a four-week pre-college program with credit and non-credit courses, instruction in study skills and individualized tutorial assistance: basic writing, basic mathematics, introduction to computers and introduction to science. Cost: $1,295

MASSACHUSETTS

BOSTON UNIVERSITY
19 DEERFIELD STREET
BOSTON, MASSACHUSETTS 02215
(617) 353-3658 V/TTY; FAX: (617) 353-9646
E-MAIL: lwolf@bu.edu or access@bu.edu
WEB SITE: www.bu.edu/disability

Learning Disabilities Services (LDS)
Summer Program: To assist students with their transition to college, LDS offers a unique summer program designed specifically for incoming freshman with disabilities. ENTRY! provides an opportunity for entering students to develop the skills necessary to reach their fullest potential in college. Students move into their assigned dormitory one week early to participate in daily learning strategies seminars, workshops and recreational activities. A special workshop is also offered to assist parents of students enrolled in ENTRY! with this important transition. Personalized support continues through the academic semester.

CURRY COLLEGE
1071 BLUE HILL AVENUE
MILTON, MASSACHUSETTS 02186-2395
(617) 333-2270; FAX: (617) 333-2018
E-MAIL: Ijiri@curry.edu **WEB SITE: www.curry.edu**

Program for Advancement of Learning (PAL)
Summer Program: The Program for Advancement of Learning (PAL) begins with Summer PAL which runs for three weeks in June or July. Students deepen their understanding of themselves, how they learn and how to monitor

their own learning. They develop knowledge that leads to greater competence, effectiveness and interdependence as a learner. Cost: $2,700. Optional

NEW JERSEY

NEW JERSEY CITY UNIVERSITY
2039 KENNEDY MEMORIAL BOULEVARD
JERSEY CITY, NEW JERSEY 07305-1597
(201) 200-2091; FAX: (201) 200-3083
E-MAIL: projmentor@njcu.edu **WEB SITE: www.njcu.edu**

Project Mentor
Summer Program: A four-week summer orientation program, which prepares students for success in an academic setting, is available to incoming freshmen students who are eligible. If a Project Mentor student participates in the summer orientation program, he/she will be expected to pay tuition and fees for any college level course for which he/she is registered. In addition, residential students participating in the summer orientation program are required to pay the cost of room and board during their summer stay. Writing in response to assigned and self-chosen readings, editing, computer applications, and mathematics instruction form the foundation of the summer curriculum. Placement testing and advising registration for the fall semester also take place.

NEW YORK

ADELPHI UNIVERSITY
BOX 701, ONE SOUTH AVENUE
GARDEN CITY, NEW YORK 11530-0701
(516) 877-4710, 1-800-ADELPHI; FAX: (516) 877-4711
E-MAIL: ldprogram@adelphi.edu **WEB SITE: www.adelphi.edu**

Learning Disabilities Program
Summer Program: A five-week diagnostic/experiential program. Students earn seven credits while receiving academic and counseling support from professional staff. Cost: $1,200 plus tuition, room and board

COLLEGE OF STATEN ISLAND – CUNY
1P-101, 2800 VICTORY BLVD.
STATEN ISLAND, NEW YORK 10314
(718) 982-2510, (718) 982-2515 TTY; FAX: (718) 982-2117
E-MAIL: nielson@mail.csi.cuny.edu
WEB SITE: www.csi.cuny.edu/disabilityservices

Disability Services

Summer Program: A summer program and all support services are offered for all students who need developmental work in reading, writing and mathematics.

CONCORDIA COLLEGE
171 WHITE PLAINS ROAD
BRONXVILLE, NEW YORK 10708
(914) 337-9300 X2361
E-MAIL: ghg@concordia-ny.edu WEB SITE: www.concordia-ny.edu

The Concordia Connection
Summer Program: A three-day intensive workshop focusing on study skills and basic college orientation is provided prior to regular freshman orientation. Cost: None

IONA COLLEGE
715 NORTH AVENUE
NEW ROCHELLE, NEW YORK 10801-1890
(914) 633-2159; FAX: (914) 633-2174
E-MAIL: lrobertello@iona.edu WEB SITE: www.iona.edu

College Assistance Program (CAP)
Summer Program: A 12-day, 9 AM to 3 PM, college transition program covering many study skills — including research paper writing, lecture note taking, text reading and note taking, stress management, learning style awareness, self-advocacy and training. Cost: $750

MANHATTAN COLLEGE
4513 MANHATTAN COLLEGE PARKWAY
RIVERDALE, NEW YORK 10471
(718) 862-7885, (718) 862-8000 TDD; FAX: (718) 862-7821
WEB SITE: www.manhattan.edu

Specialized Resource Center
Summer Program: Summer sessions overlap so that the student garners three credits while building a sense of collegiate life.

MARYMOUNT MANHATTAN COLLEGE
221 EAST 71st STREET
NEW YORK, NEW YORK 10021
(212) 774-0724; FAX: (212) 517-0419
E-MAIL: jbonomo@mmm.edu
WEB SITE: www. marymount.mmm.edu

Program for Academic Access for Students with Learning Disabilities

Summer Program: Individual tutoring is recommended and arranged by the program to strengthen preparation for the first year.

MERCY COLLEGE – DOBBS FERRY CAMPUS
555 BROADWAY
DOBBS FERRY, NEW YORK 10522
(914) 674-7324
E-MAIL: TRich@mercy.edu **WEB SITE: www.mercy.edu**

STAR Program
Summer Program: A pre-college seminar is held for students in the STAR Program. Cost: $700

NEW YORK INSTITUTE OF TECHNOLOGY
300 CARLETON AVENUE, INDEPENDENCE HALL
P.O. BOX 9029
CENTRAL ISLIP, NEW YORK 11722-9029
(631) 348-3354 or 1-800-345-NYIT
WEB SITE: www.nyit.edu

Vocational Independence Program
Summer Program: "Introduction to Independence" is a seven-week co-educational summer program for young adults with learning disabilities, between 16 and 20 years of age, who are considering post-secondary options. "I to I" provides educational, vocational, social and recreational programming designed to prepare the student for a successful transition to campus life, independent living and the work environment. The Program features a four-day trip to a place such as Montreal, Quebec, Niagara Falls, Toronto, Williamsburg, Virginia, and Virginia Beach in the final week, and a mid-summer Parents' Weekend includes a workshop on post-secondary options. Cost: $8,495

NEW YORK UNIVERSITY
240 GREENE STREET, 2nd FLOOR
NEW YORK, NEW YORK 10012
(212) 998-4979; FAX: (212) 995-4114
E-MAIL: lc83@nyu.edu **WEB SITE: www.nyu.edu/osl/csd**

Henry and Lucy Moses Center for Students with Disabilities
"Transitioning to College for Students with Learning Disabilities" workshop offered in summer and fall.

QUEENS COLLEGE – CUNY
171 KIELY HALL
65-30 KISSENA BLVD.
FLUSHING, NEW YORK 11367-1597
(718) 997-5870; FAX: (718) 997-5895
WEB SITE: www.qc.edu

Office of Special Services for Students with Disabilities
Summer Program: Throughout the summer Queens College offers students with learning disabilities academic enhancement which keeps them in the mainstream of learning. Content tutoring is available as well as an opportunity to improve memory skills, note-taking skills, test-taking strategies and overall learning abilities. Diagnostic assessments are also encouraged in order to pinpoint specific areas of weakness. Cost: None

SAINT THOMAS AQUINAS COLLEGE
125 ROUTE 340
SPARKILL, NEW YORK 10976
(845) 398-4230; FAX: (845) 398-4229
E-MAIL: pathways@stac.edu **WEB SITE: www.stac.edu**

Pathways
Summer Program: All incoming Pathways freshmen are required to attend a four-day, three-night summer program prior to the first semester. The goals are to learn the specific needs of each student, to begin preparing individuals for the academic rigors of higher education and to build a sense of trust and community within the group. The program integrates the first part of a three-credit course called Studies in Culture whose topic may vary from year to year. This aspect of the program continues into the fall semester. The summer program, which includes both field trips and classroom lectures, fosters a sense of community among the students through shared activities, while building their self-confidence and comfort within the college setting. Cost: $550–650

NORTH CAROLINA

UNIVERSITY OF NORTH CAROLINA AT CHAPEL HILL
BANK OF AMERICA BUILDING
137 EAST FRANKLIN STREET – STE 602 CB #3447
CHAPEL HILL, NORTH CAROLINA 27514-3447
(919) 962-7227; FAX: (919) 962-3674
E-MAIL: jane_benson@unc.edu or tmaitlan@email.unc.edu
WEB SITE: www.unc.edu/depts/lds

Learning Disabilities Services

Summer Orientation: Testing accommodations are provided for the Foreign Language Placement test during summer orientation for entering freshmen and transfer students who qualify for these accommodations. Accommodations for LD / ADHD students are determined on a case-by-case basis depending upon documentation, the same as during regular college sessions.

OHIO

MUSKINGUM COLLEGE
MONTGOMERY HALL
NEW CONCORD, OHIO 43762-1199
(740) 826-8280; FAX: (740) 826-8404
E-MAIL: ehenry@muskingum.edu WEB SITE: www.muskingum.edu

PLUS Program
Summer Program: Two-week residential program consisting of non-credit expository course, writing and speech. Experiences are similar to the college semester with weekend field trips and many social activities. Cost: FIRST STEP $1,500. Optional

PENNSYLVANIA

DUQUESNE UNIVERSITY
ADMINISTRATION BUILDING
600 FORBES AVENUE
PITTSBURGH, PENNSYLVANIA 15282-0206
(412) 396-6661; FAX: (412) 396-5466
E-MAIL: griggs@duq.edu
WEB SITE: www.duq.edu; www.lsc.duq.edu

Learning Skills Center
Summer Program: The program consists of a five-week pre-college experience. Students are assessed by way of diagnostic testing and they participate in developmental and / or remedial courses prior to matriculating into college. Students are then monitored by counselors throughout the school years to assist in their area of need. The program is ongoing during the academic year; it is not limited to those students who have a learning disability. Various outreach programs also have been instituted, such as Project for Academic Coaching through Tutoring (PACT) and Outreach Opportunity for marginally Performing Students (OOPS). Cost: $717

KING'S COLLEGE
133 NORTH RIVER STREET
WILKES-BARRE, PENNSYLVANIA 18711
(717) 826-5800; FAX: (717) 825-9049
E-MAIL: jaburke@kings.edu **WEB SITE: www.kings.edu**

Academic Skills Center – First Year Academic Studies Program (FASP)
Summer Program: Optional college entry program includes small classes, core requirements, tutoring, and provides orientation to college living and learning.

MERCYHURST COLLEGE
501 EAST 38th STREET, GLENWOOD HILL
ERIE, PENNSYLVANIA 16546-2071
(814) 824-2450; (814) 824-2071
E-MAIL: drogers@mercyhurst.edu **WEB SITE: www.mercyhurst.edu**

Learning Differences Program
Summer Program: A three-week, all-day program required for incoming students. Students earn three credits toward graduation. Cost: $1,700 approximately

VIRGINIA

FERRUM COLLEGE
P.O. BOX 1000, ROUTE 40 WEST
FERRUM, VIRGINIA 24088
(540) 365-4262; FAX: (540) 365-4271
E-MAIL: nbeach@ferrum.edu **WEB SITE: www.ferrum.edu**

Office of Academic Disability Services
Summer Program: Two-week summer program, August Term, devoted to intensive work on text-book reading, English, and math skills. This program is designed to facilitate academic, social, and personal growth, as well as ease the transition from high school to college for Ferrum freshmen.

WEST VIRGINIA

MARSHALL UNIVERSITY
520 18th STREET, MYERS HALL
HUNTINGTON, WEST VIRGINIA 25755
(304) 696-6252; FAX: (304) 696-3231
E-MAIL: guyerb@marshall.edu **WEB SITE: www.marshall.edu**

Higher Education for Learning Problems (H.E.L.P.)

Summer Program: The H.E.L.P. Program offers a five-week summer session. Students attend a class in the morning and then receive tutoring in the afternoon. Along with course subject tutoring, there is work on study skills, note-taking and test-taking skills and remediation. Cost: Residents – $1,000, Non-Residents – $2,200

WISCONSIN

EDGEWOOD COLLEGE
1000 EDGEWOOD COLLEGE DRIVE
MADISON, WISCONSIN 53711
(608) 663-2812; FAX: (608) 663-3291
E-MAIL: LLaz@edgewood.edu or dtobin@edgewood.edu
WEB SITE: www.edgewood.edu or
www.edgenet.edgewood.edu/lss/disability_services.htm

Learning Support Services
Summer Program: One-day required summer program is designed to plan for needed support services. Students also participate in study skills workshops and self-advocacy training that help prepare them for studies in a college environment. Cost: None

UNIVERSITY OF WISCONSIN: OSHKOSH
800 ALGOMA BLVD.
OSHKOSH, WISCONSIN 54901-8662
(920) 424-1033; FAX: (920) 424-0858
E-MAIL: kitz@uwosh.edu
WEB SITE: www.uwosh.edu/organizations/success

Project Success
Summer Program: An eight-week Language Remedial Program includes reading, spelling, writing and algebra.

UNIVERSITY OF WISCONSIN: WHITEWATER
800 WEST MAIN STREET, ROSEMAN 2021
WHITEWATER, WISCONSIN 53190
(262) 472-4788; FAX: (262) 472-5210
E-MAIL: assist@uww.edu **WEB SITE: www.uww.edu**

Project ASSIST
Summer Program: Project ASSIST offers a four-week intensive high school-to-college transition for incoming freshmen with learning disabilities. The program is a three-credit study skills course, including individual tutoring, academic advising, assessment of needs, advocacy skill instruction,

strategy instruction, social activities, orientation to campus services. Cost: In-State Residents – $1,700, Out-of-State-Residents – $2,900, includes tuition, room, board and Project Assist fee

TWO-YEAR COLLEGES

CALIFORNIA

CUYAMACA COLLEGE
900 RANCHO SAN DIEGO PARKWAY
EL CAJON, CALIFORNIA 92019-4304
(619) 660-4386, (619) 660-4239 TTY; FAX: (619) 660-4399
E-MAIL: poppy.bush@gcccd.net WEB SITE: www.cuyamaca.edu

Disabled Student Programs and Services (DSP&S)
Summer Program: The summer learning disability program includes educational assessment to determine eligibility for services and tutoring in basic skills.

PASADENA CITY COLLEGE
1570 EAST COLORADO BLVD.
PASADENA, CALIFORNIA 91106-2003
(626) 585-7127; FAX: (626) 585-7566
E-MAIL: elweller@pasadena.edu WEB SITE: www.pasadena.edu

Disabled Student Programs and Services (DSPS)
Summer Program: Provides registration assistance for fall; develops student educational contract which specifies services and accommodations.

SADDLEBACK COLLEGE
28000 MARGUERITE PARKWAY
MISSION VIEJO, CALIFORNIA 92692
(949) 582-4885; FAX: (949) 347-1526
E-MAIL: randerson@saddleback.edu or dcrary@saddleback.edu
WEB SITE: www.saddleback.edu

Special Services (Disabled Students Programs and Services)
Summer Program: College Link for high school seniors is designed primarily for students with learning disabilities and offers three courses: College Success, Self Advocacy, and Computer Access Lab for Students with Disabilities. Enrollment is through the Special Services Office.

SAN DIEGO MESA COLLEGE
7250 MESA COLLEGE DRIVE
SAN DIEGO, CALIFORNIA 92111
(619) 388-2780, (619) 388-2974 TTY; FAX: (619) 388-2460
E-MAIL: gconrad@sdccd.edu WEB SITE: www.sdmesa.edu

Disabled Students Programs and Services (DSP&S)
Summer Program: Offers tutoring and software instructional services through the High Tech Lab for all summer sessions.

SANTA ANA COLLEGE
1530 WEST 17th STREET
SANTA ANA, CALIFORNIA 92706
(714) 564-6260; FAX: (714) 285-9619
E-MAIL: choo_brooke@sac.edu or kobane_mary@sac.edu
WEB SITE: www.sac.edu

Learning Disabilities Program
Summer Program: Six week program; Cost: None

SANTA MONICA COLLEGE
1900 PICO BLVD.
SANTA MONICA, CALIFORNIA 90405
(310) 434-4684; FAX: (310) 434-3694
E-MAIL: marcopulos_george@smc.edu WEB SITE: www.smc.edu

Learning Disabilities Program
Summer Program: Assessment workshop to determine eligibility for learning disabilities program.

SIERRA COLLEGE
5000 ROCKLIN ROAD
ROCKLIN, CALIFORNIA 95677
(916) 781-0553; FAX: (916) 789-2967
WEB SITE: www.sierracollege.edu

Learning Opportunities Center
Summer Program: Sierra College offers test proctoring, liaison for incoming students and extended time for college assessment test.

SKYLINE COLLEGE
3300 COLLEGE DRIVE
SAN BRUNO, CALIFORNIA 94066-1698
(650) 738-4280, (650) 738-4329 TTD; FAX: (650) 738-4228

WEB SITE: www.skylinecollege.net

Developmental Skills Program
Summer Program: Single assessment/eligibility course offered, limited to eight to ten students; 1:1 assessment

COLORADO

COMMUNITY COLLEGE OF DENVER
P.O. BOX 173363, CAMPUS BOX 204
DENVER, COLORADO 80217-3363
(303) 556-8455; FAX: (303) 556-4563
E-MAIL: sharon.walton-hunt@ccd.edu
WEB SITE: www.ccd.edu

Special Learning Support Program
Summer Program: A Freshman Experience Class is offered for students with learning disabilities

ILLINOIS

HARPER COLLEGE
1200 WEST ALGONQUIN ROAD
PALATINE, ILLINOIS 60067
(847) 925-6266; FAX: (847) 925-6267
E-MAIL: pherrera@harpercollege.edu
WEB SITE: www.harpercollege.edu

Access and Disabilities Office/PASS (Program for Achieving Student Success)
Summer Program: ORN 101 is a one-credit two-day seminar offered for incoming freshmen.

INDIANA

VINCENNES UNIVERSITY
1002 NORTH FIRST STREET
VINCENNES, INDIANA 47591
(812) 888-4149, (812) 888-4214; FAX: (812) 888-5531
E-MAIL: summerbridge@vinu.edu or hclausman@vinu.edu
WEB SITE: www.vinu.edu

Student Transition into Educational Programs (STEP)
Summer Program: BRIDGE – Specifically designed for incoming students during the last summer session – an all inclusive academic and social pro-

gram. Contact Hope Clausman, (812) 888-4149, summerbridge@vinu.edu or hclausman@vinu.edu

IOWA

WALDORF COLLEGE
106 SOUTH 6th STREET
FOREST CITY, IOWA 50436
800-292-1903; FAX: (641) 585-8194
E-MAIL: murraym@waldorf.edu **WEB SITE: www.waldorf.edu**

Learning Disabilities Program (LDP)
Summer Program: Orientation prior to school year focuses on learning and study styles/strategies, time management, transition from high school, getting to know the college setting, and developing a support system

MINNESOTA

HIBBING COMMUNITY COLLEGE
1515 EAST 25th STREET
HIBBING, MINNESOTA 55746
(218) 262-6745
E-MAIL: shellyflaten@hcc.mnscu.edu **WEB SITE: www.hcc.mnscu.edu**

Disability Services
Summer Program: Early Start is a summer program offered to all students. It is designed especially for the inexperienced or apprehensive college student. This workshop helps students brush up on their writing and math skills and gain confidence in many other areas. Cost: None

MISSOURI

METROPOLITAN COMMUNITY COLLEGE – LONGVIEW
500 SOUTHWEST LONGVIEW ROAD
LEE'S SUMMIT, MISSOURI 64081-2105
(816) 672-2053; FAX: (816) 672-2719
E-MAIL: maryellen.jenison@mcckc.edu **WEB SITE: www.mcckc.edu**

Academic Bridges to Learning Effectiveness (ABLE)
Summer Program: Students may enroll in first-semester block of ABLE courses and/or a variety of general studies courses with support through ABLE. Cost: $35 per credit hour. Optional

METROPOLITAN COMMUNITY COLLEGE – PENN VALLEY
3201 SOUTHWEST TRAFFICWAY
KANSAS CITY, MISSOURI 64111
(816) 759-4089
E-MAIL: patricia.goodwin@mcckc.edu WEB SITE: www.mcckc.edu

Academic Bridges to Learning Effectiveness (ABLE)
Summer Program: Students may enroll in first-semester block of ABLE courses and/or a variety of general studies courses with the support through ABLE. Up to 12 first-semester students are accepted in the summer semester. Cost: $35 per credit hour. Optional

NEW JERSEY

BROOKDALE COMMUNITY COLLEGE
765 NEWMAN SPRINGS ROAD
LINCROFT, NEW JERSEY 07738-1597
(732) 224-2730; FAX: (732) 530-7417
E-MAIL: efoley@brookdalecc.edu or cfreeman@brookdalecc.edu
WEB SITE: www.brookdalecc.edu

Learning Disabilities Support Program
Summer Program: "Transition to College" is a support course for students with learning disabilities to help them prepare for the transition to college. College survival skills are introduced, e.g., communication skills, college vocabulary, reading and writing, time management, setting priorities, taking responsibility for academic tasks and active studying.

CAMDEN COUNTY COLLEGE
P.O. BOX 200, COLLEGE DRIVE
BLACKWOOD, NEW JERSEY 08012
(856) 227-7200 X4430; FAX: (856) 374-4975
E-MAIL: jkinzy@camdencc.edu WEB SITE: www.camdencc.edu

Program for the Academically Challenged Student (PACS)
Summer Program: The PACS Program offers a freshman orientation, two-credit, five-week summer class. This class provides strategies for note taking, test taking, time management, improving memory, career exploration and more.

NEW YORK

HUDSON VALLEY COMMUNITY COLLEGE
80 VANDENBURGH AVENUE
TROY, NEW YORK 12180
(518) 629-7154, (518) 629-7596 TDD; FAX: (518) 629-4831
E-MAIL: negropab@hvcc.edu **WEB SITE: www.hvcc.edu**

Disability Resource Center
Summer Program: A three-week summer course to sharpen math, reading, writing, and learning styles called "Smart Start" is available to incoming students at no charge.

ONONDAGA COMMUNITY COLLEGE
4941 ONONDAGA ROAD
SYRACUSE, NEW YORK 13215
(315) 498-2245; FAX (315) 498-2977
E-MAIL: hazzardn@sunyocc.edu **WEB SITE: www.sunyocc.edu**

Office of Services for Students with Special Needs (OSSSN)
Summer Program: A one-credit course is offered during the summer in study strategies for students with learning disabilities.

PAUL SMITH'S COLLEGE
ROUTES 86 & 30, P.O. BOX 265
PAUL SMITHS, NEW YORK 12970
(518) 327-6414; FAX: (518) 327-6369
E-MAIL: mccartr@paulsmiths.edu
WEB SITE: www.paulsmiths.edu

Center for Accommodations Services
Summer Program: Three-day orientation program; Cost: $60. Parents are included.

ROCKLAND COMMUNITY COLLEGE
145 COLLEGE ROAD
SUFFERN, NEW YORK 10901
(845) 574-4316; FAX: (845) 574-4462
E-MAIL: mzemek@sunyrockland.edu
WEB SITE: www.sunyrockland.edu

Office of Disability Services
Summer Program: "Keys For Success" – a one-credit program open only for incoming freshmen with learning disabilities. Instruction in study skills,

organizational skills, time management, test-taking strategies, note taking, summarizing, coping skills, campus orientation. Cost: $105 plus fees

OHIO

CUYAHOGA COMMUNITY COLLEGE – EASTERN CAMPUS
4250 RICHMOND ROAD
HIGHLAND HILLS VILLAGE, OHIO 44122-6195
(216) 987-2034; FAX: (216) 987-2423
E-MAIL: maryann.sender@tri-c.edu WEB SITE: www.tri-c.edu

ACCESS/DSS/Vocational Education Program
Summer Program: The summer program includes introduction to college life, time management skills, strategies for becoming a more independent student and study skills.

PENNSYLVANIA

COMMUNITY COLLEGE OF ALLEGHENY COUNTY:
ALLEGHENY CAMPUS
808 RIDGE AVENUE
PITTSBURGH, PENNSYLVANIA 15212
(412) 237-4613, (412) 237-4552 TTY; FAX: (412) 237-2721
E-MAIL: mgleser@ccac.edu WEB SITE: www.ccac.edu

Learning Disabilities Summer Pre-College Program
Summer Program: A four-week pre-college program emphasizing study skills, reading, English, and math and transition from high school to college.

READING AREA COMMUNITY COLLEGE
P.O. BOX 1706, 10 SOUTH SECOND STREET
READING, PENNSYLVANIA 19603
(610) 372-4721 X5060; FAX: (610) 607-6257
E-MAIL: mmitchell@racc.edu WEB SITE: www.racc.edu

Center for Counseling and Academic Development
Summer Program: One-credit course in "College Success Strategies" (required of all incoming students). Basic courses in reading, writing, math and study skills are offered.

VERMONT

LANDMARK COLLEGE
(COLLEGE FOR STUDENTS WITH LEARNING DISABILITIES)
RIVER ROAD, R.R. I, BOX 1000
PUTNEY, VERMONT 05346
(802) 387-6711; FAX: (802) 387-6860
E-MAIL: admissions@landmark.edu WEB SITE: www.landmark.edu

Summer Program: Three-week intensive program focusing on skills development, reading and reading comprehension, effective writing or composition skills, organizational and study skills. Students take writing, study skills and either math or special communications. All summer classes meet for an hour and fifteen minutes a day (non-credit). Cost: $3,600

VIRGINIA

NEW RIVER COMMUNITY COLLEGE
P.O. BOX 1127
DUBLIN, VIRGINIA 27084
(540) 674-3600 X4358; FAX: (540) 674-3649
E-MAIL: nrdixoj@nr.edu WEB SITE: www.nr.edu

Learning Enrichment and Achievement Program (LEAP)
Summer Prep Program: One-week introduction to college and academic strategies. Cost: $35

WISCONSIN

WAUKESHA COUNTY TECHNICAL COLLEGE
800 MAIN STREET
PEWAUKEE, WISCONSIN 53072-4698
(262) 691-5210
E-MAIL: djilbert@wctc.edu WEB SITE: www.wctc.edu

The Learning Place
Summer Program: A one-day transition class with limited enrollment. The program prepares the students with learning disabilities for the fall semester.

WISCONSIN INDIANHEAD TECHNICAL COLLEGE
1900 COLLEGE DRIVE
RICE LAKE, WISCONSIN 54868
(715) 234-7082; FAX: (715) 234-5172
WEB SITE: www.witechcolleges.com

Student Success Center Services
Summer Program: Non-credit, post-high school/pre-college Transition Assistance Program (TAP) is designed to prepare students with learning disabilities for college.

COLLEGES OFFERING SCHOLARSHIPS SPECIFICALLY FOR STUDENTS WITH LEARNING DISABILITIES

NATIONAL CENTER FOR LEARNING DISABILITIES
WEB SITE: www. ncld.org

Anne Ford Scholarship
The Anne Ford Scholarship is a $10,000 award given to a high school senior with an identified learning disability who is pursuing an undergraduate degree. The ideal candidate is a high school senior who has faced the challenges of having a learning disability; is committed to completing a college degree and setting career goals; has demonstrated perseverance; embraces new opportunities; has a well-rounded perspective shaped by experiences in school, in the community, and with family and friends; understands how a learning disability affects his/her life and recognizes the importance of self-advocacy; believes in contributing to society in a way that increases the opportunities for individuals with learning disabilities; and will feel comfortable serving as a role model for others who struggle with learning disabilities. For more information visit www.ncld.org.

FOUR-YEAR COLLEGES

ALABAMA

JACKSONVILLE STATE UNIVERSITY
700 PELHAM ROAD, NORTH
JACKSONVILLE, ALABAMA 36265-1602
(256) 782-5093 V/TDD; FAX: (256) 782-5025
E-MAIL: dmiller@jsucc.jsu.edu **WEB SITE: www.jsu.edu**

Disability Support Services (DSS)
The Heather Whitestone, Miss America Scholarship is available for any student with a documented disability who is served by Disability Support Services.

ARIZONA

ARIZONA STATE UNIVERSITY

BOX 873202
TEMPE, ARIZONA 85287
(480) 965-1234, (480) 965-9000 TDD; FAX: (480) 965-0441
E-MAIL: disability-q@asu.edu **WEB SITE: www.asu.edu**

Disability Resource Center (DRC)
All undergraduate applicants must be registered with the DRC as a qualified student with a disability and be enrolled in a full-time degree program at ASU. Scholarships range from $200 to $1,250 per semester. For an *Andrew Brown* or *Ethelmae Merriam Scholarship,* student must have a minimum 2.5 ASU cumulative GPA, submit a two-page personal statement, establish financial need, all disabilities are eligible. Along with the above criteria, other scholarships have additional requirements: For a *DRC Regents' Scholarship* students must be an undergraduate Arizona resident with 3.0 GPA. For a *Steven and Mary Rosenfield Scholarship,* students must have a documented learning disability or ADHD, be a first semester freshman, northern California resident preferred.

UNIVERSITY OF ARIZONA

P.O. BOX 210136, 1010 NORTH HIGHLAND AVENUE
TUCSON, ARIZONA, 85721-0136
(520) 621-1427; FAX: (520) 626-3260
E-MAIL: jorgera@u.arizona.edu **WEB SITE: www.salt.arizona.edu**

Strategic Alterative Learning Techniques (SALT) Center
SALT awards two needs-based scholarships to incoming freshmen. Criteria: SALT financial aid application and letter requesting consideration.

ARKANSAS

UNIVERSITY OF THE OZARKS

415 NORTH COLLEGE AVENUE
CLARKSVILLE, ARKANSAS 72830
(479) 979-1403; FAX: (479) 979-1429
E-MAIL: jlc@ozarks.edu **WEB SITE: www.ozarks.edu**

Jones Learning Center
Jones Learning Center Scholarships: Two types of scholarships are awarded - both merit and need-based. Awards range from $500 to $8,000 annually. Must maintain a cumulative GPA of 2.0.

CALIFORNIA

BIOLA UNIVERSITY
13800 BIOLA AVENUE
LA MIRADA, CALIFORNIA 90639
(562) 944-0351 X5851, (562) 777-4030 TTY
WEB SITE: www.biola.edu

Disability Services
Disability Services awards five $1,000 scholarships. The deadline is October for the Spring semester. Applications are through the Disability Services office.

CALIFORNIA STATE POLYTECHNIC UNIVERSITY: POMONA
3801 WEST TEMPLE AVENUE
POMONA, CALIFORNIA 91768
(909) 869-7659 V/TDD; FAX: (909) 869-3271
E-MAIL: clschmitt@csupomona.edu
WEB SITE: www.csupomona.edu

Disability Resource Center (DRC)
The DRC sponsors a yearly silent auction to raise money to improve services and to offer students with disabilities an opportunity to apply for scholarships.

CALIFORNIA STATE UNIVERSITY: NORTHRIDGE
18111 NORDHOFF STREET
NORTHRIDGE, CALIFORNIA 91330-8264
(818) 677-2684; FAX: (818) 677-4932
E-MAIL: sdr@csun.edu **WEB SITE: www.csun.edu**

Students with Disabilities Resources
There are approximately twenty $1,000 scholarships each year that students with any type of disability can apply for. Scholarship money is derived from philanthropic organizations throughout the community. Donors pick the students from the completed applications.

COLORADO

UNIVERSITY OF COLORADO: BOULDER
107 UCB
BOULDER, COLORADO 80309-0107
(303) 492-8671; FAX: (303) 492-5601
E-MAIL: dsinfo@colorado.edu

WEB SITE: www.colorado.edu/disabilityservices

Academic Access and Resources Program
Scherpenseel Family Scholarship: Awarded to entering freshmen in Arts and Sciences with Colorado residency, documented disability and financial need.

DISTRICT OF COLUMBIA

THE GEORGE WASHINGTON UNIVERSITY
800 21st STREET NW, MARVIN CENTER, SUITE 242
WASHINGTON, D.C. 20052
(202) 994-8250 V/TDD; FAX: (202) 994-7610
E-MAIL: dss@gwu.edu **WEB SITE: www.gwu.edu**

Disability Support Services
Barbara Jackman Zuckert Scholarship for blind students with learning disabilities, part or full-time. One scholarship per year is offered, amount varies.

FLORIDA

FLORIDA A & M UNIVERSITY
667 ARDELIA COURT
TALLAHASSEE, FLORIDA 32307
(850) 599-3180; FAX: (850) 561-2513
E-MAIL: nholmes@famu.edu **WEB SITE: www.famu.edu**

Learning Development and Evaluation Center
Thordore R. and Vivian Johnson Scholarship: $2,000 annually is offered to a student with a 2.0 GPA, 2nd semester, plus eligibility for financial aid and a documented learning disability.

FLORIDA ATLANTIC UNIVERSITY
777 GLADES ROAD, SU 133, PO BOX 3091
BOCA RATON, FLORIDA 33431
(561) 297-3880, (561) 297-0358 TTY; FAX: (561) 297-2184
E-MAIL: nrokos@fau.edu **WEB SITE: www.osd.fau.edu**

Office for Students with Disabilities
Johnson Scholarship: Up to $3,500 per year for Florida residents. *Life Long Learning Society Scholarship:* $1,000 for a student with a disability who is currently enrolled in Florida Atlantic University.

SAINT PETERSBURG COLLEGE
6605 5th AVENUE, NORTH
SAINT PETERSBURG, FLORIDA 33733-3489
(727) 341-4758; FAX: (727) 341-4770
E-MAIL: Giar.Linda@spcollege.edu WEB SITE: www.spcollege.edu

Office of Services for Students with Disabilities (OSSD)
Amy Blanton Scholarship: Up to $500 for several students with disabilities.

GEORGIA

UNIVERSITY OF GEORGIA
114 CLARK HOWELL HALL
ATHENS, GEORGIA 30602
(706) 542-8719; FAX: (706) 542-8778
E-MAIL: dshimket@uga.edu WEB SITE: www.dissvcs.uga.edu

Disability Resource Center (DRC)
Recipients of the following awards must be University of Georgia students registered with the DRC. *Joe Coile Memorial Award:* $500. Student must demonstrate Coile's quality of service, dedication and character. *Lauren Melissa Kelly Award:* $500-1,000 Hardship Award. *Gregory Charles Johnson Award:* full tuition for one academic year. Student must be a Georgia Resident, have completed 30 semester hours and have a 2.5 GPA. *Fritch Foundation:* Awards for students with disabilities, amounts vary.

ILLINOIS

SOUTHERN ILLINOIS UNIVERSITY AT CARBONDALE
CLINICAL CENTER ACHIEVE PROGRAM
CARBONDALE, ILLINOIS 62901-4615
(618) 453-2595; FAX: (618) 453-3711
E-MAIL: achieve@siu.edu WEB SITE: www.siu.edu/~achieve

Clinical Center Achieve Program
The George Scheffer Tru Value Scholarship: $500. The scholarship is awarded to a student in the roster of all incoming new students specifically enrolled in the Achieve Program. There is no application process.

INDIANA

INDIANA UNIVERSITY
DISABILITY SERVICES FOR STUDENTS
601 EAST KIRKWOOD HALL, #327
BLOOMINGTON, INDIANA 47405-2801

(812) 855-3508; FAX: (812) 855-7650
E-MAIL: ferguson@indiana.edu
WEB SITE: www.indiana.edu/~iubdss

Disability Services for Students
Life Family Scholarship Fund: Several awards are made each spring to students with learning disabilities who are registered with the Office of Disabled Student Services. Award criteria include being an Indiana or Tennessee resident with demonstrated academic excellence and financial need.

IOWA

MORNINGSIDE COLLEGE
1501 MORNINGSIDE AVENUE
SIOUX CITY, IOWA 51106
(712) 274-5191, 1-800-831-0806 X5191; FAX: (712) 274-5101
E-MAIL: tennapel@morningside.edu
WEB SITE: www.morningside.edu

Focus Program
Focus Grant – Must qualify for financial assistance; the amount awarded is half the cost of the Focus Program.

KANSAS

KANSAS STATE UNIVERSITY
202 HOLTON HALL
MANHATTAN, KANSAS 66506-1311
(785) 532-6441; FAX: (785) 532-6457
E-MAIL: dss@ksu.edu **WEB SITE: www.ksu.edu/dss**

Disabled Student Services
Educational Opportunity Scholarships: Two scholarships offered at $500 each.

KENTUCKY

EASTERN KENTUCKY UNIVERSITY
521 LANCASTER AVENUE, TURLEY HOUSE 1
RICHMOND, KENTUCKY 40475-3136
(859) 622-1500 V/TDD; FAX: (859) 622-6395
E-MAIL: disbellu@acs.eku.edu
WEB SITE: www.eku.edu/student services

Project SUCCESS
The Agee Memorial Dyslexia Scholarship is offered to a student with an estab-

lished and documented specific learning disability in reading and/or dyslexia. Two academic scholarships, consisting of $1,000 each, are awarded towards the cost of tuition to two students who meet the stated criteria. If tuition is paid for by another grant, scholarship or agency, the award will go directly to the student. One scholarship is awarded to an incoming freshman, the other to a current student in good academic standing. The scholarship recipient may only receive funds once. Students not selected may apply each academic year.

MURRAY STATE UNIVERSITY
SERVICES FOR STUDENTS WITH LEARNING DISABILITIES
P.O. BOX 9
MURRAY, KENTUCKY 42071-0009
(270) 762-2018; FAX: (270) 762-4339
E-MAIL: cindy.clemson@murraystate.edu
WEB SITE: www.murraystate.edu/secsv/ssld

Services for Students with Learning Disabilities
Many students with learning disabilities receive scholarships from Vocational Rehabilitation.

MAINE

UNITY COLLEGE
QUAKER HILL ROAD, RR 78, P.O. BOX 1
UNITY, MAINE 04988-9502
(207) 948-3131 X263; FAX: (207) 948-5626
E-MAIL: jhoran@unity.edu **WEB SITE: www.unity.edu**

Learning Resource Center
Learning Resource Center Achievement Scholarship: Up to $750 in award(s) may be given annually to a high school applicant(s) who has overcome adversity and disadvantage to succeed in high school. Eligibility requires demonstrated academic improvement and achievement in spite of one or more significant obstacles such as serious illness, physical handicap or learning disability. Problems encountered and successful efforts to overcome them should be documented with supporting letters from school officials and, if appropriate, other professionals such as physicians, tutors, rehabilitation workers and/or counselors.

MARYLAND

FROSTBURG STATE UNIVERSITY
150 PULLEN HALL
FROSTBURG, MARYLAND 21532-1099
(301) 687-4483; FAX: (301) 687-4671
E-MAIL: lpullen@frostburg.edu
WEB SITE: www.frostburg.edu/clife/dss

Disability Support Services
Delta Chi Fraternity Disabled Student Scholarships: Units of $300 are available to full-time students who have demonstrated academic ability. Applicants must be registered with Student Support Services Office.
Governor's Special Needs Scholarship for the Handicapped: Scholarship for annual tuition is offered to a Maryland resident with a bona fide and veritable handicap, a combined SAT of 750 and high school GPA of 2.7 or above. University applicants must have an academic GPA of 2.7 or above.

MASSACHUSETTS

BOSTON UNIVERSITY
19 DEERFIELD STREET
BOSTON, MASSACHUSETTS 02215
(617) 353-3658 V/TTY; FAX: (617) 353-9646
E-MAIL: lwolf@bu.edu **WEB SITE: www.bu.edu/disability**

Learning Disabilities Services (LDS)
The Office of Disabilities Services offers a limited number of scholarships for degree program students who participate in LDS's Comprehensive Strategy Tutoring Program. Students who demonstrate eligibility for need-based financial assistance through the University's Office of Financial Assistance may apply for scholarship assistance. Scholarship assistance beyond two academic semesters is not offered, but students may submit an appeal for additional financial assistance.

CURRY COLLEGE
1071 BLUE HILL AVENUE
MILTON, MASSACHUSETTS 02186-2395
(617) 333-2270; FAX: (617) 333-2018
E-MAIL: Ijiri@curry.edu **WEB SITE: www.curry.edu**

Program for Advancement of Learning (PAL)
Benjamin Gordon Scholarship, Shapiro Scholarship, Jennifer Phillips Loan. Please call for information.

FITCHBURG STATE COLLEGE
160 PEARL STREET
FITCHBURG, MASSACHUSETTS 01420
(978) 665-3427; FAX: (978) 665-4799
E-MAIL: dstevenson@fsc.edu **WEB SITE: www.fsc.edu**

Disability Services
Garrett Conrad Scholarship: $300 is awarded to a student with a disability in good academic standing, who has volunteer community service experiences.

WHEATON COLLEGE
25 EAST MAIN STREET
NORTON, MASSACHUSETTS 02766
(508) 286-8215, (508) 286-5682 TTY; FAX: (508) 286-5621
E-MAIL: mbledsoe@wheatonma.edu
WEB SITE: www.wheatoncollege.edu

Disability Services
H.C. Bowen-Smith Scholarship: $800 per year to assist financially needy students identified with probable learning disabilities to pay for testing by professionals in the area. Scholarships for diagnostic testing only.

MICHIGAN

AQUINAS COLLEGE
1607 ROBINSON ROAD SOUTHEAST
GRAND RAPIDS, MICHIGAN 49506-1799
(616) 632-2166; FAX: (616) 732-4431
E-MAIL: sweenjac@aquinas.edu **WEB SITE: www.aquinas.edu**

Academic Achievement Center
Berkowitz Scholarship for students with disabilities

WAYNE STATE UNIVERSITY
5155 GULLEN MALL, 1600 UGL
DETROIT, MICHIGAN 48202
(313) 577-1851, (313) 577-3365 TTY; FAX: (313) 577-4898
WEB SITE: www.eas.wayne.edu

Educational Accessibility Services (EAS)
Robert 0. Cork Scholarship: Amount varies. Student must be a Wayne State University student with a disability and registered with EAS, have at least a 3.0 overall GPA, have a recent transcript and a written statement. Awards are determined for two recipients who are notified in late Spring.

MINNESOTA

AUGSBURG COLLEGE
2211 RIVERSIDE AVENUE, CB #57
MINNEAPOLIS, MINNESOTA 55454
(612) 330-1053, (612) 330-1748 TDD; FAX: (612) 330-1137
E-MAIL: class@augsburg.edu
WEB SITE: www.augsburg.edu/classprogram

Center for Learning and Adaptive Student Services (CLASS)
Grace Scholarship ($1,400) to students in CLASS with financial need; *Schottenstein Scholarship* ($1,000) to students in CLASS with learning disabilities; *Lutheran Brotherhood Scholarship* ($600) to students with learning disabilities in CLASS

SOUTHWEST MINNESOTA STATE UNIVERSITY
1501 STATE STREET
MARSHALL, MINNESOTA 56258
(507) 537-6169; FAX: (507) 537-6027
E-MAIL: leach@southwestmsu.edu
WEB SITE: www.southwestmsu.edu

Learning Resources, TRIO Program
Trio Scholarships: Three $150 scholarships are awarded each year to students who receive learning resource services, are in good academic standing and who are first generation, low income and/or have a disability.

MONTANA

MONTANA STATE UNIVERSITY – BILLINGS
1500 UNIVERSITY DRIVE
BILLINGS, MONTANA 59101-0298
(406) 657-2283 V/TTY; FAX: (406) 657-1658
E-MAIL: tcarey@msubillings.edu
WEB SITE: www.msubillings.edu/dss

Disability Support Services
Disability Support Services' registered students are eligible for Montana Center Disability Scholarships. Annual number of scholarships and dollar amounts vary.

ROCKY MOUNTAIN COLLEGE
1511 POLY DRIVE
BILLINGS, MONTANA 59102-1796

(406) 657-1128, 1-800-877-8259; FAX: (406) 259-9751
E-MAIL: vandykj@rocky.edu or sas@rocky.edu
WEB SITE: www.rocky.edu

Services for Academic Success (SAS)
SAS Scholarship: $500 is awarded each year to a student who is a participant in the SAS program who has had significant challenges in pursuit of a college degree and who has financial need. Applications are available in January for the second semester.

NEVADA

UNIVERSITY OF NEVADA: RENO
DISABILITY RESOURCE CENTER 078
107 THOMPSON STUDENT SERVICES CENTER
RENO, NEVADA 89557-0072
(702) 784-6000; FAX: (702) 784-1353
E-MAIL: mzabel@unr.edu **WEB SITE: www.unr.edu**

Disability Resource Center
Educational Opportunity Award: $300 is offered to students in Junior standing with a 2.0 GPA. $1,000 scholarships are offered through the associate Student Union.

NEW HAMPSHIRE

UNIVERSITY OF NEW HAMPSHIRE
4 GARRISON AVENUE
DURHAM, NEW HAMPSHIRE 03824
(603) 862-2607 V/TTY; FAX: (603) 862-4043
E-MAIL: maxine.little@unh.edu
WEB SITE: www.unh.edu/disabilityservices

Disability Service for Students
James J. Brunelli Memorial Scholarship: $1,000

NEW YORK

HOFSTRA UNIVERSITY
130 HOFSTRA UNIVERSITY
HEMPSTEAD, NEW YORK 11549-1300
(516) 463-5038; FAX: (516) 463-4049
E-MAIL: PALS@hofstra.edu **WEB SITE: www.hofstra.edu**

Program for Academic Learning Skills (PALS)

Hofstra University awards a special scholarship to students with learning disabilities on alternate years.

JOHN JAY COLLEGE OF CRIMINAL JUSTICE
CITY UNIVERSITY OF NEW YORK
445 WEST 59th STREET
NEW YORK, NEW YORK 10019
(212) 237-8185; FAX: (212) 237-8282
WEB SITE: www.jjay.cuny.edu

Accessibility Programs for Students with Disabilities
Kitty Lund Award: One award per academic year in the amount of $500 to a junior or senior student, registered with the Office for Accessability Programs for Students with Disabilities, having a 3.0 GPA or better, and involved in extracurricular activities.

LONG ISLAND UNIVERSITY: C.W. POST CAMPUS
720 NORTHERN BLVD.
BROOKVILLE, NEW YORK 11548
(516) 299-3057; FAX: (516) 299-2126
E-MAIL: susan.rock@liu.edu **WEB SITE: www.liu.edu**

Academic Resource Center
Ed and Ginny Shorin Endowment Scholarship: $2,500 award to an Academic Resource Center student who has been successful academically and shows financial need.

NEW YORK INSTITUTE OF TECHNOLOGY
P.O. BOX 8000, NORTHERN BLVD.
OLD WESTBURY, NEW YORK 11568-8000
(516) 686-7683; FAX: (516) 686-7891
E-MAIL: cdavid01@nyit.edu **WEB SITE: www.nyit.edu**

Disability Services
Kirsch Memorial Scholarship for students with disabilities (by nomination).

NEW YORK UNIVERSITY
240 GREENE STREET, 2nd FLOOR
NEW YORK, NEW YORK 10012
(212) 998-4979; FAX: (212) 995-4114
E-MAIL: lc83@nyu.edu **WEB SITE: www.nyu.edu/osl/csd**

Henry and Lucy Moses Center for Students with Disabilities
Retentic Scholarships for students with disabilities.

ROCHESTER INSTITUTE OF TECHNOLOGY
LEARNING SUPPORT SERVICES
LEARNING DEVELOPMENT CTR., EASTMAN BLDG. (01-2355)
ONE LOMB MEMORIAL DRIVE
ROCHESTER, NEW YORK 14623
(716) 475-5296; FAX: (716) 475-5832
E-MAIL: lafldc@rit.edu **WEB SITE: www.rit.edu/sa/ldc**

Learning Support Services (LSS/LDC)
Bennett Scholarship: Scholarship awarded annually to students already in the program. Awards range from $500 to $1,500.

SAINT THOMAS AQUINAS COLLEGE
125 ROUTE 340
SPARKILL, NEW YORK 10976
(845) 398-4230; FAX: (845) 398-4229
E-MAIL: pathways@stac.edu **WEB SITE: www.stac.edu**

Pathways
Two scholarships are dedicated for Pathways students. The scholarships are renewable for four years; amounts vary.

SUNY – ALBANY UNIVERSITY
1400 WASHINGTON AVENUE, CC 130/137
ALBANY, NEW YORK 12222
(518) 442-5490; FAX: (518) 442-5589
E-MAIL: cmalloch@uamail.albany.edu
WEB SITE: www.albany.edu/studentlife/ld

Learning Disabled Student Services
Michael Corso Award: The Corso Award Fund offers up to $1,000 to students registered with Learning Disability Services for personal expenses related to continued academic success and/or the acquisition of equipment or adaptive technology. Matriculated students with a GPA of 3.0 are eligible and must present evidence of strong campus involvement and/or leadership experience, plus academic awards for high GPA.

SUNY: COLLEGE AT BROCKPORT
350 NEW CAMPUS DRIVE
BROCKPORT, NEW YORK 14420-2947
(585) 395-5409 V/TTY; FAX: (585) 395-5291
E-MAIL: osdoffic@brockport.edu **WEB SITE: www.brockport.edu**

Office for Students with Disabilities

James Francis Harris Memorial Award: Any student who has a disability is eligible to apply. A half-tuition scholarship is awarded annually to one student, sometimes two. Vocational Rehabilitation Services is also a grant resource helping students with tuition, books and tutoring.

SUNY: COLLEGE OF TECHNOLOGY AT CANTON
34 CORNELL DRIVE, CAMPUS CENTER 235
CANTON, NEW YORK 13617
(315) 386-7392; FAX: (315) 379-3877
E-MAIL: leev@canton.edu **WEB SITE: www.canton.edu**

Accommodative Services
A scholarship is available for students with learning disabilities who are enrolled in the Computer Information System curriculum, have successfully completed one year and have at least a 3.0 GPA. Accommodative Services also keeps resources of national and state scholarship information available to students with learning disabilities.

NORTH CAROLINA

UNIVERSITY OF NORTH CAROLINA AT CHARLOTTE
9201 UNIVERSITY CITY BLVD.
CHARLOTTE, NORTH CAROLINA 28223
(704) 687-4355; FAX: (704) 687-3226
E-MAIL: dissrvcs@email.uncc.edu **WEB SITE: www.ds.uncc.edu**

Disability Services
Kiwanis Club Scholarship: Awarded by the Kiwanis Club to students with disabilities.

OHIO

OHIO WESLEYAN UNIVERSITY
LEARNING DISABILITIES ASSISTANCE CENTER
61 SOUTH SANDUSKY STREET
DELAWARE, OHIO 43015
(740) 368-3280
E-MAIL: arc@owu.edu **WEB SITE: www.owu.edu**

Learning Disabilities Assistance Center
Scholarships for Central Ohio students with high ACT/SAT and specific learning disability.

UNIVERSITY OF TOLEDO
OFFICE OF ACCESSIBILITY
1400 SNYDER MEMORIAL MAIL STOP 110
TOLEDO, OHIO 43606-3390
(419) 530-4981; FAX: (419) 530-6137
E-MAIL: lyost@utnet.utoledo.edu WEB SITE: www.utoledo.edu

Office of Accessibility
Keitholtz Scholarship: $100 to $1,500 is awarded per year.

PENNSYLVANIA

EAST STROUDSBURG UNIVERSITY
200 PROSPECT STREET
EAST STROUDSBURG, PENNSYLVANIA 18301-2999
(570) 422-3954 V/TTY; FAX: (570) 422-3918
E-MAIL: emiller@po-box.esu.edu WEB SITE: www3.esu.edu

Disability Services
Krawitz Scholarship: One $500 scholarship is awarded annually to a part- or full-time student with a learning disability who is pursuing an undergraduate degree. Criteria: (1) minimum 2.3 cumulative grade point average; (2) completed a minimum of 12 credits, (3) documented learning disability.

PENNSYLVANIA STATE UNIVERSITY: BERKS CAMPUS
DISABILITY SERVICES
P.O. BOX 7009, TULPEHOCKEN ROAD
READING, PENNSYLVANIA 19610
(610) 396-6410; FAX: (610) 396-6026
WEB SITE: www.bk.psu.edu

Disability Services
Rehab Club Memorial Scholarship: Consideration for this scholarship will be given to all full-time undergraduate students with disabilities enrolled or planning to enroll in Penn State University. *David R. Martino Memorial Scholarship:* This scholarship is awarded to financially needy students with a disability who are enrolled or are planning to enroll full-time at the University. *Virginia G. Rimer Memorial Scholarship:* This scholarship will be given to outstanding graduate and undergraduate students enrolled at Penn State University who have a disability. Criteria for all these awards include demonstrated academic achievement, character, leadership and financial need.

TEXAS

SCHREINER UNIVERSITY
CAMPUS BOX 6209
KERRVILLE, TEXAS 78028
(830) 792-7256, 1-800-343-4919
WEB SITE: www.schreiner.edu

Learning Support Services Program
M.D. Anderson Foundation for students with disabilities. *Wagoner Family Endowed LSS Grant* and *John C. Hamilton Jr. Memorial Grant* are also awarded.

UNIVERSITY OF HOUSTON
307 STUDENT SERVICE CENTER
48 CALHOUN ROAD
HOUSTON, TEXAS 77204-3022
(713) 743-2255; FAX: (713) 743-5396
E-MAIL: camoruso@uh.edu **WEB SITE: www.uh.edu**

Center for Students with disABILITIES
Eric Alexander Memorial Scholarship: Amount not to exceed $1,000 per recipient. Scholarship may be broken down and given to more than one student, i.e., two students $500 each for a total of $1,000. Criteria: cumulated GPA of 2.5 or better, sophomore or upper classman, undergraduate only, full-time students who have applied for financial aid and have a learning disability according to college guidelines.

UTAH

SOUTHERN UTAH UNIVERSITY
351 UNIVERSITY BLVD.
CEDAR CITY, UTAH 84720
(435) 865-8022; FAX: (435) 865-8235
E-MAIL: alldredge@suu.edu
WEB SITE: www.suu.edu/ss/support/disability

Student Support Center/Disability Support Center
One book scholarship worth $200 is awarded. This is part of TRIO Day.

UNIVERSITY OF UTAH
CENTER FOR DISABILITY SERVICES
162 UNION BUILDING
200 SOUTH CENTRAL CAMPUS DRIVE
SALT LAKE CITY, UTAH 84112-9107

(801) 581-5020 V/TDD; FAX: (801) 581-5487
E-MAIL: info@disability.utah.edu
WEB SITE: www.utah.edu or www.disability.utah.edu

Center for Disability Services
Louise J. Snow Scholarship: Available to any student with a documented disability.

UTAH STATE UNIVERSITY
0101 OLD MAIN HALL
LOGAN, UTAH 84322-0101
800-259-2966, (435) 797-0740, (435) 797-2444 TTY; FAX: (435) 797-0130
E-MAIL: diane.baum@usu.edu WEB SITE: www.usu.edu

Disability Resource Center (DRC)
Disability Resource Center Scholarships: Unlimited number of scholarships are awarded annually for help with tuition.

UTAH VALLEY STATE COLLEGE
800 WEST UNIVERSITY PARKWAY, MAIL STOP 190
OREM, UTAH 84058-5999
(801) 863-8747; FAX: (801) 863-8377
E-MAIL: millersh@uvsc.edu or asd@uvsc.edu
WEB SITE: www.uvsc.edu

Accessibility Services Department
Five half-tuition scholarships are offered for new students on a first come, first served basis. Write for information by May 1.

WESTMINISTER COLLEGE
1840 SOUTH 1300 EAST
SALT LAKE CITY, UTAH 84105
(801) 832-2280, (801) 832-2286 TTY; FAX: (801) 832-3101
E-MAIL: gdewitt@westminstercollege.edu
WEB SITE: www.westminstercollege.edu

Disability Services Program
Joe Gunderson Memorial Scholarship: Awarded to a student in good academic standing. Preference is given to a student with a documented learning disability.

WEST VIRGINIA

MARSHALL UNIVERSITY
520 18th STREET, MYERS HALL
HUNTINGTON, WEST VIRGINIA 25755
(304) 696-6252; FAX: (304) 696-3231
E-MAIL: guyerb@marshall.edu **WEB SITE: www.marshall.edu**

Higher Education for Learning Problems (H.E.L.P.)
Scholarships are available within the H.E.L.P. Program on a limited basis to those who receive a PELL Grant.

WEST VIRGINIA WESLEYAN COLLEGE
59 COLLEGE AVENUE
BUCKHANNON, WEST VIRGINIA 26201-2995
(304) 473-8563; FAX: (304) 473-8497
E-MAIL: kuba_s@wvwc.edu or belknap_r@wvwc.edu
WEB SITE: www.wvwc.edu/stu/sass

Student Academic Support Services
Byron Barosh Scholarship, Hall Liles Scholarship, Allen Manfuso Scholarship, Victor and Gayle Mavar Scholarship Fund: These scholarships are offered to students with learning disabilities.

WISCONSIN

UNIVERSITY OF WISCONSIN: MADISON
905 UNIVERSITY AVENUE, SUITE 100K
MADISON, WISCONSIN 53715-1005
(608) 265-5467; FAX: (608) 265-2998
E-MAIL: woodbridge@wisc.edu **WEB SITE: www.wisc.edu**

McBurney Disability Resource Center
General McBurney Scholarship Program: The program is open to all currently enrolled students with disabilities. One-year awards range from $500 to $1,500. Students can apply every year they are enrolled in the university. Awards are based on scholarship, financial need and special circumstances.

CANADA

UNIVERSITY OF OTTAWA
85 UNIVERSITY, ROOM 339
P.O. BOX 450, STN A
OTTAWA, ONTARIO K1N-6N5
(613) 564-5976, (613) 564-8105 V/TDD; FAX: (613) 562-5159

E-MAIL: yruel@uottawa.ca **WEB SITE: www.uottawa.ca**

Center for Special Services (CSS)
Dr. John Davis Burton Award: Award of $1,000 is given to a student identified as having a learning disability. *Charles-Drouin Award* is for a variable amount.

SCHOLARSHIPS
TWO-YEAR COLLEGES

CALIFORNIA

BARSTOW COMMUNITY COLLEGE
2700 BARSTOW ROAD
BARSTOW, CALIFORNIA 92311
(760) 252-2411; FAX: (760) 252-1875
E-MAIL: pdedios@barstow.edu **WEB SITE: www.barstow.edu**

Disabled Students Programs and Services
Departmental scholarship of $150 to $250 is awarded annually.

BUTTE COMMUNITY COLLEGE
3536 BUTTE CAMPUS DRIVE
OROVILLE, CALIFORNIA 95965
(916) 895-2455; FAX: (916) 895-2235
E-MAIL: thorsellsu@butte.cc.ca.us **WEB SITE: www.butte.edu**

Disabled Student Programs and Services (DSP&S)
Virginia Meeks Book Scholarship: Student must be enrolled in a minimum of six semester units, three of which must be applicable to a Student Education Plan, or Associate Degree, Vocational Certificate of Achievement or transferable to a four-year university.

COLLEGE OF SAN MATEO
1700 WEST HILLSDALE BLVD.
SAN MATEO, CALIFORNIA 94402-3784
(650) 574-6433; FAX: (650) 358-6803
E-MAIL: paparelli@smccd.net
WEB SITE: www.collegeofsanmateo.edu

Assessment Center/Special Programs and Services
Patty Ramos Scholarship: $250: Basic award. Requirements: G.P.A. 2.8, full-time status, personal letter, two letters of recommendation, completed application

COLLEGE OF THE CANYONS
26455 ROCKWELL CANYON ROAD
SANTA CLARITA, CALIFORNIA 91355-1899
(661) 362-3341
WEB SITE: www.canyons.edu

Disabled Student Programs and Services
Five $100 book grants are offered per semester for students meeting the requirements. *Tommy Warner-Nolet:* Four scholarships at $250 each. *Angel Scholarship:* One $250 scholarship.

COLUMBIA COLLEGE
11600 COLUMBIA COLLEGE DRIVE
SONORA, CALIFORNIA 95370-8582
(209) 588-5130; FAX: (209) 588-5330
E-MAIL: cordovam@yosemite.cc.ca.us
WEB SITE: www.columbia.yosemite.edu

Disabled Student Programs and Services
A $1,000 annual scholarship for a currently enrolled full-time student with learning disabilities who is planning to return to Columbia College for their second year.

CYPRESS COLLEGE — ROOSEVELT CENTER
9200 VALLEY VIEW
CYPRESS, CALIFORNIA 90630-5897
(714) 484-7104 X104; FAX: (714) 826-4042
WEB SITE: www.cypresscollege.edu

Disabled Student Programs and Services
Three to four scholarships are available annually for all students with disabilities. Amounts vary from $50 to $250 per award.

DE ANZA COLLEGE
21250 STEVENS CREEK BLVD.
CUPERTINO, CALIFORNIA 95014
(408) 864-5678; FAX: (408) 864-5492
E-MAIL: waathiqpauline@deanza.edu
WEB SITE: www.deanza.edu

Educational Diagnostic Center
Seth Stauffer Memorial Scholarship: A $500 award for students in the program transferring to four-year colleges or universities. Student needs to be in good standing, completed the transfer requirements, and have success-

fully met the challenges of a learning disability. *Barbara Manriques Scholarships:* Two $750 awards for students with disabilities. *Keith Goodin Memorial Scholarship:* A $500 award for students who have overcome difficulties in mathematics. Student needs to be in good standing, successfully completed at least three math classes at this college and have a career goal, which may or may not be in the math or science fields.

FULLERTON COLLEGE
321 EAST CHAPMAN AVENUE
FULLERTON, CALIFORNIA 92832
(714) 992-7270, (714) 871-9192 TDD
E-MAIL: lcampbell@fullcoll.edu **WEB SITE: www.fullcoll.edu**

Disability Support Services
Jason Horn Memorial Scholarship: Awards vary from $100 to $200.
Frances Wahl Scholarship: Awards vary from $100 to $200.

GROSSMONT COLLEGE
8800 GROSSMONT COLLEGE DRIVE
EL CAJON, CALIFORNIA 92020-1799
(619) 644-7112, (619) 644-7980
E-MAIL: Jane.Nolan@gcccd.net **WEB SITE: www.grossmont.edu/dsps**

Disabled Student Services – Learning Development Center
Disabled Student Scholarship: One scholarship in the amount of $150 is awarded to a student with disabilities each semester.

IRVINE VALLEY COLLEGE
5500 IRVINE CENTER DRIVE
IRVINE, CALIFORNIA 92720
(949) 451-5630; FAX: (949) 451-5270
E-MAIL: czucker@ivc.edu **WEB SITE: www.ivc.edu**

Disabled Students Programs and Services (DSP&S)
Challenger's Club: Scholarships worth $100 to $250 are awarded each Spring by the Challenger's Club to students who have various disabilities.

LOS ANGELES CITY COLLEGE
855 NORTH VERMONT AVENUE
LOS ANGELES, CALIFORNIA 90029
(323) 953-4000 X2273; FAX: (323) 953-4013
E-MAIL: matransb@lacitycollege.edu
WEB SITE: www.lacitycollege.edu

Office of Special Services/Learning Disabilities Program
Jay Allen Green Memorial Scholarship Criteria: Student must have successfully completed no fewer than 12 and no more than 72 degree units at Los Angeles City College; have at least a 3.0 cumulative grade point average in all units completed at Los Angeles City College and be currently enrolled in a minimum of 9 units at Los Angeles City College; Verification of learning disability by a learning disability specialist or other qualified professional; two letters of recommendation; one page typed self-profile; up-to-date unprofessional transcript. *Rosalie S. Levine Award:* Recognizes a student with learning disabilities for exceptional accomplishment in the field of art. Criteria: Art major with a learning disability, who has completed at least one year at Los Angeles City College, and demonstrates an exceptional accomplishment in the field of art.

MOORPARK COLLEGE
7075 CAMPUS ROAD
MOORPARK, CALIFORNIA 93021-1695
(805) 378-1461; FAX: (805) 378-1594
E-MAIL: pewins@vcccd.net **WEB SITE: www.moorpark.cc.ca.us**

ACCESS (Accessibility Coordination Center and Educational Support Services)
Chris Newman Memorial Scholarship: $250

ORANGE COAST COLLEGE
P.O. BOX 5005, 2701 FAIRVIEW ROAD
COSTA MESA, CALIFORNIA 92628-5005
(714) 432-5535; FAX: (714) 432-5557
WEB SITE: www.orangecoastcollege.edu

Learning Disabilities Program
Four $300 scholarships are offered to students with learning disabilities.

OXNARD COLLEGE
4000 SOUTH ROSE AVENUE
OXNARD, CALIFORNIA 93033-6699
(805) 986-5830, (805) 488-8022 TTY; FAX: (805) 986-5928
WEB SITE: www.oxnardcollege.edu

Educational Assistance Center
A $150 award is available for students with learning disabilities. Continuing students or transferring students are eligible.

PASADENA CITY COLLEGE
1570 EAST COLORADO BLVD.
PASADENA, CALIFORNIA 91106-2003
(626) 585-7127; FAX: (626) 585-7566
E-MAIL: elweller@pasadena.edu WEB SITE: www.pasadena.edu

Disabled Student Programs and Services (DSP&S)
Five college students with disabilities will receive $200 each to assist with their educational expenses. Must have completed 15 units with an overall GPA of 2.5 or better and have a verifiable disability while receiving services from DSP&S.

SACRAMENTO CITY COLLEGE
3835 FREEPORT BLVD., ROOM A2
SACRAMENTO, CALIFORNIA 95822-1386
(916) 558-2665, (916) 558-2545; FAX: (916) 558-2670
E-MAIL: schafer@scc.losrios.edu WEB SITE: www.scc.losrios.edu

Learning (dis)Abilities Program
Scholarships are determined annually. Apply in January. Awards are made the following summer for the next academic year.

SANTA ANA COLLEGE
1530 WEST 17th STREET
SANTA ANA, CALIFORNIA 92706
(714) 564-6260; FAX: (714) 285-9619
E-MAIL: choo_brooke@sac.edu or kobane_mary@sac.edu
WEB SITE: www.sac.edu

Learning Disabilities Program
Scholarships are available for students with learning disabilities: one scholarship is $500.

SANTA BARBARA CITY COLLEGE
721 CLIFF DRIVE
SANTA BARBARA, CALIFORNIA 93109-2394
(805) 965-0581 X2364, (805) 962-4084 TTY
E-MAIL: dspshelp@sbcc.edu **WEB SITE: www.sbcc.edu**

Disabled Student Programs and Services (DSPS)
Memorial scholarships are awarded annually for up to 24 students (amounts range from $100 to $1,000). Scholarships are awarded to students with a disability who demonstrate financial need and the ability to benefit from college, and who are currently enrolled at Santa Barbara City College.

SANTA MONICA COLLEGE
1900 PICO BLVD.
SANTA MONICA, CALIFORNIA 90405
(310) 434-4684; FAX: (310) 434-3694
E-MAIL: marcopulos_george@smc.edu **WEB SITE: www.smc.edu**

Learning Disabilities Program
Several scholarships are available. Students should apply between January 1 and March 2 to receive the most assistance.

SIERRA COLLEGE
5000 ROCKLIN ROAD
ROCKLIN, CALIFORNIA 95677
(916) 781-0553; FAX: (916) 789-2967
WEB SITE: www.sierracollege.edu

Learning Opportunities Center
Several awards are made each year, ranging from $100 to $250.

VENTURA COLLEGE
4667 TELEGRAPH ROAD
VENTURA, CALIFORNIA 93003
(805) 654-6300
WEB SITE: www.venturacollege.edu

Learning Disability Program
Mike Boggs Memorial Scholarship: Annual award of $250 is given to a student with learning disabilities.

WEST HILLS COMMUNITY COLLEGE
300 CHERRY LANE
COALINGA, CALIFORNIA 93210

(559) 934-2333
E-MAIL: JoyceSmyers@westhillscollege.com
WEB SITE: www.westhillscollege.com/coalinga

Disabled Student Programs and Services (DSPS)
Stephanie Lyles Memorial Scholarship: $250. Awarded to one DSPS student each year.

FLORIDA

BREVARD COMMUNITY COLLEGE
1519 CLEARLAKE ROAD
COCOA, FLORIDA 32922
(321) 433-5598; FAX: (321) 433-5679
E-MAIL: FertelL@brevardcc.edu **WEB SITE: www.brevardcc.edu**

Office for Students with Disabilities
Melbourne Lions Club Scholarship, Rory Devalux Memorial Scholarship for students with any type of disability.

MIAMI-DADE COMMUNITY COLLEGE – KENDALL CAMPUS
11011 SOUTHWEST 104th STREET
MIAMI, FLORIDA 33176-3393
(305) 237-2767
E-MAIL: mmata@mdc.edu or mmcgrewc@mdc.edu or jsabella@mdc.edu
WEB SITE: www.mdc.edu

ACCESS Services Department
Students with a documented learning disability and a minimum of 24 credit hours may apply for scholarships from $100 to $200 for one year.

GEORGIA

REINHARDT COLLEGE
7300 REINHARDT COLLEGE CIRCLE
WALESKA, GEORGIA 30183-2981
(770) 720-5567
E-MAIL: srr@reinhardt.edu **WEB SITE: www.reinhardt.edu**

Academic Support Office
Eagles Eye: For sophomores enrolled in enhanced tutorial program.

HAWAII

HAWAII COMMUNITY COLLEGE
200 WEST KAWILI STREET
BLDG. 388, ROOM 104
HILO, HAWAII 96720-4091
(808) 933-0702 V/TTY
E-MAIL: kkane@hawcc.hawaii.edu
WEB SITE: www.hawcc.hawaii.edu

Ha'awi Kokua Program
Two scholarships awarded each semester to students who are single parents, homemakers, academically disadvantaged or students with a disability. Must have satisfactorily completed at least one semester and have a 2.5 GPA. Applications are available at the Financial Aid Office.

ILLINOIS

ELGIN COMMUNITY COLLEGE
1700 SPARTAN DRIVE
ELGIN, ILLINOIS 60123
(847) 214-7220
E-MAIL: arhoades@elgin.edu **WEB SITE: www.elgin.edu**

Disability Services
Dvorak and Lioness Scholarships for students with disabilities.

HARPER COLLEGE
1200 WEST ALGONQUIN ROAD
PALATINE, ILLINOIS 60067
(847) 925-6266; FAX: (847) 925-6267
E-MAIL: pherrera@harpercollege.edu
WEB SITE: www.harpercollege.edu

Access and Disabilities Office/PASS (Program for Achieving Student Success)
Midge C. Smith, Dan Tarisky Scholarship and the ADS Alumni Scholarships which award six – eight scholarships based on academic goals, a 2.0 GPA or higher and to some extent financial need.

JOHN WOOD COMMUNITY COLLEGE
1301 SOUTH 48th STREET
QUINCY, ILLINOIS 62305
(217) 641-4352, (217) 224-4309 TDD

E-MAIL: akers@jwcc.edu **WEB SITE: www.jwcc.edu**

Support Services Center – Disability Services
Support Services Scholarships: Amounts of $50 to $100 per semester are awarded to students with documented learning disabilities.

LINCOLN TRAIL COLLEGE
11220 STATE HIGHWAY 1
ROBINSON, ILLINOIS 62454
(618) 544-8657; FAX: (618) 544-4705
E-MAIL: haskinsb@iecc.edu **WEB SITE: www.iecc.edu/ltc**

Learning Skills Center
ABE Awards

McHENRY COUNTY COLLEGE
8900 U.S. HIGHWAY 14
CRYSTAL LAKE, ILLINOIS 60012
(815) 455-8676; FAX: (815) 455-3766
E-MAIL: balbright@mchenry.edu **WEB SITE: www.mchenry.edu**

Special Needs Program
The scholarship provides up to $500 for the fall semester and $500 for the following spring semester to be used for tuition, books and fees. Applicant should complete and submit the MCC scholarship application – one-page financial aid application and provide a letter of recommendation and documentation of disability. Scholarship is awarded to a student with a 2.5 GPA pursuing an education at MCC and involved in a community service project.

MORAINE VALLEY COMMUNITY COLLEGE
10900 SOUTH 88th AVENUE
PALOS HILLS, ILLINOIS 60465-0937
(708) 974-5711; FAX: (708) 974-8330
E-MAIL: sievers@morainevalley.edu
WEB SITE: www.morainevalley.edu

Center for Disability Services
$500 Disabilities Scholarship

PARKLAND COLLEGE
2400 WEST BRADLEY AVENUE
CHAMPAIGN, ILLINOIS 61821-1899
(217) 351-2588, (217) 353-2251 TTY; FAX: (217) 351-2581
E-MAIL: nrowley@parkland.edu WEB SITE: www.parkland.edu

Learning Resource Services Center/Disability Services
Jimm V. Scott Memorial Scholarship: Must have completed 20 hours, have a GPA of 2.5 and be enrolled in eight credit hours. Preference to journalism, music or psychology students with disabilities.

IOWA

WALDORF COLLEGE
106 SOUTH 6th STREET
FOREST CITY, IOWA 50436
800-292-1903; FAX: (641) 585-8194
E-MAIL: murraym@waldorf.edu WEB SITE: www.waldorf.edu

Learning Disabilities Program (LDP)
Philip Sigmond Memorial Scholarship: $500 – preference given to students with learning disabilities. *Elaine Anderson Memorial Award:* preference given to students with learning disabilities.

MARYLAND

THE COMMUNITY COLLEGE OF BALTIMORE COUNTY: ESSEX CAMPUS
7201 ROSSVILLE BLVD.
BALTIMORE, MARYLAND 21237-3899
(410) 780-6741, (410) 238-4601 TTY; FAX: (410) 780-6849
E-MAIL: bhunsinger@ccbcmd.edu WEB SITE: www.ccbcmd.edu

Office of Special Services
Two scholarships $100–300 for students with disabilities are determined by Office of Special Services staff.

MASSACHUSETTS

BRISTOL COMMUNITY COLLEGE
777 ELSBREE STREET
FALL RIVER, MASSACHUSETTS 02720-7395
(508) 678-2811 X2955; FAX: (508) 730-3297
WEB SITE: www.bristol.mass.edu

Center for Developmental Education/QUEST PROJECT
QUEST PROJECT Scholarship: Two scholarships are available for the academic year, $500 for the fall semester and $500 for the spring semester.

MOUNT WACHUSETT COMMUNITY COLLEGE
444 GREEN STREET
GARDNER, MASSACHUSETTS 01440
(978) 630-9316
E-MAIL: r.thibodeau@mwcc.mass.edu or j.kulig@mwcc.mass.edu
WEB SITE: www.mwcc.mass.edu

Visions Program TRIO – Student Support Services
George Wallace Foundation Scholarship: Scholarship is based on documented learning disability, minimum 2.5 GPA, completion of 24 credit hours of which at least 12 credit hours were at Mount Wachusett Community College, demonstration of financial need and display of a healthy positive attitude. Award is $500 per year.

MICHIGAN

SOUTHWESTERN MICHIGAN COLLEGE
58900 CHERRY GROVE ROAD
DOWAGIAC, MICHIGAN 49047
(269) 687-4801, 800-456-8675, FAX: (269) 782-1331
E-Mail: ssullivan.swmich.edu
Web Site: www.swmich.edu

Special Populations Program
Tuition assistance is available through the Special Populations Program by the *Carl D. Perkins Grant*: Eligible students must be enrolled in a state approved occupational program and have a financial need and be eligible for Special Populations Program.

WASHTENAW COMMUNITY COLLEGE
4800 EAST HURON RIVER DRIVE, P.O. BOX D-1
ANN ARBOR, MICHIGAN 48106-1610
(734) 973-3342; FAX: (734) 477-8517
E-MAIL: debrag@wccnet.edu **WEB SITE: www.wccnet.edu**

Learning Support Services
A scholarship is awarded to a student with a documented learning disability within the Washtenaw County School district, who has completed secondary education and is planning to attend Washtenaw Community College. Maximum amount of the scholarship is $500. Must maintain a 2.0 average and have two letters of recommendation.

MISSOURI

METROPOLITAN COMMUNITY COLLEGE – LONGVIEW
500 SOUTHWEST LONGVIEW ROAD
LEE'S SUMMIT, MISSOURI 64081-2105
(816) 672-2053; FAX: (816) 672-2719
E-MAIL: maryellen.jenison@mcckc.edu
WEB SITE: www.mcckc.edu

Academic Bridges to Learning Effectiveness (ABLE)
Pilot Club: Awarded preferably to a second or later semester student enrolled in ABLE Program and in good academic standing. *LDA of Missouri – Kansas City Affiliate:* Up to 50% of student's total expenses; must be enrolled in ABLE program and have a diagnosed learning disability. *Thomas S. Kessler Memorial Scholarship:* Awarded for tuition, books, transportation, on-campus childcare or other educational needs, as funds are available.

METROPOLITAN COMMUNITY COLLEGE – PENN VALLEY
3201 SOUTHWEST TRAFFICWAY
KANSAS CITY, MISSOURI 64111
(816) 759-4089
E-MAIL: patricia.goodwin@mcckc.edu **WEB SITE: www.mcckc.edu**

Academic Bridges to Learning Effectiveness (ABLE)
Learning Disability Association of Missouri Scholarship: Criteria: Must be Missouri resident, demonstrate financial need and have a learning disability (not due to head injury); Award amount is up to 50% of total expenses and is based on available funds.

NEW JERSEY

OCEAN COUNTY COLLEGE
COLLEGE DRIVE, P.O. 2001
TOMS RIVER, NEW JERSEY 08754-2001
(732) 255-0456; FAX: (732) 255-0458
E-MAIL: jfischer@ocean.edu or mreustle@ocean.edu
WEB SITE: www.ocean.edu

Project Academic Skills Support (PASS)
Devon Bond Scholarship: $500. Students are asked to apply through the Ocean County College Foundation at the above address for this scholarship and explain why it is needed. Awarded to students who have financial need and who are very actively working with the program.

NEW YORK

BROOME COMMUNITY COLLEGE
P.O. BOX 1017
BINGHAMTON, NEW YORK 13902
(607) 778-5234 V/TDD; FAX: (607) 778-5562
E-MAIL: pomeroy_b@sunybroome.edu
WEB SITE: www.sunybroome.edu

Student Support Services
Scholarships are available to all students with disabilities which includes students with learning disabilities.

DUTCHESS COMMUNITY COLLEGE
53 PENDELL ROAD
POUGHKEEPSIE, NEW YORK 12601
(914) 431-8037
E-MAIL: perez@sunydutchess.edu WEB SITE: www.sunydutchess.edu

Disabled Student Services
Academic Success Scholarship for student graduating from Dutchess Community College who has special learning needs. Amount: $500

HUDSON VALLEY COMMUNITY COLLEGE
80 VANDERBURGH AVENUE
TROY, NEW YORK 12180
(518) 629-7154, (518) 629-7596 TDD; FAX: (518) 629-4831
E-MAIL: negropab@hvcc.edu WEB SITE: www.hvcc.edu

Disability Resource Center
Scholarship is a need-based award, ie, books, transportation, supplies, etc., and is awarded once each semester. *Hazel Hayes Atwater Memorial Scholarship* is open to all students with disabilities. There are also departmental and other scholarships available through the Alumni Development Office. For further information please call (518) 629-7575.

ROCKLAND COMMUNITY COLLEGE
145 COLLEGE ROAD
SUFFERN, NEW YORK 10901
(845) 574-4316; FAX: (845) 574-4462
E-MAIL: mzemek@sunyrockland.edu
WEB SITE: www.sunyrockland.edu

Office of Disability Services

Harrinton Award: Annual award of approximately $1,250 may be given to a single student or to as many as three or four students with the money divided equally. *Jane Cohen Memorial Scholarship:* $500 for a full time student who has completed 24 credits with a GPA of 3.0 or better and is interested in transferring to a four-year college.

SUFFOLK COUNTY COMMUNITY COLLEGE
AMMERMAN CAMPUS
533 COLLEGE ROAD
SELDEN, NEW YORK 11784-2899
(631) 451-4045; FAX: (631) 451-4473
E-MAIL: boycem@sunysuffolk.edu
WEB SITE: www.sunysuffolk.edu

Office of Special Services
Jack Schanfeld Scholarship: For students with disabilities who meet the qualifications.

NORTH CAROLINA

WILKES COMMUNITY COLLEGE
P.O. BOX 120, 1328 SOUTH COLLEGIATE DRIVE
WILKESBORO, NORTH CAROLINA 28697-0120
(336) 838-6560; FAX: (336) 838-6277
E-MAIL: nancy.sizemore@wilkescc.edu WEB SITE: www.wilkescc.edu

Student Support Services
Students with learning disabilities are eligible for Student Support Services scholarships.

OHIO

CUYAHOGA COMMUNITY COLLEGE – EASTERN CAMPUS
4250 RICHMOND ROAD
HIGHLAND HILLS VILLAGE, OHIO 44122-6195
(216) 987-2034; FAX: (216) 987-2423
E-MAIL: maryann.sender@tri-c.edu WEB SITE: www.tri-c.edu

ACCESS/DSS/Vocational Education Program
Rhe Laub Scholarship: Established in 1989, this fund provides scholarship support to adult and working students and provides financial support for special services to students with disabilities (25 years or older, proof of employment, ACCESS department recommendation). *Ed Sparre Technology Scholarship:* Established in 2000 to provide financial support for students

who have a documented disability and need specialized adaptive equipment in order to succeed academically.

SINCLAIR COMMUNITY COLLEGE
OFFICE OF DISABILITY SERVICES
444 WEST THIRD STREET
DAYTON, OHIO 45402-1460
937-512-5113
E-MAIL: robin.moore-cooper@sinclair.edu
WEB SITE: www.sinclair.edu

Office of Disability Services
Alumni Association Scholarship for Students with Disabilities: Students must be registered with the Office of Disability Services, have a minimum 2.5 GPA and have completed 12 credit hours. They must be enrolled for at least 6 credit hours to use the award. Individuals may submit one application per quarter and will be eligible for one award per academic year.

OREGON

CLACKAMAS COMMUNITY COLLEGE
19600 SOUTH MOLALLA AVENUE
OREGON CITY, OREGON 97045
(503) 657-6958 X2324
E-MAIL: caseys@clackamas.edu **WEB SITE: www.clackamas.edu**

Disability Resource Center (DRC)
New Pioneer for Special Needs Individual Scholarship: Full tuition for the academic year. Requirements: students must be facing physical, emotional, or social challenges; must plan to enroll for and maintain at least six credits and one of the letters of recommendation submitted must be from a professional who can explain the challenge(s)

MOUNT HOOD COMMUNITY COLLEGE
26000 SOUTHEAST STARK STREET
GRESHAM, OREGON 97030
(503) 491-6923; FAX: (503) 491-7549
E-MAIL: dsoweb@mhcc.edu **WEB SITE: www.mhcc.edu**

Disability Services
Mount Hood Community College Recognition Scholarship: Scholarship is available to students with disabilities (including students with learning disabilities). Awards are based on need and GPA.

RHODE ISLAND

COMMUNITY COLLEGE OF RHODE ISLAND: KNIGHT CAMPUS
400 EAST AVENUE
WARWICK, RHODE ISLAND 02886-1807
(401) 825-2164
E-MAIL: amcmahon@ccri.edu **WEB SITE: www.ccri.edu**

Access to Opportunity
ABLE of CCRI offers two $1,000 scholarships to benefit students with physical, visual, and / or learning disabilities and used exclusively at CCRI for part- or full-time students. Requirements: Documented disability, two letters of recommendation, interview, 2.5 GPA. A scholarship for a student with a learning disability who has graduated from Community College of Rhode Island and is transferring to a four-year college or university is also available.

TEXAS

ANGELINA COLLEGE
SPECIAL STUDENT SERVICES
P.O. BOX 1768
LUFKIN, TEXAS 75902
(936) 633-5289; FAX: (936) 633-5247
E-MAIL: kbowser@angelina.edu **WEB SITE: www.angelina.edu**

Special Student Services
Vivian Ezelle Johnson Scholarships: Approximately ten scholarships are awarded per year for a value of $250 each per semester.

CEDAR VALLEY COLLEGE
3030 NORTH DALLAS AVENUE
LANCASTER, TEXAS 75134
972-860-8119; Fax: 972-860-8014
WEB SITE: www.cedarvalleycollege.edu

TRIO Special Support Services
Cedar Club: Awards six $200 awards per year to current students. Must have completed 15 hours with 2.0 GPA. Competitive. *DCCCD Foundation Scholarships*: Amount varies. *Cedar Club Scholarships:* Amount varies.

DEL MAR COLLEGE
101 BALDWIN
CORPUS CHRISTI, TEXAS 78404
(361) 698-1298; FAX: (361) 698-1092

E-MAIL: kcarrol@delmar.edu **WEB SITE: www.delmar.edu**

Special Services
Scholarship for all disabilities in the amount of $500 for full-time students with GPA above 2.0 – the higher the GPA, the more likely to get awards

NORTH HARRIS COLLEGE
2700 W.W. THORNE DRIVE
HOUSTON, TEXAS 77073
(281) 618-5481; FAX: (281) 618-7107
E-MAIL: tgarza@nhmccd.edu **WEB SITE: www.nhmccd.edu**

Disability Services Office
HouMet Diagnosticians' Scholarship: Awards are $100 to $500. Applicable to students with all types of disabilities. Apply through Financial Aid.

UTAH

SALT LAKE COMMUNITY COLLEGE
4600 SOUTH REDWOOD ROAD
SALT LAKE CITY, UTAH 84130
(801) 957-4659, (801) 957-4646 TDD; FAX: (801) 957-4947
E-MAIL: linda.bennet@slcc.edu; **WEB SITE: www.slcc.edu**

Disability Resource Center
Tuition waivers are offered to a few students with learning disabilities.

VERMONT

LANDMARK COLLEGE
(COLLEGE FOR STUDENTS WITH LEARNING DISABILITIES)
RIVER ROAD, R.R. 1, BOX 1000
PUTNEY, VERMONT 05346
(802) 387-6711; FAX: (802) 387-6860
E-MAIL: admissions@landmark.edu **WEB SITE: www.landmark.edu**

Landmark College Bridge Scholarship: Non-renewable scholarship awarded to one student with exceptional need for one year. Award ranges from $9,000 to $15,000 annually. *Endowed Scholarships:* Six awards in the amount of $1,000 based on specific criteria.

VIRGINIA

TIDEWATER COMMUNITY COLLEGE – NORFOLK CAMPUS
300 GRANBY STREET
NORFOLK, VIRGINIA 23510-1909
(757) 822-1213, 822-1226, 822-1248 TDD; FAX: (757) 822-1214
E-MAIL: jrashada@tcc.edu WEB SITE: www.tcc.edu

Learning Disabilities Services
Scholarships are available for books for students.

WISCONSIN

WISCONSIN INDIANHEAD TECHNICAL COLLEGE
1900 COLLEGE DRIVE
RICE LAKE, WISCONSIN 54868
(715) 234-7082; FAX: (715) 234-5172
WEB SITE: www.witechcolleges.com

Student Success Center Services
Special Needs Scholarship: One semester of 12 credits, 2.0 GPA and two letters of recommendation with application.

WYOMING

LARAMIE COUNTY COMMUNITY COLLEGE
1400 EAST COLLEGE DRIVE
CHEYENNE, WYOMING 82007
(307) 778-1359, (307) 778-1266 TTY; FAX: (307) 778-1262
E-MAIL: LDignan@lccc.wy.edu WEB SITE: www.lccc.wy.edu

Disability Resource Center (DRC)
Edington Family Scholarship: Scholarship for a student with a learning disability. Applicants must be graduates of a Wyoming high school and enrolled full-time at Laramie County Community College. *Association for Children with Learning Disabilities Scholarship:* Applicants must write a 50-word essay and be a graduate of a Laramie County high school.

INDEX OF COLLEGES